Press Freedom and Pluralism in Europe

in Europe

Concepts and Conditions

European C

This series s. Books
address the theory,
research, p ersity of
perspective

Series Edi
Nico Carpe
François He

Series Ad
Denis McQ
Robert Pica
Jan Servae

The aims of

a) To pro ion and
informa n about
their wc ormatics
research
b) To enco ects and
areas w
c) To stimu rch, and
to prom
d) To co-o e, with a
view to
e) To enc chers in
Europe;
f) To take
g) To deve ions and
with professional communication researchers working for commercial organizations and
regulatory institutions, both public and private;
h) To promote the interests of communication research within and among the Member States
of the Council of Europe and the European Union;
i) To collect and disseminate information concerning the professional position of communication
researchers in the European region; and
j) To develop, improve and promote communication and media education.

Press Freedom and Pluralism in Europe
in Europe
Concepts and Conditions

Edited by

Andrea Czepek, Melanie Hellwig and Eva Nowak

intellect Bristol, UK / Chicago, USA

First published in the UK in 2009 by
Intellect Books, The Mill, Parnall Road, Fishponds, Bristol, BS16 3JG, UK

First published in the USA in 2009 by
Intellect Books, The University of Chicago Press, 1427 E. 60th Street, Chicago,
IL 60637, USA

Cover designer: Holly Rose
Copy-editor: Heather Owen
Typesetting: Mac Style, Beverley, E. Yorkshire

ISBN 978-1-84150-243-4

Printed and bound by Gutenberg Press, Malta.

CONTENTS

Part Two: Conditions (Case Studies)

Introduction: Structural Inhibition of Media Freedom and Plurality across Europe

Andrea Czepek, Melanie Hellwig and Eva Nowak

In Europe, freedom of the press and an independent media system are often taken for granted. Conventionally, press freedom is defined as an absence of state intervention in media activities. All of the EU-member states today have implemented guarantees of press freedom in their constitutions and/or judicial systems. However, other factors such as economic influences, historic, cultural and social conditions also have a substantial impact on media independence and on the media's ability to fulfil their societal functions. Media systems in Europe vary widely with regard to such factors and display different problematic areas in which independent reporting and plurality of content are inhibited.

Concerns about interferences with media freedom have been increasingly raised everywhere in Europe. In Italy, the re-election of commercial television mogul Silvio Berlusconi as prime minister in 2008 revives fears of monopolization in the television sector, a strong dominance of political and commercial control of television in the hands of very few, and an opaque entanglement of political and economic interests in the media system. In Poland, attempts by the new government to successively abandon public television fees and to partially privatize public television has resulted in a fierce battle with the state television board which was appointed by the previous government (epd medien 2008). In Germany, recent cases have been revealed in which journalists' e-mail communication has been monitored – not only by the state secret service (Bundesnachrichtendienst), as happened in the case of a German Afghanistan correspondent, but also by private companies.[1]

Economic concentration and the dominance of commercial objectives in the media systems, increasing state control due to anti terrorism efforts, and new digital technologies, pose new challenges to the European media, their autonomy and their capabilities in providing a platform for free, pluralistic exchange. Thus, a closer look at preconditions for independence and pluralism in European media systems seems to be worthwhile.

This volume entails contributions and discussions from the ongoing research project 'Press Freedom and Pluralism in Europe' (PLUS). In this project, nineteen researchers from twelve countries explore and compare media systems in Europe regarding their capabilities of providing independent, pluralistic media. The book discusses definitions of the concepts of freedom of the press, media pluralism and participation in the media in Europe. It addresses the difficulties of measuring press freedom, the paradigms in defining media pluralism, as well as the possible role of training processes and approaches to self-regulation.

The case studies included illustrate chances and concerns with regard to press freedom and media plurality in Europe. The examples from EU member states in Central and Eastern Europe (Bulgaria, Lithuania, Poland, Romania), from Western Europe (Austria, France, Germany, Great Britain), Northern Europe (Finland) and Southern Europe (Italy, Spain) form a basis for future comparative research. Concerns and developments of interferences with press freedom which have been observed to be trends across Europe are structured along different realms of society: legal provisions, economic structures, political framework, historical development, social and cultural influences, traditions, and religion. Some observations:

■ Media freedom in Europe may increasingly be impeded by economic factors, such as increasing financial dependency on mass markets. Also, concentration of ownership increases dependency on fewer, more powerful media conglomerates. The tension between regulation (in order to ensure plurality and participation) and de-regulation (in order to enable an independent development of media) is discussed further on in this book.
■ Security policies, especially with regard to the prevention of terrorism, have a growing impact on media freedom (for example surveillance, data protection issues).
■ With EU-enlargement, challenges to the development of free media in post-communist states have to be addressed (for example small markets and monopolies; traditionally strong political control of the media).
■ Internet and digital media pose new opportunities, but also new challenges for media freedom. How, for example, can privacy rights be protected while free speech is guaranteed?

In its current 'White Paper on a European Communication Policy' (see Commission of the European Communities 2006), the EU-Commission demands more press freedom, plurality and citizens' participation in public communication. But how free are the media in Europe? And what are the consequences of the different economic, political and social preconditions in the European states, regarding the diversity of informational content and opportunities for citizens' participation in public discourse?

On a European level, it is widely accepted that press freedom, pluralism and participation are considered pillars of democracy and have to be protected and supported. What varies widely is how exactly these pillars should be formed and implemented: On one hand, different European institutions (European Commission, European Parliament, Council of the European Union, Council of Europe) set different priorities (for example economic liberalism vs. cultural diversity as a normative goal). On the other hand, the EU member states have developed quite different conditions in historical, cultural, economic and legal terms that are also based on differing views. The main questions are: Who 'owns' press freedom – each citizen, the journalists or the publishers? Is press freedom predominantly a right of citizens to be protected from interference by the state or does it also include an active right to information? Should press freedom include protection from other actors such as the economy? Should press freedom and plurality merely be granted or should they also be actively encouraged (for example through financial support or legal regulation which could mean involvement of the state)?

There can be no definite answers to these questions; rather, the contributions to this volume illustrate a broad spectrum of opinions and conditions in order to highlight the commonalities and differences on a European level. The team's research so far has shown that – despite all differences – there could be indeed something like a 'European consensus', for instance in embracing a rather 'positive' approach to press freedom and pluralism. As opposed to the US-American market liberal approach ('freedom from...') there seems to be wider support in Europe for a model that actively supports and regulates press freedom and media pluralism ('freedom to...') in order to ensure the representation of checks and balances, of critique and controversy, and of minority opinions and interests in a changing media world.

Theoretical background

Combining theories of political and media studies with empirical observations, Hallin and Mancini (2004) have classified media systems in western democracies into three categories: the North Atlantic liberal, the North/Central European democratic corporatist and the Mediterranean polarized pluralist model. While their approach is a very useful starting point, its shortcomings have also been widely discussed, namely the exclusion of Central and Eastern European states or, for example, the limited validity of attributing some countries to a certain model. The British media system for example, with its dominant public broadcasting, differs greatly from the North Atlantic liberal model. In other words, the inclusiveness of the approach is also its problem, given the very heterogeneous European media landscape.

In distinction to Hallin and Mancini, our approach focuses on the desired performance of media systems, and it places a stronger emphasis on the determining influence of the economic system. Our approach is based on the normative assumption that media in democratic systems serve functions such as:

- Enabling communication within and between subsystems in a complex society (system theory perspective).
- Reflecting the plurality of voices, views and values in society (critical theory perspective).
- Providing access to relevant information to all citizens.

Our project also goes beyond Hallin and Mancini's approach by including Central and Eastern European states in the study, represented here by Bulgaria, Lithuania, Poland and Romania.

Press freedom is usually considered a basic element of democratic societies, which should enable citizens to take part in the democratic process and to form an opinion on the basis of being informed about political, social and cultural events and developments. This is only possible if media offer a pluralistic choice of topics, views and voices, and access is universally granted. Pluralistic media content requires participation of a broad range of social groups including minorities.

However, press freedom, pluralism and participation are by no means concepts clearly defined and universally agreed upon. In fact, while there is a broad consensus on their importance in the democratic process, the ideas of what exactly they should entail and how they should be implemented vary widely. Thus, this book begins with a discussion of the major concepts involved: How can press freedom be defined and measured? (Markus Behmer, Andrea Czepek). Which are the different (and often contradictory) interpretations of media pluralism in Europe and among different European institutions? (Beata Klimkiewicz, Lilia Raycheva). Since autonomy on the one hand and capacities on the other hand are main prerequisites for functioning media systems, the section entitled 'Concepts' then focuses on aspects which might lead to solutions in yielding free and pluralistic media, namely defining quality in journalism education (Eva Nowak), an approach to researching gender equality with regard to access, participation and representation in the media (Elisabeth Klaus), and a discussion of self- and co-regulation concepts (Vinzenz Wyss, Guido Keel).

Legal, economic, political, historical, cultural and social conditions for free media in Europe

The case studies in this book examine the structural pre-conditions for free and pluralistic media coverage by analysing secondary data. We have developed a scheme of factors which can be defined as determinants of media systems. Rather than attempting to generalize models, we try to identify specific determinants and compare the different variations of factors in the respective states. The purpose is not merely to describe media systems but to focus on such variables that potentially influence media autonomy and pluralism.

In comparing the findings, we have found that there are some structural constraints which are a concern almost everywhere in Europe, while others can be found in certain groups of countries. Interestingly, those groups or clusters do *not* correspond equally with regard to different structural factors. There are media systems which display commonalities regarding their economic structures, but not their political framework, for example, or the other way around, and, again, varying commonalities might occur in the cultural or societal realm. While media systems in Europe are the rather heterogeneous results of different legal, economic, political, historical, cultural and social conditions, some common concerns across Europe emerge as well as some clusters with similar problems regarding the different factors, as shown in Table 1. The left column summarizes developments that can be observed in most European countries, while factors in the right column are specific in certain countries or groups of countries. The allocation of countries to the factors in the right column are only examples drawn from the cases represented in this book and are not supposed to be comprehensive; certainly, other countries could be added to some of the factors.

Our research so far has shown that the interrelations between structural conditions and the development of free and pluralistic media content are much more complex than could be assumed at first sight. Examples for this complexity considering the factors mentioned are discussed in the case studies in the second section of this book, such as:

Legal provisions
Press freedom is implemented in legal frameworks all over Europe. The EU Commission, however, regards press freedom above all economically, neglecting that press freedom and

Table 1: Pan-European trends and media system clusters regarding different conditions for media freedom and plurality.

Pan-European Developments	Media System Clusters
Legal provisions and judicial practice	
Press freedom guaranteed by constitutions	Legislation regarding media content (*France, Germany, United Kingdom*)
EU-deregulations	Legislation regarding fusion control, cross-ownership and/or foreign investments (*France, Germany, Romania*)
Anti-terrorism efforts	Strong privacy rights (*Germany, Spain*) Self-regulation institutionalized (*Finland, Germany, Lithuania, Switzerland, United Kingdom*)
Economic structures	
Regulated broadcasting market; deregulated print media market	Strong public service broadcasting systems with regulation regarding content diversity in co-existence with commercial broadcasting (dual systems) (*Austria, Finland, Germany, United Kingdom*)
Concentration of media ownership	Public television system controlled or strongly influenced by governments in co-existence with commercial broadcasting (*Bulgaria, France, Italy, Poland, Romania, Spain*)
Increasing dominance of commercial goals	Small market characteristics (*Austria, Finland, Lithuania*)
Declining resources for journalistic work	Trans-national media investments (*Austria, Bulgaria, Poland, Romania*) Fragmented media markets (*Romania, Bulgaria*)
Political framework	
EU-Commission policy norm: market deregulation	Statist/partisan approach to media policies (*Bulgaria, France, Italy, Poland, Romania, Spain*) Public-service approach to media policies (*Austria, Finland, Germany, United Kingdom*) Marketplace-of-ideas approach (*Lithuania, other states with regard to print media*)

Historical development	
Re-organization of media systems after World War II	Post-Communist transformation *(Bulgaria, Lithuania, Poland, Romania)* Aftermath of a dictatorial regime in the 20th century *(Austria, Germany, Italy, Spain)*
Social and cultural influences; tradition; religion	
Pressure and threats on media by fundamentalist groups	Prevailing journalistic culture: Watchdog, educator or commentator? Strong tradition of political taboos *(Finland, Spain)* Large ethnic minorities *(Estonia, Latvia, Romania, Germany, Spain, United Kingdom)* Social cleavage structures *(e.g. the UK's traditional social class stratification structures or Poland's urban/rural cleavage)* Influence of catholic church on media content *(Poland)*

pluralism are not only an economic but also a cultural and democratic issue. While the European Union aims at deregulating economic structures, stronger regulation regarding anti-terrorism efforts in terms of loosening privacy and journalistic rights are being discussed or planned all over Europe.

European Union policies are increasingly influencing the shape and development of media markets throughout Europe, with considerable impact on press freedom and pluralism. The European parliament has stressed the democratic role and function of media and the importance of freedom, pluralism, participation and access to media. The European Commission in its legislation and the European Court of Justice in its jurisdiction have, however, mainly focused on the economic aspects of the media market. The EU media policies have been brought together into the *i2020 initiative* and mainly pursue three goals: 'regulating the market' (mainly meaning to liberalize the market), 'stimulating the information society' (e.g. by investing in infrastructure and 'bridging the broadband gap'), and exploiting the benefits (i.e., of new technological developments and possibilities.)

In the 1980s, the rulings of the European Court of Justice (ECJ) have established that broadcasting is to be considered a service which would be governed by economic policy on the EU level rather than cultural policy which would be solely in the responsibility of the member states (Harcourt 2005: 37). Subsequently, the ECJ has interpreted the EU treaties and legislation predominantly with regard to liberalization. For instance, the Court interpreted the 'Television Without Frontiers'-Directives of 1989 and 1997 in several cases in such a way that broadcasting across borders should not be hindered, that regulation of a broadcaster's state of origin (not: transmission) should be applied and that restrictions on foreign ownership be lifted. On the other hand, the 'Television Without Frontiers'-Directives also contained provisions regarding public service goals of broadcasting, which were largely ignored by the Court's rulings. As Harcourt points out, those public interest goals (such as restriction of advertising, regulation of pluralism, protection of minors) were even thwarted by the Court in some cases.

The impact of EU treaties like the 'Television Without Frontiers'-Directive and the European Court of Justice-rulings based on these directives on European media systems has been substantial. Well known and very severe was the impact of the ECJ-rulings on satellite television in the United Kingdom. The British media Act of 1990 treated domestic and non-domestic satellite providers differently. While the domestic providers had to adhere to British media regulation regarding advertising restrictions, content and ownership rules in order to get a licence, non-domestic satellite providers did not. The ECJ ruled on the basis of the 1989 'Television Without Frontiers (TVWF)'-Directive that this unequal treatment was discriminating. The UK government changed the media Act, but in such a way that domestic satellite providers now also did not have to adhere to national media regulation, even if they catered to a British audience (unlike the terrestrial broadcasters, to which the stricter rules still apply).

The effect was immense. For one, private broadcasters in Britain can circumvent media regulation by transmitting their programming via satellite. But it has also affected media systems elsewhere in Europe: some British satellite channels transmit their programming to other states without having to adhere to respective national laws, on the grounds of the TVWF-Directive demanding unhindered broadcasting across borders. In the following years, several broadcasters have relocated to the UK and transmit their programmes from there. The ECJ has upheld that (a) such satellite providers are free to transmit their programming across borders, and (b) that they have to comply only with media legislation of the state in which their headquarters and main operations are located (in this case the UK), even if, as in the UK, the media legislation in that country itself does not comply with the TVWF-directive, and even if their programming is targeted specifically at an audience in another country.[2]

In December 2007, the 'Television Without Frontiers'-Directive was replaced by the Audiovisual Media Services Directive (AVMSD). The new directive maintains the 'country of origin'-principle for satellite broadcasters, but includes a procedure by which a consultation may take place between the state of origin of a broadcaster and the state its programming is aimed at. The resulting recommendations to the broadcaster are non-binding, but with ex-ante supervision of the EC, binding measures may be taken against a broadcaster that tries to circumvent national law. Other amendments concern advertising: the new directive generally approves of product placement, but does allow member states to enforce stricter rules; the recommendations against harmful advertising have been expanded to 'unhealthy foodstuffs'; the directive only recommends self-regulation, but it still implies some interference with media freedom, albeit regarding advertisement content.

Thus, EU media legislation and the rulings of the European Court of Justice have had an important impact on the development of media systems in Europe and are shaping the market increasingly, especially in the broadcasting sector. Mainly, by interpreting and implementing the directives, the EC and the ECJ have enhanced economic liberalization across borders, while they have paid relatively little attention to public goals such as restriction of advertising, restriction of market shares and enhancing content plurality.

In subsequent policies, the European Commission (EC) has tried to emphasize public interest goals such as securing plurality and the role of the media in the democratic process. But, as Harcourt resumes, in practice, implementation of EU policies has continued to concentrate mainly on market liberalization, also in the realm of the media. Reasons for that can be seen in a lack of democratic legitimization of EC decisions and procedures, a tendency of appointees to pursue national interests, and the EU's limited mandate with regard to policies other than economic ones. Harcourt, in her 2005 book, placed some hope in the European constitution, which was supposed to include press freedom and plurality as fundamental goals and which was intended to improve democratic participation (Harcourt 2005: 202). However, after the failure of the constitution and the failed referendum on the European Union Treaty of Lisbon in Ireland, the future of broadening the scope of the EU's mandate has currently become more uncertain.

Meanwhile, the Council of Europe has strengthened its concern with press freedom, freedom of expression and participation in its resolution 'Indicators for media in a democracy' (Council of Europe 2008), demanding a number of provisions that member states should apply in order to allow journalists to work freely and to give all political parties access to the media. The Council's resolution also states that an increasing number of court cases regarding media freedom indicate problems in this area. Beata Klimkiewicz will elaborate in her chapter on the contradicting paradigms that are guiding media policies by different European institutions, which will, in different ways, affect media freedom, plurality and participation across Europe.

At EU member state level, some states have very strong regulation of media content. In France, especially, various quotas prescribe certain content regarding French production, and proportions for certain programming such as sports and culture, not only to public but also private television and radio programming. Even the proportional allocation of airtime in public television news is regulated (about 30 per cent of news airtime is granted to the government position, the ruling party's and the opposition's perspective, respectively; it is only since 2000 that about 10 per cent of airtime is awarded to extra parliamentary views: see Thierry Vedel in this volume). In Germany, television programming is also heavily regulated, but mainly on a structural level (programme diversity is aspired to but not concretely prescribed in figures). In Romania, media ownership has to be publicly transparent, but infringements are not sanctioned, as Mihai Coman describes in his chapter. In Austria, a private initiative aiming at the transparency of representation of political party members attracts considerable attention. *ZiB Mediawatch*, published by the national newspaper *Der Standard* (2008), counts the seconds during which representatives from different political parties are shown on the main public television news, *ZiB*, on ORF public television.

In order to avoid tighter state regulation, in some countries media organizations have implemented – or have been prescribed – self-regulatory measures. An interesting case is Switzerland, where a new 'media governance' paradigm ties licensing of private broadcasters to the implementation of a quality management system (see the chapter by Vinzenz Wyss/ Guido Keel). Elsewhere, self-regulatory measures seem to have failed for now – in Austria, for instance, where the press council has been virtually dysfunctional since 2002 (see Martina Thiele's chapter).

Economic structures

A characteristic of most European media systems – in contrast to North American media – is the fact that broadcasting markets are relatively heavily regulated, and public broadcasting is often strong, whereas print media in most European countries are primarily private-commercial enterprises. Regulation in the print media sector is usually relatively low and often limited to merger control mechanisms. A justification for the stricter regulation of broadcasting compared to the printed press has been the fact that the number of adequate analogue broadcasting frequencies used to be limited. This is changing with digital distribution of radio and television, terrestrial as well as via cable and satellite. Thus, the legitimation of broadcast regulation has shifted to the public service idea of broadcasting media, which in return has raised the question whether the 'public service media' approach should or should not be applied to other media as well, for example the Internet.

Another economic characteristic which can be found all over Europe is an increasing concentration of media ownership. Commercial goals are becoming more important at the expense of democratic societal goals. This is also relevant concerning resources for journalistic work, for example fewer journalists having to provide more content, editors being outsourced and replaced by underpaid freelancers. Consequences of such measures are decreasing time for research and fact-checking and a tendency to cover mostly mainstream topics and press-relations material.

The larger Western European countries have established a dual broadcasting system with the co-existence of public and private-commercial broadcasting. However, other organizational forms have emerged, such as the private non-commercial radio stations in Austria and in some states of Germany. In the United Kingdom, satellite and cable television have become major players which, unlike terrestrial television in Britain, are only lightly regulated (see Peter Humphreys).

Trans-national investments have become an increasing trend all over Europe that does not stop at media concerns (and private equity firms) from large countries buying media business shares in smaller countries. For example, RTL bought a major share of the French private television channel M6 despite strict regulations on foreign investment in France, and the British investment group MECOM has bought newspapers not only in Germany. In general, trans-national investments are seen with some concern, regarding media freedom and plurality, because they might lead to a high level of ownership concentration, the dominance of commercial objectives (high profit margins) and uniform content. But in some cases, foreign investors are more conducive to media independence because they may be less entangled in local and regional politics and economic interests than domestic investors (see for example the conflict in Romania between the German owner *Westdeutsche Allgemeine Zeitung* (WAZ) on the one hand and the administrative council and editors' board of the newspaper *Romania Libera* on the other hand, described by Mihai Coman in his chapter).

Similarly, the correlation between ownership concentration and independence might be more complicated than generally assumed. Just to give one example: in Romania, the consolidation of media ownership since EU-membership has actually facilitated a greater independence of media reporting because, before, the very fragmented media landscape depended heavily on state advertising, whereas larger media conglomerates now are economically more independent. It seems that a minimum of market consolidation is necessary in order to safeguard financial independence of media enterprises. In Austria, the Dichand group has taken over several newspapers in Eastern Europe, whereas at the same time, the German WAZ newspaper group invested considerably in the Austrian newspaper market. The conflict and discussions in Austria following the German investment was influenced by the fear of being taken over culturally by the bigger neighbour.

Small markets face special challenges with regard to press freedom and pluralism, as Aukse Balcytiene illustrates in her chapter about the Baltic States. Because markets and populations are small, they lack both the advertisement revenues and the basis for generating sufficient public fees. One result is a high concentration of ownership and low external diversity because of the high share of fixed costs in media production. A measure to support media pluralism in such situations could be through state subsidies, which are given to print media in Finland, Romania, and Austria for example. Interestingly, while state subsidies constitute an act of state interference with the media system, they may be justified because they do not only help to maintain plurality but they may also render small media enterprises more independent from commercial pressures.

State subsidies, however, conflict with the idea of economic deregulation as the prevailing paradigm of the European Commission's economic policies. A single European media market that is highly deregulated disregards the cultural aspects of media, which the state subsidies outlined above intend to strengthen. Plurality of media decreases if media freedom is predominantly considered as commercial freedom and not as freedom of communication which would include plurality of media and plurality of voices as a public value.

The European Commission supports the idea of strong media concerns competing on the global media market. Transnational investments, not controlled by a monopolies' authority, in the long run strengthen the position of a few big media groups based in Europe. Few but strong media groups, however, weaken the plurality of views and voices within Europe and within the European countries, despite the fact that foreign investment might sometimes be a basis for journalistic independence from local political or economic leaders, as shown above in the case of Romania. A prerequisite for this positive effect of transnational media investments is that the investor promotes the idea of press freedom as a democratic goal, which might be in conflict with the goal to produce profits, at least in the short term. This is a problem with investment groups that depend on short term profits to satisfy their investors. From their point of view, media quality and public values are insignificant factors. Economic surpluses are easily produced by considerable staff reduction, as Mecom shows in Germany and the Netherlands (see Tryhorn 2008). This will lead to a decrease in quality – not least in the long run, when the investment group will probably have sold the medium.

The predominant approach of liberalizing markets within the European Union does not only affect local, regional and minorities' media in small markets which can only be produced if supported by subsidies. For some years now, state subsidies and financial support to public service radio and television have regularly been the object of the EC's efforts to deregulate the media market. The public task disappears behind the comprehensive idea of economic deregulation. However, the printed press market is obviously of minor interest to the EC. Above all, public service broadcasting is affected by EC market liberalization policies, manifested in the 'Television Without Frontiers'-directive and the telecommunications directive.

Political framework
European integration is a process which shapes and re-shapes policies in many realms and also has a substantial impact on media policies. With regard to press freedom, an obvious impact is the condition for new member states to install provisions for freedom of expression and freedom of the press as part of their democratic procedures. All new member states had to implement

such provisions and limit state involvement with the media. Media systems have changed as a result, for example in Romania, where a massive consolidation of media enterprises has taken place since joining the EU, as Mihai Coman explains in his case study about Romania.

As the current charges of corruption in Bulgaria show, however, the process is far from being completed. In Bulgaria, politicians' involvement with the media is still strong, although Bulgaria has officially adopted EU standards of freedom of the press, as Lilia Raycheva explains in her chapter about Bulgarian media.

Obviously, the dominant political paradigm determines to a large degree a country's media system and its freedom. On closer inspection, three approaches prevail in Europe, whereby in the broadcasting sector, as mentioned above, most countries have a strong public (service) system. However, there are important differences in the political approaches. A statist idea of public television is a top-down approach according to which the media (especially broadcast media) should convey government policies; an approach prevalent, for example, in France, Italy, Bulgaria and Romania. In contrast, the public service paradigm emphasizes the role of media in society and demands the diversity of society to be reflected in the media; a paradigm more prevalent in the United Kingdom, Germany and Finland. The third approach, the 'marketplace of ideas' or liberal approach, is commonly applied to print media; with regard to broadcasting, few European countries follow this approach, among them Lithuania. In Austria the societal approach to public broadcasting is broached as an issue by the audience initiative 'SOS ORF', which intends to decrease the political influence on ORF and strengthen informational content (see Martina Thiele).

Direct ownership of media organizations by politicians or political parties varies highly between European countries. In some countries, political parties or political leaders own important media organizations, most striking in this respect is Italy with Silvio Berlusconi, and also Romania, whereas in Germany, for example, there are only a few very minor shareholdings in newspapers by the German Social Democratic Party, SPD. In Spain, the influence of political parties on certain media has increased, and the big newspapers can clearly be attributed to political parties, although they are not officially owned by them.

Historical development
European media systems have been formed and reorganized after World War II. More specifically, the aftermath of a dictatorial regime plays a role in Germany, Austria, Italy and Spain, albeit with differing impact, mainly in having shaped media structures and legislation as a reaction to the totalitarian past.[3]

A recent groundbreaking experience that has reshaped European media systems is the post-communist transformation in Central and Eastern Europe. The political transformation process is not yet completed. The tradition of political influence on media is still real, and ethical values often do not play a role in public economic or political decisions. The fragmentation of media markets in Central and Eastern Europe leads to instable and insecure media publications (see Hadamik 2004).

Social and cultural influences, religion
A current pan-European development can be seen in threats to media by fundamentalist groups, either directly, as in the reaction of Islamist fundamentalists to the publication of Mohammed caricatures by the Danish newspaper *Jyllands Posten*, or also indirectly through stricter legal controls as a reaction of some governments to such threats. The question of how far religious

symbols should be respected or be potential subjects of satire is also a topic that concerns the Christian church in some countries. In Poland, Catholic Radio Maryja openly aspires to political influence.

Traditional taboos are not only challenged in matters of religion. In Spain, reporting about the Royal Family beyond official appearances has been a taboo. But recently, sparked by a public discussion about a caricature depicting Prince Felipe and his wife Letizia, and the subsequent strict reaction by the Socialist Spanish government (see Ingrid Schulze-Schneider), this taboo and with it, the legitimacy of monarchy in Spain altogether, have been publicly challenged. Finland has overcome its traditional post-war taboo on reporting critically on the Soviet Union to secure the country's neutrality and keep the big neighbour quiet, only to replace it with a taboo on criticizing EU policies in the first years of EU accession (see Inka Salovaara-Moring).

The representation and inclusion of ethnic minorities in the public media are another social concern. In Romania and Finland, for example, ethnic minorities have built up their own media market in minority languages within the country. In other countries, a substantial proportion of ethnic minorities use media from their or their parents' home countries while failing to take part in the public life of the countries they live in. The political and social effects are a lack of inclusion of all groups of society in the public sphere. Segregation of media audiences may also derive from a very stratified society, as Peter Humphreys describes in the case of the United Kingdom.

The pressure to comply with European standards, nevertheless, is rising as European integration continues. Media coverage of grievances in other countries can sometimes function as a regulative when domestic media are failing to address problems. The Swedish journalist Arne Ruth (2008) has pointed to this opportunity in the development of a European public sphere: when media report about cases in other countries, they can exert pressure on the governments and media there to react and deal with grievances they would otherwise have tried to keep from the public. One current example is the case of Slovenia and Finland, where, in September 2008, the Finnish public television station, YLE, had reported on corruption charges against the Slovenian prime minister, Janez Jansa. The Slovenian government, in return, demanded that the Finnish government should force YLE to revoke the report (Wolff 2008). This act of trying to intervene in the press freedom in another country only enhanced the public exposition of the case, as it became discussed in media across Europe. Being a member of the European Union, the Slovenian government was now faced with European public pressure to disclose the circumstances of the case and improve press freedom in their own country. Such cases are most obvious with former Communist countries, but not limited to them. During the world soccer championship in Germany in 2006, the British BBC reporter, Andrew Jennings, produced a TV report criticizing the dubious methods of the German Fifa organizers in distributing tickets. While the report was aired in Britain during the event in June of 2006, it was only aired in Germany half a year later. The fact that German public television had withheld this report from the German audience until long after the event was widely criticized. In sum, where domestic media may not be free enough to report about relevant grievances, growing trans-European attention can improve press freedom in parts of Europe where domestic media are hindered for political, economic or cultural reasons.

In conclusion, one very interesting observation is that, with reference to Hallin and Mancini, it does not seem possible to simply add a fourth model that includes the post-Communist Central and East European states' media systems. While these countries indeed share the common experience of the post-Communist transition phase, in other realms there are also great differences between them, and, rather, they can be grouped with other countries in, for example, the degree to which the media market is deregulated or which normative approaches to journalism have been adopted.[4]

Outlook

This book reflects analyses and findings discussed by a group of nineteen authors from twelve countries and from different fields at three workshops in 2007 and 2008. But our project will not end here. The next step will be to actually measure media system performance with regard to freedom and pluralism. With reference to the structural determinants, we will then be able to identify factors that hinder or further independent reporting, plurality of informational media content and a broad variety of reflected voices, views and values.

Acknowledgements

The editors wish to thank the ECREA book series editorial board for giving us the chance to present our work in this context. We also thank the Bundesministerium für Bildung und Forschung (the German Federal Ministry for Education and Research) and the University of Applied Sciences Oldenburg/Ostfriesland/Wilhelmshaven for their financial support of the 'PLUS'-project. We warmly thank our project partners and authors in this volume for the wonderful co-operation and the fruitful discussions, and we are especially grateful to Jennifer Heidrich for proofreading and to Katrin Enders for formatting the manuscript. Special thanks go to Katharina Hadamik who helped to initiate the project.

Andrea Czepek, Melanie Hellwig and Eva Nowak
Wilhelmshaven, October 2008

Notes

1. In May 2008, allegations arose that the largest German, formerly state-owned telecommunications concern Telekom had monitored its managers' e-mail communication with journalists in order to uncover whistleblowers (Spiegel online 2008). This is especially alarming considering that Telekom has to carry out the highly contested telecommunications data retention, saving all telecommunications data for six months for the purpose of criminal investigations.
2. One case for example in 1997 dealt with the Italian publisher De Agostini, which advertised a children's magazine on a satellite channel transmitted to Sweden, although advertising geared at children is illegal by Swedish law. The ECJ rejected the complaint by the Swedish media ombudsman. (Harcourt 2005: 30)
3. In Germany for example, public service broadcasting was constructed to be controlled by non-governmental boards and financed by a fee (not taxes) in order to avoid direct influence of the government or ruling party. The legislation prohibiting Nazi-propaganda was a reaction to the Nazi past.
4. see the case studies on Bulgaria by Lilia Raycheva, on Romania by Mihai Coman and, to see the differences, about the Baltic States by Aukse Balcytiene.

References

Audiovisual Media Services Directive (AVMSD) (2007): 'Directive 2007/65/EC of the European Parliament and of the Council of 11 December 2007 amending Council Directive 89/552/EEC on the coordination of certain provisions laid down by law, regulation or administrative action in Member States concerning the pursuit of television broadcasting activities'.

Cammerts, Bart and Carpentier, Nico (eds.) (2007), *Reclaiming the media. Communication rights and democratic media roles. European Communication Research and Education Association Series*, Bristol, Chicago: Intellect.

Carpentier, Nico, Pille Pruulmann-Vengerfeldt, Kaarle Nordenstreng, et al., (eds.) (2007), *Media Technologies and Democracy in an Enlarged Europe*, Tartu: Tartu University Press.

Commission of the European Communities (2006), *White Paper on a European Communication Policy*, COM(2006) 35, Brussels, 1 February 2006.

Commission of the European Communities (2007), *Commission Staff Working Document: Media pluralism in the Member States of the European Union*, SEC(2007) 32, Brussels, 16 January 2007.

Council of Europe (2008), *Indicators for media in a democracy, Resolution 1636 (2008)*, adopted by the Assembly on October 3, 2008, http://assembly.coe.int/Mainf.asp?link=/Documents/AdoptedText/ta08/ERES1636.htm. Accessed 06 October 2008.

epd medien (2008), 'Polen: Streit zwischen Regierung und TVP verschärft sich', No. 40/41, 21 May 2008.

Hadamik, Katharina (2004), *Transformation und Entwicklungsprozess des Mediensystems in Polen 1989 bis 2001*, Dortmund: Eldorado.

Hallin, Daniel C. and Mancini, Paolo (2004), *Comparing Media Systems. Three Models of Media and Politics*, New York: Cambridge University Press.

Harcourt, Alison (2005), *The European Union and the regulation of media markets*, Manchester: Manchester University Press.

Iosifidis, Petros (2007), *Public television in the digital era. Technological challenges and new strategies for Europe*, Houndmills, New York: Palgrave Macmillan.

Meier, Werner and Trappel, Josef (eds.) (2007), *Power, Performance and Politics. Media Policy in Europe*, Baden-Baden: Nomos.

Organization for Security and Co-operation in Europe (OSCE) (2003), Office of the Representative on Freedom of the Media, *The Impact of Media Concentration on Professional Journalism*, Vienna.

Ruth, Arne (2008), 'In der Nähe so fern', *Kulturreport: Europa in den Medien – Medien in Europa*, vol. 2, Robert Bosch Foundation, Stuttgart, pp. 24–32.

Sarikakis, Katharina (2004), *Powers in Media Policy. The Challenge of the European Parliament*, Bern: Peter Lang.

Spiegel online (2008), 'Spionageskandal: Telekom-Schnüffler jagten vermeintliche Verräter im Aufsichtsrat', http://www.spiegel.de/wirtschaft/0,1518,555283,00.html. Accessed 25 May 2008.

Terzis, Georgios (ed.) (2007), *European media governance. National and regional dimensions*, Bristol, Chicago: Intellect.

Terzis, Georgios (ed.) (2008), *European media governance. The Brussels dimension*, Bristol, Chicago: Intellect.

'Television Without Frontiers-Directive (TVWF)' (1997), *Directive 97/36/EC of the European Parliament and of the Council of 30 June 1997 amending Council Directive 89/552/EEC on the coordination of certain provisions laid down by law, regulation or administrative action in Member States concerning the pursuit of television broadcasting activities.*

Tryhorn, Chris (2008): 'Montgomery paper group to cut Dutch jobs', The Guardian, Friday, June 27, 2008. http://www.guardian.co.uk/media/2008/jun/27/pressandpublishing.mediabusiness. Accessed 06 October 2008.

Wolff, Reinhard (2008), 'Probleme mit finnischer Pressefreiheit. Ein echter Demokrat', *die tageszeitung*, 08.09.2008.

ZiB Media Watch (2008): http://derstandard.at/. Accessed 04 October 2008.

PART ONE: CONCEPTS

MEASURING MEDIA FREEDOM: APPROACHES OF INTERNATIONAL COMPARISON

Markus Behmer

Introduction

Every year on 3 May the 'World Press Freedom Day' is celebrated. It was proclaimed by the UNESCO in 1992, to mark the ratification of the 'Windhoek Declaration'. It was adopted one year later, during a regional UNESCO conference, when media representatives and experts had demanded independence, freedom and pluralism of the press.

Even sixteen years after Windhoek, 3 May is not a red-letter day, a day for joyful statements – rather, it offers the opportunity for critical appraisal. Freedom of the press is an ideal, yet oppression of that freedom is still reality in many places. Furthermore, since September 11 2001, freedom of communication and media has even suffered setbacks, worldwide. The fight against terrorism has often been a plea for constraints of media freedom all over the world. In Russia, the media are controlled and exploited by the president and powerful economic groups; the lives of journalists who gave critical reports from Chechnya were threatened. In China – and not only there – access to the Internet is strictly controlled; critical net activists are arrested. In Iraq the media are still in a sorry state. In Columbia journalists are kidnapped or murdered; in Cuba they are imprisoned on a massive scale.

This list could be continued for some time. In western democracies as well, even in Western Europe and in Germany, there is, here and there, cause for concern, for instance, when editorial offices are searched on suspicion of betrayal of state secrets, or telephones of journalists are wiretapped, or critical coverage of firms is omitted on account of pressure by advertisers. Of course, one has to think in relative terms here: phone bugging operations are alarming, but may not be equated with the arresting of critical journalists; the closing of websites due to pornographic or racist contents does not equate with acts of official pre-censorship in the run-up to elections.

To begin with, it should only be noted that the elementary human rights to gain information from a multitude of various sources and to communicate freely are under threat in many places, in different ways and to different extents. The most massive breaches of these (as of other) basic rights are to be found in those regions which are commonly (albeit in an unduly trivializing or at least strongly abbreviated manner) referred to as the 'Third World' – and particularly in conflict areas.

The International Freedom of Expression Exchange (IFEX) features the most comprehensive collection of breaches to the basic rights concerning communication around the globe on the World Wide Web. It gives numerous current alerts almost daily. That the cases shown on the pages of IFEX usually deal with injustice is not only self-evident but also clear under international law.

Media freedom and international law

Article 19 of the UN Universal Declaration of Human Rights states: 'Everyone has the right to freedom of opinion and expression; the right includes freedom to hold opinions without interference and to seek, receive and impart information and ideas through any media regardless of frontiers.'

These words are worth being remembered again and again. However, Article 19 is only a general manifesto which needs to be substantiated in two ways: first, its content is rendered more precisely by further inter- and transnational conventions, such as Article 10 of the 'European Human Rights Convention' of the European Council (1950), the Helsinki Final Act of the Conference for Security and Co-Operation in Europe (now OSCE) from 1975, the UN Millenium Development Goals, the Conventions of the World Trade Organisation WTO, the International Telecommunication Union (ITU) and other UN sub-organizations, particularly in the various media declarations of the UNESCO. The later ones show how difficult it is to reach a worldwide consensus, even regarding the basic implications of Article 19. The work of the UNESCO communications department was paralysed or overshadowed by disputes over the unconditional 'free flow of information' versus a better-balanced worldwide flow of information aided by a 'New World Information and Communication Order' for at least two decades in the seventies and eighties (see for example Rohn 2002; Breunig 2000).

The second area of implementation or realization of Article 19 concerns national law. Christian Tietje clarifies this in the International Media Handbook of the Hans Bredow Institute: 'Just as in the jurisdiction of the international system in general, so it is in the areas of communication law, the states still being the protagonists as to jurisdiction and its enforcement' (Tietje 2002: 17). Here it can be observed that freedom of communication is part of the basic rights catalogue in almost all constitutions on earth.

A detailed survey was carried out by Christian Breunig in 1994 in which he analysed, amongst other things, the contents of the constitutions of 160 states. 143 states guarantee – or at least guaranteed then – one or more freedom(s) of communication in their constitutions. In sixteen constitutions, freedom of speech was assured explicitly; in 21, the freedom of speech and opinion; in 58, the freedom of the press; in 60, the freedom of information; and in 103, freedom of opinion (Breunig 1994: 308).[1] However, as is often the case, it would be wrong to equate 'quantities to qualities'. Even if freedom of the press is not explicitly mentioned, it does not mean that it does not exist. The term 'press freedom' is not found in the constitution of

Sweden, for example, even though its press enjoys more freedom than in almost any other state on earth. And being printed in the constitution does, by no means, signify that it is implemented *de facto*. That is proven by the example of North Korea, ruled by one of the world's most repressive regimes. Another example: the freedom of broadcasting is only mentioned in two of the constitutions analysed by Breunig's *expressis verbis*: in the German 'Grundgesetz' – and in the constitution of the Islamic Republic of Iran.

Often, constitutions contain limitations to the chartered freedom of communication which 'abrogate the positive content basic rights' (Breunig 1994: 307). And it is not rare for arbitrariness to prevail despite any particular legislation. A comparative law analysis alone, therefore, can not offer sufficient insight into the media situation. This observation is further underscored by the fact that the basic understanding of press freedom can differ significantly.

In authoritarian systems press freedom is often subsidiary to other government aims. In the German Democratic Republic, for instance, one had to look upon freedom of the press as the freedom from economic constraint as well as the possibility (or rather the duty) of taking part in the build up of socialism (see, for example, Holzweißig 1997). In the Development Media Concept, which to this day is advocated at least implicitly in many states of the so-called Third World, the media are, to a certain extent, allocated the task to first and foremost cooperate in the formation of a nation after the era of colonization. According to this view, the media's primary tasks are nation-building and, finally, contributing to social and economic development – pluralism and freedom of the press are often looked upon as second-rate, sometimes even as detrimental (Stevenson 1994: 231–59). For instance, in strongly religious-orientated states, the media almost voluntarily make a taboo out of numerous topics and events. In Turkey there is paragraph 301 of the penal law, which assesses 'defamation of Turkishness' as an element of offence – as many will be aware of after the murder of Hrant Dink and the arguments about Orhan Pamuk.

With reference to Jean-Jacques Rousseau, it can be said that the press is free – but in many places and in many ways, it is in bonds. How can these bonds be more precisely defined? How can freedom of the press and the media situation be focused on in an international comparison?

Comparing media freedom around the world: A short inspection of four surveys
Up until the last four or five years, internationally comparative media research did not, unfortunately, rank very highly, at least in German communication science. In 2002, Hans Kleinsteuber mentioned that it is in a 'yet embryonic state' (Kleinsteuber 2002: 42). Since then the situation has improved,[2] but even in the 'strongholds' of international media research, such as in the United States and in Great Britain, comparison has been only a side show of research for a long time. Methodical problems, such as the general question of various systems being comparable or the exact categories of comparison to be operationalized in comparative research, for the most part, still ,need to be clarified. There is a need for special clarification depending on the subject of research; the complexity is therefore high, the qualifications the researcher has to fulfil, immense. The British Media Researcher Sonia Livingstone points out: 'In personal communication, comparative projects are described as "exhausting", "a nightmare" and "frustrating", though also "exhilarating" or "stimulating"' (Livingstone 2003: 481). Cross-national comparisons are 'exciting

but difficult, creative but problematic' (Livingstone 2003: 478). The field of studies is correspondingly clear. But currently the prominence of comparative media research is growing:

> Funding bodies and policy imperatives increasingly favour comparative research. Stimulated also by the phenomena of globalization and the concomitant rise of globalization theory, researchers in media, communication and cultural studies increasingly find themselves initiating collaboration or invited to collaborate in multinational comparative projects. (Livingstone 2003: 477)

This general result applies also to freedom of the press as the subject of examination. Thus, for a long time, there were only a few international comparative studies to comply with exact scientific demands (see, for example, Holtz-Bacha 2003). In the last few years, this situation has become much better and there is a series of studies which attempt, sometimes extensively, international comparison of the limitations of press freedom. The concrete focus is somewhat different in each case, as is the research instrument.

I would briefly like to introduce four of these studies. I will describe their methodical approach and also mention problems or inevitable shortcomings. Finally, I would like to refer to a few of the results of these studies before reaching a conclusion. The four studies I will briefly present are:

- 'Freedom of the Press: A Global Survey of Media Independence' by Freedom House (last edition: Deutsch Karlekar 2007a)
- 'World Press Freedom Index' by Reporters Without Borders (2007b)
- 'Media and Democracy Report' by the Konrad Adenauer Foundation (2005)
- 'African Media Barometer' by the Friedrich Ebert Foundation in cooperation with the Media Institute of Southern Africa (MISA) (2006/2007).

Other studies worth mentioning are, for example, 'News Media and Freedom of Expression in the Arab Middle East' edited by the Heinrich Boell Foundation (2004) and 'The World Press Freedom Review' of the International Press Institute (2006).

Freedom House: 'Freedom of the Press'
Let us begin with the oldest established survey, the study by the Washington based NGO Freedom House, conducted annually since 1980: 'Freedom of the Press: A Global Survey of Media Independence'. The survey considers communication and media freedom in more than 190 states, according to almost constant criteria and is an 'important instrument for metering continuously the global development of press freedom', as Christina Holtz-Bacha rightly emphasizes (Holtz-Bacha 2003: 408). The survey is published every year on 3 May, the 'World Press Freedom Day', when some media interest is guaranteed. The results are presented in form of brief country reports, an overview article (Deutsch Karlekar 2007b), sometimes some longer reports on special topics or problems, and always global and regional charts and scales. Since 2004, Freedom House compiles a ranking, too, in which every state gets a concrete position in the table of media freedom (or, as the case may be, bondage), although it cannot represent a scientifically correct scaling. The survey always attracts great attention, but it is not

without controversy. For example, it is criticized for incorrect scaling and some methodical difficulties (for example Becker 2003: 109). Furthermore, Freedom House is sometimes accused of having a pro-American bias (for example UN 2001) – not least because more than three quarters of the NGO's resources derive from federal grants of the US government (Freedom House 2007a: 24).

The final most simple, perhaps also most trivial, approach here is to differentiate between free and not free states. This is the approach which Freedom House takes in its annual inquiry. The result for 2007 shows that 72 out of 195 countries and territories examined were rated 'free' (having a 'free' media system), nine fewer than 2001; 59 fell under 'partly free' and 64 under 'not free', two more than six years before. The situation seems even more alarming when one does not differentiate according to the number of states but according to the number of inhabitants: less than one fifth (18 per cent) of the world population of 6.5 billion people live in states with a free press, but more than two fifths (43 per cent) live in systems characterized as not free (Freedom House 2008).

How is the survey carried out? 23 'methodology questions' are bundled up into three top categories. Top category A includes the normative frame: the legal situation comprising laws and regulations which influence the media content. Top category B includes the transformation of the legal status into factual action and the threat to media and journalists, also the political pressure, control by the executive, violence against media, and, generally, the working conditions relevant for the content. Lastly, top category C includes the economic situation, that is the economic pressure and control as well as concentration tendencies which influence contents (Freedom House 2007b).

The worst possible score is 30 points in categories A and C, and 40 in category B. All in all, results are presented within an assessment range from 0 (completely free) to 100 (completely not free). Optimum values not exceeding 12 points are currently reached by Finland, Iceland, Belgium, Denmark, Norway, Sweden, Luxembourg, and Switzerland; negative values of at least 90 points by Eritrea, Burma, Cuba, Libya, Turkmenistan, and – with 97 points, ranking last – North Korea (Freedom House 2007c).

So how are the free, the partly free and the not free media systems distributed on the globe? Freedom House offers a descriptive world map (Freedom House 2007d). 'Free' states are coloured in green, 'partially free' ones in yellow, the 'not free' ones in blue. One recognizes at first glance a conglomeration of blue, that is 'not free' states, particularly in Africa, in the Arabian region, in South and East Asia, as well as in the Caribbean (including Cuba and Haiti) – thus, in large parts of the Third World, though this is in addition to many successor states of the Soviet Union (such as Russia, Belarus, and Moldova, also the only European states). The green areas on the map, on the other hand, concentrate in the highly developed states of the 'North', particularly in North America and Europe. It is a shame, by the way, that a state which has been a founding member of the European Union was only listed as partly free in 2006: Italy under Berlusconi (Freedom House 2006).[3] The new EU member states Romania and Bulgaria were still considered only partly free in the 2007 survey.

Sources for the evaluation of each country were correspondent reports and statements from travellers, research results by staff members of Freedom House, expert inquiries, analyses of reports from aid organisations and public agencies as well as current reports of NGOs, and finally analyses of local and international media themselves. The data is sent to New York and evaluated there. However, the exact basis of the data and the concrete procedure of evaluation are not made public. Peter Schellschmidt of the Friedrich Ebert Foundation critically remarks: 'The outcome is often far removed from the lived reality in the countries under review. Such surveys are also likely to be incomplete' (Schellschmidt 2005b: 2). For instance, the inquiry does not really include the possibilities of access to the media – and the quality of coverage in the media is hardly considered, either.

Reporters Without Borders: 'World Press Freedom Index'
The second survey is more limited in its explanatory ability regarding general media freedom and particularly the plurality of the media. The 'World Press Freedom Index' of Reporters Without Borders or Reporters Sans Frontières (RSF) has been published annually at the end of October since 2002. Its focus is much tighter – it is concerned with the endangerment of journalists at work. A ranking of all examined states is compiled as well. In 2007, 169 states were listed. The outcome of the ranking tends to result in findings similar to the (more precise) Freedom House survey. Here, too, the Scandinavian states and Belgium rank as the ten countries with the most freedom – and at the end of the list we again find Burma, Cuba, Turkmenistan, North Korea and – in the last position – Eritrea (RSF 2007b). As to the details, there are, however, some evident differences which can not be referred to here at full length. Just two examples: Slovakia ranks as an excellent third in the RSF index – and only at position 33 in the Freedom House table; the United States are placed at 48 in the RSF ranking – and are ranked at 16 by Freedom House.

The RSF table was drawn up by having at least three experts, mostly journalists, lawyers or scientists, from each country answer a questionnaire consisting of 50 questions.

Their answers were collected in Paris, collated and, where necessary, researched. But the RSF does not disclose who those experts are or how they were chosen – which, of course, is understandable. In the questionnaire, the physical endangerment or threatening of journalists is quite dominant: the first thirteen questions relate to how many journalists in the previous year were murdered, put into jail, tortured, threatened, attacked or had to flee. These questions are allotted up to 49 points of the worst possible score of 122 points. The other 37 questions (for the most part only to be answered with yes or no) aim at the application of certain laws, the dealing with censorship, the state's possession of media and its influence, the possibilities of coverage for foreign journalists and so on (RSF 2007d).

Konrad Adenauer Foundation: 'Media and Democracy Report'
A much more complex questionnaire has been developed by the political scientist Karl-Rudolf Korte (Duisburg) and his team for the 'Media and Democracy Report' of the Konrad Adenauer Foundation. It was published in 2005. At the beginning of his report, Korte also describes a basic problem of international comparative research in general. 'Every international comparative survey has to deal with the conflict between range (i.e. the generalisation of results) and empirical accuracy. The range of scientific statements increases with the number of objects under scrutiny' (KAF 2005: 13).

Accordingly, he then says about the Freedom House survey:

Causes which are specific to each country are not fully taken into account so that a wide range can be achieved. The studies...provide important data on the global development

...However...they deliver little information about the characteristics of each country that are responsible for a friendly or hostile media climate. Thus, studies with a wide range of indices are of limited use for practical work in political consulting...So far they have been unable to satisfactorily explain different levels of media freedom. (KAF 2005: 14)

When, however, only few countries are included in a study, or only case studies on certain states are carried out, these may turn out to be much more precise but 'To have a small number of cases, however, is also a disadvantage because comparisons cannot be made and the range of generated hypotheses is too low' (KAF 2005).

Therefore, Korte and the Konrad Adenauer Foundation steered a middle course. Only fourteen states were examined, fourteen case studies carried out. The states under scrutiny were Argentina, Belarus, Bolivia, Cambodia, Democratic Republic of Congo, Egypt, India, Indonesia, Jordan, Mexico, Nigeria, Russia, South Africa and Tunisia. The KAF Team elaborated a systematic questionnaire with 30 main questions and numerous questions of detail (KAF 2005: 21–31). They are summed up to five 'main indicators':

- ■ 'General conditions' of the media scene (like the literacy rate, the proportions of state-run and publicly run media, the ownership of media companies and so on)
- ■ 'Legal environment' (freedom of expression, regulation of media coverage, licences, monopolies and cartels and so on)
- ■ 'Political conditions' (for example illegal state repression, self-censorship, obstacles to Internet access)
- ■ 'Economic pressures' (for example state subsidies for private media, economic barriers to establishing a newspaper)
- ■ 'Non-state repression' (for example, the question of whether the state authorities can effectively protect journalists). (KAF 2005: 15–20)

All things considered, this is a very comprehensive approach. However, here too, there seems to be a discrepancy between the sophisticated scientific instrument and its application in research.

As Korte describes:

The KAF Democracy Report is characterised by a qualitative research design. The data was collected by interviewing local experts in the chosen countries using a 'half-open questionnaire'. This choice of experts proved to be advantageous because they were able to combine their detailed knowledge of the political and social situation in each country with an objective standard of measurement. (KAF 2005: 15)

But again, who these experts are is concealed – and probably, unavoidably so. It is by all means possible that the individual KAF offices which carried out the survey *in situ* practised a more pragmatic approach and did not demonstrate the same accuracy in every country. However, the country reports are all fairly extensive – each comprising around twenty pages – and they offer good information. Yet there are differences in regard to certain details. The comparative composition, the conclusions at the end of the publication are, unfortunately, rather succinct (just about four pages). The conclusions made are not really very profound. For instance, 'Political repression of the media comes in waves', 'Non-state repression and economic pressure pose an increasing threat to media freedom', 'The correlation between the level of media freedom and literacy levels' is weak and 'economic pressures are the main source of self-censorship' (KAF 2005: 312–15).

Friedrich Ebert Foundation and Media Institute of Southern Africa: 'African Media Barometer'
Another very sophisticated instrument has been put together by the Friedrich Ebert Foundation (FES) in cooperation with the Media Institute of Southern Africa (MISA) which is the basis of its 'African Media Barometer'. They, too, have decided for a smaller selection of countries: Sixteen sub-Saharan states[4] were examined and finally ranked. But their method is a bit different from the methodical approach of the other studies. The FES explains:

> The process is both simple and intensive. So far, panels of ten people each in 16 countries have met for a retreat over a long weekend: half of them personalities from civil society (academics, trade unionists, clerics from different faith communities, jurists, human rights activists, members of women's groups), the other half working in or on the media (journalists, publishers, media lobbyists, media academics). The panel participants are chosen carefully, depending on the experience, knowledge and merits they bring to the discussion as well as the fact that their word counts for something in their respective societies. They are not just attending another seminar talk shop or answering questions put to them. They themselves are the experts, compiling their knowledge and their assessments in a targeted and focused process. The moderator (the only outsider) has just one part to play: to moderate the discussion. The assessment is determined by the panel participants only. Their guide is a list of 42 indicators, home-grown in Africa and not just made up somewhere in Berlin or Washington. (Schellschmidt 2005b: 3)

Further on, 'benchmarks' have been formulated as 'ideal goals' covering four sectors (Schellschmidt 2005b: 4):

1. Freedom of expression, including freedom of the media, are effectively protected and promoted.
2. The media landscape is characterized by diversity, independence and sustainability.
3. Broadcasting regulation is transparent and independent; the state broadcaster is transformed into a truly public broadcaster.
4. The media practise high levels of professional standards.

At the end, each panel participant could allocate one point to each of the four areas in the worst case and five points in the best case. According to the average value of ten evaluations, a ranking of the sixteen countries was developed.

All things considered, this seems to be a rather explorative approach. Much comes out of the discussion and depends on the quality of it. And mutual interaction or manipulation of the panel participants cannot be ruled out. A combination with less reactive methods would probably make sense here – including foreign experts, as well. And again, the quality of coverage in the media is not scientifically analysed.

But the results are, of course, very interesting and the research done by the Friedrich Ebert Foundation has produced a number of good country reports as well.

Problems and shortcomings
Now it would certainly be interesting to go into details of the studies and to compare the evaluation of selected states in each survey. Unfortunately, there is not enough room for that. However, we can conclude that the best rated country in the 'African Media Barometer', that is Mali, also ranked best in the study of Freedom House as the country with the most liberal media system in Africa – at position 51. The RSF also ranked Mali at position 51 – but quite far behind Namibia, Ghana, South Africa, Cap Verde, and Togo (and sixteen places below the ranking in the 2006 survey). This alone reveals that within the various studies there are some differences which are worth looking at scientifically – particularly with regards to the development of an even better research instrument.

An interesting first step into this direction has recently been taken by the American communication scientists Lee B. Becker, Tudor Vlad and Nancy Nusser. In a comparative study they examined four measures – namely those by Freedom House and Reporters Without Borders as well as two other ones which have not yet been mentioned: one by the International Research and Exchanges Board (IREX), situated in Washington like Freedom House, and another one by the New York journalists' rights organization Committee to Protect Journalists (CPJ). Becker, Vlad and Nusser tried to find considerable consistency in the four measurements. In order to do so they carried out a complex quantitative comparative study of the four surveys – and reached the conclusion that there are high correlations between the findings: 'The empirical analyses of the numerical ratings...shows that at least the first three of these organizations largely come to the same conclusions about the media' (Becker, Vlad and Nusser 2007: 18).[5] As 'one of the notable deficiencies of the existing indices', however, it is noted 'that they are heavily oriented toward application. Little effort has been made to define the theoretical concepts being used. Mostly, one must guess about what it is that the organization is actually trying to measure' (Becker, Vlad and Nusser 2007: 19). And, finally, Becker, Vlad and Nusser (2007) conclude: 'The relationship of the existing measures...to other measures is virgin territory. The findings of this analysis suggest it is a territory worthy of exploration.'[6]

Apart from the theoretical challenges, it still seems relatively easy to draw up a catalogue of criteria. A good and comprehensive guideline could be provided, for instance, by 'Media Development Indicators' which were submitted by the International Programme for the Development of Communication (IPDC) of the UNESCO in March 2008. Therein they develop 'a framework for assessing media development' which comprises five principal categories and an elaborate list of key indicators. These principal media development categories deal with the following questions:

- Is there 'a system of regulation and control conducive to freedom of expression, pluralism and diversity of the media'?
- Are there sufficient 'plurality and diversity of media, a level economic playing field and transparency of ownership'?

■ Do the media feature 'as a platform for democratic discourse'?
■ What about the professionalism of journalism? Is there a 'professional capacity building and supporting institutions that underpins freedom of expression, pluralism and diversity'?
■ Is 'the infrastructural capacity...sufficient to support independent media'? (IPDC 2008: 10)

Even if one pinned down what is to be measured and developed an instrument to operationalize it (for example based on these IPDC categories and numerous indicators to be specified in detail and under inclusion of the questionnaires of Freedom House, Reporters Without Borders or the Konrad Adenauer Foundation) there would still remain a vast number of problems in the details.

One little example is that it is certainly a tautology that the murder of journalists is one of the gravest breaches of press freedom and it should be possible to precisely investigate the number of murdered journalists. Yet, it does not appear to be quite that easy.

The Committee to Protect Journalists quotes the number of journalists killed in 2007 to be 64 (CPJ 2008), the Vienna based International Press Institute reports 91 'media employees' murdered in its 2007 census (IPI 2007), the World Association of Newspapers reports as many as 95 (WAN 2007) and the sad number investigated by the Reporters Without Borders is 87 journalists killed plus twenty media assistants (RSF 2007). Why are there such discrepancies? For one thing, it is not consistently defined who should be accepted as a 'journalist' in the statistics: Should cameramen, technical media staff, administrative staff, local couriers, 'part-time reporters' be included? Secondly, a different classification can occur depending on whether a journalist has actually been killed during or because of their work or for other reasons – that is, whether or not they were killed in their 'function' as journalists. And thirdly, it cannot be excluded that not all cases could be investigated.

Conclusion

Methodical problems and difficulties in data collection are numerous, obviously. Therefore, the value of the rankings is limited, at least as far as strong scientific criteria are concerned. The RSF survey is primarily an (expedient) instrument for the purpose of public relations. It is very efficient in bringing public attention to the important concerns and the deserving work of the NGO in the service of freedom of journalists all over the world. The more sophisticated Freedom House survey shows a certain American basic adjustment that could lead to some distortion. The FES inquiry follows an explorative, qualitative approach, which makes it more difficult to generalize the data. And concerning the ambitious KAF questionnaire – as with most of the surveys – we can derive some problems by implementing it in practice.

But all these surveys provide valuable service. Jonathan Becker notes: 'It is at least fortunate that a number of organizations...are tracking developments closely and bringing them to world's attention' (Becker 2003: 112).

What can be deduced from their surveys for future study?

The four presented studies do certainly give good clues for the drafting of a questionnaire. This questionnaire must necessarily be very complex – as complex as the 'phenomenon, freedom of the press'. However, it is equally important that not only is the census instrument very complex, but that during the data collection itself this complexity is not reduced too much. To this end, more than just a few experts need to be included. A multi-methods design seems appropriate: A combination of expert interviews, data evaluations, group discussions and analyses of media content – and tight cooperation with an international research team. 'International cooperation matters', is one of the core wisdoms from the study of the Konrad Adenauer Foundation (KAF 2005: 312). And this cooperation should work in all phases of the research process up to the examination and interpretation of the results.

Early on, questions like these have to be clarified: What should the concrete avail of the survey be? Should the situation in various countries 'only' be described? Should indicators be found which best serve to indicate the dangers to press freedom? Will it be possible to describe the role of the media in the transition process more precisely? Should the results be of direct use in a political debate? Or should it give valuable clues as to where NGOs or the international community of states can specifically help or intervene?

At any rate, system comparison makes sense in many ways. Thus, specifics of one's own system are only recognizable by confrontation with other systems. System comparisons can also have a heuristic function: questions pertaining to the various systems can be asked, detailed studies stimulated. Comparative science is, therefore, not only basic research but it also allows for showing concrete development chances – and also dependencies. Failures and problems can be uncovered. Thus, specific possibilities of counselling in politics as well as in business may appear. Comparative research in press freedom can, in the ideal case, make a contribution to the improvement of the currently very dissatisfying realization of the elementary basic human right of Article 19, already quoted at the beginning. It is obvious that there are many problems and open questions during research – a long process of discussion is necessary – and certainly some pragmatism as well.

Notes

1. A very comprehensive worldwide comparative study as to the status quo of Freedom of Information, was recently proposed by Tony Mendel (commissioned by the UNESCO). Apart from a general overview on the problem position it contains concrete research on the legal situation in fourteen different states (see Mendel 2008).

2. So some textbooks and miscellanies recently have been published – for example Melischek, Seethaler and Wilke 2008; Thomas 2007; Esser and Pfetsch 2003; Hepp and Löffelholz 2002.

3. Italy was ranked at position 79 with a rating of 35 points. In the 2007 survey Italy enhanced its position, now being ranked at position 61 with 29 points.

4. The countries under scrutiny were Angola, Botswana, Ghana, Kenya, Lesotho, Madagascar, Malawi, Mali, Mozambique, Namibia, Senegal, South Africa, Swaziland, Tanzania, Zambia and Zimbabwe.

5. Only the CPJ measure is not really comparable to the others because its measurements are almost exclusively directed towards 'attacks on the press'.

6. The author is presently working on a more extensive study to explore this 'virgin territory' more closely and to create a better theoretical basis for future comparative studies at the same time.

References

Becker, Lee B., Vlad, Tudor and Nusser, Nancy (2007), 'An evaluation of Press Freedom Indicators', *International Communication Gazette*, 69:1, pp. 5–28.

Becker, Jonathan (2003), 'Review Article: Keeping Track of Press Freedom', *European Journal of Communication*, 18:1, pp. 107–12.

Breunig, Christian (1994), *Kommunikationsfreiheiten. Ein internationaler Vergleich*, Konstanz: Universitätsverlag Konstanz.

Breunig, Christian (2000), '50 Jahre Kommunikationspolitik der UNESCO', in Brüne, Stefan (ed.), *Neue Medien und Öffentlichkeiten. Politik und Telekommunikation in Afrika, Asien und Lateinamerika*, Hamburg: Deutsches Übersee Institut, pp. 99–114.

Committee to Protect Journalists (CPJ) (ed.) (2007), 'Attacks on the Press. A Worldwide Survey', Washington D.C., http://www.cpj.org/attacks06/pages06/aop06index.html. Accessed 7 February 2008.

Committee to Protect Journalists (CPJ) (ed.) (2008), 'Journalists Death Hit Decade Peak', http://www.cpj.org/Briefings/2007/killed_07/killed_07.html. Accessed 7 February 2008.

Deutsch Karlekar, Karin (Freedom House) (ed.) (2007a), 'Freedom of the Press 2007. A Global Survey of Media Independence', Lanham et al., http://www.freedomhouse.org/template.cfm?page=362. Accessed 7 February 2008.

Deutsch Karlekar, Karin (2007b), 'Press Freedom in 2006: Growing Threats to Media Independence', in Deutsch Karlekar, Karin (Freedom House) (ed.), *Freedom of the Press 2007. A Global Survey of Media Independence*, Lanham et al., http://www.freedomhouse.org/uploads/fop/2007/fopessay2007.pdf. Accessed 7 February 2008.

Esser, Frank and Pfetsch, Barbara (eds.) (2003), *Politische Kommunikation im internationalen Vergleich. Grundlagen, Anwendungen, Perspektiven*, Wiesbaden: Westdeutscher Verlag.

Freedom House (2006), 'Table of Global Press Freedom Rankings', Washington and New York, http://www.freedomhouse.org/template.cfm?page=271&year=2006. Accessed 7 February 2008.

Freedom House (ed.) (2007a), '2006 Annual Report', Washington and New York, http://www.freedomhouse.org/uploads/special_report/49.pdf. Accessed 7 February 2008.

Freedom House (2007b), 'Methodology', Washington and New York, http://www.freedomhouse.org/template.cfm?page=350&ana_page=339&year=2007. Accessed 7 February 2008.

Freedom House (2007c), '2007 Freedom of the Press World Ranking', Washington and New York, http://www.freedomhouse.org/template.cfm?page=389&year=2007. Accessed 7 February 2008.

Freedom House (2007d), 'Map of Press Freedom', Washington and New York, http://www.freedomhouse.org/template.cfm?page=251&year=2007. Accessed 7 February 2008.

Freedom House (2008), 'Press Freedom Losses Outnumber Gains Two to One in 2007', Washington, http://freedomhouse.org/template.cfm?page=70&release=649. Accessed 29 April 2008.

Friedrich Ebert Foundation and Media Institute of Southern Africa (eds.) (2006/07), 'African Media Barometer', http://www.misa.org/mediabarometer.html; http://www.fes.de/in_afrika/pl_namm.htm. Accessed 7 February 2008.

Hafez, Kai (2002), 'International vergleichende Medienforschung: Eine unterentwickelte Forschungsdimension', in Hafez, Kai (ed.), *Die Zukunft der internationalen Kommunikationswissenschaft in Deutschland*, Hamburg: Deutsches Übersee Institut, pp. 59–94.

Heinrich Boell Foundation (ed.) (2004), 'Walking a Tightrope. News Media and Freedom of Expression in the Arab Middle East' (Report compiled by Layla Al-Zubaidi), Bonn, http://www.boell-meo.org/download_en/media_study.pdf. Accessed 7 February 2008.

Hepp, Andreas and Löffelholz, Martin (eds.) (2002), *Grundlagentexte zur transkulturellen Kommunikation*, Konstanz: Universitätsverlag Konstanz.

Holtz-Bacha, Christina (2003), 'Wie die Freiheit messen? Wege und Probleme der empirischen Bewertung von Pressefreiheit', in Wolfgang R. Langenbucher, (ed.), *Die Kommunikationsfreiheit der Gesellschaft.*

Die demokratischen Funktionen eines Grundrechts (*Publizistik*-Sonderheft 4/2003), Wiesbaden: Westdeutscher Verlag, pp. 403–12.

Holzweißig, Gunter (1997), *Zensur ohne Zensor. Die SED-Informationsdiktatur*, Köln: Bouvier Verlag.

International Press Institute (IPI) (ed.) (2006), 'IPI World Press Freedom Review', Wien, http://www.freemedia.at/cms/ipi/freedom.html. Accessed 7 February 2008.

International Press Institute (IPI) (2007), 'IPI Death Watch 2007', http://www.freemedia.at/cms/ipi/deathwatch.html?year=2007. Accessed 7 February 2008.

International Programme for the Development of Communication (IPDC) (2008), 'Media Development Indicators: A Frework for Assessing Media Development', Paris: UNESCO, http://portal.unesco.org/ci/en/files/26032/12058560693media_indicators_framework_en.pdf/media_indicators_framework_en.pdf. Accessed 20 April 2008.

Kleinsteuber, Hans J. (2002), 'Mediensysteme im internationalen Vergleich: Ein Überblick', in Hafez, Kai (ed.), *Die Zukunft der internationalen Kommunikationswissenschaft in Deutschland*, Hamburg: Deutsches Übersee-Institut, pp. 39–58.

Konrad Adenauer Foundation (ed.) (2005), ‚KAF Democracy Report 2005: Media and Democracy', Bonn, http://www.kas.de/publikationen/2006/7532_dokument.html. Accessed 7 February 2008.

Livingstone, Sonia (2003), 'On the Challenges of Cross-National Comparative Media Research', *European Journal of Communication*, 18:4, pp. 477–500.

Melischek, Gabriele, Seethaler Josef and Wilke, Jürgen (eds.) (2008), *Medien & Kommunikationsforschung im Vergleich. Grundlagen. Gegenstandsbereiche, Verfahrensweisen*, Wiesbaden: Verlag für Sozialwissenschaften..

Mendel, Toby (2008), 'Freedom of Information. A Comparative Legal Survey', Paris: UNESCO, http://portal.unesco.org/ci/en/ev.php-URL_ID=26267&URL_DO=DO_TOPIC&URL_SECTION=201.html. Accessed 20 April 2008.

Reporters Without Borders (ed.) (2007a), 'Annual Report 2007', Paris, http://www.rsf.org/IMG/pdf/rapport_en_bd-4.pdf. Accessed 7 February 2008.

Reporters Without Borders (ed.) (2007b), 'World Press Freedom Index', Paris, http://www.rsf.org/article.php3?id_article=24025. Accessed 7 February 2008.

Reporters Without Borders (RSF) (2007c), 'Press Freedom Barometer 2007', Paris, http://www.rsf.org/article.php3?id_article=24909. Accessed 7 February 2008.

Reporters Without Borders (RSF) (2007d), 'Questionnaire for compiling a 2007 world press freedom index', Paris, http://www.rsf.org/article.php3?id_article=24046. Accessed 7 February 2008.

Rohn, Walter (2002), *Regelung versus Nichtregelung internationaler Kommunikationsbeziehungen. Das Beispiel der UNESCO-Kommunikationspolitik*, Wien: Verlag der Österreichischen Akademie der Wissenschaften.

Schellschmidt, Peter (2005a), 'The African Media Barometer. A new instrument in media development cooperation', Bonn, http://library.fes.de/pdf-files/bueros/namibia/03267.pdf. Accessed 7 February 2008.

Schellschmidt, Peter (2005b), 'The African Media Barometer – gauging the state of freedom of expression and freedom of the media through self-assessment', Bonn, http://library.fes.de/pdf-files/iez/04253.pdf. Accessed 7 February 2008.

Stevenson, Robert L. (1994), *Global Communication in the Twenty-First Century*, New York and London: Pearson.

Thomaß, Barbara (ed.) (2007), *Mediensysteme im internationalen Vergleich*, Konstanz: Universitätsverlag Konstanz.

Tietje, Christian (2002), 'Grundzüge und rechtliche Probleme einer internationalen Medienordnung', in Hans-Bredow-Institut (ed.), *Internationales Handbuch Medien 2002/2003*, Baden-Baden: Nomos, pp. 15–36.

UN (2001), 'NGO Committee hears arguments for, against Freedom House', Press Release NGO/432; 25 May 2001, http://www.un.org/News/Press/docs/2001/ngo432.doc.htm. Accessed 7 February 2008.

World Association of Newspapers (WAN) (2007), 'Media employees killed in 2007', http://www.wan-press.org/rubrique.php3?id_rubrique=873. Accessed 7 February 2008.

Pluralism and Participation as Desired Results of Press Freedom: Measuring Media System Performance

Andrea Czepek

Introduction

Freedom of the press is not an end in itself but serves a function in a democratic society. Journalism needs to be independent from the state, but also from overwhelming economic interests to provide diverse, complete and correct information to the citizens and enable universal participation in public discourse.

The term 'press freedom' is related to the concept of freedom of expression. In the broader sense, it encompasses freedom not only of print media, but also electronic and other public media. Conventionally, it is understood primarily as freedom from government control. The concept of press freedom was developed in the context of economic liberalization and the emergence of a free market in Britain – independent information was seen as a necessary condition for free trade. Absolute 'press freedom' demands that newspapers and other mass media organizations in a given state can operate and convey information without government interference. This is an important condition for press freedom. However, freedom from government control alone does not guarantee the free exchange of information and a pluralistic public debate. The common understanding of press freedom focuses on press freedom as commercial freedom, whereas in a context of consolidating and enhancing democratic processes, freedom of the press is seen as the opportunity for every citizen or societal group to be informed and have their voices heard and views reflected in public debate.[1]

The existing indices which are used to 'measure' press freedom in different countries are often superficial, biased and unsystematic, as Markus Behmer has pointed out in his previous chapter. Conventional indices emphasize freedom from government control and tend to neglect other aspects, such as other structural and direct factors that influence press freedom, thus disregarding to some extent the complexity of the issue. In addition, they often lack scientific consistency, a major challenge for any such index as Bindé has noted (Bindé 2005: 161). So, what could be a different way of determining press freedom?

Structural conditions

First of all, structural pre-conditions need to be analysed on a broader basis. Merely stating whether or not press freedom is guaranteed by the constitution and simply counting cases of censorship and harassment against journalists does not alone suffice to describe the state of press freedom in a country. In a complex society, the different sub-systems, such as political, economic and other sub-systems (religion, education), interact with media systems, and their competing objectives overlap and influence those of the media system. This is especially true since the media have the function of enabling communication between sub-systems and are therefore strongly interconnected with the other sub-systems. Various dependencies influence media organizations and have to be taken into account when looking at the degree of independence a media system enjoys. Of course, *legal provisions* are essential, but the judicial practice is also relevant.

Increasingly important are the *economic structures*. Dependency on market mechanisms such as high return margins limits the freedom of journalists and their reporting. In liberal democracies such economic conditions become main constraints to freedom of the press. Freedom of the press and of the media, in a broader context, thus also includes (relative) independence from economic influences.

The *political framework* also needs to be looked at more closely. What are the government's political objectives towards the media? Which political goals are dominant at the moment, and in what relation can they be seen to press freedom? For instance, security policies might prevail at a certain time and may render freedom rights secondary. A special concern in most European countries have been anti-terrorism measures that have interfered with media freedom, for instance when journalists are subject to surveillance or are forced to reveal their sources.

Furthermore, constraints on press freedom might be based on the *historical development* in a country. The historical experiences shape media structures and the conditions around them. In Germany, for example, Nazi propaganda is illegal by punitive law, which is a direct reaction to the Nazi past. But there are more indirect consequences as well, such as the re-structuring of the media landscape in Germany after the Second World War: due to the fact that many traditional publishers did not receive printing licenses from the Allied Forces directly after the War, new actors (such as Bertelsmann and Springer) could develop in the vacant space. In Greece, Spain and Portugal, media systems are still shaped by the aftermath of their relatively recent totalitarian rule. And in the post-Communist countries the impact of the past and the transition phase itself contribute to specific concerns with press freedom and plurality.

When comparing media systems and media freedom, social, cultural, traditional, and religious issues are often neglected, but they play an important role. The *social structures* of a country may be reflected in different ways in the media system. In the United Kingdom, for example, a relatively stratified class society results in a rather segregated newspaper market with different print media types (tabloids vs. 'quality' press) catering to different groups of society. Another aspect is the question of how minorities and disadvantaged groups are represented in the media, have access to them and find their views and concerns reflected in public media. *Cultural factors* might include the dominant communication culture, which might have an impact on public discourse, as well as a tradition of taboos. Cultural traditions, such as the degree of communal organization of the citizens, may contribute to certain media traditions. In Italy, for example, where involvement of the citizens in communal and church associations, unions and political parties is very high and such alignments are closely knit, journalism reflects this partisanship by also being closely aligned with distinct associations' interests and positions. However, in other countries such as Germany, where such partisan involvement is not as common and less stable, journalism is expected to be more neutral and internally pluralistic. The possible impact of *religion* on media freedom is highlighted by the discussion surrounding the publication of the so called 'Mohammed caricatures' in Denmark, but the influence of Christian churches on European journalism can also be an intervening factor, for example when defining norms of morality and taboos.

In sum, a first step in analysing the state of press freedom in a country can therefore be to analyse such structural pre-conditions, which we attempt to do with the case studies in this book. The structural conditions vary in each country and create unique situations which are shaped by unique combinations of the conditions in these realms, but despite all differences, the comparison also shows commonalities (and common concerns) among some countries and, as decisions and policies on the European level become more and more relevant, even Europe-wide.

Content pluralism

The project group formed by the authors of this volume will not, however, stop at looking at the structural conditions. The basic idea of a new index for press freedom suggested here is that press freedom in a country can be measured by exploring the *outcome* in addition to the structural conditions: is the system producing diverse, critical informational (journalistic) content? And is a broad public able to participate, as consumers and as producers, in the information exchange? There are two assumptions: for one, societies are complex and diverse; a variety of different views and interests exist in every society. Thus, a democratic media system should reflect this diversity and give all groups of society the opportunity to be represented and voice their views and interests. The second assumption is: if a lack of pluralistic media content and restrictions of access to informational media content are observed, this could indicate that freedom of the press is inhibited. It could therefore be possible to measure press freedom by determining whether (informational) media content is diverse and whether all groups of society are represented and have access to the public media – in short, whether media systems perform with regard to their societal functions.

An unregulated media market tends to produce monopolies or, at least, very dominant media conglomerates; a development that reduces the chances for other groups to voice their opinions and interests, especially if they do not cater to a mass market or address citizens as consumers. Looking at media content, an unregulated, concentrated media market would cater to such mass markets rather than minorities and deliver content that has a monetary value or can be sold (to advertisers and consumers). However, the correlation between external pluralism (meaning plurality of media ownership) and content diversity has not yet been sufficiently proven. Media concerns even argue that they ensure diversity by 'saving' smaller media enterprises from bankruptcy when they acquire them. It cannot be assumed that a very concentrated media market or very market oriented media policies *per se* lead to less independent, less diverse media. In addition, diverse media ownership alone does not guarantee press freedom and pluralism, as many examples in the case studies later on in this volume show.

The approach of measuring content pluralism as one indicator for media freedom may also help with another critical issue. Self censorship is often a concern in journalism, induced by various dependencies on the political and economic system. But it is difficult to measure self-censorship. Thus, pluralism of media reporting can be an indicator because high diversity of media content indicates a low level of self-censorship. The analysis of content diversity in relation to the structural independence will be the next step of research that the project group will undertake beyond the analyses included in this book.

Journalistic independence

One issue that is often discussed in the context of press freedom is whose freedom press freedom is, that is, who has the privilege to claim that right? In practice, not everybody can participate equally in the public discourse. But even if one considers only the media organizations themselves, it may be asked whether the proprietor of a newspaper, for example, has the right to exercise press freedom, or whether each individual journalist has this right (even in opposition to the newspaper's owner). Merrill makes a distinction between 'press freedom' as an institutional freedom from government control, and 'journalistic freedom' as an individual freedom of journalists from interference by editors and publishers (Merrill 1989: 34).

Another critical aspect of the concept of press freedom is that press freedom is not only a freedom *from* (for example government control), but also a freedom *to* – a freedom to report or not to report, a freedom to convey certain messages and opinions and not others. From this standpoint, the discussion about a 'responsible use of press freedom' arose. Freedom from external interference, certainly, is the foundation for an ethical use of the media, because one can only act ethically if one is free to choose. But in addition, journalists are often required to make responsible decisions about what to report about. They have to consider the possible effects of their reporting on others.

For example, in 1984, UNESCO published a list of ten principles of professional ethics in journalism (see Nordenstreng 1984). The list was developed by several international journalism organizations and is supposed to serve as an 'inspiration' for national or regional codes of ethics. Those principles encompass not only demands for free access to objective, unbiased, and accurate reporting, but also ethical standards for journalists. They state that the journalist is accountable not only to those controlling the media, but to the public at large, and that journalists should respect privacy, human dignity, democracy and equality. They also state that journalists should be committed to the elimination of war, apartheid, oppression, colonialism and neo-colonialism, poverty, malnutrition and diseases, and that they should promote a New World Information Order. These goals go much further than the western idea that a free media in a 'marketplace of ideas' would function automatically. They are based on the acknowledgment that further guidance is needed, and that freedom also comes with responsibilities.

While the UNESCO objectives go quite far and could be interpreted as contradicting press freedom in some regards (consequently, the US government rejected the initiative for a new information order in favour of a 'free flow of information' – with a dominance of a handful of north-western news agencies processing most of the world's news), discomfort with an absolute free market approach to press freedom remains, nevertheless. In order to avoid public interference with media freedom and still ensure ethical reporting, self-regulation by media institutions might be a third way[2] towards ensuring freedom of the press and responsibility which is discussed by Vinzenz Wyss and Guido Keel in this volume.

Participation

The question of who is actually free to communicate leads to another factor that is relevant when determining the state of press freedom: the possibilities for participation. Press freedom does not fulfil its democratic functions if it is only freedom for the very few. As the UNESCO World Report points out, 'knowledge societies in the twenty-first century will only be able to usher in a new era of sustainable human development if they ensure not only universal access to knowledge, but also the participation of all in knowledge societies' (Bindé 2005: 159). Is access to the media an elite privilege? Or is it open to the public? Does everyone have access to a wide range of information, are there possibilities to place information or actively produce media content? Only if a broad public and all relevant groups of society have access to diverse media and the potential of being heard, is press freedom really achieved.

Index of press freedom

Whether media systems are relatively free, and produce diverse, critical information, can be measured with an index based on these considerations that could be applied to media systems in different countries. When evaluating press freedom, five factors could be looked at:

- *Structural conditions* (legal, political, economic, historical and cultural)
- *Organizational prerequisites* (organizational objectives, internal structure, self- and co-regulation)
- *Individual journalistic freedom* (influence exercised, degree of harassment, censorship and self-censorship)
- *Content pluralism* as an indicator for press freedom
- *Possibilities for participation* (access to the media; active as producers and passive as consumers/recipients).

Systematic data collection

One aspect was to include more factors into the scope of examination. The other critique of conventional measures is a methodical one: The data collection process in the current indices is often arbitrary and unsystematic. It would be an improvement to obtain the necessary information about the situation in different countries in a systematic and scientific way. The values could be comprised to indicate the relative level of press freedom in a country, and the development can be compared over time. Thus, a content analysis will be an important instrument in the future implementation of the index, as well as systematic surveys. The following table suggests a systematic evaluation of the index, which could be conducted in various countries and yield a more differentiated picture of the status quo of press freedom in a country, and be used to compare major problems, constraints and possible solutions.

Table 1: Index of press freedom.

Structural conditions
- Legal provisions and implementation
- Economic structures
- Political framework
- Historical developments
- Social, cultural, religious and traditional influences

Organizational prerequisites
- Organizational objectives and values
- Internal structure
- Self- and co-regulation

Journalistic independence
- Occurrence of repressions by the state or other organizations against journalists and/or media organizations
- Cases of censorship
- Occurrence of harassment and intimidation of journalists, media organizations
- Self-censorship
- Resources / employment conditions
- Education

Plurality – Scope and diversity of media content / i.e. informational content
- E.g., are certain controversial topics neglected?
- Are opposing views displayed?
- Is there critique of government and other organizations' policies?
- Are minorities' perspectives represented?
- Is there a broad variety of topics and views represented?

Participation – Access to the media / possibilities for participation in public discourse
- Passive access: who has access as a recipient? (There could be restrictions, e.g. technical, economic, lack of education, distribution restrictions)
- Active access:
  a) Who has access to media content production?
  b) Who are the sources and actors referred to in media reporting?
- Empowerment: media education and literacy

Outlook

The thesis underlying this index is that content pluralism and universal participation in public debate are desired characteristics of democratic media systems. The question is whether media systems and the actors within them are autonomous enough to pursue these goals, and this again can be determined by measuring their performance in terms of plurality and participation.

Table 2: Index of press freedom: Method and Evaluation.

	Method of data collection	Values (examples)
		Production
Legal and structural conditions	■ Secondary Analysis	*Macro level* 0 = no legal provisions for press freedom or many restrictions; majority of media under state control or very monopolized. 1 = legal guarantees for press freedom exist but in practice many restrictions are applied; certain diversity in media ownership but strong state control or control of few large media organizations etc. 2 = few legal restrictions; various media owners (state and others) etc. 3 = no legal restrictions, little concentration in media markets, high diversity of media owners etc.
Organizational prerequisites	■ Secondary Analysis ■ Survey	*Meso level* 0 = organizational objectives are focused on economic goals and/or particular interests; organizational structure is hierarchical and restrictive; possibly strong regulation. 1 = some commitment to societal objectives (dissemination of information, enable communication, reflect pluralistic views), but economic and/or partisan interests prevail. 2 = societal/democratic objectives are dominant at least in some media organizations, economic/partisan interests secondary; organizational structures allow some autonomy to organization members. 3 = most media organizations focus on societal objectives, structure allows universal and diverse access, functioning self-regulation.
Journalistic independence	■ Survey among journalists; media organizations ■ Secondary sources	*Micro level* 0 = repressions against journalists are frequent, censorship and self-censorship occur 1 = repressions and censorship occur, but some journalists are able to report critically without being intimidated. 2 = repressions occur, but the majority of journalists can report freely. 3 = there are no cases of harassment or censorship.

	Service	
Content Pluralism/ Scope and diversity of informational media content	■ Content Analysis	0 = media report one-sided, government policies are not criticized, opposing views are not displayed, large segments of society are not represented. 1 = some criticism of the government or other major organizations occurs, but government-sided, uncritical or elite-oriented reporting dominates. 2 = diversity and critical reporting dominate vs. biased reporting. 3 = there is an overall diverse reporting; many relevant topics and opinions can be voiced, differing interests are displayed, there is criticism and control of state and economic policies.
	Citizens	
Participation	■ Content Analysis ■ Survey ■ Secondary analysis (e.g. statistical and demographic data)	0 = active and passive access to media is reserved to a small elite. 1 = there are possibilities to participate, but large segments of the society are excluded from public discourse. 2 = there are many possibilities to access media, but some groups are excluded because of structural, political, educational or economic reasons. 3 = broad active and passive participation is possible for most relevant social groups.

In this book, we mainly address the first three factors, which represent three levels of conditions shaping the freedom and plurality of a media system: system-wide structural conditions, the level of media organizations, and the individual level of media actors with regard to information content, for example journalists. The other two factors, content diversity and participation chances, will be subject to future research of the work group.

Notes

1. UNESCO for example pursues four goals with its communication and information policies 'Towards Knowledge Societies': freedom of expression, universal and equal access to information, education for all and cultural diversity (see Bindé 2005).
2. On the discussion of reconciling freedom and regulation, see McQuail 2003.

References

Bindé, Jérôme (2005), *Towards Knowledge Societies*, UNESCO World Report, Paris: UNESCO.

Mcquail, Denis (2003), *Media Accountability and Freedom of Publication*, Oxford: Oxford University Press.

Merrill, John C. (1989), *The Dialectic in Journalism. Toward a Responsible Use of Press Freedom*, Baton Rouge: Louisiana State University Press.

Nordenstreng, Kaarle (1984), *The Mass Media Declaration of UNESCO*, Norwood, NJ: Ablex.

Is the Clash of Rationalities Leading Nowhere? Media Pluralism in European Regulatory Policies

Beata Klimkiewicz

Only where things can be seen by many in a variety of aspects without changing their identity, so that those who are gathered around them know they see sameness in utter diversity, can worldly reality truly and reliably appear.

Hannah Arendt (Arendt 1958: 57)

Introduction

Media pluralism is one of those terms in European media policy that generates broad respect for its undisputed merits, and its importance for the process of democracy and identity formation at the European level is generally agreed upon. These processes are closely related to the media exposure of distinctive opinions on European matters, as well as values and cultural representations that influence them. Media pluralism contributes to the richness of European public opinion and identity formation, yet its complexity is liable to ambiguity. A variety of interpretations, the manifold character and ever-changing circumstances provide for a wide range of how the concept itself is being used in the formulation of policy objectives and rationales, as well as in policy implementation.

The proposed contribution aims at the conceptual analysis of media pluralism as it has been used and operationalized in European media policy. Three aspects will be observed in this respect: vocabulary used, ways of reasoning and development of a policy process itself. The chapter argues that problematization of media pluralism stems from two different standards of rationality (cutting across geopolitical divisions), and that carries with it the implication of ambivalence of policy-making and ambiguity of the language in which policy process is negotiated.[1] An important question to be addressed points to the potential of this tension for identity formation at the European level.

Media pluralism: Definitions and approaches in media policy
Conceptual interpretations
The context and scale of media pluralism, as well as its relations and interdependencies with the political system and larger society, define the way and discourse through which the term itself is conceptualized and operationalized as a policy rationale. Media pluralism is approached at a number of layers: a macro level of media systems (media ownership and service structures, entry costs and conditions), a meso level of media institutions (media performance, professional practices, user access and the way the user interacts with the content and services), and a micro level of media contents. Media pluralism is also interpreted through conceptual dichotomies or alternatives such as external/internal, proportional/open, organized/spontaneous, polarized/moderate, evaluative/descriptive or reactive/interactive/proactive. The table below illustrates this conceptual framework:

In the context of media policy, the operational definition of media pluralism has most notoriously developed around the axis of the external/internal dimension. Wijayananda Yayaweera described it as 'the end of monopolies of any kind and the existence of the greatest possible number of newspapers, periodicals and broadcasting stations reflecting the widest possible range of opinion within the community' (Yayaweera 2005). Using different wording but the same distinction, the UK White Paper 'A New Future for Communications' referred to diversity as the range of different programmes and services available to viewers and listeners. Plurality, on the other hand, was viewed as referring to the choices viewers and listeners are offered between different providers of such services (Department of Trade and Industry 2000). Most comprehensively, the notion of media pluralism has been elaborated by the Council of Europe and its advisory committees (later successively used and modified by other European institutions). The Activity Report of the Committee of Experts on Media Concentration and Pluralism (MM-CM 1994) conceives of pluralism as 'internal in nature, with a wide range of social, political and cultural values, opinions, information and interests finding expression within one media organization, or external in nature, through a number of such organizations, each expressing a particular point of view' (see also Jakubowicz 2006a).

The frequently drawn distinction between *external* 'plurality of autonomous and independent media' and *internal* 'diversity of media contents available to the public' seen from the media supply point of view revealed a problematic relationship between the two dimensions. Namely, the research has not, to date, unanimously proved that this relationship is causal and direct. A strong link between plurality of ownership and diversity of content cannot, in practice, be easily demonstrated. Although some researchers sustain that extensive media concentration leads to promotion of corporate values and political preferences of media owners and advertisers in media contents (Bagdikian 2000), others convincingly argue that a direct link between media concentration and content diversity cannot be identified in quantitative terms (Ward 2006). Most commentators also agree that media pluralism is a multidimensional issue and should not be confined to mere plurality of ownership and diversity of content.

Table 1: Definitions of media pluralism.

External	■ plurality of independent and autonomous media outlets and providers. ■ multiple centres of ownership, production, performance and distribution control.
Organized	■ media pluralism is organized in a segmented structure of media outlets and providers representing different social groups, cultural communities and political orientations. ■ a strong link to institutions representing these groups and interests.
Internal	■ diversity of media contents, services and sources reflecting and generating a broad variety of opinions, views, representations and values of social, ethical, political and cultural nature.
Spontaneous	■ media system is structured more spontaneously. ■ media representation of a multiplicity of competing interests and values is individualized.
Proportional (Representative)	■ media pluralism proportionally reflects existing population's preferences; political and cultural division in a society; ethnic, linguistic and religious population's structure.
Polarized	■ media are identified with ideologically opposed tendencies; distinct cultural, ethnic, religious traditions (ethnic, cultural, religious cleavages are deep). ■ advocacy and commentary-oriented journalism.
Open	■ media pluralism equally or openly reflects population's preferences; political and cultural division in a society; population's ethnic, linguistic and religious structure.
Moderate	■ ideological distance represented by the various media is narrow, tendencies toward the centre are stronger. ■ cultural, ethnic, linguistic differences are not projected into the media structure.
Descriptive	■ describes media pluralism conceptual and factual features, indicators, aspects.
Reactive	■ media pluralism reflects diversity of opinions, political views, identity choices, cultural representations among users through media performance, services, content, structural aspects,
Evaluative	■ evaluates descriptively identified features.
Interactive	■ media pluralism results from a variety of interactions between media users and providers.
Proactive	■ media pluralism generates and actively shapes diversity of opinions, political views, identity choices, cultural representations among users through media performance, services, content, structural aspects.

Source: MM-CM 1994; McQuail 1992; Van Cuilenburg and Van der Wurff 2000; Kekes 1996; Hallin and Mancini 2004.

The potential of media pluralism
The traditional concept of media pluralism is being challenged by the changing media ecology and societal transformation resulting from the impact of the digital revolution, convergence and multiplicity of media platforms, services and providers. In this new context media pluralism presents the *potential* of full usage and exploitation, which depends on individual users, their ability to read the 'media script' (also critically and alternatively to the production routines), and to generate their own messages, ways of distribution and interaction with the media services. The potential of media pluralism can be conceived through its 'building blocks' and the capacities these blocks are able to mobilize. Thus it is considered a *condition conducive to* the balance between multiple centres of media control, compensation of multiple sources of information, competition between multiple opinions and views, socialization through multiple forms of media access and participation, as well as recognition and representation of multiple values and choice between multiple forms of interaction.

Table 2: Potential of media pluralism: Key aspects and capacities.

'Building blocks'	Capacities
Multiple centres of media control	Balance
	Shared control
Multiple sources	Complementarity
	Compensation
Multiple opinions and views	Competition
	(Discursive, not instrumental)
Multiple access and participation	Socialization
Multiple values	Recognition and representation (not fragmentation)
Multiple forms of interaction	Choice

An important capacity of the media pluralism potential is a balance between multiple centres of media control. These are not necessarily identical with the ownership structures, although the latter definitely play a most influential role when it comes to the development of media networks (usually very centralized due to complex technological conditions and investment needed). The centres of control vary in the extent to which they balance ownership and provider control with journalistic and content producer autonomy and independence, and more generally, with regulatory constraints. Subscription systems handled by digital providers are often criticized for the exclusive use of proprietary technical solutions and the lack of service interoperability, resulting in the increased control exercised both over subscribers and producers (Nissen 2006). It is therefore relevant in this context to what degree multiple competing centres of media production, performance and delivery 'mutually control themselves' and whether there is a broad respect for this limited or shared media control.

The compensation of multiple sources is linked to a 'communicating vessels effect', which a media user is able to activate. Media pluralism potential may be used more effectively if a media user at a disadvantage with respect to one source of information is able to compensate for this lack by exploiting his access to a different source. In an era of source-recycling, when the same sources are re-packaged and used across the full range of media platforms and distributed by different divisions of the same conglomerate, clear identification and recognition of the sources has crucial significance. The competition between multiple opinions and views is another key capacity of the media pluralism potential. Proliferation of the content on new platforms does not in itself guarantee pluralism. Freedom of choice is an essential possibility, which can be exercised if the choice is made between different options. It is also important *how* this choice is made. Jadwiga Staniszkis (2006) warns that competition between different opinions and views should be discursive in its nature to raise the quality of a public discussion. The competition, which resembles a stock exchange where diversity becomes instrumental and rational arguments can not be developed due to technocratic procedures or journalistic routines, leads to meaningless diversity (Staniszkis 2006: 8–9).

Multiple access to and participation in an exchange of media images, words, and representations defines a process of socialization and shapes models of behaviour. Media use is woven into the fabric of everyday life; the media substitute social activities and change the character of social institutions (Schulz 2004). In such highly media-pervaded societies, the potential of media pluralism depends on the quality of socialization accompanied and strengthened by media literacy skills, such as the competence to distribute ideas in different media formats, an ability to critically read media contents and to oppose, when necessary, biased and harmful media representations. Media pluralism is also often described through the capacity of recognition and representation of multiple, often conflicting, values. Yet this polarized media projection of values can reinforce existing prejudices, or widen the gap between different communities. Furthermore, it may contribute to a fragmented society, in which individuals interact primarily with those in the same identity community, and are exposed mostly to those opinions with which they already agree (Hoynes 2002). Thus, the potential of media pluralism may be effectively used if the representation and recognition of multiple values does not lead to fragmentation and ghettoization.

Finally, full exploitation of media pluralism potential depends on choices made among multiple forms of interactions with the media. The fact that media users may increasingly control how and when they interact with media services stimulates diversity. The users are free to decide on the proportion of attention they choose to pay to passive (push) or interactive (pull) media use, which issues they want to scrutinize and contribute to interactively, and which contents they prefer to receive passively. Yet, an interactive future is certain to produce new types of monopoly (bottlenecks controlled by private suppliers) and new forms of exclusion (low level of media literacy) that can only be tackled with purposeful and positive intervention, to remedy information and media access asymmetry (see for example Graham and Davies 1997; Freedman 2005; Collins and Murroni 1996). Moreover, interactive services are still not universal. Gaps in Digital literacy, in particular, internet and computer skills, are still important especially for groups at risk, those with low education, economically inactive and the older population (EC, DG Information Society and the Media 2007: 5).

Media pluralism comes into being through relations and context in which it is involved. It is also conditionally linked to the public sphere and articulation of issues of common concern. In media policy, the relevance of the concept itself is marked by its potential. In other words, it is important how the potential of media pluralism is seen to be activated and how connections between its 'building blocks' and capacities are to be stimulated in policy language, way of reasoning and development of a policy process itself.

Inclusive and autonomous approach

In media policy thinking, media pluralism is regarded in the broader social and political context as a contribution to deliberative democracy or as a fundamental condition for a democratic public sphere (see Habermas 1995, 1996; McQuail 1992; Cavallin 2000: 105–70). Primarily concerning a variety of views, opinions, and attitudes of a political, religious, and ethical nature, such diversity serves as a founding rationale for defenders of public service broadcasting, and other structural measures promoting a more interventionist articulation of pluralism. Yet pluralism is also seen in economic, technocratic or professional terms – as increasing freedom of choice for the consumer, freedom of operation for the industry, and the right to self-regulation and institutional autonomy; in other words, in opposition to interventionist public regulation.

The two perspectives on conceptualization of media pluralism for the purpose of media policy can be examined through the role of functional differentiation (Luhmann 2000; Alexander 1981: 17–51). In the first *inclusive* approach, the media (whose role it is to contribute to appropriate functioning of a democratic system) are not seen as functionally differentiated from other spheres of social life (politics, culture, civil society) or social bodies (political groups, the state, interest groups). The media, as with central institutions of the public sphere, are expected to identify and politically expose problems (a warning function), but also to thematize them and offer possible solutions (a problematizing function). Although their capacity to solve these problems seems limited, it is to be utilized to oversee the further treatment of problematic areas by the actors of a political system (Habermas 1996: 359). Thus, the inclusive option asserts that the media are institutionally connected to social and political organizations, such as political parties, interest groups, churches, and cultural organizations. Media pluralism is to be best structured and achieved at the level of a media system as a whole, through the existence of a range of media outlets or organizations reflecting the points of view of different groups or cultural representations, rooted in different traditions of a society. Such a system, characterized by a dominant presence of external (and organized) pluralism, will obviously be considered to have a high level of political and cultural parallelism (the extent to which a media system reflects the major political and cultural division in society) (Hallin and Mancini 2004: 28). The advocacy status of civic, cultural, religious, alternative or politically-oriented media can also presuppose that alternative portrayals will be used which may differ from the canons of professional journalism (Dahlgren 1995: 156–9).

The *autonomous* approach assumes that the media are in a process of becoming autonomous systems and networks due to functional differentiation. Thus, the media are functionally differentiated from other systems within a society and their institutional relations with the state, political groups, cultural and social organizations are significantly dispersed. Differentiation does not mean that the media system is detached from the sphere of politics and other arenas of social life. Media networks and their applications increasingly organize and shape relations between the different actors of political and social systems. As a result, these relations can be interpreted both as political and as relations between information and communication (Van Dijk 2006). The autonomous approach can also be characterized by the growth of professional norms, self-regulation and the degree of universalism in national civil cultures (Hallin and Mancini 2004: 79). The trend towards differentiation is, to a large extent, driven by economic factors and commercialization. Media pluralism could be best manifested through the dominance of internal pluralism, achieved within each individual media outlet or organization. A system characterized by a dominant role of internal pluralism will have a low level of political and cultural parallelism, and particular media outlets will aim at maintaining universal provision and neutrality, as well as focusing on the experience and perspective of the 'common' citizen (Hallin and Mancini 2004: 79). Another question related to growing media autonomy (autonomy from a political system but not economic forces), is whether other cultural and social fields will lose their own autonomy as they are increasingly influenced and 'colonized' by the mass media (see Habermas 1996; Bourdieu 1998; Meyer 2002).

The normative frameworks and grounds for policy options described above are rooted in different standards of rationality rather than interests. Jadwiga Staniszkis (2004) points out that 'rationality' refers to the way of reasoning which is logical and correct in light of given rationales and method of reality problematization. Hence, different or even conflicting choices of two parties using different rationales may be perfectly rational, given the different logic and way of reality conceptualization. Conflict of interest, on the other hand, refers to a situation in which different parties function within a framework of the same rationale but propose different choices or solutions (Staniszkis 2004: 19). Inclusive and autonomous approaches to media pluralism conceptualization draw, to a certain extent, main and conflicting lines between European institutions and pressure groups incapable of establishing a common *modus operandi* concerning the regulatory framework for securing media pluralism in Europe.

Competitive globalization: European Commission

Cultural diversity and competitiveness
The European Commission's approach towards media diversity has been governed by the logic of *competitive globalization* – 'media diversity' is important as it contributes to competitiveness of European ideas, cultures, languages – and most crucially – media and communication industries as a whole, on the global scene. This strategy shares many common characteristics with the belief in autonomy of 'differentiated' media systems and in the lack of reasons for instruments stimulating external pluralism. One of the symptomatic features is also the acceptance of internal pluralism measures, in cases where they can strengthen competitiveness.

Some aspects of media diversity have been defined and used to protect a common European media space against US imports and to support European dominant media players. The concept of 'cultural diversity' has served as an argument for state aid to the film and audiovisual industries as well as support for measures concerning European works and requirement of independent production during the drafting of the new Audiovisual Media Services (AVMS) Directive (European Commission 2005a). In its issue paper on cultural diversity, the Commission called for creation of incentives increasing the distribution of European co-productions: 'Positive likely impacts in cultural terms might be a deeper understanding of Europe's cultural diversity and richness and a wider acceptance of the European integration process' (European Commission 2005b: 4). In this sense, the promotion of European works, co-productions and works made by independent producers has been increasingly perceived and interpreted as an essential contribution to the nurturing of cultural diversity, both within and outside Europe, and as a pertinent way of correcting proportions between media representations of cultures on a global scale.

The relational perspective strengthens the view on cultural diversity as a key value shared by all Europeans, which needs to be constantly reaffirmed in subsequent media regulatory designs. In this process, cultural diversity contributes to fostering a European awareness and a feeling of collective belonging, intrinsically and conditionally linked to the progress of the Union.[2] It is interesting to observe how the once highly contentious European quota issue has transformed in the alchemy of media policy making and implementation into a widely accepted media policy instrument. Despite different approaches to cultural diversity and some criticism of implementation and monitoring functions, a gradual consensus that the rules on the promotion of European and independent production have provided a stable and flexible framework for the protection of cultural diversity (seen of course from the perspective of European culture) has not been harmed. Herein, 'cultural diversity' has conceptually functioned as a European cultural projection: it has been the conscious effort of media policy makers and industry to place recognizable images and representations of European culture (through diverse cultural expressions) in the global public sphere.[3]

Yet the widening of the new AVMS Directive's scope to non-linear audiovisual media services brings far less agreement, although it can be perfectly justified from the position of European *cultural competitiveness* in the global context. The potential of non-linear audiovisual services to replace linear services upholds, in view of the Commission, regulatory commitment to promotion and distribution of European works – and thus promotion of cultural diversity – on non-linear services. In its Audiovisual Media Services Directive, the Commission proposes that media service providers *promote* production of, and access to, European works (European Parliament and the Council 2007: 27–45). The new directive suggests that such a promotion might, for example, take the form of financial contribution for the production and rights acquisition of European works, or of the share and/or prominence of European works in the catalogue of programmes offered by the on-demand audiovisual media service (Article 3i). In a process of reporting to the European Parliament and the Council on the application of Paragraph 1, the Commission is expected to take into account the objective of cultural diversity (European Parliament and the Council 2007: 42). Due to the risk of bypassing these regulatory requirements by companies set up outside the European Union, the weight of cultural diversity promotion carries a more symbolic than pragmatic significance and might be, in the future, more closely related to public media services than non-linear services in general.

Pluralism as an 'added' value
During the 1990s, 'media pluralism' was conceptualized by the Commission merely through anti-concentration and media ownership policies (in fact, stimulating external pluralism). Attempts to introduce such media pluralism regulation have been discreetly passed down by the Commission to the competence of the Member States, equally reluctant to limit mergers of dominant national players. Thus, (external and structural) media pluralism was not seen as a value to be generated through European Union media policy instruments, but rather as an 'added value' to be addressed by other European (Council of Europe) or national institutions (European Commission 2005c).

In 1992, at the request of the European Parliament, the European Commission published a Green Paper: 'Pluralism and Media Concentration in the Internal Market'. Its main purpose was to assess the need for Community action on the question of concentration in the media (television, radio, press) and to evaluate different approaches of involved parties (Commission of the European Communities 1992). The results of the consultation process reaffirmed divergent standpoints of the involved bodies. The European Parliament, the Economic and Social Committee, the journalists' federations and the trade unions emphasized that the need to safeguard media pluralism as such justified action at the EU level. In the opinion of these bodies, there was a risk that pluralism of media may be affected, in particular, by media concentration and cross-ownership (Commission of the European Communities 1994). Media industry representatives also supported the need for action, but with different argumentation, pointing to global competitiveness and the impact of new technologies. Weighing the divergent positions, the Commission concluded that an initiative on media ownership might prove necessary (Commission of the European Communities 1994: 6).

A second round of consultations resulted in circulation of a discussion paper prepared by DG Internal Market, proposing a possible draft directive on media pluralism in 1996. In the course of the discussions, the document's focus was modified from 'Concentrations and Pluralism' to 'Media Ownership' in the Internal Market. Gillian Doyle (2002: 164) points out that this signalled a move to deflect the focus from pluralism (where the Commission's competence would be uncertain) towards removing obstacles to the Internal Market. Even with such significant modifications and flexibility, the initiative was rejected. Underscoring the difficulty to propose any kind of rules of harmonization between the EU Member States on media pluralism, the Commission has withdrawn from this policy area, emphasizing the importance of the added value of additional European actions.

The failure in this case did not only stem from profound tensions between contradictory policy agendas of the involved parties. In the regulatory debate, the separate concepts of media pluralism and media ownership elided, although they are obviously not identical. 'Media pluralism' served as a conceptual shell used most often in reference to anti-concentration measures and media ownership. This limitation goes even further than confining media pluralism to external media pluralism, as it excludes a number of important structural aspects. One of them is, for instance, the form of financing. Diversity of media owners will not result in much difference in terms of content if these media are all financed by advertising. There is historical evidence that advertising is, in fact, a limited source, growing at about the same rate as the over-all economy. Thus, if policy looks towards media to serve as an engine for creating new economic opportunities and jobs, it should focus on the development of media that is not supported by advertising (Galbi 2001). Other important aspects are mutual relations and interdependencies between media structures and a larger society. This also implies diverse ways of interacting with media, as the direction of interaction ultimately changes the vectors of media pluralism (pull, not push) and the modes through which the media operate in a larger system.

Publication of the EP report on media pluralism following the EP's 'Resolution on the risks of violation, in the EU and especially in Italy, of freedom of expression and information' (European Parliament 2004),[4] and drafting of AVMS Directive, provided a new opportunity for redressing the issue. 'The issue of media concentration is back on the political agenda', wrote Aidan White, Secretary General of the European Federation of Journalists in the EFJ report 'Media Power in Europe: The Big Picture of Ownership' (European Federation of Journalists 2006). The report once again links media concentration to media pluralism, concluding that pluralism is not an issue to be left to local politicians, but is a European issue that requires a European response. 'The European response' according to repeated claims of the European Parliament and interest groups, however, took a slightly different direction. This was a certain result of coping with heterogeneous interests represented by a diversity of organizations, but more importantly following the logic of an autonomous approach, in which all policies affecting the media are to be tested against the editorial freedom and the economy of the media industry (DG Information Society and the Media 2006; see also Commission of European Communities 2005a).

In a series of meetings with the publishing industry,[5] it became apparent that the industry representatives clearly aimed to prevent any new legislation to regulate media concentration and pluralism at the European level (see European Publishers Council 2005), and demanded the recognition of the publisher's competitive position in a process of drafting policies aimed at other media market players (such as AVMS Directive) (European Publisher's Forum 2005). The publishing industry has also unitedly reminded the Commission that there has not been a competence for the European Union to intervene on matters of media pluralism beyond its current rules on competition and merger regulation, and this should remain so (ENPA 2005). The Commission's approach concerning competitiveness of the EU Publishing Sector plainly demonstrates that this is the key perspective which media policy is being 'filtered through'. The Staff Working Paper on 'Strengthening Competitiveness of the EU Publishing Sector' recognizes that the productivity of the publishing and printing industries in the European Union is higher than in the United States. However, this sector is seen to be under strong economic pressure, due to the increasing digitization of content, changing consumer patterns and modes of distribution. Publishers have not yet been able to build the business models necessary to exploit online distribution; their online publications are frequently cross-subsidized by print revenues (Commission of European Communities 2005a). Thus, media policy should support sustainable competitiveness, bringing together the economic, environmental and social (high rates of employment) objectives of the European Union, in order 'to enhance pluralism and culture at the European level' (Commission of European Communities 2005a: 30).

The audiovisual industry has raised equally strong arguments. Regulatory priorities were exposed straightforwardly by James Murdoch (2005), CEO of British Sky Broadcasting during the Liverpool Audiovisual conference:

Nobody can seriously say that there is a problem with plurality when there are hundreds of TV news channels, millions of news websites and weblogs, and – perhaps – more importantly the ability for citizens to access information in an unmediated way direct from its original source...I fully accept that big companies in any industry will come under intense scrutiny and have to show that they are competing fairly, but I do hope that the old argument of equating bigness with a lack of plurality is consigned to the old world.

Nicolas de Tavernost, President of the Association of Commercial Television in Europe, backed his deregulatory stand during the ACT conference 'TV 2010 – Digital & Beyond'[6] by putting emphasis on new competition from telecom and broadband industries: Broadcasters do not want favourable treatment, we just want an end to discriminatory regulation against our businesses' (ACT 2006).

This reasoning – rooted in the *competitive globalization approach* – presented one of the main lines developed in the Issues Paper 'Media Pluralism – What should be the European Union's Role', prepared for the discussion on the new AVMS Directive during the European Audiovisual Conference in Liverpool:

A balance between the safeguard of media pluralism in Europe and the possibilities for European companies to compete globally is crucial if we want a European presence at the global 'top table' in the communications and media sector, especially in view of trade deficit of around $8bn p.a. with the U.S. (European Commission 2005c: 5)

Karol Jakubowicz (2006b: 5) emphasizes that the only explanation for issuing the document, which shows, in fact, no intention to deal with media pluralism, could be that the European Commission was trying to demonstrate to the European Parliament that it had made a strong commitment to take up the issue.

Yet 'added' value approach to media pluralism has not only reactive, but also proactive potential in the multi-level EU media policy-making. Following the logic of *competitive globalization*, Commission policy activities and discourses benefit from adding the 'value of media pluralism' to strengthen the Commission's bargaining position vis-à-vis external actors (both industry representatives and various interest groups). A good example can be adding the 'value of media pluralism' to the project of the new AVMS Directive, promoted through the three major measures which contribute to media pluralism: an obligation for Member States to guarantee the independence of national regulatory authorities; the right of broadcasters to receive 'short reporting'; and promotion of European works and content from independent European producers (European Commission, DG Information Society and the Media 2005).

On 16 January 2007 the Commission published a staff working document 'Media Pluralism in the Member States of the European Union', indicating further steps in a policy process regarding this matter (Commission of the European Communities 2007). The document sustains a familiar argument against submitting a Community initiative on pluralism at present, but it emphasizes a necessity to closely monitor the situation. The monitoring process is to involve an independent study on media pluralism indicators (2008) and communication from the Commission concerning these indicators (2009). Thus, 'concrete' indicators of assessing media pluralism present a crucial methodological category used for developing a more sophisticated risk-based monitoring mechanism, including such areas as:

■ Policies and legal instruments that support pluralism in MS
■ The range of media available to citizens in different MS
■ Supply side indicators on the economics of the media. (Commission of the European Communities 2007: 17–18)

The idea to monitor conditions of media pluralism in the EU Member States integrates the Commission's decision-making with European Parliament's and Council of Europe's priorities, concerning policy on media pluralism. At the same time, this integration is compensated by gains in autonomy vis-à-vis media industry and interest groups. The monitoring is not likely to bring a significant qualitative change in current EU media policy-making guided by the rationality of competitive globalization, but will present a potential base for more substantial policy change (which the Commission may or may not use), depending on a critical mass of information needed for the initiation of new solutions.

Internal pluralism: A domain of public service broadcasting?
Internal pluralism regulation usually refers to the legal obligation of media providers to render pluralism within their contents and services. This kind of regulation has been historically central, although not exclusive, to the model of public service broadcasting. The protocol on the system of public broadcasting appended to the EC Treaty by the Treaty of Amsterdam links PSB to the democratic, social and cultural needs of each society and to the requirement to protect media pluralism (European Commission 1997). Werner Rumphorst (2006) points out that this relation to media pluralism is very specific and 'internal' in its nature. It may be plausibly argued that any media outlet, even the most polemical one, contributes to media pluralism. But the PSB is singled out from the external plurality of other media outlets in its normative task to ensure impartial, comprehensive and quality information contributing to the formation of well informed citizenship (Rumphorst 2006). Thus, the public status of PSB justifies intervention in the broadcaster's programming autonomy in the interest of media pluralism and cultural diversity. This is well transposed to the programming obligations of PSB in most European countries, which frequently require the transmission of a specific proportion of culture-related programmes, promotion of local culture and works, and often the broadcasting of programmes representing all the regions in a given country (Ader 2006: 7). Moreover, internal pluralism is reflected in the PSB's normative attempt, as Karol Jakubowicz (2006c) puts it, to meet audience's needs as 'complete human beings', offering a full range of services generating from different collective identities (citizens; members of different social groups, communities, minorities and cultures; consumers and users of information, education, advice and entertainment).

The Protocol allows the Member States to finance PSB on the grounds of these democratic, social and cultural needs, but the ways they are interpreted and understood are marked by a profound ambiguity. Complaints brought up since the beginning of the 1990s by private broadcasters, regarding an unfair competitive regime giving privileges to PSB, provide compelling evidence of growing tension between the wish to permit PSB to fully realize their mission (and thus provide for internal pluralism within their services) and the general rules of European competition and state aid policy. Media industry consortia have repeatedly emphasized a growing discrepancy between the mission statements and the actual activities of Europe's PSB (ACT, AER and EPC 2004), and the distortion of markets (due to collecting advertising revenues in addition to state aid) in excess of what is acceptable to private operators to be able to effectively compete with PSB (European Publisher's Forum 2005). The fact that PSB is the third most subsidized 'industry' in Europe adversely affects, in view of the private stakeholders, the whole media market in Europe, including the press and Internet publishing, not only private TV and radio broadcasters (see European Publishers Council 2005).

In its assessment of public financing for PSB in the past, the Commission examined whether public financing applies to measures that are essential for fulfilment and continuation of the public service mission on the basis of Article 86 (2) EC. The Commission approved such financing in the case of public broadcasting channels 'Kinderkanal' and 'Phoenix' in Germany (State Aid – Germany 1999: 3), a 24-hour news television channel with licence fee in the United Kingdom (State Aid –

United Kingdom 2000: 6), the public financing of the nine BBC's digital television channels (BBC's digital curriculum) (State Aid – United Kingdom 2003: 6) and the financing of the creation of an international news channel in French (State Aid – United France 2005). The Commission, however, raised objections in the case of public financing of the Danish public broadcaster TV2. On the one hand, the Commission accepted the broadly defined public service broadcasting task under which TV2 ensured internal pluralism of its services providing a mix of programmes on culture, sport, entertainment and news on several television channels. On the other hand, the Commission found that TV2 had been overcompensated by State funding and that the State compensation was not proportionate to the net cost TV2 had to bear in fulfilling its public service mission (European Commission 2004). Similarly, in 2006 the Commission found that the Dutch public broadcaster NOS had been overcompensated by State funding and ordered them to pay back 76.3 million Euro to the Dutch government (European Commission 2006). Thus, within the framework of the EU competition policy, and having a crucial impact on the EU media policy in general, internal pluralism remit is being tested and discussed through the logic of economic competition, one of the crucial components of the *competitive globalization* approach.

The tension between PSB and private operators is becoming intense, not only because PSB institutions fail to distinguish sharply enough between internal pluralism remit and the commercial activities, but also because of discussion on the role of PSB in a new digital environment. The central point here revolves around the legitimacy of new non-linear services to be offered by PSB organizations and the controversial idea to confine PSB remit to traditional linear broadcasting. In its communication on the application of state aid rules to public service broadcasting, the Commission states that:

> the public service remit might include *certain* services that are not 'programmes' in the traditional sense, such as online information services, to the extent that...they are addressing the same democratic, social and cultural needs of the society in question. (European Commission 2001: 8, emphasis added.)

Commissioner Reding reaffirmed this position, stating that PSB are free to develop activities other than traditional broadcasting and make available socially valuable content on other platforms, however the scope and financing of such activities should be clearly defined by the Member States (Reding 2006). Public service broadcasters see their involvement in new media platforms and services, such as online content services, necessary to safeguard media pluralism and fulfil fundamental European policy objectives in the digital environment, for example social cohesion, cultural diversity and public information services (EBU 2006). Moreover, the legacy of PSB commitment to internal pluralism is linked to the paradoxes of new digital environment and operations: mere quantity of platforms, channels, thematically fragmented services does not automatically bring more media pluralism and diversity. New private platform providers increasingly control the revenue stream of programme makers and the COPE paradigm (Create Once – Publish Everywhere) economically privileges programming schemes that can be traded in many countries and localized more easily in multiple versions, thus reducing cultural specificity and profound diversity.

Yet some of the recent interpretational attempts of the Commission support the assumption that in a multichannel media environment (catering both to specialist and universal interests and tastes), PSB does not necessarily have to provide internal pluralism through a whole range of non-linear services, but should rather focus predominantly on traditional linear or related services in fulfilling their mission. Verena Wiedemann points out that, in its letter to the German Government, DG Competition has assumed online services of the public service broadcasters permissible only if 'closely linked' to the traditional broadcasting services. Moreover, contents made available by PSB on mobile platforms should be inadmissible *per se* in the view of DG Competition (Wiedemann 2005). In other words, mobile platform services are apparently regarded by the Commission as being outside an area that can be considered as 'services of general interest' (Nissen 2006: 27).

It might be too early to assess this regulatory direction, but some Commission declarations demonstrate the necessity to limit public financing of PSB to the *strict minimum* and call for a comprehensive reform of state aid rules in light of the Lisbon strategy. In closing the existing procedures under EC Treaty state aid rules (Article 88 (1)) and following changes made to the financing of public broadcasters in France, Italy and Spain, the Commission concluded: 'Financing of public broadcasters should not exceed the strict minimum necessary to ensure the proper execution of the public service mission, should not unduly benefit commercial activities (cross-subsidies) and should be transparent' (European Commission 2005d). A key concept emerging from the debate on state aid rules reform in the context of the Lisbon Strategy is a 'market failure', seen as a situation where the market does not lead to an economically efficient outcome. One of the areas where markets do not achieve economic efficiency is public goods. These are beneficial to a society but are not normally provided by the market, given that it is difficult or impossible to exclude anyone from using the goods. The Commission recognizes *some* types of public broadcasting to fall into this category (Commission of the European Communities 2005b: 7, emphasis added).

The Commission has certainly not questioned media pluralism as a rationale justifying the special status (and thus also financing from state aid) which PSB enjoys within the national context of Members States. It seems that some online services can be accepted by the Commission to meet democratic, social and cultural needs and to protect media pluralism in MS societies. Yet this 'national dimension' of EU media policy making is being increasingly tested through the logic of economic competition and counterbalanced with the globally oriented competitive approach. The economic and pro-competitive course of action with regard to state aid policy not only aims at reducing the general level of state aid, but requires the justification of any support, including that of providing internal pluralism within the services of PSB, by market failure. The rationality of *competitive globalization* confines internal pluralism measures to the question of competition, state aid rules and delimitation of PSB remit unless PSB is not redefined in a transnational democratic constellation (as institutions fostering well-informed pan-European citizenship) and new digital environment (as Public Service Media or Public Media Services, not Public Service Broadcasting).

A catalyzer of democratic participation: European Parliament and the Council of Europe

European Parliament
Unlike the Commission, other European institutions (mainly the European Parliament and Council of Europe), interest groups and professional institutions (International Federation of

Journalists) have repeatedly highlighted the importance of media pluralism for the democratic nature of the European media landscape and expressed the need to formulate a common regulatory approach at the EU level. This is seen to be indispensable in order to accommodate growing tensions between:

- Processes of media concentration and the citizens' rights to receive information from diverse and independent sources
- PSB status and EU competition and state aid policy
- Structural media diversity and high costs of market entry
- Unequal representation of minorities and pressure from advertisers in favour of mainstream audiences
- Journalistic autonomy and political influences.

Despite its weak legislative powers, the European Parliament has more frequently initiated Community media policy than the Commission or the Council (Verhulst and Goldberg 1998: 17–49). In particular, the Parliament has pressed for action to pursue policies protecting media pluralism. Throughout the 1990s, it adopted an impressive number of reports which were developed into resolutions addressing various facets of media pluralism. The first more concrete and policy-shaped discussions on the issue revolved around a series of party-specific initiated documents and motions for resolutions. Katharine Sarikakis (2004) emphasizes that, despite internal and ideological differences, the European Parliament did not find it difficult to reach consensus on two major issues: the definition of the problem itself and the action that needed to be taken in terms of policy.

Although some MEPs highlighted positive aspects of media concentration, the conviction was broadly shared that unlimited media concentration might endanger the independence and freedom of journalists and thus, the right of citizens to access information from diverse and transparent sources. The formation of the conception of media pluralism has been gradual and has taken on form in the course of subsequent documents and discussions. Its conceptual frame was rooted in normative democratic expectations, while the causal and direct relation between media concentration and diversity of opinion was perceived as an eventual hindrance to democratic performance. This interpretation of the emerging notion of media pluralism is embedded in the Resolution on Media Takeovers and Mergers (European Parliament 1990: 137) referring to many 'worrying examples' of concentration which could readily be observed in national and transnational European media landscapes.

Proposals to implement *complex* media pluralism regulation at the EU level were formulated in the Resolution on Media Concentration and Diversity of Opinions (European Parliament 1992: 44). The Parliament called on the Commission to submit a proposal for a directive harmonizing national restrictions on media concentration and enabling the Community to intervene in acts of concentration that endanger pluralism on a European scale. Secondly, the Parliament proposed the creation of the European Media Council with an advisory function to: monitor the development of the European media landscape (also in a global context); ensure transparency of media ownership; and provide the Commission with reports, recommendations and proposals concerning media developments and policy in Europe. Finally, the Parliament called for actions to improve journalistic independence and freedom. The proposals included drafting a framework directive safeguarding journalistic and editorial independence in all media, and the approval of a European Media Code setting basic standards of professional ethics (European Parliament 1992: 44; see also European Parliament 1994a: 177).

Further EP resolutions, such as the Resolution on the Commission Green Paper 'Pluralism and Media Concentration in the Internal Market' (1993) (European Parliament 1994a: 177), Resolution on concentration of the media and pluralism (European Parliament 1994b: 157) and Resolution on Pluralism and Media Concentration (European Parliament 1995: 133), accompanied the debate over the Commission's Green Paper 'Pluralism and the Media Concentration in the Internal Market' (1992) and its 'Follow-up' (1994), and reaffirmed the position arguing for complex regulatory measures. After the double rejection of the draft directive by the College of Commissioners, parliamentarists themselves admitted that media pluralism is 'without doubt the biggest failure of the EP' (Sarikakis 2004: 132). The media pluralism regulatory initiative did not prove successful in the 1990s, even though the Parliament had renewed efforts to address the issue.

Still, in the following years, media pluralism remained on the EP's media policy agenda. In 2004 the EP adopted the Resolution on the risks of violation, in the EU and especially in Italy, of freedom of expression and information (European Parliament 2004: 1026).[7] Examining the situation in selected Member States and focusing on Italy in particular, the resolution proposes that the Commission review the existing powers as well as the monitoring of public broadcasting, in order to adopt pertinent measures ensuring the protection of media pluralism. The European Parliament stresses in the resolution that free and pluralist media reinforce the principle of democracy on which the Union is founded. This is closely linked to the conception of EU citizenship – citizens have the right to stand and vote in municipal and European elections in a Member State of which they are not a national. Hence, the European Union has a political, moral and legal obligation within its fields of competence to ensure that the rights of EU citizens to free and pluralist media are respected (European Parliament 2004: 1027).

There are other pragmatic reasons which justify the specification by the European Union as to the minimum conditions to be respected by Member States to ensure an adequate level of media pluralism. One of the reasons is, according to the European Parliament, the lack of recourse of the Community courts by individuals when an absence of pluralism in the media has been determined (European Parliament 2004: 1027). This direction of reasoning clearly demonstrates that media pluralism is seen by the European Parliament as a fundamental value of the European Union in sustaining and reinforcing its democratic ideals. As the recognition of this value facilitates the democratic participation of its citizens, it should, in the words of the EP, affect the institutional practice of the European Union and its Member States (European Parliament 2004).

Council of Europe

Premises of democratic participation brought to the foreground numerous policy initiatives that were developed in order to set up common media pluralism standards within the framework of the Council of Europe. One of the fundamental incentives in this respect has been a positive action approach with regard to Article 10 ECHR. In this sense, Article 10 has functioned not only as a guarantee against interventions by states in the field of freedom of expression and freedom of the media, but it has also encouraged a positive action approach to ensure the citizen's right to be fully and impartially informed, and to receive the information from diverse and independent sources (Voorhoof 1998: 35–57).

This approach has been supported by a significant volume of resolutions, recommendations and declarations adopted by the Parliamentary Assembly and by the Committee of Ministers, many of which stressed the importance of the active implementation of Article 10 ECHR for the appropriate development of media pluralism and access to diversity of information sources. Most of these documents are not legally binding, but they do set down a number of principles and strategies suggested to Member States for further implementation. The table below illustrates a thematic spectrum and level of complexity reflected in numerous measures designed to protect media pluralism. A chronological ordering of these documents shows how closely CoE's objectives in this matter were linked to given historical circumstances and developments, such as democratization of media systems in Central and Eastern Europe. Sustained democratic premises induced both the Committee and Assembly to repeatedly call Member States' attention, in order to adopt recommended measures protecting various aspects of media pluralism, and ultimately unfreeze implementation idleness.

Already in the 1970s, the Committee of Ministers and Parliamentary Assembly recognized a risk affecting the diversity of the press landscape due to a wave of major mergers and business failures in the press sector. Many daily newspapers had ceased publishing or were bought up by rival papers. The Committee of Ministers reacted to this development with a Resolution (74) 43 to help endangered newspapers and the Parliamentary Assembly adopted Recommendation 747 (1975) on the internal freedom of the press (Möwes 2000). In 1981, the Committee of Ministers set up the Steering Committee on the Mass Media (CDMM), which has created a succession of subordinate bodies to deal with the issue of media concentration and pluralism (Jakubowicz 2006a).

The first of them, a Committee of Experts on media concentrations and pluralism (MM-CM), was established in late 1991 to conduct an in-depth examination of media concentration phenomena with the help of a network of national correspondents. One of the important questions addressed by empirical research was the necessity of implementation of harmonized measures at the European level in order to rectify negative effects of concentrations on political and cultural pluralism. The fundamental differences of opinions within the Committee of Experts rendered it impossible to support such harmonization. Instead, the Committee observed that the trend towards ever larger media units has made it increasingly difficult to trace ownership and information sources. Finally MM-CM drew up guidelines designed to promote transparency in the media, which the Committee of Ministers adopted as Recommendation No. R (94) 13 on Measures to Promote Media Transparency. The lack of consensus concerning direct influence of media concentration on pluralism has not impeded further CoE's commitment regarding these issues, but required to redress them in a more complex setting. A work of the Group of Specialists on Media Pluralism (MM-S-PL) established in 1999 has been symptomatic in this respect. The Group elaborated a text adopted by the Committee of Ministers as Recommendation No. R (99) 1 on Measures to Promote Media Pluralism. In this document, media pluralism is conceived as a catalyzer of democratic participation, which is manifested in three principal normative aspects: individuals should have access to pluralistic media content; the media should enable different groups and interests in society – including minorities – to express themselves; and democracy should be enhanced and consolidated by the existence

Table 3: Media pluralism related resolutions, recommendations and declarations adopted by the Parliamentary Assembly and by the Committee of Ministers of the Council of Europe.

Committee of Ministers	Parliamentary Assembly
*2007 – Declaration on protecting the role of the media in democracy in the context of media concentration *alerts member states to the risk of misuse of power of the media in a situation of strong concentration of the media and new communication services, and its potential consequences for political pluralism and for democratic processes	
*2007 – Recommendation Rec (2007) 3 on the remit of public service media in the information society *recognizes the continued full legitimacy and specific objectives of public service media in the information society	
*2007 – Recommendation Rec (2007)2 on media pluralism and diversity of media content *reaffirms that media pluralism and diversity of media content are essential for the functioning of a democratic society and are the corollaries of the fundamental right of freedom of expression and information as guaranteed by Article 10 ECHR *stresses the need to revise this issue in the context of new technological developments	
*2006 – Declaration on the guarantee of the independence of public service broadcasting in the member states *reaffirms the vital role of PSB as an essential element of pluralist communication and of social cohesion which seeks to promote, in particular, respect for human rights, cultural diversity and political pluralism	*2004 – Recommendation 1641 (2004) on public service broadcasting *recognizes that PSB offers a variety of programmes and services catering to the needs of all groups in society and recommends the Committee of Ministers to adopt a new major policy document on PSB
*2006 – Recommendation Rec(2006)3 on the UNESCO Convention on the protection and promotion of the diversity of cultural expression *recommends that member states ratify, accept, approve or accede the UNESCO Convention	

*2003 – *Recommendation Rec (2003) 9 on measures to promote the democratic and social contribution of digital broadcasting*
*recalls that the existence of a wide variety of independent and autonomous media, permitting the reflection of diversity of ideas and opinions, is important for democratic societies

*2000 – *Recommendation No. R (2000) 23 on the independence and functions of regulatory authorities for the broadcasting sector*
*recognizes the importance of genuine independence of the regulatory authorities for the broadcasting sector

*2000 – *Declaration on cultural diversity*
*recalls the commitments of MS to defend and promote media freedoms and media pluralism as a basic precondition for cultural exchange

*1999 – *Recommendation No. R (99) 1 on measures to promote media pluralism*
*stresses the importance for individuals to have access to pluralistic media content and recommends the States to promote political and cultural pluralism by developing their media policy in line with Article 10 ECHR

*1996 – *Recommendation No. R (96) 10 on the guarantee of the independence of public service broadcasting*
*reaffirms the vital role of PSB as an essential factor of pluralistic communication

*1994 – *Recommendation No. R (94) 13 on measures to promote media transparency*
*recalls that media pluralism and diversity are essential for the functioning of a democratic society

*2003 – *Recommendation 1589 (2003) on freedom of expression in the media*
*asserts that media concentration is a serious problem across the continent and asks the Committee of Ministers to urge all European states to ensure the plurality of the media market through appropriate anti-concentration measures

*2001 – *Recommendation 1506 (2001) on freedom of expression and information in the media in Europe*
*highlights that a pluralist and independent media system is essential for democratic development, and that the current market restructuring might lead to further concentration restricting media pluralism

*1999 – *Recommendation 1407 (1999) on media and democratic culture*
*states that sheer quantity of information does not by itself provide variety and quality, and recognizes the problem of the delicate relationship between freedom of expression and the citizen's right to objective, undistorted information

*1991 – *Recommendation 1147 (1991) on parliamentary responsibility for the democratic reform of broadcasting*
*recommends national parliaments to revise broadcasting regulation to ensure pluralism at least at the level of the overall media landscape

*1975 – *Recommendation 747 (1975) on media concentrations*
*draws up a model statute to secure internal freedom of the press and sets up criteria for an

Committee of Ministers	Parliamentary Assembly
and recommends that the governments promote media transparency	establishment of CoE's information centre on mergers and business failures in the press sector
*1982 – Declaration on freedom of expression and information *supports the existence of a wide variety of independent and autonomous media reflecting diversity of ideas and opinions	*1974 – Resolution (74) 43 on press concentration *recommends certain measures of public aid to the press

of a multiplicity of autonomous and independent media outlets at the national, regional and local levels (Council of Europe 1999). These three dimensions refer to the conceptualization of media diversity proposed by Denis McQuail. Being itself a broad principle, diversity can be fulfilled by the mass media in three ways: by reflecting differences in society (diversity as reflection); by giving access to different points of view (diversity as access); and by offering a wide range of choice (diversity as choice) (McQuail 1992: 144).

The main findings of the MM-S-PL in the course of its mandate were summarized in the 'Report on Media Pluralism in the Digital Environment' (Council of Europe 2000). The document has not proposed any immediate regulatory action, but has brought up differentiated issues that demand response from Members States, especially in the context of rapidly changing digital environment.[8] A wider media diversity perspective has been at the centre of focus of the subsequent Advisory Panel on Media Diversity (AP-MD), set up in 2001, and reflected in two Panel's reports 'Media Diversity in Europe' (Council of Europe 2002) and 'Transnational Media Concentrations in Europe' (Council of Europe 2004). The Group of Specialists on Media Diversity (MC-S-MD), continuing the work of the Panel, has concentrated on the ongoing assessment and monitoring of conditions affecting cultural diversity and media pluralism, especially in the context of digital environment and democratic performance.

New technological developments and implementation difficulties urged the Council of Europe to revise instruments proposed in the already existing recommendations. On 31 January 2007 the Committee of Ministers of CoE adopted three new documents referring to media pluralism: Recommendation Rec (2007) 2 on Media Pluralism and Diversity of Media Content; Recommendation Rec (2007) 3 on the Remit of Public Service Media in the Information Society; and the Declaration on Protecting the Role of the Media in Democracy in the Context of Media Concentration. In the Recommendation Rec (2007) 2 on Media Pluralism and Diversity of Media Content, the three basic dimensions of media pluralism are re-formulated, especially with regard to the positive interpretation of Article 10 and the role of media transparency in well-informed policy making, as well as critical media analysis by citizens (Council of Europe 2007). The Recommendation links requirements concerning freedom of expression with media pluralism: demands of the Article 10 of ECHR can be fully satisfied only if citizens are given the possibility to form their own opinion from diverse sources of information. Transparency of media ownership is seen as an important precondition for well-informed decisions and analysis by regulatory authorities and the public (Council of Europe 2007).

A brief account of ways in which media pluralism is exposed in documents of European Parliament and the Council of Europe reveals fundamental similarities. In the case of both institutions, the logic of setting up media pluralism standards involves harmonizing or balancing the forces of globalization (outside the European Union) with a stimulation of democratic participation and more pro-active citizenry (inside the European Union). This citizenry is not to be nationally, but rather transnationally defined to articulate and cope with common issues now emerging across national boundaries. Despite the fact that both institutions involve a representative set of societal interests in the policy formulation process, the difficulties are found in the implementation and transposition stages. This is related not only to ensuring that all member states adopt the standards agreed upon, but also that they support transposing these standards into harmonized rules and measures, both at European and national levels.

The question of a structural asymmetry

These different (and in many aspects conflicting) ways of looking at media pluralism problematization led to 'seesaw' efforts to introduce and abandon media pluralism regulatory measures at the European level. The problem, however, does not only seem to be rooted in a structural asymmetry of EU policies that have made pro-market deregulatory 'negative integration' far easier to achieve than market-correcting regulatory and 'positive integration'. Fritz Scharpf argues that 'negative integration' refers to the removal of barriers – like tariffs – or other obstacles to free and undistorted competition. 'Positive integration' on the other hand concerns reconstitution of an economic system of regulation through market-correcting measures (Scharpf 1999: 45). In general, Scharpf emphasizes structural asymmetry of EU governance (with an overwhelming role of 'negative integration') and asserts that *aquis communitaire* have done little to increase the institutional capacity for 'positive integration' and problem solving (Scharpf 1999: 157).

This regulatory asymmetry has been repeatedly echoed by other scholars when analysing EU or European media policies. With regard to public service broadcasting, concern for media pluralism, and cultural policy, Alison Harcourt has stressed the essentially closed, 'technocratic', top-down, market-making, 'deregulatory' nature of EU media policies (Harcourt 2004). Similarly, Venturelli underlines the absence of legislative clarification on positive information rights such as political rights, and a dominance of negative free-speech rights justifying deregulatory and liberalizing policies in the media sphere, which contrast with mechanisms for supporting media production (European quota) (Venturelli 1998). Dennis McQuail and Jan van Cuilenburg (2003) see normative grounds for deregulatory asymmetry in a new communications policy paradigm. The new paradigm results from such developments as technological and economic convergence, and the merging of the branches of computing, communications and content (publishing). The emerging policy paradigm for media and communications is mainly driven by an economic and technological logic. This media policy shift legitimizes the retreat from regulation where it interferes with market development or technological objectives, and it gives higher priority to economic and technological welfare over social-cultural and political welfare when priorities have to be set (Van Cuilenburg and McQuail 2003: 181–207).

The structural asymmetry in European media policies is not exclusively rooted in a dichotomy between pro-market (deregulatory or negative measures) and market-correcting (regulatory or positive measures) or a dichotomy between economic and political/cultural objectives. Both pro-market and market correcting measures may be used for the same rationale as is the case of *competitive globalization*. Namely 'this objective' guides the European Commission's policies on media pluralism/diversity (as it is understood and incorporated in media policy language) in both deregulatory (reluctance towards harmonizing 'media pluralism' anti-concentration measures) and market-correcting directions (protection of cultural diversity through European quota, European co-productions and production by independent producers).

The dividing line comes rather from two different ways of perceiving and conceptualizing media networks in a context of larger societies or political systems. In other words, policy on media pluralism is rooted in two different standards of rationality: one seeing the media as an increasingly politically autonomous and differentiated system, playing a central role in a process of competitive globalization; the second perceiving the media as a part of a deliberative democratic system. The first option is constructed in the (external) global context, especially vis-à-vis challenges of global economic competition, cultural and linguistic imperialism, and technological convergence. The second approach refers to the (internal) European political and civic space, recognized mainly through the concept of European citizenship. In the case of the former, policy debates are most decisively influenced by the media industry – seen as a main and autonomous subject of eventual regulation. In the sense of the latter, the crucial role in the debate is played by civic and non-governmental organizations, political parties, media expert institutions and the journalistic environment.

In the conceptual framework of competitive globalization, media pluralism is divided into other partial categories to be dealt with in different policy areas ('cultural diversity' through audiovisual policy measures, 'media pluralism' through ownership and competition rules, and 'internal pluralism' through general policy towards PSB and state aid rules). In the framework of democratic participation, media pluralism is conceived in complex terms and is to be addressed in one common regulatory model. Some might argue that there is a contradiction in positing one common normative model for safeguarding media pluralism, as media pluralism in itself implies diversity of media types, organizations, ways of operation and interaction with the audience. This is namely the argument used by non-linear services providers striving for no, or minimal, regulations, on the grounds that different audiences have different expectations, therefore the same rules cannot be imposed on all media. The position of the UK Broadband Stakeholder Group helps to explain further consequences of this stand: 'New audio-visual content services, made possible through innovation in digital technology and the internet, should be given time to evolve and develop rather than being shackled by premature and unnecessary intervention by the EU' (Williams 2005).

It is also interesting to see whether media pluralism is recognized as a value in both models of rationality. Undoubtedly, media pluralism is a value on which democratic participation is founded. At the same time, it is the objective for which the process of democratic participation is striving. On the other hand, within the model of competitive globalization, media pluralism functions as an added value to be generated by 'other' institutions through 'different' objectives. One common theme for both approaches is a search for a new media policy paradigm in existing schemes. As regards the latter, a 'new' paradigm is, to a certain extent, modelled on other policy fields; therefore a gradual reduction of media specific measures is one of its most characteristic features. In the case of the former, it is not merely a plea for reconstruction of the 'old' public service media policy paradigm, but rather an attempt at its redefinition in a new transnational political constellation and digital environment.

Table 4: Models of rationality, within which media pluralism is being used as a media policy conception and objective.

	Competitive globalization	Democratic participation
Media	Autonomous Increasingly autonomous and differentiated system	Inclusive Part of deliberative democratic system
Context	External Global economic competition, cultural and linguistic imperialism, technological convergence	Internal European political and civic space, european citizenship
Main Commentators	Media industry	Civic and non-governmental organizations, political parties, media expert institutions, journalistic environment
Regulatory framework	Fragmented 'Cultural diversity' – audiovisual policy measures, 'Media pluralism' – ownership and competition rules, 'Internal pluralism' – general policy towards PSB and state aid rules	Complex
Value orientation	Added value	Core value and objective
Media policy paradigm	Reduction Of media specific measures	Redefinition Of 'old' public service media policy paradigm in a new transnational political constellation and digital environment
Institutional framework	European commission	European parliament Council of europe

Conclusions

Let us return to the initial question: Is the clash of rationalities leading nowhere? The effects of the clash may be both negative and productive: both standards of rationality – competitive globalization and democratic participation – provide at once limits and impetus for European media policy concerning media pluralism. The tensions between the two poles render media policy language its ambiguity (media pluralism conceptualized through autonomous and inclusive approach) and media policy activities its ambivalence (fragmented regulatory actions, or soft measures, such as monitoring, and a complex framework for enforcing common, harmonized standards at the European level). Both ambiguity and ambivalence stimulate an opportunity of internal change. The clash between the two standards of rationality brings, on the one hand, the risk of destructive institutional competition and policy to a deadlock, but on the other, creates a potential for the reform that would not be possible in a unified structure.

The policy concerning media pluralism has been seen as one of the biggest failures of EU institutions (both the Commission and Parliament). Despite the increasing need for harmonized European rules on media pluralism, the European Union still lacks the formal powers (especially if member states' interests strongly diverge) and the institutional capacities necessary to enforce the compliance with the rules and their transposition in the member states. The most important regulatory instrument continues to be competition law, which, while strong and intrusive, is limited in scope and is a poor substitute for other regulatory powers and capacities (Grande and Eberlein 2005: 89–112). The Council of Europe's continuous efforts to repeatedly address the need for common standards on media pluralism have not, so far, brought a legally binding outcome.

Yet the clash of rationalities through which the issue of media pluralism is being conceptualized provides an alternative route of harmonization, especially through defining the limits of both standards. One such limit is confining media pluralism to the issue of media concentration or a structural, external dimension, often equated with media ownership. The relevance of the concept of media pluralism in media policy is increasingly marked by its potential and modes of activation. Its traditional and static framing is challenged by the ongoing identification, the sense of which depends on mutual relations and interdependencies. Thus, the potential of media pluralism is conditionally linked to capacities that can be mobilized through its 'building blocks', such as multiple centres of media control, sources of information and so on. At the same time, its full usage is increasingly determined by individuals, their ability to critically read media content, and to generate their own messages, as well as modes of delivery and ways of interaction.

These new interpretational dimensions challenge centres of gravity in media policy-making. The idea to regulate media pluralism at the structural level (prevention of concentration through anti-concentration rules, imposing diversity on media actors) is being replaced by soft and indirect regulatory levers, such as monitoring, transparency, and promotion of media literacy. Through information exchange and networking, both EU institutions and the Council of Europe are developing harmonized strategies focusing predominantly on information and competence (for example, support for media literacy). An individualized and interactive character of media use amplifies the possibility to better safeguard media pluralism through supporting citizens and interest groups with special knowledge, enabling them to more easily establish their relations with mainstream media, get their messages heard, and have their cultural expressions represented and opinions addressed. In this sense, more appropriate than providing fish, it seems more appropriate to equip media users with the angling-rod and the know-how to use it.

The fact that media pluralism is rationalized in different ways, and that tension exists between these ways, does not decrease its potential or block the chance for vital policy-making. The important question is, however, whether 'policy bridges' are built between divergent practices rooted in different standards of rationality, and whether they, in consequence, activate media pluralism potential. This multirationality and multifunctionality of the media policy process itself creates a complicated, multi-layered setting that in certain circumstances brings a harmonized solution with it and strengthens European institutions vis-à-vis external actors. An instructive example would be the promotion of cultural diversity (in regulatory practice European works, independent productions and co-productions) as a key value shared by all Europeans, and a regulatory rationale that needs to be constantly reaffirmed in subsequent media regulatory designs. On the other hand, European institutions have not established a harmonized approach enabling the redefinition of PSB's role in the transnational democratic constellation (as institutions nurturing well-informed *pan-European* citizenship) and in the new digital environment. Thus, they have not challenged the coherence of testing EU media policy through the logic of economic competition and a globally oriented competitive approach.

Finally, the clash of rationalities, resulting in ambiguity of policy language and ambivalence of policy action, changes the patterns of democratic legitimacy. Accompanied by institutional interdependencies and functional convergence, European media policy-making creates structural gaps in democratic control. This participation-limiting legitimacy stands in contrast to a trust-demanding social and public policy system in Europe (Merelman 2003: 286–7). The sophistication and complexity of the policy process demands that Europeans be willing to trust unknown solutions. In other words, the legitimacy dilemma reflects the contradiction between stimulating citizen trust in policy-making and the lack of participatory openness and transparency of policy-negotiating systems.

Notes

1. A close relationship between ambiguity of language and ambivalence of political conduct was distinguished and conceptualized by Michael Oakeshott (1996).
2. For more on this perspective see the report of the Department for Culture, Media and Sport (2005).
3. For more on cultural projection see Merelman 1995.
4. More on the Resolution see in the section *A catalyzer of democratic participation: European Parliament and the Council of Europe (European Parliament)*.
5. These included: European Publishers' Forum 2005 (annual meeting), 6 December, Brussels; Editors-in-Chief meeting with Information Society and the Media Commissioner Viviane Reding, Brussels, 23 September 2005 and the second meeting on 23 October 2006.
6. The conference was organized in Brussels on 27 April 2006.
7. The Resolution was followed by the publication of 'Final report of the study on "the information of the citizen in the EU: obligations for the media and the Institutions concerning the citizen's right to be fully and objectively informed"', prepared by the European Institute for the Media on behalf of the European Parliament, 31 August, 2004.
8. The report reflects in part results of the study on 'Pluralism in the multi-channel market: suggestions for regulatory scrutiny' prepared on behalf of MM-S-PL to explore the means by which media pluralism can be maintained or even strengthened in the digital future.

References

ACT, AER, EPC (2004), 'Safeguarding the Future of the European Audiovisual Market: A White Paper on the Financing and Regulation of Publicly Funded Broadcasters', available at http://www.epceurope. org/presscentre/archive/index.shtml. Accessed 3 October 2006.

ACT (2006), ACT Conference *TV 2010: Digital&Beyond*, http://www.acte.be/usermodule/en/act.asp. Accessed 3 October 2006.

Ader, T. (2006), 'Cultural and Regional Remits in Broadcasting', *IRIS Plus Legal Observations of the European Audiovisual Observatory*, No. 8.

Alexander, J. C. (1981), 'The Mass News Media in Systemic, Historical and Comparative Perspective', in E. Katz, and T. Szecskö, (eds.), *Mass Media and Social Change*, Beverley Hills: Sage Publications, pp. 17–51.

Arendt, H. (1958), *The Human Condition*, Chicago: The University of Chicago Press.

Bagdikian, B. (2000), *The Media Monopoly*, 6th edition, Boston: Beacon Press.

Bourdieu, P. (1998), *On Television*, New York: The New Press.

Cavallin, J. (2000), 'Public Policy Uses of Diversity Measures', in J. Van Cuilenburg, and Van der Wurff, R. (eds.), *Media and Open Societies: Cultural, Economic and Policy Foundations for Media Openness and Diversity in East and West*, Amsterdam: Het Spinhuis, pp. 105–70.

Collins, R. and Murroni, C. (1996), *New Media, New Policies*, Cambridge: Polity.

Commission of the European Communities (1992), 'Pluralism and Media Concentration in the Internal Market: An Assessment of the Need for Community Action', Commission Green Paper, COM (92) 480 final, Brussels, 23 December 1992.

Commission of the European Communities (1994), 'Follow-up to the Consultation Process relating to the Green Paper on "Pluralism and Media Concentration in the Internal Market – an Assessment of the Need for Community Action"', COM (94) 353 final, Brussels, 5 October 1994.

Commission of the European Communities (2005a), Commission Staff Working Paper: 'Strengthening Competitiveness of the EU Publishing Sector, The Role of Media Policy', SEC(2005) 1287, Brussels, 7 October 2005.

Commission of the European Communities (2005b), 'State Aid Action Plan: Less and Better Targeted State Aid: A Road Map for State Aid Reform 2005-9', COM (2005) 107 final, Brussels, 7 June 2005.

Commission of the European Communities (2007), Commission Staff Working Document: 'Media Pluralism in the Member States of the European Union', SEC (2007) 32, Brussels, 16 January.

Council of Europe (1999), 'Recommendation No. R (99) 1 of the Committee of Ministers to Member States on Measures to promote Media Pluralism'.

Council of Europe (2000), 'Report on Media Pluralism in the Digital Environment', adopted by the Steering Committee on the Mass Media in October 2000, Strasbourg, CDMM (2000) pde.

Council of Europe (2002), 'Media Diversity in Europe', Report prepared by the AP-MD, H/ APMD (2003)001.

Council of Europe (2004), 'Transnational Media Concentrations in Europe', Report prepared by the AP-MD, AP-MD (2004).

Council of Europe (2007) 'Recommendation Rec(2007)2 of the Committee of Ministers to member states on media pluralism and diversity of media content'.

Dahlgren, P. (1995), *Television and the Public Sphere: Citizenship, Democracy and the Media*, London: Sage Publications.

Department for Culture, Media and Sport (2005), *Liverpool Audiovisual Conference: Between Culture and Commerce*, 20–2 September.

Department of Trade and Industry (2000), 'A New Future for Communications. The White Paper', http://www.citi.gov.uk. Accessed 3 October 2006.

DG Information Society and the Media (2006), 'Task Force for Co-ordination of Media Affairs', http://europa. eu.int/information_society/media_taskforce/index_en.htm. Accessed 15 October 2006.

Doyle, G. (2002), *Media Ownership. The Economics and Politics of Convergence and Concentration in the UK and European Media*, London: Sage Publications.

EBU (2006), 'EBU Comments to the EC Commission's public consultation paper on Content Online in the Single Market', DAJ/HR/jmc, 23 October 2006.

ENPA (2005), 'ENPA Response to the Commission Issues Paper on Media Pluralism – What Should Be the European Union's Role?', http://ec.europa.eu/comm/avpolicy/docs/reg/modernisation/issue_papers/contributions/ip6-enpa.pdf. Accessed 10 October 2006.

European Commission (1997), 'Protocol on the System of Public Broadcasting in the Member States', 2 October 1997, O.J. 1997, C 340.

European Commission (2001), 'Communication from the Commission on the application of State aid rules to public service broadcasting', 2001/C 320/4.

European Commission (2004), 'Commission Decision of 19 May 2004', C(2004) 1814 final, 19 May 2004.

European Commission (2005a), 'Impact Assessment – Draft Audiovisual Media Services Directive', COM (2005) 646 final.

European Commission (2005b), 'Issues Paper for the Liverpool Audiovisual Conference: Cultural Diversity and the Promotion of European and Independent Audiovisual Production', Brussels: DG Information Society and Media.

European Commission (2005c), 'Issues Paper for the Liverpool Audiovisual Conference: Media Pluralism – What should be the European Union's role?', Brussels: DG Information Society and Media.

European Commission (2005d), 'State aid: Commission closes inquires into French, Italian and Spanish public broadcasters following commitments to amend funding systems', IP/05/458, 20 April 2005.

European Commission (22 June 2006), 'Press Release: Commission orders Dutch public service broadcaster NOS to pay back €76.3 million excess ad hoc funding', (IP/06/822).

European Commission, DG Information Society and the Media (2005), 'Why and how Europe seeks pluralism in audiovisual media', http://europa.eu.int/information_society/services/doc_temp/tvwf-sht5_en.pdf. Accessed 10 September 2006.

European Commission, DG Information Society and the Media (2007), 'Measuring progress in e-inclusion, Riga Dashboard', reports on progress in the achievement of policy targets set by the Ministerial Declaration signed in Riga on 11 June 2006, http://ec.europa.eu/information_society/activities/einclusion/docs/i2010_initiative/rigadashboard.doc. Accessed 3 February 2008.

European Federation of Journalists (2006), 'Media Power in Europe: The Big Picture of Ownership', http://www.ifj.org/pdfs/EFJownership2005.pdf. Accessed 10 October 2006.

European Parliament (1990), 'Resolution on Media Takeovers and Mergers', O.J. C 68, 19 March 1990, p. 137.

European Parliament (1992), 'Resolution on Media Concentration and Diversity of Opinions', O.J. C 284, 2 November 1992, p. 44.

European Parliament (1994a), 'Resolution on the Commission Green Paper "Pluralism and Media Concentration in the Internal Market"', O.J. 1994, C 44, 14 February 1994, p. 177.

European Parliament (1994b), 'Resolution on concentration of the media and pluralism', O.J. 1994, C 323, 21 November 1994, p. 157.

European Parliament (1995), 'Resolution on Pluralism and Media Concentration', O.J. C 166, 3 July 1995, p. 133.

European Parliament (2004), 'Resolution on the risks of violation, in the EU and especially in Italy, of freedom of expression and information', O.J. C 104 E, 30 April 2004.

European Parliament and the Council (2007) 'Directive 2007/65/EC of the European Parliament and the Council of 11 December 2007 amending Council Directive 89/552/EEC on the coordination of certain provisions laid down by law, regulation or administrative action in Member States concerning the pursuit of television broadcasting activities', O.J. 2007 L 332.

European Publishers Council (2005), 'Memorandum on Pluralism and Media Concentration addressed to the Members of the European Parliament's Intergroup on the Press, Communication and Freedom', http://www.epceurope.org/issues/MemorandumPluralismMediaConcentration.shtml. Accessed 20 October 2006.

European Publisher's Forum (2005), '21st Century Publishing in Europe "Promoting Knowledge, Information and Diversity": Calls for Action', Brussels, 6 December 2005, http://europa.eu.int/information_society/media_taskforce/doc/publishing/calls_for_action.pdf. Accessed 20 October 2006.

Freedman, D. (2005), 'Promoting Diversity and Pluralism in Contemporary Communication Policies in United States and the United Kingdom', International Journal of Media Management, 7: ½, pp. 16–23.

Galbi, D. (2001), 'Communications Policy, Media Development and Convergence', Federal Communication Commission, http://www.galbithink.org/media.htm. Accessed 15 October 2006.

Giddens, A. (1991), The Consequences of Modernity, Stanford: Stanford University Press.

Graham, A. and Davies, G. (1997), Broadcasting, Society and Policy in the Multimedia Age, Lutton: John Libbey.

Grande, E. (2001), Institutions and Interests: Interest Groups in the European System of Multi-Level Governance, Working Paper No. 1/2001.

Grande, E. and Eberlein, B. (2005), 'Beyond delegation: transnational regulatory regimes and the EU regulatory state', Journal of European Public Policy, vol. 12 (1), pp. 89–112.

Habermas, J. (1995), The Structural Transformation of the Public Sphere. An Inquiry into a Category of Bourgeois Society, Cambridge, Mass: The MIT Press.

Habermas, J. (1996), Between Facts and Norms: Contributions to a Discursive Theory of Law and Democracy, Cambridge, Mass: The MIT Press.

Hallin, D. C. and Mancini, P. (2004), Comparing Media Systems: Three Models of Media and Politics, Cambridge: Cambridge University Press.

Harcourt, A. (2004), The European Union and the Regulation of Media Markets, Manchester: Manchester University Press.

Hoynes, W. (2002), 'Why media mergers matter', openDemocracy, 16 January 2002, http://www.opendemocracy.net/debates/article-8-24-47.jsp. Accessed 13 October 2006.

Inglehart, R. (1990), Culture Shift in Avanced Industrial Societies, Princeton: Princeton University Press.

Jakubowicz, K. (2004), 'Ideas in Our Heads: Introduction of PSB as Part of Media System Change in Central and Eastern Europe', European Journal of Communication, 19 (1), pp. 53–74.

Jakubowicz, K. (2006a), 'Media Pluralism and Concentration: Searching for a Productive Research and Policy Agenda (in the light of the Council of Europe Experience)', paper presented at the Working Group 3 meeting of COST Action A30, Budapest, 22–3 September 2006.

Jakubowicz, K. (2006b), 'Revision of the European Convention on Transfrontier Television in the Context of International Media Policy Evolution', paper presented during the meeting of Working Group 3 of COST Action A30, Budapest, 22–3 September 2006.

Jakubowicz, K. (2006c), 'Public Service Broadcasting: The Beginning of the End, or a New Beginning?', presentation at the EBU-MTV conference 'From Secret Service to Public Service', 3 November 2006.

Karp, J.A., Banducci, S. A. and Bowler, S. (2003), 'To Know it is to Love it. Satisfaction with Democracy in the European Union', *Comparative Political Studies*, 36:2, pp. 271–92.

Kekes, J. (1996), *The Morality of Pluralism*, Princeton: University of Princeton Press.

Luhmann, N. (2000), *The Reality of the Mass Media*, Stanford: Stanford University Press.

McQuail, D. (1992), *Media Performance: Mass Communication and the Public Interest*, London: Sage Publications.

Merelman, R.M. (1995), *Representing Black Culture: Racial Conflict and Cultural Politics in the United States*, New York: Routledge.

Merelman, R.M. (2003), *Pluralism at Yale: The Culture of Political Science in America*, Wisconsin: Wisconsin University Press.

Meyer, T. (2002), *Media Democracy: How the Media Colonize Politics*, Cambridge: Polity.

MM-CM, Council of Europe's Committee of Experts on Media Concentrations and Pluralism (1994), 'The Activity Report of the Committee of Experts on Media Concentrations and Pluralism', submitted to the 4th European Ministerial Conference on Mass Media Policy, Prague, 7–8 December 1994.

Möwes, B. (2000), *Fifty Years of Media Policy in the Council of Europe: A Review*, 6th European Ministerial Conference on Mass Media Policy, Cracow (Poland), 15–16 June 2000, MCM (2000) 003.

Murdoch, J. (2005), Speech to the 2005 European Audiovisual Conference, 21 September 2005.

Nissen, Ch. S. (2006), *Public Service Media in the Information Society*, the Report prepared by the Group of Specialists on PSB in the Information Society (MC-S-PSB), Strasbourg: Media Division, Directorate General of Human Rights, Council of Europe.

Oakeshott, M. (1996), *The Politics of Faith & the Politics of Scepticism*, New Haven and London: Yale University Press.

Petković, B. (ed.) (2004), *Media Ownership and its Impact on Media Independence and Pluralism*, Ljubljana: Peace Institute.

Reding, V. (2006), 'The Role of Public Service Broadcasters in a Vibrant and Pluralist Digital Media Landscape', speech at the joint EBU-MTV's conference 'From Secret Service to Public Service', Budapest, 3 November 2006, http://ec.europa.eu/comm/commission_barroso/reding/docs/speeches/ebu_mtv_20061103.pdf. Accessed 20 November 2006.

Rumphorst, W. (2006), 'The Requirements for the Independence of Public Service Television', paper presented at the EBU-MTV conference 'From Secret Service to Public Service', Budapest, 3 November 2006.

Sarikakis, K. (2004), *Powers in Media Policy: The Challenge of the European Parliament*, Oxford: Peter Lang.

Scharpf, F. (1999), *Governing in Europe: Effective and Democratic?* Oxford: Oxford University Press.

Schulz, W. (2004), 'Reconstructing mediatization as an analytical concept', *European Journal of Communication*, vol. 19 (1).

Staniszkis, J. (2004), *Władza globalizacji*, Warszawa: Wydawnictwo Naukowe 'Scholar'.

Staniszkis, J. (2006), 'Pluralizm i władza', *Dziennik/Europa – Tygodnik Idei*, No. 42, 21 December 2006, pp. 8–9.

State Aid – France (2005), N 54/2005, C 2005 1479 final of 7 June 2005.

State Aid – Germany (1999), NN 70/98, O.J. 1999, C 238, p. 3.

State Aid – United Kingdom (2000), NN 88/98, O.J. 2000, C 78, p. 6.

State Aid – United Kingdom (2003), N 631/01, O.J. 2003, C 23, p. 6.

Van Cuilenburg, J. and McQuail, D. (2003), 'Media Policy Paradigm Shifts: Towards a New Communications Policy Paradigm', *European Journal of Communication*, 18 (2), pp. 181–207.

Van Cuilenburg, J. and Van der Wurff, R. (eds.) (2000), *Media and Open Societies: Cultural, Economic and Policy Foundations for Media Openness and Diversity in East and West*, Amsterdam: Het Spinhuis.

Van Dijk, J. (2006), *The Network Society: Social Aspects of New Media*, London: Sage Publications.

Venturelli, S. (1998), *Liberalizing the European Media: Politics, Regulation and the Public Sphere*, Oxford: Clarendon Press.

Verhulst, S. and Goldberg, D. (1998), 'European Media Policy: Complexity and Comprehensiveness', in L. d'Haenens and F. Saeys, (eds.), *Media Dynamics and Regulatory Concern in the Digital Age*, Berlin: Quintessenz Verlags GmbH, pp. 17–49.

Voorhoof, D. (1998), 'Guaranteeing the Freedom and Independence of the Media', *Media and democracy*, Strasbourg: Council of Europe Publishing, pp. 35–57.

de Vreese, C.H and Boomgaarden, H.G. (2006), 'Media Effects on Public Opinion about the Enlargement of the European Union', *Journal of Common Market Studies*, 44:2, pp. 419–36.

Ward, D. (2002), *The European Union Democratic Deficit and the Public Sphere: An Evaluation of EU Media Policy*, Amsterdam: IOS Press.

Ward, D. (2006), *Final Report on the study commissioned by the MC-S-MD 'The Assessment of content diversity in newspapers and television in the context of increasing trends towards concentration of media markets'*, MC-S-MD (2006) 001, Strasbourg: Council of Europe.

Dietrich, W. (2002), 'Media Pluralism and European Regulation', *European Business Law Review*, 13 (5), pp. 459–87.

Wiedemann, V. (2005), 'Legislating and regulating for pluralism', paper presented at the European Parliament's Seminar on *Pluralism not Concentration: an EU Media Policy*, 7 April 2005, Brussels.

Williams, G. (2005), 'What is the Television Without Frontiers Directive?', *Free Press*, No. 148, September/October.

Wijayananda, Y. (2005), 'Vibrant democracy needs independent and pluralistic media', an interview with Yayaweera, Director of the International Programme for the Development and Communications, UNESCO, 3 May 2005. http://topics.developmentgateway.org. Accessed 20 October 2006.

THE CHALLENGES OF ICT TO MEDIA PLURALISM[1]

Lilia Raycheva

Introduction

In March 2000, the European Council in Lisbon set up an agenda for the economic and social renewal of Europe. Realizing that the continent is facing a paradigm shift driven by globalization, the EU Heads of States and Governments agreed to make the European Union 'the most competitive, dynamic and inclusive knowledge-driven economy by 2010'. It was noted then that 'the knowledge economy is profoundly changing the types of skills required for work and that information technologies can help reduce long-term structural unemployment' (European Council 2000). In 2005, following the Commission's mid-term review of the Lisbon agenda, a comprehensive strategy for the Information Society 2005–10 was launched.

Further on, the 'i2010 – a European Information Society for growth and employment' initiative was adopted by the European Commission on 1 June 2005 as a framework for addressing the main challenges and developments in the sector of information, communication and media industries up to 2010. The initiative contains a range of EU policy instruments envisaged to encourage the development of competitive digital economy, such as regulatory instruments, research and partnerships with stakeholders. It also promotes ICT as a key driver of social inclusion and better quality of life.

'i2010' has three main policy objectives:

■ To create a single European information space, which will secure an open and competitive internal market for the digital economy (electronic communication and media services) both for industry and consumers.
■ To strengthen investment in innovation and research in ICT and to encourage the industrial application of ICTs.
■ To foster inclusion, better public services and quality of life through the use of ICT. (EC 2005).

The creation of a single information space started with the upgrading of EU rules on audiovisual content services. Practices have demonstrated considerable progress: telecommunication providers already offer broadcasting services and content providers supply communications services. The goal is for the consumers to be able to watch audiovisual content anytime, anywhere, and on all technical platforms (TV, computer, mobile phone, personal digital assistant and so on). Broadband, triple play and quadruple play, fixed-mobile convergence, fibre rollouts, and mobile TV are the new challenges to the media markets. Next generation networks, capable of offering speeds that can support Internet and high-definition TV (IPTV, VOIP, mobile TV, Web 2.0) are on the way. This entire exciting variety of technological options and services needs regulatory certainty in developing a common internal market for electronic communications (Reding 2007).

This gives rise to the question: How well does the traditional media system with its main social pillars, such as plurality and diversity, fit into the newly developed situation, in which geopolitical boundaries are becoming ever more conditional?

The perspective of mediamatics

Theoretical verification and legal regulation of the traditional mass media developments have difficulty in keeping pace with the headlong progress of new technologies. The type and pace of these changes will predetermine the further development of the Information Society and will present mankind with challenges in many aspects. We are on the threshold of change in the very paradigm of the mass media system: technologically, financially, administratively, creatively and, above all, socially.

Of all factors affecting the building rate of the new type of society, the technological one is undoubtedly the most active. Arrangement and processing of information have been optimized and the speed of communication has increased. The mass scale advent of digital electronics and computer software in everyday life presumes the introduction of new schemes and mechanisms for the creation, distribution and consumption of information. The range of traditional communication products and services is steadily expanding. Moreover, the satellite links, digitalization and new information technologies have brought to the fore the question of convergence in communications development on various levels.

In its 1997 'Green Paper' the European Commission defined convergence as follows:

■ Ability to transfer kindred services on different platforms.
■ Bringing together of such large-scale public works as the telephone, television or personal computers.

The 'Green Paper' also identified the basic characteristics of the Internet and digital technologies that challenged the applied grounds for the existing media regulation in a converged marketplace: the overcoming of scarcity, the interactive merge between publisher and consumer, user-driven status, and decentralized (horizontal) communication. Thus, it prompted media industries that, in the vast growing technological era, they would be predominantly governed by market mechanisms and economic objectives for achieving wider social, economic and general policy aims (EC 1997: 18).

The 'Green Paper' has set clear goals on the convergence policy in audio vision. The information and communication technologies have outpaced regulation and have set up an economic basis for the convergence of entire industries: the electronic, entertainment and media industries. In this sense, Santiago Lorente sees two stages in technological development: 'convergence between telecommunications and informatics (telematics) and between telematics and audio-vision (mediamatics)' (Lorente 1997: 119).

Being the backbone of the knowledge society, broadband provides access to advanced public services and diverse multimedia content for information, entertainment, training and work. Broadband access has become a prerequisite for a wide range of issues, from economic growth to social inclusion. The move to broadband will fundamentally add new phenomena to the Internet experience, such as 'user-generated' content sites and advanced 'digital ecosystem' technologies (EC 2006a).

It is the Single European Information Space pillar of i2010 that combines regulatory and other instruments for the creation of a modern, market-oriented regulatory framework for the electronic communications, with an emphasis on the audiovisual policies, radio spectrum management, and the process of switchover to digital TV. In 2006, at the ITU's Regional Radiocommunication Conference (RRC-06) in Geneva, a treaty was signed according to which the transition period from analogue to digital broadcasting should end on 17 June 2015. The new Digital Plan based on broadcasting standards known as T-DAB (for sound) and DVB-T (for TV) will replace the analogue broadcasting plans which had existed for Europe since 1961 (ITU 2006).

The switchover from analogue to digital broadcasting is expected to create new distribution networks and expand the potential for wireless innovation and services. Just prior to the reform of the EU telecom rules, on 29 March 2007, the European Commission published its twelfth report on the EU telecom market. It pointed out that although the consumers have more choices in a sector with almost €290 billion in revenues, the full potential of the EU internal market still remains untapped (EC 2007a).

In 2007, the ITU held its World Radiocommunication Conference 2007 (WRC-07) under the motto: 'Bringing all radio services together'. The Conference adopted an international treaty, known as 'Radio Regulations Governing the Use of the Radio-Frequency Spectrum and Satellite Orbits'. These regulations were revised and updated to meet the global demand for radio-frequency spectrum efficiency. Digital broadcasting was among the 30 agenda items addressed at WRC-07 (ITU 2007).

In the final documents of RRC-06 and WRC-07, as well as in other documents, special attention was focused on various aspects of the digital dividend. Priority was assigned to the public orientation of the digital dividend usage. According to the EC 'Communication on Reaping the Full Benefits of the Digital Dividend in Europe: a Common Approach to the Use of the Spectrum Released by the Digital Switchover', the transition from analogue to digital broadcasting and HD services has been regarded as a possibility to increase media pluralism, growth in media content production, and higher-quality and more interactive services for viewers. Thus, digital dividend is related, above all, to the support of existing broadcasting services in a fully digital environment, with special attention to public service obligations (EC 2007b).

In early 2008, the Committee of Ministers of the Council of Europe adopted a 'Declaration on the Allocation and Management of the Digital Dividend and the Public Interest'. According to this, the Member States must declare that they 'should acknowledge the public nature of the digital dividend resulting from the switchover and the need to manage such a public resource efficiently in the public interest, taking account of present and foreseeable future needs for a radio spectrum' (CoE 2008).

Despite the general progress of broadband developments, access to the new services in remote and rural regions appears to be limited because of high costs resulting from low density of population and remoteness. With this in mind, in March 2006 the European Commission published the communication 'Bridging the Broadband Gap', which refers to territorial differences in broadband access, speeds, quality of service, prices and use between urban and rural/remote areas, as well as between more/less developed areas in Europe (EC 2006b). This is a direct move towards the protection of fundamental democratic achievements, such as freedom of expression and access to information.

The contemporary European audio-visual policies

Protection of freedom of expression and promotion of media pluralism are two of the most important democratic pillars of contemporary society. The necessity of sustaining these social achievements was already underlined in the first pan-European documents. In 1950, these intentions were outlined in Article 10 (Freedom of expression) of the Convention for the Protection of Human Rights and Fundamental Freedoms (CoE 1950a).

About half a century later, Article 11 (Freedom of expression and information) of the Charter of Fundamental Rights of the European Union reaffirmed that:

1. Everyone has the right to freedom of expression. The right shall include freedom to hold opinions and to receive and impart information and ideas without interference by public authority and regardless of frontiers.
2. The freedom and pluralism of the media shall be respected. (EUP 2000)

Within the meaning of the 'Treaty of Rome' – the founding document of the European Union – broadcasting is considered a service. The requirement for freedom of movement of goods and services across the frontiers of the Member States is a basic requirement for achieving the pan-European objectives (EU 1957). Some thirty years later, revising the Treaty of Rome, the Single European Act (SEA) added new momentum to European integration by completing the internal market (EU 1986). According to the 'General Agreement on Trade in Services' (GATS), the audiovisual services sector has become the subject of multilateral trade negotiations since January 2000. The sector includes motion picture and video tape production and distribution services, motion picture projection services, radio and television services, radio and television transmission services, and sound recording (WTO 2000).

As the main intergovernmental organization at a pan-European level dealing with the democratic dimensions of communication, the Council of Europe (CoE) has been consistently active in setting common standards for media developments. Attention to these developments has become particularly strong since the 1990s with the rapid progress of information and communication technologies, which stimulated the media concentration process (CoE 2007a).

The acts of the Council of Europe important for the audio visual developments are the legally binding European treaties or conventions, many of which are open to non-member states, as well as the acts of the:

■ Parliamentary Assembly
■ Committee of Ministers
■ Steering Committee on the Media and New Communication Services (CDMC)
■ Standing Committee of Transfrontier Television
■ European Court of Human Rights.

Mostly significant for the audiovisual sector are the European Convention for the Protection of Human Rights and Fundamental Freedoms and the European Convention on Transfrontier Television (ECTT).

Article 10 of the European Convention for the Protection of Human Rights and Fundamental Freedoms provides the right of everyone to freedom of expression, which includes the right 'to hold opinion and to receive and impart information without interference by public authority and regardless of frontiers'. This freedom is subject to certain restrictions that are 'in accordance with law' and 'necessary in a democratic society' (CoE 1950b).

The aim of the ECTT is to facilitate, among the parties, the transfrontier transmission and the retransmission of television program services (CoE 1989). It lays down a set of minimum rules in areas such as the responsibility of broadcasters in regard to programming matters, including the European content of programming; advertising, teleshopping and sponsorship, as well as the protection of certain individual rights. Application of the ECTT mostly relies on mutual cooperation between the parties.

The ECTT and the amending Protocol, on the one hand, and the newly adopted Audiovisual Media Service Directive (which has replaced the Television without Frontiers Directive), on the other, have similar objectives, although the intention of the AVMS Directive as an instrument of the European Commission is to create a common market in broadcasting.

Alongside the European Parliament and the Council of the European Union, the European Commission is one of the three main institutions governing the European Union. The primary role of the European Commission is to propose and implement the legal basis for the European Union. The Commission is also responsible for adopting technical measures to implement legislation adopted by the Council and, in most cases, the Parliament. It monitors the Member States' compliance with the Union's agreed Treaties and Directives, taking action against those in default. The Commission is intended to be a body independent of the Member States. It consists of 27 Commissioners, one from each Member State of the European Union, supported by an administrative body of the Directorates-General (EC 2007c).

The EU Directorate General for the Information Society and Media was expanded as of January 2005 to include the media (which were formerly under DG for Education and Culture). DG InfSo deals with the research, policy and regulation of the areas of information, as well as with communication technology and media. It defines and implements the regulatory framework for services based on information, communication and audio-visual technologies. Its regulation has cultural, societal and economic objectives, and covers some of the largest economic sectors in Europe. Furthermore, it fosters the growth of the content industries drawing on Europe's cultural diversity. 'i2010 – European Information Society for Growth and Employment' is currently the main ruling policy document of DG InfSo (DG Infso 2005).

The European Union as one of the largest economic and political entities in the world is a supranational and intergovernmental alliance of 27 states with 495 million people (EUROSTAT 2007) and a combined nominal GDP of €11,295 ($15,183) billion in 2007 (EU GDP 2007).

Following the rigorously developing TV and radio market, the need to set some minimum regulatory standards applicable to all Member States was felt. Thus on 3 October 1989 the European Union came up with the Television without Frontiers Directive 89/552/EEC. This Directive constitutes the legal EU framework aimed at coordination of certain provisions laid down by law, regulation or administrative actions in the Member States concerning the pursuit of television broadcasting activities. It aims to ensure free movement of broadcasting services within the internal market and at the same time to preserve certain objectives of public interest, such as cultural diversity, the right to reply, consumer protection, and protection of minors. It is also intended to promote the distribution and production of European audiovisual programmes, and to ensure, whenever possible, that they are given a majority position in the programme schedules of the television channels (EC 1989).

Parallel to these actions, a report 'Europe and the Global Information' (largely known as the 'Bangemann Report') proved to be extremely influential in starting the discussion on the future European communications policy, by pointing out that the building of a European Information Society would be market-driven (EC 1994).

In the process of implementation of the TVWF Directive it was impossible to adopt decisions, contradictory to the norms of the ECTT. The fact that the Amending Protocol of the ECTT was adopted after the revision of the Directive in 1997 can serve as an illustration of the coordinated actions of the European Union and the Council of Europe in the audiovisual area. This Protocol practically reflected the amendments to the Directive. The current discussions of the revision of the ECTT are in tune with the newly adopted AVMS Directive. As a matter of fact, this process started quite a time ago: since 2001 the effectiveness of the articles of the Convention and the Directive has been thoroughly analysed.

In the five years since the TVWF Directive was amended, the European audiovisual sector has dramatically changed. The convergence of technologies has provided interweaving of linear and non-linear services. The expansion of fixed broadband, digital TV and 3G networks has rapidly changed the viewers' habits. The vertical structure of audio-visual programming was gradually displaced by horizontal fragmentation of the audiences, who wished to follow their own viewing time schedule. Technological progress has made a strong impact on the business models of the media industry. A need for modernization and adjustment of the regulatory framework was felt in this new situation of a rigorous market and technological developments.

After a long and intensive discussion, more coherent measures for reinforcing the pan-European audiovisual policy were proposed to the Community legislator, taking into account the objective of creating a pro-competitive, technologically driven and growth-oriented environment for the development of the audiovisual sector. A broad consensus on the scope, European works, co- and self-regulation, and independence of the national media regulators was achieved. Thus, the amending Directive was adopted on 11 December and entered into force on 19 December 2007. Member States have two years to transpose the new provisions into national law, so that the modernized legal framework for audiovisual media services will be fully applicable throughout the European Union by the end of 2009.

The AVMS Directive offers an updated and comprehensive legal framework that covers all linear (broadcasting) and non-linear (on-demand) audiovisual media services, provides less detailed and more flexible regulation and modernizes rules on TV advertising to better finance audiovisual content. The AVMS Directive also upholds the basic pillars of Europe's audiovisual model, such as cultural diversity, media pluralism, and protection of minors, consumer protection, and intolerance of incitement to racial and religious hatred. It acknowledges that:

> audiovisual media services are as much cultural services as they are economic services. Their growing importance for society, democracy – in particular by ensuring freedom of information, diversity of opinion and media pluralism – education and culture justifies the application of specific rules to these services.

In particular, the new Directive underlines the importance of promoting media literacy, the development of which can help people 'exercise informed choices, understand the nature of content and services and take advantage of the full range of opportunities offered by new communication technologies' (EC 2007d). Thus, people will be better able to protect themselves and their families from harmful or offensive material.

The field both of the ECTT and the AVMS Directive is very flexible and dynamic. That is why the work on their improvement is an ongoing process. In particular, the revision of both instruments by the participating parties concerns:

- The scope of the Convention and Directive (the broadening of traditional television broadcasting towards the ICT audio-visual services).
- The duties of the parties to the Convention and the Directive.
- The broadening of the jurisdiction and scope of regulatory practices, involving co-regulation and self-regulation.
- The freedom of reception and retransmission, including intended and unintended transfrontier distribution.
- The developments of advertising techniques (advertising, sponsorship, teleshopping, product placement and so on).
- The protection of rights granted by the Convention and the Directive (such as the right to information and cultural objectives, media pluralism, right to reply, protection of minors and respect for human dignity) and so on.

The rapid change of the audiovisual market requires a thorough refining of the existing norms in the Convention and the Directive under a broad consensus. The question is whether the regulatory changes should anticipate or follow the practices.

Promotion of media pluralism and content diversity

For many years already, one of the constant objectives in achieving a sustainable democratic environment on a pan-European level has been the persistent promotion of media pluralism and diversity of media content. Both the Council of Europe and the European Union have been very active and productive in discussing the issue through a number of recommendations, resolutions, declarations, opinions, communications, research papers, and so on, prepared to reflect the rapidly changing media sector.

One of the first pan-European documents attempting to define the concept of pluralism, is the Commission's Green Paper 'Pluralism and Media Concentration in the Internal Market' COM (92) 480 of 23 December 1992.

The variety of expressions used containing the word 'pluralism'– pluralism of the media, pluralism in the media, the pluralist nature of the expression of currents of thought and opinion, pluralism of information, pluralism of the press, plurality of the media – shows that there is no common understanding of the concept. However, two common features do emerge from a legal analysis of the European Convention on Human Rights as interpreted by the European Court of Human Rights and of national laws:

- The concept of pluralism serves to limit the scope of the principle of freedom of expression.
- The purpose of such limitation is to guarantee diversity of information for the public. (European Communities 1992).

The phenomenon of media pluralism and content diversity has been unceasingly a central issue of European policy-making. In 2007 both the European Commission and the Council of Europe published a number of documents concerning problems in the media environment arising from the rapid technological developments in the audiovisual area.

On 16 January 2007, the Information Society and Media DG of the European Commission initiated a three-step approach to 'Media pluralism: the need for transparency, freedom and diversity in Europe's media landscape'. This new programme points out that the media pluralism debate should concentrate not only on the grounds of media ownership but also on the transparent mechanisms, which will guarantee access of the citizens to varied information so that they can form opinions without being influenced by one dominant source. A key issue in this process is the functioning of the media as genuinely independent.

Presenting the three steps, the Information Society and Media Commissioner Viviane Reding underlined especially that:

while the media face radical changes and restructuring due to new technology and global competition, maintaining media pluralism is crucial for the democratic process in the Member States and in the European Union as a whole. This requires a sound understanding of the economic and legal reality of today's European media landscape, which our three-step approach seeks to achieve. (EC 2007e)

Two weeks later, on 31 January 2007, the Committee of Ministers of the Council of Europe adopted three documents concerning the further promotion of media pluralism and content diversity in the new digital environment:

- 'Declaration on protecting the role of the media in democracy in the context of media concentration'.

■ 'Recommendation Rec (2007) 2 on media pluralism and diversity of media content'.
■ 'Recommendation Rec (2007) 3 on the remit of public service media in the information society'.

'The Recommendation Rec (2007) 2 to Member States on media pluralism and diversity of media content' stipulates that the Governments of the Member States shall consider including in national law or practice:

■ Measures promoting structural pluralism of the media, such as: ownership regulation; public service media, other media contributing to pluralism and diversity; access regulation and interoperability, other support measures.
■ Measures promoting content diversity, such as: promotion of wider democratic participation and internal diversity; allocation of broadcasting licensees and must carry/offer rules; support measures; enhancing awareness of the role of the media.
■ Media transparency.
■ Scientific research. (CoE 2007b).

The challenges to television

Media pluralism is usually linked to the democratic performances of society. However, a greater number of media outlets does not necessarily mean that diversity of content has been achieved. The concept of pluralism can be defined both in terms of its function and in terms of its objective. Concerning television, media pluralism can be assessed through the number and types of channels, the number and structure of their owners, the editorial content of the broadcasts, and the access of different societal groups to programming.

Over recent years, media concentration has been considered the main threat to media pluralism. Concentration in the ownership structure of mass media industries usually suggests a state of monopoly/oligopoly, or large-scale owners in a given media industry. Concentration of media ownership suggests also the presence of media conglomerates, such as Disney, CBS, Time Warner, News Corp, Bertelsmann AG, Viacom and General Electric, which together own over 90 per cent of the media market (Concentration of media ownership 2007).

Fear of the negative consequences of media concentration is mainly connected with the availability of less diverse opinion in the media and with fewer opportunities for certain minority groups (including ethnic, religious, cultural, linguistic groups and so on) to reach the broad public through media. Both of these problems are considered significant obstacles to the development of a healthy, competitive media market. A major concern is also whether a consolidated media market (especially on a local level) can be accountable and dependable in serving public interest, especially in times of crisis and in cases of emergency. The ultimate results of such a media market consolidation is viewed as a poorly-informed public, restricted to reduced options of media array, which offer mainly information supporting the media owners' interests. Increased concentration of media ownership may also lead to censorship of critical debate on certain problems, to the absence of a wide range of issues of public interest and to increased commercialization of content. However, extensive research into the issue of media concentration and pluralism could not identify in quantative terms a direct link between media concentration and content diversity (Ward 2006: 1).

In some cases consolidated capital may even have a positive effect on pluralism. It may ensure more effective competitiveness against the media conglomerates, maintain reduced costs of operation, increase diversity of content supply to an extended area, and provide for more and more differentiated products and services, thus better answering the demands of the public.

Comparing the two sides of the problem, it should be noted that 'approaching the issue of media pluralism solely from the perspective of media ownership concentration is unproductive' (Jakubowicz 2006).

A prevailing trend in contemporary society is the growing number of TV channels which carry out the external (structural and market) pluralism. In this case, regulatory measures may be directed at organizing such relations between the various media companies so as to ensure a degree of autonomy between them. In the contemporary world, the media are clogged with unvaried entertainment formats in form and content. The form of presentation certainly has its powerful say in television, but if deprived of content, it becomes nondescript and unpromising. Along with this, some programmes that are meaningful for public interest are neglected, owing to a lack of attractiveness as compared, for example, with reality shows. Thus it becomes evident that realization of the principle of structural pluralism is tightly bound to the meaningfulness of content in the TV programmes. If we fail to find such a combination of diversity and quality, we will be doomed to endless switching from channel to channel, seeking in vain for something meaningful in the ocean of flickering TV images: pluralism is meaningless in such a situation (Raycheva et al. 2003). In this case, the measures may be directed either at the internal organization of the media company whose control structure will have to represent the various currents of opinion, or at the editorial content of the broadcasts.

From the viewpoint of content, guaranteeing of political and cultural pluralism merits special attention.

Concerning political pluralism, television often acts as the main subject of political manipulation, especially before elections. The starting point in this process is the selection, processing and distribution of information.

A fundamental assumption in contemporary political science is that authorities rely on information resources. The skill of sifting out meaningful from immaterial information enhances the power potential. The possibility to distribute information, in one's own interpretation at that and with channels to boot, or to withhold some of it, multiplies the power capacity (Bauman 1998: 21). Direct exercise of such power is a prerogative of the media. That is why, when powerful media fall under the control of economic or political power groups, this significantly deforms democracy.

Concerning cultural pluralism, there are two risks in this sphere: one is diluting the national cultural identity and uniqueness, the other is national encapsulation. Multiculturalism is rife with the danger of forcing in and taking up foreign models. Transnational TV formats gain ever larger territories in the poorer countries, displacing their cultural traditions and threatening main public values. Thus, pluralism may turn into its own opposite by losing entire styles, epochs, national models, and favourite works of other generations along the way. In this sense, it is important to preserve cultural identities, the letters and the languages in the EU integration processes. The constitutional rights of minority groups (ethnic, religious, cultural, linguistic and so on) to education and information in their mother tongue are also part of the cultural pluralism of the media.

Contemporary television is a convergent phenomenon, combining the intellectual product with technological potential, market mechanisms, regulatory practices and the response of audiences. Along with this, television is both a reflection and an embodiment of the post-modern concept, with its key characteristics of fragmentation, intertextuality, simulation and plurality. Fragmentation is intrinsic to television owing to its programmed and multi-channel character. Intertextuality received a boost with the advancement of digitalization. The principle of simulation in fact reversed the situation of television mirroring society into society mirroring television. Contrary to these three characteristics, however, pluralism cannot be viewed as intrinsic to television. Pluralism is determined by the tasks set for television, and the manner it deals with these tasks.

There is, however, a problem that comes to the fore: greater opportunities for selection carry weight only if there is something to choose from. What is the use of the great number of channels if they are filled with the same programmes, or with similar tastelessness? That is, the pluralism of content has been reduced to nil.

Conclusion

The significance and role of television in the contemporary world have grown enormously with the development of new platforms for the distribution of audio-visual content. Television continues not only to inform audiences but to shape their views as well. Moreover, it catalyses rather than reflects public processes, thus creating preconditions for reformatting the very society to the extent that society begins to reflect the developments on the TV screen. This mutual interpenetration is aided by diffusion of some other activities kindred with the media world. The political elite are quick to use the media for their PR purposes. For the economic elite, the media are the main distributors of their advertisements. The needs of the public are increasingly forced out of the media. Paradoxically enough, governments engage in regulatory protection of public service television, which is supposed to be their most vehement critic. Self-regulation has, as yet, failed to become the public ombudsman and corrective of commercial influence. Even enhanced interactivity could hardly pull the recipients out of their assigned role of users and consumers. The Internet environment is aiding the fragmentation of audiences, but still fails to change the prevailing vertical communication model. The moment it succeeds would probably bring about large functional restructuring of the traditional mass-media system.

Rapid technological developments of the information and communication industries outline the need to modernize the regulatory framework and practices. The new Audiovisual Media Service Directive will be implemented in the national legal framework within two years and the revision of the European Convention on Transfrontier Television is on its way. Modernization can be viewed from several perspectives:

- *In political terms*, the development of free and unhindered transmission of audiovisual services on a pan-European level governed by a common legal framework is important for pursuing EU objectives. In view of the democratic, social and cultural significance of the media, policy-makers and public authorities should enforce adequate measures to ensure transparency in the media sector and prevent conflicts of interest which pose a threat to the independence and plurality of the media.
- *In technological terms*, the turbulent progress of information and communication technologies is challenging the concept of traditional broadcasting, which is limited to the number of analogue

channels. The rapid spread of cable systems, broadcasting satellites and low-power TV has expanded the offer of diverse programs. Digital technologies, broadband and web casting increase the number of channels, providing the viewers with multiple choices of programs and audio-visual services. The contemporary audiovisual reality becomes more and more complex with the interweaving between linear and non-linear services. A key question in the context of the digital switchover refers to the task of determining the best use of the spectrum dividend.

- *In economic terms*, the expanding tendency towards deregulation and privatization in broadcasting leads to predominance of the commercial structures. The media content becomes more and more dependent on market mechanisms. Thus, the merger control at the European, as well as at national level, should be complemented with specific measures to protect and promote media pluralism.

- *In regulatory terms*, the tendencies to merge media, telecommunications and entertainment industries lead to changes in the legal basis of the regulatory approaches (in structure and duties of the regulatory authorities, in methods of regulating – regulation, co-regulation and self-regulation – and in audiovisual content, subjected to regulation). In this sense, it is of great importance to outline the parameters of the 'regulatable' content.

- *In social terms*, the quantity of programmes on offer leads to fragmentation, demassification of the audiences of the traditional broadcasting (one-to-many), thus opening ground for non-broadcasting and interactive audio-visual services. Furthermore, the Information Society services offer their products in a 'one-to-one' mode. Through citizen journalism and citizen media, individuals can produce and disseminate information and opinions that are marginalized by the mainstream media. The broad impact of media on the general public in real time is reduced due to asymmetric communication offered by diverse electronic sources. This new communication environment needs an energetic developing of media literacy programmes.

- *In professional terms*, the rapid introduction of the technological innovation is challenging the traditional formats, styles, and modes of programming. The process of media convergence as well as interactivity tendencies raises serious questions in the managing of editorial content. The significance of self-regulation and application of ethical codes of conduct become ever more important for journalist practices. Public service broadcasters should contribute to media pluralism by providing a diverse range of quality programmes. Media organizations should develop better accountability systems in order to strengthen professional values, editorial and journalistic independence and quality journalism.

The new pan-European moves for further promoting media pluralism and content diversity in the audiovisual sector are of major economic, social and cultural importance: TV is still the most significant source of information and entertainment for 98 per cent of the European households that watch television on the average of more than three hours per day. However, bearing in mind the rapid technological developments in a highly competitive market, a major concern about the vitality of the new regulatory rules may be how long the pillars of Europe's audiovisual model (cultural diversity, protection of minors, consumer protection, media pluralism, and intolerance against racial and religious hatred) will be protected. And all of this makes ever more obvious how the compression of historical time dictates the new pace of the communication process with the good, the bad and the unexpected challenges of ICT.

Note

1. The topic has been analysed by the author in the following publications: *Tracing the Digital Switchover in Enlarged Europe*. A chapter in Urban, Agnes; Sapio, Bartolomeo and Turk, Tomaž (eds.), *Digital Television Revisited. Linking Users, Markets and Policies* (2008), Budapest (Hungary): COST Action 298 'Participation in the Broadband Society', pp. 155–64; *Television: The Good, the Bad and the Unexpected Challenges of ICT*. Presented at the International transdisciplinary conference organized by COST Action 298 'The Good, the Bad and the Unexpected. The User and the Future of Information and Communication Technologies', Moscow, Russian Federation, 23–5 May 2007, http://www.costa30.eu/?q=node/32. Accessed 20 May 2008.

References

Bauman, Z. (1998), *Globalization. The Consequences for Man*, Sofia: LIK.

Concentration of media ownership (2007), http://en.wikipedia.org/wiki/Concentration_of_media_ownership. Accessed 15 April 2007.

Council of Europe (CoE) (1950a), 'Convention for the Protection of Human Rights and Fundamental Freedoms' as amended by Protocol No 11, http://conventions.coe.int/Treaty/en/Treaties/Html/005.htm. Accessed 15 April 2007.

Council of Europe (CoE) (1950b), 'European Convention for the Protection of Human Rights and Fundamental Freedoms', http://www.echr.coe.int/NR/rdonlyres/D5CC24A7-DC13-4318-B457-5C9014916D7A/0/EnglishAnglais.pdf. Accessed 15 April 2007.

Council of Europe (CoE) (1989), 'European Convention on Transfrontier Television', http://conventions.coe.int/Treaty/EN/Treaties/Html/132.htm. Accessed 15 April 2007.

Council of Europe (CoE) (2007a), 'An Overview', http://www.cid.bg/en/right/genoverview.htm. Accessed 15 April 2007.

Council of Europe (CoE) (2007b), 'Recommendation Rec (2007) 2 to member states on media pluralism and diversity of media content', https://wcd.coe.int/ViewDoc.jsp?id=1089699&BackColorInternet=9999CC&BackColorIntranet=FFBB55&BackColorLogged=FFAC75. Accessed 15 April 2007.

Council of Europe (CoE) (2008), 'Declaration of the Committee of Ministers on the allocation and management of the digital dividend and the public interest', https://wcd.coe.int/ViewDoc.jsp?Ref=Decl(20.02.2008)&Language=lanEnglish&Ver=0002&Site=COE&BackColorInternet=9999CC&BackColorIntranet=FFBB55&BackColorLogged=FFAC75. Accessed 8 April 2008.

DG Infso (2005), http://en.wikipedia.org/wiki/Directorate-General_for_Information_Society_and_Media. Accessed 15 April 2007.

EU GDP, International World Monetary Fund (2007), http://www.imf.org/external/index.htm. Accessed 15 April 2007.

European Commission (EC) (1989), 'Council Directive 89/552/EEC of 3 October 1989 on the coordination of certain provisions laid down by Law, Regulation or Administrative Action in Member States concerning the pursuit of television broadcasting activities', http://ec.europa.eu/comm/avpolicy/reg/tvwf/index_en.htm. Accessed 15 April 2007.

European Commission (EC) (1994), 'Europe and the global information society', The Bangemann Report, http://europa.eu.int/ISPO/infosoc/backg/bangeman.html. Accessed 15 April 2007.

European Commission (EC) (1997), 'Green Paper on Convergence of the Telecommunications, Media and Information Technology Sector, and the Implication for Regulation towards an Information Society Approach', Com(97)623, http://europa.eu.int/ISPO/convergencegp/greenp.html. Accessed 15 April 2007.

European Commission (EC) (2005), 'What is i2010?', http://ec.europa.eu/information_society/eeurope/i2010/what_is_i2010/index_en.htm. Accessed 15 April 2007.

European Commission (EC) (2006a), 'The Commission's "Broadband for all" policy to foster growth and jobs in Europe', http://europa.eu/rapid/pressReleasesAction.do?reference=MEMO/06/132&format=HTML&aged=0&language=EN&guiLanguage=fr. Accessed 15 April 2007.

European Commission (EC) (2006b). 'Bridging the broadband gap. Communication from the Commission to the Council, the European Parliament, the European economic and social committee and the Committee of the Regions', Sec (2006) 354 SEC (2006) 355, http://eurlex.europa.eu/Lex.Uri.Servsite/en/com/2006/com2006_0129en01.doc. Accessed 15 April 2007.

European Commission (EC) (2007a), 'Telecoms: Consumers have more choice, but full potential of EU's internal market remains unexploited', http://ec.europa.eu/information_society/newsroom/cf/itemlongdetail.cfm?item_id=3304. Accessed 15 April 2007.

European Commission (EC) (2007b), 'Communication from the Commission to the Council, the European Parliament, the European economic and social committee and the Committee of the regions: Reaping the full benefits of the digital dividend in Europe: a common approach to the use of the spectrum released by the digital switchover', http://ec.europa.eu/information_society/policy/radio_spectrum/docs/ref_docs/com/com_dd_en.pdf. Accessed 8 April 2008.

European Commission (EC) (2007c), http://en.wikipedia.org/wiki/European_Commission. Accessed 15 April 2007.

European Commission (EC) (2007d), 'Directive 2007/65/EC of the European Parliament and of the Council amending Council Directive 89/552/EEC on the coordination of certain provisions laid down by law, regulation or administrative action in Member States concerning the pursuit of television broadcasting activities'. http://eur-lex.europa.eu/LexUriServ/LexUriServ.do?uri=CONSLEG:1989L0552:20071219:EN:PDF. Accessed 8 April 2008.

European Commission (EC) (2007e), 'Media Pluralism: The need for transparency, freedom and diversity in Europe's media landscape', http://ec.europa.eu/information_society/media_taskforce/pluralism/index_en.htm. Accessed 15 April 2007.

European Communities (1992), 'Pluralism and Media Concentration in the Internal Market – An Assessment of the Need for Community Action. Green Paper', COM (92) 480 final, http://aei.pitt.edu/1156/. Accessed 15 April 2007.

European Council (2000), 'The Lisbon European Council – an agenda of economic and social renewal for Europe', Contribution of the European Commission to the special European Council in Lisbon, http://ec.europa.eu/growthandjobs/pdf/lisbon_en.pdf. Accessed 15 April 2007.

European Parliament (EU P) (2000), 'Charter of Fundamental Rights of the European Union', http://www.europarl.europa.eu/charter/pdf/text_en.pdf. Accessed 15 April 2007.

European Union (EU) (1957), 'Treaty Establishing the European Community', http://europa.eu.int/eur-lex/en/treaties/dat/EC_consol.html. Accessed 15 April 2007.

European Union (EU) (1986), 'The Single European Act', http://europa.eu/scadplus/treaties/singleact_en.htm. Accessed 15 April 2007.

EUROSTAT (2007), 'Population and Social Conditions', http://epp.eurostat.ec.europa.eu/portal. Accessed 15 April 2007.

ITU (2006), 'Digital broadcasting set to transform communication landscape by 2015'. http://www.itu.int/newsarchive/press_releases/2006/11.html. Accessed 9 April 2007.

ITU (2007), 'ITU World Radiocommunication Conference concludes after four weeks. International treaty sets future course for wireless', http://www.itu.int/newsroom/press_releases\2007\36.html. Accessed 8 April 2008.

Jakubowicz, K. (2006), 'Media Pluralism and Concentration: Searching for a Productive Research and Policy Agenda (in the light of the Council of Europe Experience)', prepared for presentation during the meeting of Working Group 3 of COST Action A 30, Budapest, 22–3 September 2006.

Lorente, S. (1997), 'The Global House: New Opportunities in Automation and Information', in Caby, L. and Vedel, Th. (eds.), *Telecommunications. Changing Relationships in an Information Society*, TIC Trends in Communication, No 3, Amsterdam: Boom Publishers.

Raycheva, L.; Jukova, D. and Karaivanov, G. (2004), 'Transparency and pluralism in the process of digitalization – challenges to the regulatory authorities', http://www.cem.bg/r.php?sitemap_id=111&id=415. Accessed 15 April 2007.

Reding, V. (2007), 'Telecommunication markets in Europe: Growth and investment need competition', http://ec.europa.eu/information_society/policy/ecomm/tomorrow/index_en.htm. Accessed 15 April 2007.

Ward, D. (2006), 'The assessment of content diversity in newspapers and television in the context of increasing trends towards concentration of media markets', final report on the study commissioned by the MC-S-MD, MC-S-MD(2006)001, Directorate General of Human Rights, Council of Europe, Strasbourg: Media Division, www.coe.int/t/e/human_rights/media/1_Intergovernmental_Co-operation/MC-S-MD/MC-S-MD(2006)001_en.pdf. Accessed 15 April 2007.

WTO (2000), 'General Agreement on Trade in Services', http://www.wto.org/English/tratop_e/serve/audiovisual_e/audiovisual_e.htm#top. Accessed 15 April 2007.

Press Freedom and Pluralism on the Micro Level: Journalistic Qualifications and Professionalization

Eva Nowak

Professionalization as a supportive factor for press freedom and pluralism

To meet the standards of the journalistic role in a democratic society, professional socialization is a decisive factor on the micro level of prerequisites. Regarding structural prerequisites, press freedom and pluralism depend on law and constitution, politics, cultural and economic influences on a macro level (see McQuail 1992: 99ff. and Czepek 2005: 19ff.). On a medium level, it also depends on media ownership, the medium and its concept, including target group, thematic choice, the role of interest groups – be it political, religious, economic or other – and the organisation and decision-making processes within the media companies. These structural prerequisites have an influence on press freedom and pluralism. They are, however, not a guarantee. A journalist's every-day decisions about whether to choose a certain topic and how to cover it – one-sided, critical, with in-depth research or superficially – do not exclusively depend on these structural questions. In countries with a good structural basis for press freedom and pluralism, journalists, nevertheless, might not always use the possibilities they have. This might result from economic pressure of, or on, the media company and the concept of the medium itself (medium level). On a micro level, press freedom and pluralism, however, also depend on how a journalist defines his or her professional role and on the quality of journalistic skills which are vital to fulfil this role.[1]

The journalistic role in a democratic society is often defined as (see Hallin and Mancini 2004 and Czepek 2005):

- A watchdog who has a control function within a society
- A neutral reporter on events and developments to enable a fact-funded formation of opinions, and as
- A commentator to contribute to different views in a concept of external pluralism.

A precondition for the development of a journalistic role, decision making criteria, and journalistic routines, is the professionalization of journalists. This article discusses which qualification aims support the journalistic role in the democratic sense and thus support press freedom and pluralism. Which competences are needed to achieve these qualification aims? And potentially, how do different types of journalistic professionalization processes, like journalism schools, university studies or training on the job, support the relevant competences and qualification aims?

Professionalization, competences and qualification

Journalistic qualifications describe the functional requirements for working successfully as a journalist (see Kron 2004: 238). Regarding the training process, these functional requirements can be transferred into qualification aims, which are found at the end of a successful professionalization process. The definition of these aims depends on the definition of the journalistic role, here the role in a democratic society as described above.

To fulfil these qualifications, a journalist needs certain competences.[2] These competences describe a disposition for journalistic action. The expression 'key competences' hints at the fact that competences are a precondition in meeting qualification. Competence in this sense includes knowledge, values and behavioural standards (see Weischenberg 1995: 492). Apart from a range of competences, journalistic action requires ability, willingness and the possibility to act.

Figure 1: Analytic matrix on journalistic competences. *Source: Nowak 2007: 93.*

Thus competences are not a guarantee but a prerequisite to fulfilling journalistic qualifications (see Schobel 2005: 106).

The advantage of distinguishing qualification aims and competences lies in the possibility of structuring journalistic training more adequately. Gaining competences is a dynamic process; for example competences lead to additional competences because they form a network (see Erpenbeck and Heyse 1999: 26). Qualification aims are less flexible because they are defined at a specific moment for a certain situation. Qualification aims of the 1980s are only partly the same as qualification aims today, because society as well as media has changed. Nevertheless, journalists may have gained competences in the 1980s that enable them to fulfil the qualification aims of today's media world.

So after defining qualification aims, competences have to be identified and trained in, which then leads to journalistic qualifications.

Defining journalistic qualification aims

The definition of the journalistic role as a watchdog, neutral reporter and commentator is a value-based decision for a democratic society. This decision includes a responsibility not only for the journalistic product but also for the effect of journalistic production on society. This understanding of the journalistic role comprises basic journalistic skills, for example being able to apply journalistic routines and programmes like organizing, presenting, gathering, selecting and checking information (see Rühl 1980). Mastering these routines and programmes will enable a journalist to fulfil everyday tasks like the production of a medium. This is the basis for journalistic work.

However, it takes more to be a good journalist:

- Detailed knowledge about one or more fields of reporting in order to be able to check experts' arguments and recognize contexts and problems
- Systematic reflection in order to be able to gain a certain independence of opinions and manipulations by politicians, companies, lobby associations, apparent victims and so on
- An analytical and distanced approach to topics of reporting as well as the medium, the journalistic working process and the media system. This supports the journalistic freedom and responsibility.

These qualifications are fundamental for the journalistic role in a democratic society. Reflection and an analytical and autonomous approach enable journalists to adapt to changes in the media and to react adequately to new situations. Journalistic routines, like gathering, selecting, checking and presenting information in combination with systematic reflection, support pluralistic reporting and gives motivation for well-grounded research and to *actively* choose and consider topics, views and problems outside the mainstream, instead of only reacting to PR- or event-driven impulses.[3]

This leads to three sections of journalistic qualifications:

1. Production – being able to produce a medium
2. Development and reflection – being able to develop a medium
3. Autonomy and responsibility – being able to integrate democratic values.

The following paragraphs analyse which qualifications belong to these sections and how they can support press freedom and pluralism:

Production involves

- Being able to produce journalistic quality.
- Being able to fulfil journalistic programmes and role requirements.
- Being able to deal with journalistic organizations.
- Gaining specialized knowledge in a certain field of reporting.

This list of qualifications enables a journalist to do his or her everyday work, independent of the state of press freedom and pluralism in the country he or she is working in. This depends, of course, in some points, on the definition of journalistic roles, programmes and journalistic quality (see Weischenberg 1998). If the journalistic role is defined as a must-be-critical role, then this is already an important qualification for the support of press freedom and pluralism.

Apart from these definitions, with these qualifications, a journalist can produce a good article or TV item on the professional level but possibly avoid certain topics or situations to avoid problems with advertising clients, the editor in chief, politicians or the biggest employer in the region. This would touch on the question of press freedom or pluralism. The level of reflection needed for this first section of qualification aims is relatively low.

The second section, *development and reflection*, involves

- Analysing and reflecting regularly on one's own journalistic work and the media system.
- Being able to transform this reflection into journalistic action and thus react adequately to unknown situations.
- Being able to develop journalism according to changes in society, technology, media use and so on.

These qualifications enable a journalist to adapt to future qualifications in a transforming world. It is the view beyond the end of one's own nose. However, the way journalism is developed and the quality of the reaction to a new situation depend on values. An editor-in-chief, for example, could react to a decrease in copies sold by avoiding critical or complicated topics, or he/she could decide to write more positively about, for instance, big local industries. This is a reflection-based reaction to a new situation, but the value behind the decision is merely economic and does not include the values of press freedom and pluralism. This second section, therefore, is also not decisive for press freedom and pluralism. However, the third one is:

Autonomy and responsibility involves

- Taking responsibility for one's own work, its consequences for people and society.
- Being able to act according to journalistic ethics.
- Keeping internal autonomy independent of media companies, political parties, religious groups, economic pressure and so on.

Autonomy is a counterproductive journalistic qualification in a society that suppresses pluralism and press freedom. Autonomy and responsibility support the freedom of speech, the pluralism of topics and a critical approach as part of the journalistic role. Thus, to support press freedom and pluralism, journalistic professionalization must involve the training of autonomy on a basis of journalistic ethical standards.

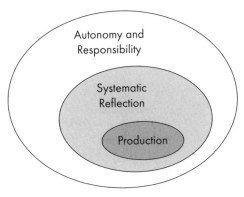

Figure 2: Three sections of qualification aims.

Training of relevant competences

To achieve qualification aims, an organized professionalization process[4] trains certain competences which have first to be identified (see Figure 1). The analytical basis for identifying the relevant competences is a matrix developed by the author (Figure 3) (see Nowak 2007: 91–8).

This matrix shows that to achieve operational competence, for example to actually work successfully as a journalist, a combination of professional competences, expert and orientation knowledge and key competences are needed. The three sections of qualification aims refer to all elements of this matrix. It is easy to see that from 'production' over 'reflection' to 'autonomy and responsibility' the key competences gain importance:

- 'Production', as a sector of qualification aims, includes the training of competences such as methodological and technical skills, knowledge of media and specialized and general knowledge. Among the key competences, the first row plays the important role: learning competence, personal, social and communicative competences and creativity as well as the ability to organize from the second row.
- 'Reflection' as a sector of qualification aims includes – apart from the competences mentioned under 'production' – all professional competences and, among key competences, the ability to reflect and to analyse.
- 'Autonomy and responsibility' as a sector of qualification aims moreover needs the key competences value orientation and readiness to take responsibility.

From a didactic point of view, this means that qualification aims that support press freedom and pluralism cannot only be trained through traditional lectures where a professor or instructor

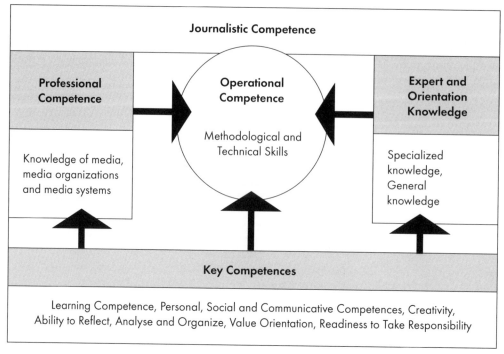

Figure 3: Analytic matrix on journalistic competences. *Source:* Nowak 2007: 93.

passes on his/her knowledge by reading or disclaiming a script. This might work with knowledge transfer, although even here integrating new information into previous knowledge, and thus into the mid- and long-term memory, will be difficult without applying other didactical methods (see Edelmann 2000: 280). With the training of journalistic skills and key competences it is nearly impossible to limit teaching methods to traditional lectures: operational competence requires the operational processes of acquiring these competences.

Based on the concepts of Krathwohl, Bloom and Masia (1967), learning target taxonomies, which limit teaching methods to lectures, would mean to only train cognitive learning targets. On this basis, the author has developed an advanced model of learning targets (see Nowak 2007: 155–61) including:

- Cognitive learning targets: thinking, knowledge, problem-solving, intellectual abilities.
- Operational learning targets: observable skills.
- Affective learning targets: emotions, values, opinions, attitudes, motivation.

This indicates that, in traditional lectures, operational and affective targets cannot be tackled. However, all types of targets are vital for training journalistic competences as described above. Writing articles or interviewing people needs operational learning targets, as they are operational competences. Training value-orientation and readiness for responsibility is only possible by also applying affective learning targets. Cognitive, operational and affective learning targets do not coexist independently, but have to be trained in a combination of theory and practice. This illustrates the analytical matrix of competences in this article (see Figure 3). The integration of theory and practice demands interactive and open didactical methods such as discussions, working groups, projects and problem-oriented learning instead of mere top-down methods like lectures (see Terhart 2005: 89–90).

Adequate forms of journalistic training

Competences supporting press freedom and pluralism can only be trained in an interactive and project-based learning environment, integrating theory and practices, as operational and affective learning targets take centre stage. But which forms of journalism training support this approach?

Fröhlich and Holtz-Bacha (2003) identify four categories of countries that represent their *dominant* system of journalism education:

- Journalism training mainly on a university level (Finland, Sweden, Spain, United States, Canada).
- Journalism training in stand-alone journalism schools which are sometimes linked with university level (Denmark, Norway, the Netherlands, Italy).
- Journalism training on a university level as well as in stand-alone journalism schools (France, Germany,[5] Ireland, Portugal).
- Journalism training primarily as training on the job (Great Britain, Austria).

The problem with these categories is that they are not sharply defined and that they are based on the analysis of a limited range of countries in Western Europe and North America. Hiebert and Gross (2003: 257ff.) describe journalism education in Eastern Europe as still being in transformation, as the journalistic role in the society as well as educational structures are still being discussed.

In the following, I will give an analysis of potential concerning the support of press freedom and pluralism in different types of journalistic training.

Training on the job is, in many countries, a common access to professional journalism (see Fröhlich and Holtz-Bacha 2003). It means that journalists-to-be have little or no theoretical training but learn to be a journalist while they are already working as one. They learn by example with, as role models, their colleagues, who give information and comment on the beginners' work. Qualification aims are not explicitly set but the aim is usually to be accepted as a journalist – to get a contract – or, from the other point of view, to integrate a beginner as a useful colleague into the team. Concerning qualification aims, training on the job emphasizes the production section and neglects development/reflection and autonomy/responsibility. Although the competences that belong to the production section will be imparted, profound knowledge and experience is a matter of coincidence and thus not a reliable part of this form of journalistic training. Training on the job is, therefore, not an adequate form of journalistic training for the support of press freedom and pluralism.

Traineeships are the organized form of training on the job. Qualification aims are usually set; a minimum amount of theoretical training is often included. Although traineeships do not depend on fortunate coincidences as much as training on the job, they are still not an adequate form of journalism training for the support of press freedom and pluralism. The negative points mentioned under 'training on the job' also apply, to a considerable degree, to traineeships. Reflection, responsibility and, to a certain degree, autonomy, however, might better be trained in traineeships rather than in unorganized training on the job, as long as seminars are included covering these topics. The question is to what depth they are covered. The training of journalistic autonomy, however, depends highly on the employer and his/her ethical and democratic values. If profit maximization is the highest value, the trainee will not be encouraged to develop an autonomous and responsible journalistic role.

Non academic journalism schools are often owned by media companies; some are owned by non-profit organizations or churches, or are private and commercial. Journalism schools offer an ambiguous picture, not only in terms of ownership but also in terms of their focus on media, topics and teaching methods. In Germany, journalism schools often emphasize practical training and neglect the theoretical background. Nevertheless, they enjoy a good reputation because of their emphasis on the practical training of methodological and technical skills, including reflection on journalistic products and ethical standards. Journalism school alumni can often easily start working as journalists, as they have had a good training in production-based competences. Professional competences are often limited to the journalistic product. The qualification aim of 'responsibility' is often important in journalism schools. The role of 'autonomy' as a qualification aim depends on ownership, as described above under 'traineeship'.

Universities vary as much as non-academic journalism schools. As a tendency, however, many universities offer a purely academic education, which enables alumni to pursue a career at a university or research institute. A good academic education in mass communication theory, however, does not necessarily train a student to work as a journalist. Older journalists often recommend studying any subject at a university and then entering journalism by training on the job. This obviously disregards the integration of theory and practice and especially of professional competence. Universities, however, have the potential to fulfil all relevant qualification aims and standards of training competences mentioned above, as long as they integrate theory and practice and agree to train journalists and not academic researchers, as the competences needed differ.

Vocational training cannot be a unique source of journalistic training as argued under 'traineeship' and 'training on the job'. It is, however, important for the adaptation of competences to changes in media and society in the sense of life-long learning. This is especially important for the sections on 'production' and 'reflection/development'.

This comparison of forms of journalistic training shows that different types of training have differing potential to support press freedom and pluralism. Journalism schools, and especially universities, have a high potential to support press freedom and pluralism, although many might not use their potential.

Conclusions

The contribution of journalistic professionalization to press freedom and pluralism lies in a clear connection between production skills, reflection and responsibility, with an emphasis on responsibility. An organized training process such as universities and journalism schools offer can, however, only support press freedom and pluralism when the training processes fulfil certain requirements. Traditional lectures in front of large groups support, above all, cognitive learning. Competences like reflection, value orientation and responsibility require open learning methods which support affective involvement of students, like discussion, working groups, projects and problem-oriented learning (POL). Nevertheless, the central prerequisite for a training process which supports press freedom and journalism is the definition of the journalistic role as autonomous and critical.

Notes

1. For professionalization, socialization and role development see Saxer and Kull 1981: 29; Weischenberg 1995: 494ff.; Gruber 1975: 71–2 and Heinz 2002: 397–8.
2. 'Competence' can also be defined as a natural, inborn ability, in contrast to 'performance' as a learnt ability. This distinction, however, is not flexible enough to describe a training process as qualification aims change with changes in the media and in society. Gaining competences is neither inborn nor static but a dynamic process.
3. This shows that prerequisites on the macro- and the medium level as defined in the beginning of this article are vital for journalistic action on the micro level.
4. Concerning the concept of professionalization see Ronneberger and Rühl 1992 and Weischenberg 1995.
5. In Germany, however, the most common way to enter journalism is via a traineeship called 'Volontariat' with a duration of between one and a half and two years. They are supposed to include some weeks of theoretical training. Although the word 'Volontariat' implies a non-paid internship, it is usually a job with a fixed salary. However, academic training has been gaining relevance since the mid 1970s.

References

Bloom, Benjamin S. (ed.) (1966), *Taxonomy of educational objectives: the classification of educational goals, handbook, 1, cognitive domain*, New York: McKay.

Czepek, Andrea (2005), *Pressefreiheit und Pluralismus in Sambia*, Münster: Lit Verlag.

Edelmann, Walter (2000), *Lernpsychologie*, Weinheim: Beltz; PVU.

Erpenbeck, John and Heyse, Volker (1999), *Die Kompetenzbiographie. Strategien der Kompetenzentwicklung durch selbstorganisiertes Lernen und multimediale Kommunikation*, Münster: Waxmann.

Fröhlich, Romy and Holtz-Bacha, Christina (eds.) (2003), *Journalism Education in Europe and North America. An International comparison*, Cresskill/NJ: Hampton Press.

Gruber, Thomas (1975), *Die Übernahme der journalistischen Berufsrolle. Eine sozialwissenschaftliche Analyse*, Nürnberg: V. d. Nürnberger Forschungsvereinigung.

Hallin, Daniel C. and Mancini, Paolo (2004), *Comparing Media Systems: Three Models of Media and Politics*, Cambridge: Cambridge University Press.

Heinz, Walter R. (2002), 'Berufliche und betriebliche Sozialisation', in Hurrelmann, Klaus and Ulich, Dieter (eds.), *Handbuch der Sozialisationsforschung*, 6th edition. Weinheim and Basel: Beltz, pp. 397–415.

Hiebert, Ray and Gross, Peter (2003), 'The Remaking of Eastern European Journalists', in Romy Fröhlich, and Christina Holtz-Bacha, (eds.), *Journalism Education in Europe and North America. An International Comparison*, Cresskill/NJ: Hampton Press, pp. 257–82.

Krathwohl, David R., Bloom, Benjamin S. and Masia, Bertram B. (1967), *Taxonomy of educational objectives: the classification of educational goals; handbook. 2: Affective domain*, New York: McKay.

Kron, Friedrich W. (2004), *Grundwissen Didaktik*, München and Basel: Reinhardt.

McQuail, Denis (1992), *Media Performance. Mass Communication and the Public Interest*, London; Thousand Oaks and New Delhi: Sage.

Nowak, Eva (2007), *Qualitätsmodell für die Journalistenausbildung: Kompetenzen, Ausbildungswege, Fachdidaktik*, Dortmund: Eldorado.

Ronneberger, Franz and Rühl, Manfred (1992), *Theorie der Public Relations*, Opladen: Westdeutscher Verlag.

Rühl, Manfred (1980), *Journalismus und Gesellschaft*, Mainz: v. Hase & Koehler.

Saxer, Ulrich and Kull, Heinz (1981), *Publizistische Qualität und journalistische Ausbildung*, Zürich: Publ. Seminar d. Univ. Zürich.

Schobel, Kurt (2005), 'Curriculumplanung anhand von Lernzielen/Anmerkungen zur Kompetenzdebatte', in Ulrike von Holdt, Christiane Stange, and Kurt Schobel, (eds.), *Qualitative Aspekte von Leistungspunkten: Chancen von Bachelor- und Masterstudiengängen*, Bielefeld: Univ.-Verl. Webler, pp. 101–15.

Terhart, Ewald (2005), *Lehr-Lern-Methoden. Eine Einführung in Probleme der methodischen Organisation von Lehren und Lernen*, Weinheim: Juventa-Verlag.

Weischenberg, Siegfried (1995), *Journalistik. Bd. 1: Mediensysteme, Medienethik, Medieninstitutionen*, Opladen: Westdeutscher Verlag.

Weischenberg, Siegfried (1998), *Journalistik. Bd. 2: Medientechnik, Medienfunktionen, Medienakteure*, Opladen: Westdeutscher Verlag.

Media Systems, Equal Rights and the Freedom of the Press: Gender as a Case in Point

Elisabeth Klaus

Equal rights regulations and affirmative action are sometimes thought of as restricting the freedom of the press. In this article I will contradict this argument and instead claim that the provision of equal rights is a decisive indicator of press freedom in the media. The focus will be on the gendering of the media system and on gender equality, but much of what I say is applicable to issues of race/ethnicity, class and age as well as religious rights. Gender issues today are very much intertwined with issues of ethnicity and class and I will refer to this off and on in my discussion.

Press freedom: Controlling or extending the rights of individuals and groups
Tied to the principle of public/ness, press freedom is related to the establishment of a democratic public sphere, which allows citizens to communicate freely and without censorship. In his insightful study on the 'The Principles of Publicity and Press Freedom' (2002) Splichal has critically evaluated the emergence of press freedom in its historical and philosophical relationship to the principles of publicity. The major principles of publicity were freedom of thought and freedom of expression, both being directed against the secrecy prevailing in feudal society. Splichal points out that freedom of the press was originally conceived as an extension of these two principles and promised to help fulfil Kant's goal of achieving the common good by allowing for a common reasoning. These ideas are at the core of the idea of enlightenment. They have formed the shaping of the European nation-states and also count among the founding principles of the European Union. Critical theories of the public sphere, prominent among them Habermas' analysis of public discourse, have relied on these ideas as well.

Splichal points out that the idea of press freedom diverted from its original focus and often came to be thought of as the pursuit of freedom *by* the media. Thus, it no longer served as an *extension* of the publicity principles by granting the individuals' rights to freedom, but as a means for controlling mass behaviour. Especially when it is linked to freedom of enterprise and private ownership, freedom of the press can be a powerful force restricting, not enhancing public debate. In countries where the media system is highly concentrated, be it as a state monopoly or by private ownership, grave danger exists of excluding particular social groups and rendering oppositional opinions invisible. On this ground, Splichal (2002: 83–5), Hamelink (2004) and others have called for introducing a right to communicate to the Universal Declaration of Human Rights. It would distract from the main topic of this volume to elaborate further on this idea. Suffice it to say, when I mention press freedom in this article I do not refer to its historical occurrence as a restricting force in the public discourse, but as an idea facilitating it by extending the principles of publicity. Freedom of the press, hence, does not primarily refer to freedom *by the press*, but to the freedom of publication of ones opinions and views *by the citizens through the media*. Realizing press freedom then entails the rights of individuals and social groups to receive all the relevant information necessary in order to participate freely in the public decision-making process and to form, express, and finally publicize their opinions. The degree to which these rights are guaranteed is a decisive measure for the degree of press freedom in a society.

The realization of freedom of the press thus encompasses two aspects: there is a legal aspect that entails the formal right to receive and transmit information without the interference of the state or other outside authority and guarantees an independent press. The other aspect requires a more in-depth look at the media system and addresses the prerequisites for participation and inclusion in the media, both as subjects to speak and have one's opinions heard, and as objects to be talked about and be represented in a non-discriminatory fashion. When seen as a guarantor of freedom of thought and freedom of expression, freedom of the press is linked both to the content of the media (does it provide adequate information?) as well as to the participation in media and communications (do the different social groups have access to the media or are some of them excluded?). This more substantial aspect, then, brings us to the discussion of a normative framework for the realization of freedom of the press in the case of women.

At the very influential Fourth World Conference on Women held in Beijing in 1995, at which the European Union played a very active role, twelve critical areas of concern for women and for the improvement of women's rights across the world were identified (Beijing 1995). 'Women and the Media', Section J, was based on the 'Toronto Platform for Action' (Toronto 1995), drafted at the UNESCO symposium 'Women and the Media, Access to Expression and Decision-Making'. In its preamble the Toronto Platform called for 'new opportunities for the participation of women in communication and media and for dissemination of information about women'. It held that it was necessary to increase the number of women in all areas of the media, but especially in the technical and decision-making fields. The range of action recommended went from facilitating training for young women to a recognition of the importance of women's media networks and alternative media produced by women. Obviously all of these are connected to the shaping of the media system.

With regards to media content, the Toronto Platform called for an improvement of the largely negative and stereotyped portrayal of women, and it condemned pornography and sexism. To this end, gender-awareness programmes targeting media professionals of both gender and gender-sensitive editorial policies, including the adequate use of language, was recommended. The platform furthermore suggested the introduction of media-monitoring bodies for editorial content and for advertisement. The demand for diversity features prominently in the Platform for Action. Achieving diversity both with regards to the access to media by women of different social backgrounds and lifestyles as well as with regards to their representation constitutes an important goal in the document. Following to a large extent the suggestions of the UNESCO symposium in Toronto, the Beijing Platform for Action named two major strategic objectives to provide for gender equality in the media:

- *Strategic Objective J.1.* Increase the participation and access of women to expression and decision-making in and through the media and new technologies of communication.
- *Strategic Objective J.2.* Promote a balanced and non-stereotypical portrayal of women in the media. (Beijing 1995)

I will focus on these two goals, one being concerned with access and participation and the other with representation, and ask to what degree these have been achieved. To this end, I will first present results from the Global Media Monitoring Project (2005) with a focus on the data that refers to the European participants. Then I will introduce the analytic concepts proposed by feminist scholars, which allow us to assess the gendering of the media both with regards to its occupational dimension and its content dimension. Based on this overview of gender studies research, in the conclusion, issues and questions are identified that need to be addressed when asking to what degree the two strategic objectives are fulfilled by the media system in different countries. In 2005 the European Union evaluated the outcome of the Beijing Platform of Action and established indicators for its successful implementation, but this was not yet done for the area of concern, 'Women and the Media' (see Roadmap 2006). A realistic assessment of these issues would help in determining factors that hinder or facilitate the fulfilment of press freedom for all citizens and for the different social groups they belong to.

Press freedom and the gendering of international media systems

A global average: Europe in the Global Media Monitoring Project
The Global Media Monitoring Survey collected data on the gendering of the world's news media on inconspicuous days in 1995, 2000 and 2005 (GMMP 2005). In 2005, data from 76 countries was gathered, among them 24 European countries. A number of Eastern European countries that had not participated in the two previous surveys were represented. The data provide a good overview of the gendering of the news, but is not reliable in every detail, monitoring only a single day in the media's news reporting. Also, the national findings are based on different samples and sample sizes, but weighting measures have been introduced to account for these differences. The data, furthermore, has been collected on the basis of the same coding scheme and for a clearly defined body of news stories. Despite the above mentioned limitations, the GMMP now constitutes the most comprehensive data base and provides the best comparative data not only on a global scale, but also as regards the European countries (see Gallagher 2001). The GMMP 2005 comprises an impressive number of 12,893 news stories taken from television, radio and newspapers worldwide. About a third

of these were collected and analysed in Europe. Both participation and representation of men and women in news stories is addressed.

As to the issue of *participation and access*, the first objective of the Beijing Platform for Action, the GMMP shows that women and men present the news in about equal proportions and this was true for all three years in which the survey was conducted. The number of female reporters is traditionally much lower than that of female presenters, but the GMMP notes a steady increase in the percentage of news items reported by women: from 28 per cent in 1995 to 31 per cent in 2000, reaching 37 per cent in 2005. However, these data need to be differentiated, with female reporters gaining much more ground in radio and television than in newspapers and reporting considerably more on local events than on national or international ones. The European percentages, calculated as the average for the participating 24 countries, lag a few points behind the global ones, but the diversion is small.

Table 1 presents the combined figures for news presenters and news reporters in the different countries and shows stark differences among them. Germany has the lowest percentage of women news presenters and news reporters with just 27 per cent, followed by the United Kingdom, the Netherlands, Belgium and Portugal, where under 40 per cent of the personnel in the news rooms are women. On the other end of the spectrum are Georgia and Serbia and Montenegro with 80 and 74 per cent female news presenters and reporters respectively. In thirteen countries – just over half of the total – the differences between women and men are only small, with women's participation ranging from 45 to 55 per cent. There is a slight tendency, then, for Western European countries to lag behind in women's employment in the media when compared to Northern, Central and Eastern Europe. One possible explanation of this focuses on the tradition of public service broadcasting in Western European countries. This appears paradoxical since public service TV was meant to ensure plurality in news and access of all social groups to broadcasting, but feminist scholars have pointed out that public service broadcasting was at the same time tightly linked to a pedagogy of information that favoured elite politics and 'hard news' and neglected other issues (for an overview see Klaus 2005: 235–40). But the great differences between reporters and presenters in the different countries and with regard to the different media need to be kept in mind, so that a single explanation for the variation is certainly inadequate.

When looking at the characteristics of news presenters on television, a striking pyramid emerges with regards to age. Within the younger age groups the percentages of female presenters is much higher than in the older ones. Women seem to vanish successively from the screen, the older they get. There are only two topics that women report on more frequently than men. These are the weather and stories on poverty, housing and welfare. With regards to celebrity news as well as arts and entertainment, the number of female reporters is just a little smaller than that of their male colleagues. On the other end, sport is the least likely to be reported on by women, with four out of five stories being told by a man. Women are also underrepresented in reporting on politics and government. The GMMP concludes: 'Overall, male journalists report at the so-called "hard" or "serious" end of the news spectrum such as politics and government...Female journalists are more likely to work on the so-called "soft" stories' (GMMP 2005: 19). However, it should be stressed that, with the exception of sports, the differences are in no way overwhelming or always clear-cut. The GMMP results suggest that women now have a greater share in the making of the news, but the design does not allow for a look at the decision-making level of the media. Also, the rather high percentage of women presenting and reporting news stories is counteracted by the low number of women represented in the news.

Table 1: News presenters and reporters and news subjects in Europe.

Europe	News presenters and reporters				News subjects			
	Women		Men		Women		Men	
	N	%	N	%	N	%	N	%
Austria	29	48%	31	52%	21	12%	160	88%
Azerbaijan	55	45%	68	55%	13	15%	73	85%
Belgium	47	37%	80	63%	79	31%	179	69%
Bosnia-Herzegovina	84	51%	82	49%	57	15%	324	85%
Croatia	58	46%	68	54%	108	26%	313	74%
Estonia	47	49%	48	51%	45	24%	142	76%
Finland	41	47%	47	53%	114	29%	277	71%
Georgia	24	80%	6	20%	10	19%	43	81%
Germany	88	27%	239	73%	146	22%	505	78%
Hungary	32	50%	32	50%	25	12%	185	88%
Ireland	70	54%	60	46%	84	26%	234	74%
Italy	676	52%	624	48%	244	14%	1502	86%
Malta	49	42%	69	58%	59	17%	295	83%
Netherlands	31	36%	54	64%	47	24%	147	76%
Norway	63	44%	80	56%	81	26%	229	74%
Portugal	73	37%	124	63%	73	20%	299	80%
Romania	87	52%	80	48%	39	23%	133	77%
Serbia and Montenegro	132	71%	54	29%	62	17%	311	83%
Spain	124	49%	127	51%	153	22%	552	78%
Sweden	122	51%	119	49%	112	30%	262	70%
Switzerland	52	46%	60	54%	35	17%	175	83%
Turkey	188	39%	297	61%	127	19%	559	81%
United Kingdom	118	35%	217	65%	131	25%	401	75%
Uzbekistan	26	55%	21	45%	9	15%	51	85%
TOTAL		48%		52%		21%		79%

Source: GMMP 2005: 135 and 120–1 (newly arranged and partly recalculated).

The *representation* of women as news subjects is strikingly low and lags far behind their role in everyday life. Only 21 per cent of news subjects are women and in only 10 per cent of the news are women central to the stories. They are more important in stories on crime and violence at the periphery of the news. Also, they appear much more often as celebrities, royalty or as 'ordinary people', while experts and spokespersons are overwhelmingly men. Women are largely absent from the area of politics and economy, and even more surprisingly also seldom featured in education, child-care, consumer issues or HIV-AIDS. Only 4 per cent of the news stories explicitly deal with equality issues, which are conspicuously absent in the reporting on politics and economy. At the same time, news stories are twice as likely to reinforce (6 per cent) blatant gender stereotypes as to challenge (3 per cent) them. The GMMP concludes:

> Blatant stereotyping is alive and well in news reporting around the world. Nor is it limited to the gratuitous display of female flesh – although there are plenty of examples of this. Sexist reporting extends to a very wide range of stories – including sport, crime, violence, and even politics. (GMMP 2005: 20)

The GMMP summary notes a link between the gender of the news reporter and the news subject, with women relating more stories that feature women and also more often raising gender equality issues, but this could also be an effect of the topics women report on. A gender-sensitive language is often lacking from the stories and where a differentiation between men and women would be appropriate, as for example in the case of the consequences of social childcare arrangements or the average figures for pension rights, such figures are rarely presented.

Table 1 highlights the representation of women as news subjects in Europe. The overall average in the European countries for which data was provided is 21 per cent and thus identical to the global average. But again, a closer look at the table reveals great differences between the different countries. Belgium, Sweden and Finland are the leaders with about 30 per cent of the news subjects being women. Austria and Hungary are on the other end of the continuum, featuring only 12 per cent of female subjects in their news. Just a little higher are the percentages for Italy and Azerbaijan, Bosnia-Herzegovina and Uzbekistan. In half the countries women make up 20–30 per cent of the news subjects. Most Western European countries are in this group, while the Eastern and Southern European countries represented in the survey display figures below the average. The Northern European countries have the best score when looking both at the percentage of women among the news personnel and as news subjects.

In summary, the GMMP shows that women seem to have made greater progress in the newsroom than in their representation in news stories. But a division of labour seems to exist with men reporting in the more central areas of news. Also, women appear more frequently on television and are on the average much younger than their male colleagues. It needs to be kept in mind that the GMMP cannot look at the level of decision-making and provides mostly quantitative data. The gendering of the news to the disadvantage of women is especially obvious when looking at the content of media and the subjects that are allowed to speak. Overall, only one in five news subjects is a woman and fewer appear as experts. However, while blatant stereotyping and sexism still exist, they are found only in a minority of the news stories. On the other hand, the GMMP found incidences of male and female reporters that actively support gender equality. Feminist media studies have tried to make sense of the different findings and provide theoretical concepts that help to explain the relationship between women and the media and to consider this relationship in their respective social and cultural contexts.

The occupational dimension: Participation and access of women to the media
Lünenborg (1997) and Gallagher (1990) have systematically collected comparative data on the employment of women in journalism in Western European countries, and Gertrude Robinson (2005) has done the same for the United States and Canada and contrasted these

findings with some of the European data. These authors provide a frame for analysing the gendering of the media system (see also Ross and Byerly 2004). Very little systematic data exists on other parts of Europe. Lünenborg (1997: 119–31) points out that the percentage of female journalists had been especially high in the Eastern European countries prior to the demise of communism. Today, a lot of variation exists in the different transformation states, but it seems that in the majority of countries the percentage of female journalists declined dramatically after 1989.[1] In the German Democratic Republic, for example, the number of female and male journalists was about equal, but after the unification of Germany the percentage of women declined drastically to about 30 percent, and thus to the level of the West German employment figures.

Despite such differentiation, however, the discrimination of women in the media work force has been a common feature across the European countries and was also visible in the Eastern European communist countries (Lünenborg 1997; also Ross 2005; Zoonen 1998). The existing data reveals a *vertical segmentation* between men and women employed in media and communications. The concept of a vertical segmentation was introduced by Neverla and Kanzleiter (1984) as an important feature of the labour market and refers to the gender hierarchy in existence in the media. The more a position is associated with competence, privilege and decision-making power, the higher will be the percentage of men holding this position. The reverse is true as well: the lower a job in the media's hierarchy, the more likely it becomes that a woman will hold it. In all the countries for which such data exist, a majority of the secretaries in the media offices are women, while they are much less represented on the editorial staff and only rarely own media businesses. Within journalism the pyramid shows up when comparing the percentage of women and men that are employed as trainees, as full-time journalists or as editors-in-chief. Recent surveys conducted in Germany and Austria suggest that very little progress has been made with regards to the representation of women in the latter group (Weischenberg, Malik and Scholl 2006; Kaltenbrunner et al. 2007). Another indicator of vertical segmentation of the journalist work force is that of wage difference, with women in the same jobs earning less than their male colleagues (Allen 2004: 124).

Neverla and Kanzleiter (1984) identified another form of gender division in the media workforce, which they called *horizontal segmentation*. They found that there were areas of women's and men's employment that mirrored the traditional division of labour between the sexes (also Zoonen 1998: 34). While the percentage of female journalists was high in the family and health departments, it was very low in the areas of sports, politics and business. There is an ongoing debate among German communication scholars as to the extent of horizontal segmentation in today's media. Lünenborg (2001) has pointed out that studies often present a misleading picture of female employment when providing percentages only. Since women are a majority of the work force only in lifestyle, health or family departments, it appears that they are employed solely at the margins of journalism. But these are generally also small departments and when Lünenborg recalculated the actual employment figures, it immediately became obvious that women, just like their male colleagues, work overwhelmingly in the areas of local news, politics or economy and thus are firmly positioned in the centre of the profession. Lünenborg concluded that many studies overestimate gender differences because they treat gender as an all-encompassing, ever-present variable of individuals while at the same time neglecting the multi-dimensional aspects of the gender category.

In Germany, Austria, the United States as well as in many other countries, the vertical segmentation specifically has not diminished as much as one could have expected, given the fact that for a number of years now the majority of trainees in journalism education are female and women enter the journalistic workforce with a more solid educational background than their male colleagues. Feminist scholars have blamed the gendering of journalism for this situation. Gender is not only a personal system, socializing the individual, but also a structural force that is shaping social institutions and value systems. The gendering of media and journalism includes the high regard for values such as objectivity (Allen 2004: 120–2) and an elite orientation, but can also be seen in the gendered climate of the newsroom (Robinson 2005; Ross 2005), in the competitive structuring of media and communication (Weish 2003), in male-centred career networks and work schedules that are antagonistic to family life (for an overview see Klaus 2005: 177–80). This is the reason why the number of women in higher education or in journalism training does not automatically translate into more women gaining decision-making positions in media and communication. The GMMP and other research indicates that some progress has been made in the employment of women, but almost nothing is known about the chances for minority women or transgender women to gain access to the media workforce, which appear to be very slim.

At least two things are needed to change the male dominance in the journalistic workforce and to allow women a fair share in the decision-making processes. One has to do with standards for gender equality within the media organizations and the other with equal access to communication and media policies. In Germany, the greatest advances in the employment figures of women in media have been made in those businesses where affirmative action and gender mainstreaming policies were introduced, as was the case in the WDR, a public German broadcaster situated in Cologne. A commitment to gender equality is almost invariably tied to the existence of women's media organizations or networks of feminist journalists, who formulate common demands and interests. It is the political arena where the most important decisions on the media system are made. The number of women in the political decision-making bodies, in governments, parliaments and political parties can have an influence on media and communication policies. In some countries female politicians and women's organizations are represented on regulatory media boards. Such decision-making power at the level of the media and of politics also increases the chances of women and women's organizations to influence the representation of women by the media.

The content dimension: The representation of women by the media
A balanced and non-stereotypical portrayal of women was the second objective put forth in Beijing (1995). The lack of women as subjects in news stories has been a clear finding of the GMMP. In none of the participating countries is there a balanced gender portrayal. Quite a few indicators confirm the existence of gender stereotypes in the news, such as the lack of women as experts and spokesperson, and their attribution to the 'softer' news items and to the private issues. Already in 1978, when Gaye Tuchman summarized the feminist research findings, she concluded that the portrayal of women was not a mirror of society, but lagged far behind the social changes that had occurred. According to Tuchman, the portrayal of women was characterized by their *symbolic annihilation and trivialization* in the media.

The *symbolic annihilation* can best be seen in the marginal status of women in political reporting and in a language-use that renders women invisible. In many countries the masculine forms are favoured in the media. For example, in the German-speaking countries journalists claim overwhelmingly that the masculine form is the generic neutral, despite evidence to the contrary, and that to add the female form would also be awkward. In the context of the EU-funded project 'Gender, Politics and Media: Challenging Stereotypes, Promoting Diversity, and Strengthening Equality' (2005)[2] Pantti (2005) has provided an excellent overview of previous European studies conducted in this area. The results show that symbolic annihilation is firmly linked to the *trivialization* of women and many of the findings reverberate the results of the GMMP. Pantti concludes that the media images discriminate against women in politics by a variety of means such as:

- Their invisibility
- The specific topic selection, whereby women appear in 'soft news' and men in 'serious' or 'hard news'
- The firm connection made between women and their family status
- The focus on the looks, styles and appearances of female politicians
- A gendered use of language when characterizing politicians
- The framing of female politicians in the context of gender in contrast to their colleagues.

The symbolic annihilation and trivialization resulting from a focus on the styling and on the private lives of female politicians, and their stereotypical portrayal by the media creates a double-bind situation for women in politics, who appear as incapable politicians when they act feminine and as anti-feminine, and thus not to be trusted, when they act like men.[3] In contrast, male politicians were not placed in such a gendered frame, as Pantti (2005) remarks: '(M)en are more likely than are women to be described in gender-neutral terms'. In this way, men, their actions and areas of interests are conceptualized as the norm in political and public life, while women appear as the diversion from it. In an EU-project focusing on 'The Role of Mass Media in (Re)Distribution of Power' (Latvia 2004) the absence of references to their gender in the reports on male politicians has been fittingly called the 'silencing of gender'.

In her comprehensive discussion of the lack of advances made towards an adequate portrayal of women by the media since the Beijing Conference, Pandian (1999) used mostly data from outside of Europe, but much seems to apply here as well. Aside from the scarcity of information on women, the lack of women as news subjects and their stereotyping, Pandian identifies *negative and derogative images of women* as an important problem area, hindering the fulfilment of the goals articulated in Beijing. Many European studies have painted the same picture with women often being used as sex objects in advertisements. They are also much more frequently portrayed as passive victims than as active subjects. Violence against women in media is frequently sexualized (Röser 2000). In this way it is tied to pornography and linked to an irresponsible reporting on sexual violence against women (Zoonen 1994; see also Allen 2004: 136–41).

Examples of inadequate reporting on male violence against women can be found in German and Austrian news stories on the murder of a woman by her ex-partner. While women nowadays are rarely portrayed as bringing about their punishment by lewd or promiscuous behaviour, those stories almost invariably appear under the headline of a 'family tragedy'. Thus the crime is equated with other tragic occurrences such as accidents, fatal illnesses or natural disasters that befall a family unit. The silencing of gender can be seen at work in this example since the social reasons for these crimes, which are rooted in the existence of a power relationship between the sexes and in the prevalence of traditional concepts of masculinity, are thus rendered invisible. Such gender stereotyping has very real consequences for the women and men in the audiences. In a German study, Röser (2000) has shown how media violence that reinforces the imbalance of power between men and women is perceived as a threat by female viewers in real life, hindering their freedom of movement in the public realm.

Alternative gender portrayals are rare in the news, but there seems to be some more progress in the fictional programs. Klaus and Kassel (2005) found that Austrian entertainment series in 2004 featured a wide variety of traditional as well as non-traditional gender images with genres being directed at young people and comedies presenting a more modern image of women's lifestyles and career options. However, according to that research, not much progress has been made in regards to the verbal and nonverbal interactions of men and women in the different series that tended to be conventional, with women portrayed as the weaker sex and the caretaker of men and children, while men were portrayed as much stronger and protective, but also as less caring in the family context. As has been found in other countries, very little coverage is given to equality issues and alternative images of women in all types of media content in Austria (Klaus and Kassel 2007). This points to the necessity of supporting the publishing by different women's groups of alternative media that can counter some of 'the irrelevance of mainstream media content to the real lives of women' (Pandian 1999: 464).

When compared to the occupational arena, the rate of change with regards to the gender portrayal in media seems to be even slower. The search for explanations for the persistence of vertical and horizontal segmentation in the media workforce and for the annihilation and trivialization of women by the media has led to new research questions. Pantti (2005) points out that research on the relationship between gender, media, and politics initially focused on the (in) visibility of women, then analysed the specific coverage of female politicians and finally turned to questions of *gendered mediation* by the media. The feminist research agenda has altogether shifted from a sole concern with media representation of women to a more differentiated approach that focuses on the multiple ways in which gender is constructed by the media. This has lead to a greater scrutiny of professional norms and working procedures in journalism and of the hierarchies of values in effect in media content.

The objectivity norm and the norm of fast reporting in the news selection process has been especially questioned by feminist scholars, as has the devaluation of entertainment programmes that are more closely associated with female audiences, and the unqualified condemnation of the recent changes in news production (Lünenborg 1997). News values do not lend themselves to a discussion of structural factors, either, and this means that social problems of inequality and exclusion are rarely addressed. In Germany and Austria researchers have suggested to add xenophobia/ethnicity and misogyny/gender as news values, with foreigners and women having less chance of appearing in news stories than native citizens and men, even if the events concerned display the same number of news factors (for example Prenner 1995). Few media professionals are aware of these implicit biases in the news rooms and production departments. The European 'Screening Gender'-Project[4] supported by the European Union and organized by five European public broadcasters between 1997 and 2000 as well as the 'Gender, Politics, and Media'-Project mentioned above developed material for comprehensive gender-awareness training of the media staff using different examples from media content. Also, some organizations of female journalists have put out guidelines for the use of gender-sensitive language by media in their countries.

Ethical standards for media and journalism that include principles for an adequate, non-sexist, and non-discriminatory gender portrayal could be installed by legislation or by a voluntary self-monitoring of the media. Some countries introduced an ombudsman or organizations that provide opportunities for audiences to take action against sexist, violent and derogatory media images. In Germany as well as in Austria regulatory bodies exist at which protest against advertisements can be directed. Charges of discriminatory or sexist practices always feature prominently in the complaints raised, but the ruling triggers only moral sanctions. A similar function for journalism is held by the 'Deutsche Presserat', which serves as a self-regulatory body for media content, but it is called a 'toothless tiger' since its sanctions are not binding. Undoubtedly, restrictive measures need to be complemented by a conscious effort to diversify gender images and to support gender equality in society. In order to achieve this, alternative, feminist, and minority media should be subsidized, and provisions should be taken to allow that voices from civil society can also be heard in mainstream media. Germany, for example, requires private TV stations to give a time slot to independent media production companies and both Germany and Austria have a triadic structure in their broadcasting systems, with community media being supported as a third pillar besides private-commercial and public stations.

Conclusions: Prerequisites for equality in the media system

The two strategic objectives laid out by the UN are obviously interlinked. Only when women in the media are portrayed as actively engaged in politics, work, and public affairs, will women in the audiences be encouraged to participate in all areas of social life. The social responsibility of the media extends to portraying a wide variety of gender and sexual relationships, thus enabling women and men to make informed choices from the great variety of options open to them today. This goal can better be achieved when more women are present at all levels of media production, but also if women can actively engage as audiences with the media content available. This requires that women have the technical means as well as the competences to access and to choose from all media content. In many countries women still have less access to the Internet and have even less often the technical skills or the self-esteem to successfully use ICTs for their information and publication needs. This problem has been addressed in terms of the Digital Divide, which has narrowed considerably in the Western European countries, but which is still wide open in technologically and economically poorer countries and in those states where a stricter gender division prevails.

Press freedom can only be realized to its full extent when all citizens have equal access to the media. As gender research has shown in the case of women, no country has as yet achieved this goal. But there are important differentiations between the countries. In order to compare and evaluate the extent of gender equality, and thus the degree of the realization of press freedom in the different countries, a number of indicators have proven useful. While women should be treated as a social group and their status analysed in comparison to that of men, also necessary is a more differentiated approach which addresses the situation of women of different ethnic groups and class backgrounds and of diverse sexual orientations and lifestyles. Comparative data that need to be collected include:

Indicators for participation and access to the media

- Number of women in media workforce
- Percentages of women in different areas of media and hierarchical positions
- Wage differences between men and women
- Representation of different social groups in decisions making bodies for media content and media policy
- Representation of women and women's groups in regulatory media bodies
- Representation of women with regards to media ownership
- Extent of the digital divide and measures to counteract it.

Indicators for gender equality in media content

- Representation of women as subjects in news stories
- Representation in different subject areas
- Rules against pornography and sexual violence in media content
- Financial and other support for alternative media and community programming
- Gender training for editorial staff
- Rights of audiences to shape media content by ombudsmen or monitoring bodies.

To overcome the structural barriers for the participation of women in media and a non-discriminatory gender portrayal by media, conscious measures need to be taken. Vertical and horizontal segmentation of the labour force, as well as the symbolic annihilation and trivialization in the media, is a result of a dualistic gender regime in effect in society. Although men are also affected by gender stereotyping, the construction of gender by the media supports a power imbalance that discriminates against women. Undoubtedly, progress, albeit much too slow, has been made towards a better representation of women both at the level of the workforce and of media content in many countries. Although statistics on this are much needed, it is safe to say that the progress that has been made favours middle-class, heterosexual, Christian and native-born women, while migrant women, lesbians, Islamic and working-class women are still largely absent from the media workforce as well as from media content.

Notes

1. Pantti (2005) reports the same in regard to the number of women holding a political office.
2. See Portraying Politics 2006 for detailed information on the project and the resulting research and training toolkit.
3. Women in journalism who enter male-dominated fields and positions face a similar double-bind situation.
4. Detailed information on 'Screening Gender. Promoting Good Practices in Gender Portrayal on Television' including the training tool kit can be found on the Internet (see Screening Gender 2000).

References

Allen, S. (2004), *News Culture*, 2nd edition, Maidenhead and Berkshire: Open University Press.
Beijing (1995), 'Beijing Declaration and Platform for Action', Adopted by the Fourth World Conference on Women: 'Action for Equality, Development and Peace', Beijing, 15 September 1995, A/CONF.177/20

(1995) and A/CONF.177/20/Add.1', University of Minnesota, Human Rights Library, http://www1. umn.edu/humanrts/instree/e5dplw.htm#three. Accessed 1 April 2008.

Gallagher, M. (1990), 'Women and Men in Broadcasting. Prospects for Equality in the 90s', A Summary Paper of the EBU/EC Conference, Athen, 7–10 November 1990.

Gallagher, M. (2001), *Gender Setting: Cultivating Vulnerability in an Uncertain Age*, London: Routledge.

GMMP (2005), 'Global Media Monitoring Project. Who makes the news?', http://www.whomakesthenews. org/who_makes_the_news/report_2005. Accessed 1 April 2008.

Hamelink, C. J. (2004), *Human Rights for Communicators*, Cresskill and N.J.: Hampton Press.

Kaltenbrunner, A., Karmasin, M., Kraus, D. and Zimmermann, A. (2007), *Der Journalisten-Report*, Wien: Facultas.

Klaus, E. (2005), *Kommunikationswissenschaftliche Geschlechterforschung. Zur Bedeutung der Frauen in den Massenmedien und im Journalismus*, 2nd edition, Wien: Lit.

Klaus, E. and Kassel, S. (2004), 'Männer- und Frauenbilder in Unterhaltungsserien des ORF-Fernsehprogramms. Literaturrecherche und Inhaltsanalyse', in ORF Markt- und Medienforschung, *Publikumsratstudie 2004. Zur Wahrnehmung von männlichen und weiblichen Rollenbildern in den ORF-Unterhaltungsserien und deren Identifikationspotentiale aus der Sicht der ZuschauerInnen*, Wien, Januar 2005, pp. 5–52.

Klaus, E. and Kassel, S. (2007), 'Das Frauen- und Männerbild im österreichischen Fernsehen. Ein Überblick über die vorliegenden Forschungsergebnisse', in C. Steininger and J. Woelke, (eds.), *Fernsehen Österreich 2007*, Konstanz: UVK, pp. 301–21.

Latvia (2004), 'The role of mass media in the (re)distribution of power', Center for Gender Studies, University of Latvia, Report for the project 'Mass media in the (re)distribution of power', funded by the European Union in terms of the Community Framework Strategy on Gender Equality (2001–5), http://www. medijuprojekts.lv/uploaded_files/7_Latvia_ResRep_media_ENG.pdf. Accessed 1 April 2008.

Lünenborg, M. (1997), *Journalistinnen in Europa. Eine international vergleichende Analyse zum Gendering im sozialen System Journalismus*, Opladen: Westdt. Verlag.

Lünenborg, M. (2001), 'Geschlecht als Analyseperspektive in der Journalismusforschung. Potenziale und Defizite', in E. Klaus, J. Röser, and U. Wischermann, (eds.), *Kommunikationswissenschaft und Gender Studies*, Opladen: Westdt. Verlag, pp. 124–43.

Neverla, I. and Kanzleiter, G. (1984), *Journalistinnen. Frauen in einem Männerberuf*, Frankfurt a.M. and New York: Campus.

Pandian, H. (1999), 'Engendering communication policy: key issues in the international women-and-media arena and obstacles to forging and enforcing policy', in *Media, Culture and Society*, 21:4, pp. 459–80.

Pantti, M. (2005), 'Literary review for the project Gender, Politics and Media: Challenging Stereotypes, Promoting Diversity, Strengthening Equality', http://www.portrayingpolitics.net/research.php. Accessed 1 April 2008.

Portraying Politics (2006), http://www.portrayingpolitics.net. Accessed 1 April 2008.

Prenner, A. (1995), *Zur Konstruktion von Männerrealität in den Nachrichtenmedien*, Bochum: Brockmeyer.

Roadmap (2006) 'Communication from the Commission to the Council, the European Parliament, the European Economic and Social committee and the Committee of the Regions – A Roadmap for equality between women and men 2006–10 – COM(2006)92 final', http://ec.europa.eu/employment_ social/gender_equality/gender_mainstreaming/roadmap_en.html. Accessed 1 April 2008.

Robinson, G. J. (2005), *Gender, Journalism and Equity. Canadian, U.S., and European Perspectives*, Cresskill: Hampton Press.

Röser, J. (2000), *Fernsehgewalt im gesellschaftlichen Kontext. Eine Cultural Studies-Analyse über Medienaneignung in Dominanzverhältnissen*, Opladen: Westdt. Verlag.

Ross, K. (2005), 'Women in the boyzone. Gender, news and herstory', in S. Allen, (ed.), *Journalism: Critical Issues*, Maidenhead and Berkshire: Open University Press, pp. 287–98.

Ross, K. and Byerly, C. (eds.) (2004), *Women and Media. International Perspectives*, Malden: Blackwell.

Screening Gender (2000), 'Screening Gender. Promoting Good Practices in Gender Portrayal on Television', http://www.yle.fi/gender/. Accessed 1 April.

Splichal, S. (2002), *Principles of Publicity and Press Freedom*, Oxford: Rowman & Littlefield.

Toronto (1995), 'Toronto Platform for Action', Adopted by the participants in the International Symposium: 'Women and the Media, Access to Expression and Decision-making', held in Toronto (Canada) from 28 February to 3 March 1995, http://www.un.org/esa/gopher-data/conf/fwcw/bground/unesco.txt. Accessed 1 April 2008.

Tuchman, G. (1987), 'The Symbolic Annihilation of Women by the Mass Media', in G. Tuchman A.K., Daniels and J. Benét, (eds.), *Hearth and Home. Images of Women in the Mass Media*, New York: Oxford University Press, pp. 3–38.

Weischenberg, S., Malik, M. and Scholl, A. (2001), *Die Souffleure der Mediengesellschaft. Report über die Journalisten in Deutschland*, Konstanz: UVK.

Weish, U. (2001), *Konkurrenz in Kommunikationsberufen. Kooperationsstrukturen und Wettbewerbsmuster im österreichischen Journalismus*, Wiesbaden: Deutscher Universitäts-Verlag and GWV Fachverlage.

Zoonen, L. v. (1994), *Feminist Media Studies*, London, Thousand Oaks and New Delhi: Sage.

Zoonen, L. v. (1998), 'One of the girls? Or the changing gender of journalism', in C. Carter, G. Branston, and S. Allen, (eds.), *News, gender and power*, London: Routledge, pp. 33–56.

Media Governance and Media Quality Management: Theoretical Concepts and an Empirical Example from Switzerland

Vinzenz Wyss and Guido Keel

Introduction

By exploring and comparing media systems in Europe in terms of their capabilities to provide independent and pluralistic media, freedom is conventionally defined as the absence of state intervention. But by asking the question of how the different media systems in Europe vary regarding freedom, pluralism and participation, we also have to ask whether media policy and media regulation incite the media to fulfil their societal functions, such as to contribute to the observation and synchronization of society. For this societal role, media's independence and freedom are crucial preconditions. On the other hand – especially under the terms of commercialization (see Meier and Jarren 2001) – it can also be seen that the media normally act according to their own imperatives and rules, and these rules are not necessarily those which foster the normatively assigned societal role. That is why political systems – governments – are implementing regulatory frameworks. In the media sector regulation is required, for example, when it comes to opening markets, when media are abusing their power, or when regulation is required in order to attain specific quality goals such as diversity or the protection of minors and so on.

From this point of view, media regulation does not necessarily mean a limitation of freedom by the state, but a strengthening and support of freedom and pluralism. Based on that perspective, we discuss in this article the potential of co-regulation as a modern form of regulation. As McGonagle (2002: 2) writes, trends such as media convergence and internationalization of the media require new forms of regulation. In the search for these new, more consistent and adequate forms of regulation, the notions of self- and co-regulation instead of traditional state-dominated regulatory systems have been introduced to the debate. These new forms of regulation usually occur first in the environment of new technologies – the online world – while regulation concerning traditional media tends to stick with more traditional forms of regulation. The Report of the US President's Working Group on Unlawful Conduct on the Internet stresses the role of the private sector as a crucial actor to protect children online, to support self-regulatory consumer protection initiatives as well as to coordinate and cooperate with law enforcement authorities (WGIG 2005).

The White Paper on European Governance, published by the European Commission, mentions the term co-regulation as an example of better regulation that 'combines binding legislative and regulatory action with measures taken by the actors most concerned' (European Commission 2001: 21). In a co-regulatory system, the public authorities accept that the protection of societal values can be left to self-regulatory mechanisms and codes of conduct. This is exactly the basic assumption of the new concept of 'Media Governance', which implicates the intermediation of the steering and control effort by state regulation authority and the principle of media autonomy. A central requirement of 'Media Governance' is the implementation of a quality management system that systematically treats the interests of the stakeholders and functions as an instrument to establish a culture of responsibility, or media accountability.

In this article we give a quick overview, with reference to the corresponding literature, of the main requirements of 'Media Governance'. In a second step, we describe the main principles of a quality management system for media organizations. In Switzerland the media regulation and supervisory authority – the Federal Office of Communication (OFCOM) – has applied the co-regulation concept by linking the guaranteeing of broadcasting licenses to the implementation of quality management systems within the media organization. We discuss in this context the results of a study commissioned by OFCOM that shows the state of quality control practices among Swiss private broadcasting organizations and the conclusions drawn by OFCOM for the broadcasting licensing and regulation process. Subsequently, we present some empirical evidence concerning the first effects of this new co-regulation process in Switzerland and draw some conclusions with regard to the potential of the 'Media Governance' concept. Finally, we offer an outlook on future research needs in this field on an international level.

From media policy to Media Governance

There are many rather different concepts of regulation implemented internationally. Some fields of regulation are completely handed over to industry self-regulation, while others remain subject to traditional government regulation. In the media sector, the regulatory opportunities of the state are generally limited, because state regulation in that field conflicts with the principle of freedom of the media and might be seen as inappropriate censorship. In the current theoretical discussion about the right concept, new models – such as 'regulated self-regulation' – are seen as the 'third path' in media policy (see Puppis 2007). In these new concepts the role of the state moves away from hierarchical control to a modulation of processes going on within society (see Schulz and Held 2001). In the scientific discussion about effective media policy and an adequate regulation system, this third path is outlined under a new buzzword: 'Media Governance' (see Donges 2007). This concept is likely to become a promising model for co-regulation in the media sector. McQuail (2003: 91) defines this modern form of regulation as follows: 'Media Governance covers all means by which the mass media are limited, directed, encouraged, managed or called into account, ranging from the most binding law to the most resistible of pressure and self-chosen disciplines.'

'Media Governance' is a plurivalent concept which includes the setting of rules, their implementation and the sanctioning as an outcome of private actors negotiating with the regulator and other societal stakeholders. Meier (2006: 203) distinguishes three different perspectives: governance for, governance within, and governance by the media. In this article we focus on the relation between the first and second perspective and understand 'Media Governance' according to Hamelink and Nordenstrang (2006: 7) as a 'framework of practices, rules and institutions that set limits and give incentives for the performance of the media'. Furthermore, we assess the potential of media regulation to actively encourage the media to enforce social and corporative objectives.

According to Jarren (2007) 'Media Governance' aims at the creation of a new social order within the special function of media in society. In spite of the guaranteed autonomy of the media, other civic actors have the opportunity to participate in the policy-making process. Thus, on the one hand, media policy restricts the influence of the state on media structure, but on the other hand, media policy secures the orientation of the media towards the needs of society. In other words, 'Media Governance' has to assure the autonomy of the media but at the same time take care that the media organizations assume responsibility within this autonomy. That means that media organizations and professional groups are obliged to establish a dialogue, negotiation processes and forms of self-obligation like codes of conduct, mission statements or ethical codes. In order to do this, the following should act as the guiding principles (see Jarren 2007: 141–2):

1. Freedom of communication and professional independence: On the level of the single media organization this could mean separation of the commercial administration and the editorial board but also the implementation of professional rules of autonomy as they are written down in the guidelines of press councils.
2. Responsiveness of the media organization relating to all (not only political) stakeholders: For example on the organizational level, this could mean the involvement of different civic interest groups in the media observatory, or, on the level of media coverage, pluralism by selecting a variety of themes and differing opinions.
3. Equal Access to the media for all interest groups.
4. Media Accountability: Media organizations are obliged to observe the rules that are stipulated by organized interests within the society.

This social order as a culture of responsibility has to be constituted in a social process. In this process of co-regulation, new organizations or initiatives can arise within the media system or within the single media organization. Social actors who contribute to this process of self-control within the media system are, for example, press councils, journalism schools or other institutions of professional education. Media observatories or media awards could be part of this system. Within the media organization, responsibility can be located on different levels: the media organization as a whole, the ownership, the management and the individual journalist. Within the media organization, ethics committees or quality committees communicate both within the organization and between the organization and society. They correspond with new forms of self-obligation and self-control. The involvement of citizens or special representatives of interest groups can provide a way to organize social responsibility in the media parallel to the influence of the market and the state.

Most of the existing co-regulation has been established to protect minors or to regulate advertising. Both objectives are suitable for co-regulatory measures. However, other fields would also be suitable; for instance, some co-regulatory systems for the implementation of ethics or quality management systems in broadcasting or in the press.

The implementation of quality management systems as precondition
Quality management required
'Media Governance' in the sense of co-regulation is not independent from a priori defined political or cultural rules and agreements, nor is it only an ex post instrument. Rather, co-regulation can be an instrument of quality assurance during the production process within the media organizations. Only if the rules of external regulation are linked with self-regulation can media policy then be an effective instrument of quality assurance within media organizations (see Gottwald et al. 2006). Therefore, the implementation of a comprehensive quality management system within media organizations is an important precondition for 'Media Governance' and can be an outcome of co-regulation. A quality management system, which includes the establishment of visible and transparent schedules of responsibilities on the level of the media organization and the newsrooms, is part of this culture. This also includes the constitution and communication of transparency rules, quality norms, principles and standards as well as procedures involving the civic society or recipients (see Jarren 2007: 142). A quality management system that treats the interests of the stakeholders systematically can be seen as an instrument to establish a culture of responsibility or media accountability. On the organizational level, the culture of media responsibility can be encouraged by a Media Accountability System as proposed by Bertrand (2000).

Along with the idea of 'Media Governance', concepts of quality management are gaining in importance. In this process, quality goals must be stated by management in a way that they can be measured in an evaluation process. Quality assurance itself is an ongoing process with preventive, accompanying, and ex post elements. The process of quality assurance is primarily established and driven by the management. It allows for persistent evaluation in the sense of self-control to see whether the organization's performance (for example its programme) meets the goals and standards set by themselves in accordance with the broader regulatory framework. On the editorial level, maintaining quality includes all the systematically planned procedures which contribute to determining journalistic production processes or services, or improving and adjusting them to previously defined requirements – quality goals. Quality assurance thereby helps to define corrective measures to meet the set standards and to overcome deficits. To develop, steer and ensure quality in media companies, suitable management concepts which develop the corresponding structures and create internal guidelines are necessary.

Concepts of media quality management
Quality management concepts exist in various forms: one example is the self-evaluation model of the European Foundation for Quality Management (EFQM 2008) which meets the requirements of the Total Quality Management (TQM) philosophy and was considered as the framework for the continuous improvement of organizational quality management (see Wyss

2002). The TQM approach defines quality as the goal of a comprehensive management strategy in which all of the individual strategies of the editor in chief are aimed at raising quality by developing quality criteria, putting them into practice and maintaining them. In particular, the three main goals – comprehensiveness, regularized procedures and performance assessment – mark the TQM approach as a particularly ambitious one (see Meckel 1999: 43–4). The goal of TQM is not just about meeting standards; the quality management process associated with it is continuous. This presupposes that a media company regularly acquires information about its environment, its competitors and customers, and adjusts to the requirements of the relevant stakeholders. Finally, quality management requires a control procedure. An improvement can only be recognized as such if concrete quality goals are formulated at the outset, against which the currently achieved quality standard can be measured.

Up to now, there is no media company noted for the application of the EFQM model. But since 2003 two International Standards exist: ISAS BC 9001:2003 for broadcasters and ISAS P 9001:2005 for the press and Internet content providers (see Certimedia 2008). These standards were developed by the Media and Society Foundation – a Swiss-based initiative of prominent international media professionals – which gathered the main principles universally shared by media organizations regarding quality management (see Media Society Foundation 2008). The foundation justifies this initiative as follows:

> Commercial and political pressures are threatening media's credibility and weakening its influence on society. Media transparency and accountability are needed to establish a trusting relationship between the media and its readers, listeners or viewers, but also its numerous other stakeholders, i.e. its own staff, the advertisers, the public at large, the civil society, public authorities, etc. The time has come for the media to claim its commitment to its own professional and ethical standards and demonstrate that it is enforcing the values it is upholding. (Media Society Foundation 2008)

All requirements of International ISAS Standards are specific to media companies and intended to be applied by all organizations and their suppliers, regardless of type (television and radio broadcasters, Internet content providers), status (private, public service or community broadcasters) and size. To date, only three companies worldwide comply with the requirements of the ISAS Standard (see Certimedia 2008): Trans TV (Indonesia's leading commercial television channel), Canal Once (Mexico's public cultural channel), and Latvijas Radio (Latvia's national radio station). The ISAS Standards are based on ISO 9001:2000. Research by Wyss (2002) and Hermes (2006) has shown that it makes little sense to use the ISO 9001:2000 Standard – which is widespread in other industries – for media organizations without adapting it to the peculiarities of the media industry.

Standards of media quality management
All the concepts of quality management have in common that an evaluation of the quality assurance practice has to focus on certain standards. If media organizations want to contribute to the process of quality assurance systematically, they have to communicate these standards. In addition, by implementing a quality management system the media organizations have to commit to a culture of responsibility as well as identify and pursue crucial quality-focused

processes. A quality management system thus includes at least (1) a transparent quality policy and (2) resources processes (see Wyss 2002):

(1) Quality policy
The management should provide evidence of its commitment to well-defined core values. The quality policy of the management should be formalized in the form of a widely disseminated document that is reviewed at least once a year. This document could, for example, include an editorial charter that guarantees the independence of the media organization from any kind of power, be it political, economical or other. A code for programmes or a mission statement, an ethical code or a quality manual includes, for example, professional norms of quality journalism, such as pluralism of opinions and points of view, the promotion of gender equality, consideration for minority groups, promotion of diversity and so on. A code of advertising allows for transparency as a crucial quality standard in journalism. The management should clearly describe the organization's relationship with such constituencies as owners/shareholders, political authorities and advertisers.

(2) Resources and processes
The management should identify and document all the processes having a direct impact on the quality of editorial content, the relationship with advertisers, the relationship with external suppliers of content, the measurement of audience figures and listeners/viewers' satisfaction, and the management of human resources. The organization should have clear rules of recruitment and professional development options for all its employees. Specifically, the organization should have training opportunities, transparent recruitment and lay-off procedures, and encourage employees to suggest quality improvements. The organization should pay particular attention to the measurement of audience figures, audience satisfaction, and stakeholders' complaints. The management should establish an in- or/and out-house critic, or a 'content evaluation commission' to scrutinize the newspaper, or monitor the programme. The management should put in place a quality or ethics committee and mediation mechanisms (for example ombudsman) to deal with external complaints. The management could establish a press council, for example regular meetings of professionals from the media and representative members of the community. All these are elements which contribute to a quality management system.

While there is an intensive discussion among media scientists on the functionality and adequacy of quality management systems, the ongoing debate has hardly affected the media organizations so far. Recent research on the establishment and implementation of forms of quality assurance paint a bleak picture: Research in the German-speaking countries show that such initiatives are very seldom or only rudimentarily implemented in media organisations. Hermes (2006: 238–40) found in a survey of German news organizations that they are still far from a comprehensive quality culture or a deliberate use of quality management approaches. With the exception of public broadcasters, only one third of all news organizations have defined quality goals in mission statements or editorial handbooks. Research by Siegrist (2006) and Wyss (2007) on the state of quality management in daily newspapers and among private broadcasters finds the same for Switzerland.

According to Wyss (2002), the low level of quality management among media organizations can be explained by the fact that in media business the dominance of cost management hinders the discussion about journalistic quality and its maintenance. The trend to increased commercialization of the media industry results in a process by which media organizations and editorial production processes are increasingly dictated by economic logic rather than journalistic principles. The more the media operate according to the logic of economy, efficiency and profit maximization, the less we can expect the implementation of a quality management system which systematically takes into consideration the interests of the stakeholders. Therefore, it remains doubtful if media organizations will make an effort on their own to establish quality management systems, if external media regulation – legal provisions – does not support this process. That is why Ladeur (2000) asks for a media policy and regulation which fosters forms of editorial quality management, and Jarren (2007: 134) raises the point that it always takes public debate and sometimes the threat of measures by political actors to institutionalize self-control.

The case of Switzerland
Problem analysis: The attempt of OFCOM
OFCOM recently made a first step in the direction of 'Media Governance'. This media regulation body handles questions related to telecommunications and broadcasting (radio and television). In this sphere, OFCOM fulfils all regulatory tasks concerning electronic media. In 2007, after the implementation of the new law on Radio and TV (nRTVG), the radio and TV licences in Switzerland were re-assigned. According to Article 38 and Article 43 nRTVG, the licensing of media organizations is dependent on the fulfilment of certain performance standards by these organizations. The constitutional mandate requires a broadcasting system which contributes to education and cultural development, free development of opinions as well as to entertainment. The implementation of this constitutional provision takes place on two levels: firstly, SRG SSR idée suisse as a public broadcaster is to provide for this service on a national and language-regional level. Secondly, private broadcasters are in a position to deliver these services on a local level.

Why did OFCOM decide to use media self-responsibility or co-regulation in the implementation of the nRTVG and to require self-regulation from private broadcasters? This decision has a history which shows how, in several steps, private actors, with a mandate of the state, have set their own rules and made sure they were implemented and sanctioned. It has become obvious that a lack of self-regulation is to be overcome by means of co-regulation.

OFCOM made a first important step when it formulated the programme mandate to prepare the implementation of the nRTVG. To do this, OFCOM commissioned and published two media science studies on the professional structures in private broadcasting and on quality assurance within these organizations. The Institute for Media Science and Media Research at Zurich University was mandated to realize a survey (online-survey of 44 radio stations and eighteen TV stations, or 449 individuals; see Bonfadelli and Marr 2007). The Institute for Applied Media Studies at Zurich's University of Applied Science (IAM) analysed, with observation, document analysis and interviews, the mechanisms and practice of quality assurance in eleven radio and television stations selected for this purpose (see Wyss 2007). The gathered data was to support OFCOM in implementing the nRTVG in an adequate manner according to the structural realities of the situation in Switzerland. The study was to result in suggestions on how Swiss private broadcasters could meet the imperatives of quality assurance. The practical goal of the research project was to identify models for best practice strategies that should be considered when formulating the licensing requirements.

The need for such research was obvious, since earlier corresponding scientific studies on the state of quality management in media organizations showed that there was only indirect reference to society: forms of participation (for example press councils or ombudsmen) hardly existed, and quality management that integrated the interests of stakeholders was hardly implemented (see Wyss 2002). The research commissioned by OFCOM reinforced these impressions. Elements of quality assurance (for example programme planning, programme feedback, documents such as editorial guidelines or charters) exist in many organizations; however, a continuous and systematic quality assurance hardly ever takes place (see Bonfadelli and Marr 2007). 58 per cent of all production directors find programme feedback and quality assurance very important and another 30 per cent find it important. To what extent these merely remain lip service depends heavily on the role which quality assurance plays in editorial everyday life. In eight out of ten organizations, mission statements exist.

71 per cent of all stations have an editorial charter, and in six out of ten stations, a document defines ethical standards. Less than half of all stations have explicit guidelines on how to deal with PR activities.

Since paper doesn't blush, the existence of these documents says little about everyday practice. More telling are the findings of the second qualitative study on the practical implementation of quality assurance procedures which was carried out parallel to the interviews (see Wyss 2007). The results from that research are to result in suggestions how Swiss private broadcasters could meet the imperatives of quality assurance as well. The study showed that the volume of documents, such as mission statements or manuals, in the analysed media organizations is considerable; however, they differ greatly in content and form and have no common concept regarding journalistic quality. In the various stations there are very different ideas concerning the function of these guidelines. The documents provide only vague and approximate quality definitions. For example, the editorial concept of one station states:

> The relevance depends on the target group and the emotional involvement of the members of that group. There is no absolute or abstract relevance. There is no importance except for that of those of our listeners who belong to the majority of our target group (thus not children, not other journalists, not university graduates).

Another station makes a difference between a 'performance mission statement' and a 'financial mission statement', which fully aligns the programmes with 'today's and future needs of the market' and with 'profit'. There is hardly a specific positioning by the distinctive quality of goals among the stations.

In the research, the news organizations' resource problems became obvious. Absence due to training leads to a shortage in manpower. Stations depend heavily on the intrinsic motivation of the mostly very young employees. In Swiss private radio and TV stations every other person is 30 years old or younger. Only 16 per cent are older than 40. The average age is about 33. The relation between young journalists – often with only basic training – and trainees is 1:1 at some stations. Nearly 20 per cent of all interviewees have had no journalistic training at all. At these private stations, training is something the employees have to seek themselves, rather than having the station provide it for them. Only half of the stations offer internal or external training.

The available resources such as time or expert knowledge are rather weak. Work pressure is generally high. With a monthly salary of CHF 5200, the median income in this media sector is not only well below the overall median income for journalists (CHF 7200), but is even below the median for all employees in Switzerland (CHF 5550).

Also concerning quality assurance processes, the qualitative and quantitative picture presents itself rather poorly: periodic programme feedback following emission takes place in seven out of ten cases. The editors are well aware of the importance of an approval process to avoid mistakes; however, such a process takes place only occasionally. Only in every other station is the systematic countercheck of PR information provided to the station on a regular basis. The stations analysed rarely evaluate listener and viewer feedback. The legally stipulated ombudsman has hardly any practical relevance. Because of the usual lack of resources, stations do without systematic media research, although most stations express a need for qualitative data or specific research.

Standards of quality assurance by OFCOM
For private broadcasters, only those organizations that have the potential to meet the requirements of a defined mandate are recognized for broadcasting licences. This mandate, however, leaves flexibility for individual interpretation. According to OFCOM, this requires – besides other elements – organizational forms of quality management. The programme autonomy guaranteed by the constitution prevents programme standards from being too detailed. That is why the mandate only describes these standards as abstract requirements concerning the programme content and completes these standards with requirements for the production process, which should enhance the likelihood that the programmes meet the constitutionally-required standards.

Thus, the requirements concerning quality assurance do not directly refer to the journalistic quality of a single production, or even a single news story, but to the organizational structures and processes which bring about these programmes. The organizations are obliged to establish a quality management system which – with regard to the journalistic production of programmes – includes the following (see UVEK 2007: 3, Article 6):

1. Quality goals and standards concerning form and content of the programme. They are to reflect the programming mandate and to specify the goals and standards of the single organization. These goals and standards are to be included in documents such as mission statements, editorial guidelines or editorial handbooks. The goals are to be made known among all employees. They are predominantly related to the quality dimension's relevance, as well as diversity of topics, opinions and actors.
2. Defined processes which allow for an ongoing control of whether stated quality goals are met. This includes for example briefings, production approval processes and institutionalized programme feedback, all in relation to the above mentioned goals and standards. Furthermore, the result of this feedback is to be made accessible for all employees.
3. Sufficient personal resources to fulfil the programming mandate. As far as human resources are concerned, training to meet the defined programme requirements is to be implemented.

Performance reviews with employees and written-down agreements on goals to be achieved help communicate the quality standards.

In July 2007, the Federal Council defined the VHF radio and local TV coverage areas with performance obligations and specified the number of licences. In September 2007, OFCOM put the licences out to tender. The deadline for submission of candidatures was December 2007. After this, OFCOM opened the public hearing on 52 radio and 20 TV licence applications. This process of public hearing ('Vernehmlassungsverfahren') can be seen as well as a kind of co-regulation. Up to this point, broadcasters could exercise significant influence on the implementation of the co-regulation process. Their 72 candidatures for the total of 54 licences could be consulted on the OFCOM website (OFCOM 2008) during the licensing process. OFCOM as the regulating body hopes that, thanks to this process, the goals brought about in the quality agreements and self-declared performance standards will be discussed more thoroughly internally. Furthermore, they wish to trigger a public debate on issues of media quality as well.

First effects: Empirical evidence
This article was written during the public-hearing phase. Thus it is possible to draw a first conclusion by carrying out a documentation analysis. This following analysis applies to 72 candidatures for the licences and focuses only on the elements of quality assurance. In their applications, the stations had to provide information beyond the quality management system, on various aspects of their business such as the rules of procedure, organizational charts, responsibilities, financial holdings and investments, nature of planned programme, information on production process and financing of programme and so on. With this information, they mostly delivered promises. These documents show what is planned to be installed in the following months until the first round of quality management evaluation.

All stations, without exception, state in their applications that they approve of the relevance of editorial quality management systems to optimize and improve the editorial performance. Roughly 60 per cent of all stations explicitly refer to the concept of Total Quality Management – a concept that in connection with media organizations had been an almost unknown term in Swiss and German editorial offices until recently (see Wyss 2002; Hermes 2006). 15 per cent of all TV stations and 8 per cent of all radio stations even refer to the EFQM model. Two thirds of all organizations reinforce in their applications the intention to have their quality assurance system regularly evaluated by an external body. 20 per cent of all TV stations and 13 per cent of all radio stations even consider an ISO certification.

In their applications, the programme providers went extensively into preventive, accompanying and corrective measures of intra-organizational quality assurance.

Table 1 lists the various measures along the logic of the assurance process. More than 90 per cent of all stations were able to supplement their application with an editorial mission statement. That is 15 per cent more than before OFCOM's intervention. 85 per cent of the TV stations and 73 per cent of the radio broadcasters have published journalistic guidelines – for example, printed in an editorial handbook. One third of all stations claims that these documents are regularly updated and amended, which is an indicator for the continuity and systematic approach of this quality assurance measure. At least every third station refers to the

Table 1: Quality Management Instruments.

	TV (N=20) in %	Radio (N=52) in %
1. Preventive measures		
Editorial mission statement	95	90
Editorial Handbook/Journalistic Guidelines	85	73
Training, external or internal	95/ 85	82/ 87
Management by Objectives (Quality goals)	70	60
Evaluation of employee satisfaction	15	0
Programme and issue planning	100	88
2. Measures accompanying the production process		
Briefings by superiors	50	46
Editorial conference	80	77
Approval of single broadcasts (Countercheck)	65	48
3. Corrective measures		
Feedbacks, internal or external	85 / 50	92 / 27
Ombudsman	5	6
Audience research	45	37
Evaluation of viewer / listener feedback	50	38

'Rights and Duties of Journalists' issued by the Swiss Press Council. Of course these documents cannot be seen as proof that the employees know the content of the policy. 25 per cent of all organizations say that discussions about their quality policy take place in internal events dedicated to this cause.

An exact analysis of the provided documents that refer to rules in the sense of quality goals and norms shows that they are based on only an approximate understanding of journalistic quality. According to OFCOM's requirements, all stations promise in their rules and regulations the existence of an independent editorial status, which is aimed at guaranteeing editorial independence in relation to the publisher or commercial management. The quality criteria discussed in the documents (mission statements and handbooks) mostly refer to the news, and focus on the quality dimension's relevance, diversity, adequacy, and comprehensibility as well as the provision of specific journalistic content for a certain regional community (for example to strengthen identity or enable a dialogue). More than half the stations identify relevance as a central quality goal, without giving any further information on what it stands for. To a similar extent, descriptions of quality criteria such as accuracy, correctness, balance, objectivity and transparency, or the separation of editorial and commercial programmes are found. Also mentioned are news values which create relevance, such as proximity (regional reference), timeliness, emotionality, conflict and prominence. With regard to the quality dimension of diversity, most stations simply repeat the demands from the programming mandate, without further specifying these terms. Other quality goals such as reduction of complexity, orientation, analysis, scrutiny or providing of background information are hardly mentioned.

Another preventive measure mentioned in the documents is employee training. In that respect, OFCOM made specific demands: the broadcasters must prove that they offer their employees the opportunity for training. In earlier studies, it was repeatedly stated that over half the journalists considered the opportunities for training in their editorial teams to be inadequate (see Wyss 2002). Now, between 85 and 95 per cent of all stations state that they see internal or external training as a central quality assurance instrument and thus want to pay special attention to it. Other key points here are the evaluation of recruitment and personnel policy and of measures of employee satisfaction. The document analysis showed, however, that only 70 per cent of all TV stations and 60 per cent of the radio broadcasters manage according to agreed objectives or carry out regular performance appraisal. Only 20 per cent could provide corresponding questionnaires. Only 15 per cent of all TV stations say that they have regular employee satisfaction surveys. All TV stations and 88 per cent of all radio stations stated in their applications that they intend to make efforts to improve their programme and issue planning.

Looking at measures accompanying the production process renders a sobering picture. Only half the stations have quality-oriented employee briefings previous to the production process. Eight out of ten stations stress the relevance of their editorial conference. In the discussion of guidelines, the conference is cited as one of the most important instruments to ensure quality. Only 15 per cent make an effort, however, to protocol these discussions and to make the content accessible to the employees who are not present. Approval of single broadcasts before their emission, according to the TQM principle of 'preventing rather than correcting mistakes', is also far from being standard procedure.

Internal criticism of programmes is undoubtedly one of the most important corrective quality assurance measures. However, only 3 out of 10 stations have corresponding checklists which could be used for such feedback processes, but in 4 out of 10 cases, such feedback is written down and accessible for everybody. Less common are measures where external experts are invited to provide feedback. Interesting in that respect is that only 5 per cent of all stations refer to their already-existing ombudsman – the media organizations are required by law to provide one – as quality assurance institutions. Audience research for quality assurance is relevant to only 45 per cent of all TV stations and to 37 per cent of all radio stations. The evaluation of viewer and listener feedback does not seem to be systematically implemented everywhere.

Conclusions and outlook

The case of Switzerland as presented here shows that the implementation of concepts of co-regulation does indeed have the potential to engage media organizations in the sense of 'Media Governance', to have them make their quality goals transparent and identify quality oriented processes. The case proves that previous to the intervention by the regulatory body many media organizations made far less effort concerning quality assurance than afterwards. However, the analysis of the licence applications shows that many of the promised quality assurance processes have not yet been implemented. Some mission statements or charters were only produced immediately before putting together the application and had not been put in practice. Only the evaluation commissioned by the regulatory body will show to what extent the media organizations' intentions are just acts of hypocrisy. Because media organizations usually strive for economic and financial goals as well, it remains doubtful whether a holistic quality management will be able to cope with these inconsistencies and streamline all organizational processes to achieve journalistic quality. Rather, it can be assumed based on Brunsson's (2002) concept 'The Organization of Hypocrisy' that in their quality management the duality between economic and journalistic goals is carried on and media organizations professionally feign: 'To talk in a way that satisfies one demand, to decide in a way that satisfies another, and to supply products in a way that satisfies a third' (Brunsson 2002: 27). At the same time, scepticism is also justified towards the regulator: although co-regulation is a concept which has considerable political resonance and can be interpreted as an initial step towards deregulation, the concept could also be seen as a 'charade' by the state, 'which would ostensibly convey the impression of an inclusive approach to law-making, but in reality ensure a covert continuation of the State-dominated status quo' (McGonagle 2002: 4).

Finally, this article shows that an analysis of media systems regarding their capabilities to provide independent and pluralistic media should focus not only on the absence of state intervention. Rather, it could be shown that co-regulation has the potential to strengthen and enhance media performance. If media organizations implement an effective media quality management system, it is more likely that the principles of 'Media Governance' can be achieved. So, by considering the 'Media Governance' perspective, to evaluate media systems also means to investigate whether the most important media organizations in a country have implemented concepts of co-regulation, which includes an effective quality management system.

References

Bertrand, C.-J. (2000), *Media Ethics and Accountability Systems*, New Brunswick (NJ) and London: Transaction Publishers.

Bonfadelli, H. and Marr, M. (2007), 'Journalistinnen und Journalisten im privaten Rundfunk der Schweiz. Ergebnisse einer Online-Befragung im Auftrag des BAKOM – Forschungsbericht', IPMZ der Universität Zürich, http://www.bakom.admin.ch/themen/radio_tv/00509/01188/01811/index.html?lang=de. Accessed 15 February 2008.

Brunsson, N. (2002), *The Organization of Hypocrisy. Talk, Decisions and Actions in Organizations* [1st Edition 1989], Abingdon and Oxfordshire: Wiley.

Certimedia (2008), 'ISAS BC 9001 & P 9001', http://www.certimedia.org/en/isas-bc-9001–p-9001. html. Accessed 20 February 2008.

Donges, P. (2007), 'Medienpolitik und Media Governance', in P. Donges (ed.), *Von der Medienpolitik zur Media Governance?*, Köln: Halem, pp. 7–23.

European Commission (2001), 'European Governance – a White Paper', http://eur-lex.europa.eu/ LexUriServ/site/en/com/2001/com2001_0428en01.pdf, p. 21. Accessed 15 February 2008.

Gottwald, F.; Kaltenbrunner, A. and Karmasin, M. (eds.) (2006), *Medienselbstregulierung zwischen Ökonomie und Ethik. Erfolgsfaktoren für ein österreichisches Modell. Studien zur Medienpraxis*, Wien: Lit.

Hamelink, C. J. and Nordenstreng, K. (2006), 'Towards Democratic Media Governance', in E. de Bens (ed.), *Media Between Culture and Commerce*, Bristol: Intellect Books.

Hermes, S. (2006), *Qualitätsmanagement in Nachrichtenredaktionen*, Köln: Halem.

Jarren, O. (2007), 'Die Regulierung der öffentlichen Kommunikation. Medienpolitik zwischen Government und Governance', *Zeitschrift für Literaturwissenschaft und Linguistik*, 37, 2007/146, pp. 131–53.

Ladeur, K.-H. (2000), 'Rechtliche Möglichkeiten der Qualitätssicherung im Journalismus', *Publizistik*, 45, 2000/4, pp. 442–61.

McGonagle, T. (2002), 'Co-Regulation of the Media in Europe: The Potential for Practice of an Intangible Idea', *Iris plus*, 2002/10, 4, http://www.obs.coe.int/oea_publ/iris/iris_plus/iplus10_2002.pdf.en. Accessed 15 February 2008.

McQuail, D. (2003), *Media Accountability and Freedom of Publication*, Oxford: Oxford University Press.

Meckel, M. (1999), *Redaktionsmanagement. Ansätze aus Theorie und Praxis*, Opladen: Westdeutscher Verlag.

Media Society Foundation (2008), 'The Media and Society Foundation', http://www.media-society.org. Accessed 15 February 2008.

Meier, W. A. (2006), '"Media Ownership Governance": Plattform für einen Risikodialog über Medienmacht', in F. Marcinkowski, W.A. Meier and J. Trappel (eds.) (2006), *Media and Democracy. Experiences from Europe*, Bern: Haupt Verlag AG.

Meier, W.A. and Jarren, O. (2001), 'Ökonomisierung und Kommerzialisierung von Medien und Mediensystem. Einleitende Bemerkung zu einer (notwendigen) Debatte', *Medien & Kommunikationswissenschaft*, 49, 2001/2, pp. 145–58.

OFCOM (2008), http://www.bakom.ch/index.html?lang=en. Accessed 13 May 2008.

Puppis, Manuel (2007), 'Media Governance as a Horizontal Extension of Media Regulation: The Importance of Self- and Co-Regulation', *Communications*, 32, No 3, pp. 330–6.

Schulz, W. and Held, Th. (2001), *Regulated Self-Regulation as a Form of Modern Government. Study commissioned by the German federal Commissioner for Cultural and media Affairs. Interim Report*, Hamburg: Hans Bredow Institute for Media Research.

Siegrist, N. (2006), 'Wie sichern Tageszeitungen ihre journalistische Qualität? Eine Untersuchung am Beispiel von fünf Schweizer Regionalzeitungen', unveröffentlichte Lizenziatsarbeit, IPMZ der Universität Zürich.

UVEK (2007), 'Ausschreibung der Radio- und TV-Konzessionen', in Das Eidgenössische Departement für Umwelt, Verkehr, Energie, Kommunikation (ed.), *Ausschreibung der UKW- und TV-Konzessionen*, http://www.bakom.admin.ch/themen/radio_tv. Accessed 15 February 2008.

Working Group on Internet Governance (WGIG) (2005), 'Report of the Working Group on Internet Governance', (http://www.wgig.org/docs/WGIGREPORT.doc) http://www.wgig.org/docs/WGIGREPORT.pdf. Accessed 15 February 2008.

Wyss, V. (2002), *Redaktionelles Qualitätsmanagement. Ziele, Normen, Ressourcen* (Forschungsfeld Kommunikation, Band 15), Konstanz: UVK-Medien.

Wyss, V. (2007), 'Qualitative Analyse der Strukturen zur redaktionellen Qualitätssicherung im privaten Rundfunk in der Schweiz 2006. BAKOM – Forschungsbericht', IAM of the Zurich University of Applied Sciences Winterthur, http://www.bakom.admin.ch/themen/radio_tv/00509/01188/01811/index.html?lang=de. Accessed, 15 February 2008.

PART TWO: CONDITIONS (CASE STUDIES)

ASSESSING PLURALISM AND THE DEMOCRATIC PERFORMANCE OF THE MEDIA IN A SMALL COUNTRY: SETTING A COMPARATIVE RESEARCH AGENDA FOR THE BALTIC STATES

Auksė Balčytienė

Introduction

The principal function of news media is to support democratization: to ensure that different opinions are heard and different interests can access media, and to act as a watchdog. Murdock and Golding (1989), for example, identify three kinds of relations between communications and citizenship. First, people must have access to information: they must be able to use media in order to register criticism, mobilize opposition and propose alternative courses of action. In other words, freedom of information and expression must be at the core of the fundamental rights. Second, people must have access to the broadest possible range of information, interpretation and debate in areas that involve political choices. This implies that pluralism of media actors offering diverse content is a necessary precondition for practising citizenship. Third, they must be able to recognize themselves and their aspirations in the range of representation offered across available media. From here, it follows that scholarly debate on media pluralism and diversity should focus on how democracy should work. Therefore, a number of critical questions must be asked, such as who gets access to the public sphere and has the power to set the public agenda; attention should also be paid to what is represented in media discourse, and how.

Indeed, the concept of 'media pluralism' has many aspects. It deals both with diversity of media structure (actors) and diversity of content (voices available in media). Therefore, media pluralism has to be understood as a complex concept covering all measures that ensures citizens' access to a variety of information sources, opinions and voices.

A very common approach to studying media pluralism is to concentrate on media ownership plurality (diversity of firms taking part in media business). Indeed, this approach is strongly inspired by an ongoing media-structural change and development towards more mixed ownership forms (cross-media and diagonal concentrations) on both a national and international scale. As claimed by many, the process of media concentration leads to an enormous opinion-forming power and its outcomes may be dangerous for democracy (Humphreys 1996; Meier and Trappel 1998). Media concentration may result in a skewed public discourse where only certain viewpoints are represented and others are silenced. The subsequence of such a process may be rather severe. A few strong media players may become very powerful and control the majority of newspapers, TV stations and also Internet news portals.

It is not difficult to see that in the media pluralism discussion two factors, namely the size and wealth of the news market, become of major significance (Doyle 2002). Indeed, in smaller countries, external media pluralism such as diversity of media actors can be more difficult to achieve. Hence, one must then look into internal pluralism. For policy drafters, in such context, a principal question needs to be answered – what is to be supported (plurality of actors or plurality of voices) and through which measures? In spite of justified worries, one has to take into account the fact that only a few players are present in a small market may not in itself threaten media pluralism. The way media content is produced, namely what kind of voices and how many of them are represented in media, also has an impact on the overall level of plurality in the media. Media companies may have and respect internal codes that promote diversity of opinion; in addition, certain measures, such as codes and agreements between editors and owners, academic media criticism, public debates on changes in the media sector, as well as other measures, may be considered to safeguard an implied abuse of power.

In the context of ongoing debates about media systems homogenization (i.e. increasing deregulation and media marketization, ongoing commercialization of content and marketing of politics) (Curran and Myung-Jin 2000; Hallin and Mancini 2004; Plasser 2005), the question on how to ensure media pluralism and democratic performance has emerged with a new urgency. A number of questions, therefore, need to be asked: which specific contextual conditions must media meet to promote democracy? In other words, is the market sufficient to support media external diversity? Are media companies strong enough and do they have enough expertise and resources to produce original quality content as opposed to imported information materials (thus, aiming at internal diversity)?

Also, it has been reported that aside from media structural changes and possible maladies associated with the process of diminishing plurality through an increase of media concentration, and possible pressures associated with this (such as abuse of power through possible commercial or political interests), another process is noticeable, namely the proliferation of mixed discourses. To put it more precisely, promotional content and PR-based writing proliferates, in conventional as well as in the Internet media (Scott 2005). As a result, diversity of content (voices and opinions represented) is vanishing: very often readers come across the same articles in different dailies; TV viewers watch the same news reports on different TV stations; and the Internet media readers find the same breaking news across different online news portals. There are many reasons for this. On the one hand, media firms tend to save resources and not produce all their articles or programmes themselves (especially news stories that are related to foreign news reporting). Rather, they tend to rely on outside agencies that supply information, photos, infographics, and so on. On the other hand, the breaking character of some news media (online news portals) adds new requirements onto production: news needs to be filled on a regular and frequent basis, thus the easiest way to adhere to such a request is to fill the news hole with news agency, promotional and PR-based writing (Scott 2005; Balčytienė and Harro-Loit, in press). Provision of such inputs does not necessarily affect the quality of editorial content as long as it is balanced with original production (news, editorials, analysis, commentaries, investigative journalism, news features and so on).

As regards journalism, the media pluralism and diversity debate deals with a normative goal to reflect diversity in society, on the one hand, and gives access to and acts as a forum for different interests, on the other hand (Jonsson 2002). Thus, in the media pluralism discussion another perspective also needs to be addressed, namely the role of the audience. A central question here is whether different news media should select and present the same events and in the same way. Indeed, diversity should deal either with variation in the selection of news (selecting news and setting public agenda) or variation in the presentation of the same news events (changing news discourse by framing stories and adding different voices and opinions). As Jonsson (2002) poses, to decide what is desirable in this context is a complex matter: if the audience only uses one news channel then there is nothing wrong if all news media report on the same event in the same way. But if people subscribe to several newspapers, watch several TV news programmes or access different news portals and come across the same news, then this becomes problematic. The question then deals with diversity of voices in different media, namely the variations in the media discourse across different news channels.

To sum up, the goal of this article is to review media performance in the Baltic States according to a normative ideal of democratization. To achieve such an aim, the article looks into media structures from a perspective of media pluralism and diversity. It aims to investigate the circumstances under which liberal regulation and increasing media competition, as well as other factors associated with free market logic, lead to media pluralism and professionalization of journalism (autonomy and independence of media from external and internal pressures, also media accountability), and when it fails to achieve this.

Media 'made in the Baltic countries': Similarities and differences

A very natural approach is the tendency to treat the three Baltic countries as one region. As will be demonstrated, differences exist in media structures of the three countries: since the transition to a free market economy and consolidated democracy there are divergences (due to historical, social, cultural and technological reasons) observed across the media systems of the three countries. At the same time, in spite of differences, media systems and journalism practices of the three Baltic countries can be researched as belonging to a single group with defining characteristics, such as each country having a small market (geographically and linguistically restricted) and a very recent history of political, economic and social transformations.

Despite the fact that in the Baltic States the sizes of news markets, their recent histories as well as media regulation climates are comparable, differences influencing the journalism culture in Lithuania, Latvia and Estonia still exist. For example, from the point of view of language, the news market in Lithuania is small but homogeneous, while in Latvia and Estonia the markets are even smaller and split between two language groups (Latvian or Estonian and Russian) (see Table 1).

Table 1: Baltic Media Indicators (1 Euro = 3.4528 Lithuanian Litas, LTL; 15.646 Estonian Kroons, EEK).

Indicators	Estonia	Latvia	Lithuania
Population and major linguistic groups	1.34m (2007) 68.6% Estonians, 25.7% Russians, 3.3% Ukrainians and Belorussians	2.27m (2008) 59% Latvians, 28% Russians, 4% Belorussians, 2% Poles, 1% Lithuanians, 5% other	3.38m (2007) 84.6% Lithuanians, 6.3% Poles, 5.1% Russians, 1.1% Belorussians, 2.9% other language groups
Reading culture (first dailies in the national languages, newspaper reach according to WAN)	Luhhike Oppetus (1766) WAN: 68.5%	Latviesu Arste (1768) WAN: 64.7%	Nusidavimai Dievo karalystéje (printed in Lithuania Minor, 1823) WAN: 56% (2006)
Media regulation climate	No company or person may simultaneously own a TV station, a radio station and a daily or weekly paper No restrictions on foreign ownership No provisions in the broadcasting act against political organizations owning media Concentration is controlled by general Competition Law	Each broadcasting organization, except public broadcasting organizations, may not produce more than three programmes No restrictions on cross-media ownership The monopolization of electronic mass media in the interests of a political organization (party), etc. is not permitted Non-EU ownership of a mass media is restricted to 49 % Restrictions against political advertising	There is no restriction against foreign ownership or as to the structure of capital of media It is a duty of media firms to indicate changes in media ownership structure There are no restrictions on cross-media ownership A political party may not be the owner of a Broadcaster State should create equal legal and economic opportunities for honest competition of public information producers and disseminators No restrictions on cross-media ownership Restrictions against political advertising
Media advertising revenues (2006)	1355m EEK	76m LVL	430m LTL
Total number of newspapers, number of dailies (WAN, 2006)	143 (2006) No. of dailies: 16	130 (2006) No. of dailies: 22	325 (2005) No. of dailies: 22
Major dailies, their average circulation numbers (000): data	Postimees (mainstream), 65–9 SL Õhtuleht (tabloid), 63–5 Eesti Päevaleht (mainstream), 35–9	Diena (quality/mainstream), 33–52 (weekend edition) Latvijas Avïze (quality/	Vakaro žinios (tabloid), 130 Lietuvos rytas (mainstream), 50–130 (weekend edition)

publicly provided by newspapers	Äripäev (business daily), 22–6 Postimees in Russian, 15–20	mainstream), 45–8 Vesti Sevodņa (mainstream), 23–9 Vakara Zinas (tabloid), 12 Vesti Segodna (in Russian, mainstream), 39	Respublika (tabloid) Kauno diena (regional), 40 L.T. (tabloid) Lietuvos žinios (mainstream), 20 Verslo žinios (business daily), 10
Number of TV broadcasters	4 (3 national, 1 local)	28 (4 national)	31 (4 national, 1 regional,
Number of radio broadcasters	32 (4 national, 16 regional, 12 local)	41	48 (10 national, 6 regional, 35 local)
Major Internet news portals and their types	Delfi.ee (online-only news portal) Postimees.ee (news portal of Postimees) Sloleht.ee (news portal of SL Õhtuleht) Epl.ee (news portal of Eesti Päevaleht) Etv.ee (news portal of ETV)	Delfi.lv (online-only news portal) TVnet (online-only news portal) Apollo.lv (online-only news portal) Politika.lv (specialized news and analysis online-only news portal) Dialogi.lv (specialized news and analysis online-only news portal)	Delfi.lt (online-only news portal) Lrytas.lt (news portal of Lietuvos rytas) Alfa.lt (online-only news portal) Balsas.lt (online-only news portal) Vz.lt (news portal of Verslo žinios) Bernardinai.lt (online-only specialized news portal) Lrt.lt (news portal of LRT)
Internet penetration	69%	56%	52.9%
Free media (free dailies)	Linnaleht	5 min (in Riga and metro area, in Lat and Rus) Rītdiena (nationally, the biggest newspaper – 173 thousand subscribers for year 2008, but it has not come out this year due to financial problems, future is uncertain)	15 min (in major cities: Vilnius, Kaunas, Klaipėda) Miesto žinios (in Vilnius)
Major media groups and ownership types	Eesti Meedia (owned by Schibsted, cross-media) Ekspress Grupp (print media) Bonnier Business Press (print media) Ühinenud ajakirjad (print media, Finnish owners) Moles (print media) Modern Times Group (MTG) (broadcast media) Metromedia International (radio) Sky Media (radio)	AS Diena (Bonnier Media, print media) Santa (magazines) Lilit (magazines) Petits (print media) MTG (broadcasting) News Corp Europe (broadcast media)	Lietuvos rytas (cross-media) Achemos grupė (cross-media) Respublikos leidiniai (print media) Žurnalų leidybos grupė (Schibsted, magazines) Verslo žinios (Bonnier Media, print media) Modern Times Group (MTG) (broadcast media) Diena Media News (previously owned by Orkla Media, print media) MG Baltic (cross-media) M-1 (radio)

As in many countries worldwide, television in the Baltic States is an important medium of information for citizens. The broadcast market has public service providers and private owners. In Estonia, the public service broadcaster ETV already seized advertising in 2002 – the main reason being attempts to promote the development of domestic TV channels by creating better funding opportunities for the private broadcasting sector. In all three countries, private broadcaster TV3 (which is a Baltic-Scandinavian network owned by the Modern Times Group from Sweden) is the most popular, with around 25 per cent of audience share. The public service station takes only third place in each country (with only around 12 per cent of audience share). Although viewers in Estonia consider national television news programmes to be important sources of information, agenda-setting is carried out primarily by newspapers (television news programmes often just broadcast the main newspaper stories). This creates a paradoxical situation: although the influence of television on public opinion is very significant – at least in terms of the importance Estonians attribute to it as a source of news – TV channels in Estonia do not appear to take advantage of this position (OSI and EUMAP 2005).

Newspapers in Estonia have the biggest advertising revenues (more than 40 per cent of the media advertising market), while in Lithuania and Latvia television has the largest share of advertising (around 40 per cent). Another important characteristic of the Lithuanian news environment (also detected in Latvia) is the large number and wide availability of regional and local TV channels, many of them also having local news programmes. Radio in the Baltic countries is strongly commercialized and orients itself towards entertainment. In Lithuania there is a 24-hour news radio (Žinių radijas), while in other countries music channels dominate.

Estonia is described as a small country, promoting an online life style (almost two thirds of the population are Internet users), while Lithuania is a less Internet-oriented country with only half of the population (53 per cent) using the Internet. In Estonia, as in the Scandinavian countries, traditional newspapers are the strongest online news providers. Besides the online-only *Delfi. ee*, the three portals of national dailies (*Postimees, Eesti Paevaleht* and *SL Ohtuleht*) are among the five most visited websites in Estonia. In Lithuania, in contrast to Estonia, there is only one daily (*Lietuvos rytas*) that has a stronger voice online (with *Lrytas.lt*). The need for online news in Lithuania is met by mainstream (*Delfi.lt, Alfa.lt, Balsas.lt*) as well as specialized (*Bernardinai. lt*) news portals. Latvia, too, has mainstream (*Delfi.lv, TVnet.lv*) as well as specialized news and analysis portals (*Politika.lv, Dialogi.lv*).

In all three countries, free newspapers are in the lists of the Top Five most read dailies. The arrival of free dailies is a fairly new thing in the Baltic countries which has challenged the identities of print newspapers (especially in Lithuania). New challenges, however, are emerging in this context: How to deal with free media? How free is the free media and who pays for free news, broadcasting and journalism online?

Fruits and roots of liberalism

In Europe, there is no universal model to categorize media policies (ideas enshrined in media regulation) according to the many diverging parameters. There is no unanimous agreement, and different forms of regulation are applied across different countries. In the Baltic States, there is an obvious stress on the ideals of free market and liberalism.

Three fundamental things affect media pluralism and the diversity climate in the Baltic countries: (1) the role of the state is fairly constricted, (2) market logic is highly promoted and (3) media accountability is weak. On the one hand, if assessed structurally, liberal regulation of media creates an open space for media firms to compete with one another, making it possible for citizens to access all kinds of content both offline and online. On the other hand, the logic of the market is dictated by media firms and the outcome of that is rather disappointing: media production is guided by the principle of 'producing content as cheaply and quickly as possible'.

Media culpa
Baltic journalism is facing strong pressures: different players are involved in media production, distribution and consumption; technological changes, too, translate into a variety of transformations (digitization, convergence) affecting audience segmentation. Indeed, the number of news channels (free newspapers, broadcasting time, online news portals and specialized magazines) is increasing in all countries. As a result of these changes, scholars (not only in the Baltic States) are now discussing the need to preserve professional journalism, whereas media mainly produce mixed content, concentrate on more sensational and more entertainment-oriented reporting and blur boundaries between news and advertising (Erjavec 2005; Balčytienė and Harro-Loit 2007). Mixed discourses proliferate in magazines, broadcast media and online. Therefore, different policy proposals are suggested, ranging from formalization of professional training (emphasizing media analysis techniques and critical reflection skills as well as the importance of journalistic and editorial autonomy) to media literacy education in schools.

Indeed, the media climate in the Baltic States is very competitive. A negative outcome of this is the fact that journalism is mainly driven by a consumerist approach. Expenses of producing serious media such as local news or investigative reporting in a small country are becoming extremely high. Therefore, some media, suffering from bottom-line pressures, tend to overlook professional requirements by producing hybrid media. This trend supports a number of worries also outlined in different studies. For example, experience in different countries shows potential negative effects of too much or unregulated competition: as a result of 'savage deregulation', certain content becomes marginalized, for example foreign reporting or investigative journalism. It has also been experienced that over-strong competition results in a decline of diversity and quality. This is because competing providers make different trade-offs: in a small country, demand for non-mainstream information is potentially smaller than in larger markets. Thus with increasing competition, reluctance to invest in new products and quality becomes rather strong, and professionalism suffers.

Larger and wealthier markets (with greater resources available for the provision of media) can afford a greater diversity of output than smaller markets. Therefore, for smaller markets, a particular concern is the availability of resources to support the production by domestic media groups of original content as opposed to imported production. In a small market, shortage of funds causes a decline in (expensive) foreign news coverage and foreign news quality; research studies prove that only few media companies have foreign correspondents and invest in foreign news reporting (Balčytienė et al. 2007; Tammpuu and Puulerits 2007).

Despite trade-offs associated with content, one more outcome associated with this trend is an increase in media power. Media acts as 'watch dog' and demands transparency from the other institutions in the society. In a small country where liberalism is promoted in policies but professionalism of media is weak, the media itself, as observed rather often, remains the most opaque.

Unwanted state

In the Baltic countries, the participation of the state in the matters of media is fairly constricted. The intervention of the state, which can be assessed in the frameworks of state as owner, regulator or financer of media, can be of different degrees – it can vary from a low to a high level of control (see, for example, Hallin and Mancini 2004). Compared to other countries in the region (for example, the Scandinavian countries), the voice of the state in the Baltic States is silenced. Media regulation in the Baltic countries is very liberal: there is no restriction as to the structure of capital of media, but it is compulsory that changes in ownership structures be indicated. There are no restrictions on cross-media ownership; however, regulation requires the state to create equal legal and economic opportunities for honest competition of media. In addition, the state must ensure that no single person can occupy a position of monopoly or abuse such a dominant position. There are no restrictions against foreign ownership. A political party or organization may not be the owner and operator of a broadcaster.

Indeed, to adequately assess the reasons of promotion of certain restrictions (on the one hand) and liberalism (on the other hand) in media policies, it is crucially important to go back into the early 1990s and study historical preconditions for such steps. In the 1990s, immediately after the political breakthrough, the fundamental goal of the Baltic countries was to create national systems of media and no other alternatives to liberalism were perceived as acceptable. Because of still-active memories of the communist past, when everything was under very strict supervision and state control, state participation in the matters of media was treated as totally unacceptable; certain steps were also taken to limit political affiliation (for example, through ownership) of media (Tapinas 1998).

The emergence of liberal regulation, changing journalism and the scepticism of media towards outside criticism has resulted in a complex situation. Very often, media plays a role of 'attack dog' rather than of 'watch dog'. At the same time, however, any attempts to impose stricter regulation and de-liberalize the media market, for example by introducing restrictions on cross-media ownership, would be interpreted as an unpopular move: in European media politics as well, there is a general tendency towards neo-liberal policy promoting de-regulation, competition and openness.

The trend towards the homogenization of media systems, with increasing commercialism and other market-led fashions, has become worldwide. In this respect, media marketization in the Baltic States has its own character. As practice reveals, the new democracies have not yet completely disengaged from soviet histories: in all three countries, civil society structures are not sufficiently developed and media cultures are too weak to withstand different kinds of (economic or political) pressures (Dimants 2005; Baerug 2005; Balčytienė, 2007; Lauk in press). Indeed, the new democracies have jumped into the free market model practically unprepared in practices of professionalism and accountability. Although the Scandinavian models of self-regulation were 'exported' to their Baltic neighbours, the period of adaptation did not happen immediately (see, for example, Harro-Loit and Balčytienė 2005; Rossland 2005). In contrast, in the Scandinavian countries, media has traditionally been seen first and foremost as a social institution: the Nordic countries have cherished the ideal of social responsibility as part of the media system, thus, even with commercial goals being promoted, there are certain measures (such as a long tradition of professionalism and agreements protecting editorial autonomy from influence by media owners as well as public control) which secure pluralism and protect diversity ideals from being misused (see, for example, Lund 2007; Nord, in press).

Culture of communication

Media does not operate in a vacuum. Whether or not media can accomplish its functions and objectives does not depend on media alone. Media does not act from some independent, outside world on individuals and society; rather, media organizations and activities are embedded in social power relations (McQuail 2000).

In a small news market, these power relations acquire unique aspects; for example, journalists' relationships with sources are built upon a certain logic of proximity. In addition, different news-worthiness criteria affect news management and the production routines of journalists working in small or large media firms.

Journalists' relationships with their political or business news sources are based on a certain culture which affects media performance. One of the outcomes of this proximity is that media carefully monitors national political life. In the early 1990s, media went through a process of diversification along ideological lines. However, this was a very short period and soon (in the mid 1990s) business discovered media as an important sphere for ownership. As a result, political affiliations were erased from the flag lines of dailies. Indeed, newspapers proclaim themselves to be free and independent, but in reality, media in the Baltic States has not fully separated itself from the fields of politics and business. Media is carefully monitoring the national political agenda. Political actors, too, seek to have a hand in media: through financial grants (by prepaid advertising) they force the media to take an appropriate position; in addition, politicians use media for political news management. Business, too, is tempted to control media: on the one hand, this is done for purposes of self-defence, on the other hand, to ensure that targeted news about the business itself reaches the public.

This creates a tricky situation where media becomes an instrument in the hands of different actors (politicians and businessmen) aiming to achieve their aspirations. The tendency to accept a publicly-hidden agenda is reminiscent of the Italian media system (also of other southern European countries) where partisanship of media is strong, a strong integration between media and political elites exists and professional consolidation of journalists is low. However, the situation in the Baltic States is a bit different. The Baltic countries have developed a strong orientation to *laissez faire*; they have developed a weak-state tradition. Indeed, in a competitive environment there should be nothing wrong with different business companies owning different media. The existence of diversity of media actors balances business interests and therefore creates external pluralism. Within one medium, it is important to bring a wider spectrum of news and information in order to reach a wider readership. This creates internal pluralism. Such logic, however, looks nice only in theory. In reality, especially in a small news market where the reach of newspapers and readership of dailies is fairly low, only few people buy or subscribe to more than one newspaper. As already mentioned, a tendency is emerging where many rival media (the largest national dailies, TV news programmes) start to compete with the same kind of (hybrid) content as competition increases.

Discussion and further research needs

The three indicated characteristics of the Baltic news markets – being small, with liberal regulation and weak accountability – create a complex situation. The logic of the market is highly valued: liberal regulation opens new fields and forms for media development. The journalistic culture of Lithuania, Latvia or Estonia is affected by the liberal-media model (media competition is highly promoted, state plays a restricted role), but weaker historic journalistic traditions, as well as a weak civil society, a young system of self-regulation and lack of tradition of professional journalism, has created obvious drawbacks.

The size and wealth of the market is a decisive parameter which needs to be taken into account when discussing media changes, development and journalism culture from a comparative perspective. As demonstrated above, small news markets face different challenges and problems than big markets. For example, an important factor necessary for the media to carry out its democratic functions (provide information, create public forums and observe those in power) is availability of resources, namely a rich advertising market, and different forms to fund media (subsidies from the state, tradition of public funding and so on). Also, media performance is strongly affected by the culture of political communication (journalists' relationships with sources and how these are maintained.)

To assess in comparative perspective how media actually serve democracy (also where media fail to meet the democratic performance expectations of the media) requires a number of critical questions to be posed: Does media perform its democratic functions adequately? Whom do media serve – itself (media owners, advertisers), audiences (consumers or citizens) or government?

As mentioned, the parameter of proximity acquires rather different nuances in a small than in a large market. Therefore, it becomes important to investigate how the size of the market affects the culture of political communication: What aspects of news management are observed in a small news market? What channels (formal or informal) are used by journalists in their communication with political and business news sources? Related to this, one more aspect needs to be covered, namely the web of relationships between different interest groups and media, and the effect of these on the development of normative journalistic culture. In other words, it becomes crucially important to ask: Is there a dialogue between social groups and media? Whose power dominates?

Indeed, contemporary media systems are rapidly changing, with many challenges affecting national media structures and journalism cultures and culminating with more or less similar results, such as increased commercialization of the media, growing power of news sources or changes in news production and presentation and so on. Thus, the comparative research perspective becomes vital.

References

Baerug, R. (2005), 'Hidden Advertising and TV Journalism in the Baltic Countries and Norway', in Baerug, R. (ed.), *The Baltic Media World*, Riga: Flera, pp. 58–90.

Balčytienė, A. and Harro-Loit, H. (2007), 'How to Preserve Journalism?' Paper presented at the conference *Comparing Media Systems. West Meets East*, 23–5 April 2007, Wroclaw, Poland.

Balčytienė, A. and Harro-Loit, H. (in press), 'Between Reality and Illusion: Revisiting the Democratic Function of Baltic Journalism Online', *Journal of Baltic Studies*.

Balčytienė, A.; Vinciūnienė, A. and Janušaitė, K. (2007), 'The Case of Lithuania', in AIM Research Consortium (eds.), *Understanding the Logic of EU Reporting from Brussels*, Bochum: Projekt Verlag, pp. 103–11.

Curran, J. and Myung-Jin, P. (2000), *De-Westernizing Media Studies*, London: Routledge.

Dimants, A. (2005), 'Editorial Censorship in Baltic and Norwegian Newspapers', in Baerug, R. (ed.), *The Baltic Media World*, Riga: Flera, pp. 121–45.

Doyle, G. (2002), *Media Ownership*, London: Sage.

Erjavec, K. (2005), 'Hybrid Public Relations News Discourse', *European Journal of Communication*, 20:2, pp. 155–79.

Hallin, D., and Mancini, P. (2003), 'Americanization, Globalization, and Secularization: Understanding the Convergence of Media Systems and Political Communication', in Esser, F. and Pfetsch, B. (eds.), *Comparing Political Communication*, Cambridge: Cambridge University Press, pp. 25–45.

Hallin, D. and Mancini, P. (2004), *Comparing Media Systems: Three Models of Media and Politics*, Cambridge: Cambridge University Press.

Harro-Loit, H., and Balčytienė, A., (2005), 'Media Accountability Systems: Ecological Viewpoint', in R. Baerug, (ed.) The Baltic Media World, Riga: Flera, pp. 25–40.

Humphreys, P. (1996), *Mass Media and Media Policy in Western Europe*, Manchester: Manchester University Press.

Jonsson, A.M. (2002), 'More of the same or is there something more? Diversity in a changing television market: A Swedish example', *IAMCR 23rd Conference*, Barcelona.

Lauk, E. (in press), 'Freedom for the media? Issues of journalism ethics in Estonia', *Informacijos mokslai*.

Lund, A.B. (2007), 'Media Markets in Scandinavia: Political Economy Aspects of Convergence and Divergence', *Nordicom Review: Media Structures and Practices. As Time Goes by*, 28, pp. 121–35.

McQuail, D. (2000), 'Democracy, Media and Public Policy; Concluding Note', in Van Cuilenburg, J. and R. Van der Wurff (eds.), *Media and Open Societies*, Amsterdam: Het Spinhuis, pp. 257–62.

Meier, W. and Trappel, J. (1998), 'Media Concentration and the Public Interest', in D. McQuail and K. Siune (eds.), *Media Policy: Convergence, Concentration and Commerce*, London: Sage, pp. 38–60.

Murdock, G. and Golding, P. (1989), 'Information Poverty and Political Inequality: Citizenship in the Age of Privatized Communications', *Journal of Communication*, 39:3, pp. 180–95.

Nord, L. (in press), 'Swedish Media Between Politics and Market', *Informacijos mokslai*.

Plasser, F. (2005), 'From Hard to Soft News Standards? How Political Journalists in Different Media Systems Evaluate the Shifting Quality of News', in *Press/Politics*, 10:2, pp. 47–68.

Rossland, A. (2005), 'Accountability Systems and Media Ethics: Landscapes and Limits', in Baerug, R. (ed.), *The Baltic Media World*, Riga: Flera, pp. 14–25.

Scott, B. (2005), 'A Contemporary History of Digital Journalism', *Television & New Media*, 6:1, pp. 89–126.

Tammpuu, P. and Puulerits, E. (2007), 'The Case of Estonia', in AIM Research Consortium (eds.), *Understanding the Logic of EU Reporting from Brussels*, Bochum: Projekt Verlag, pp. 15–23.

Tapinas, L. (1998), 'The Legal Framework', in H. Schmid (ed.), *Understanding the Media in the Baltic Countries*, Düsseldorf: European Institute for the Media, pp. 148–65.

OSI and EUMAP (2005), 'Television across Europe: Regulation, policy and independence', Report retrieved from http://www.eumap.org/topics/media/television_europe. Accessed 4 February 2008.

MEDIA IN POLAND AND PUBLIC DISCOURSE

Ryszard Filas and Paweł Płaneta

Public discourse is a process of creating, strengthening and disseminating the system of social meanings. Their recognition occurs mainly through the analysis of its elements which refer to texts or their social background, for example discourse participants/institutions. Ideological, political and institutional backgrounds influence the public discourse, for example the socially created system of communicational representations; the coherent system of meanings in different domains.

Public discourse is related to how the mass media function. In modern societies, people mainly derive their knowledge about issues crucial for the community from the media, the most important source of cognitive models of reality. So the media create the systems of representation that have developed socially in order to make and circulate a coherent set of meanings regarding an important topic area. In this sense, the public discourses that are present in the media are the platforms to disseminate opinions, attitudes and values (van Dijk 1995: 107-26).

Universally available and properly functioning media – media which fulfil their social responsibilities – play a crucial role as pillars of liberal democracy. Independent mass media which represent the society remain an important element of the public sphere. This article is devoted to particular segments of the Polish media system – the printed press, the private and public broadcasting and the journalists – as institutions of public discourse.

A few years after the collapse of Communism, the *press readership model* in Poland changed completely. In the People's Republic of Poland the readership was mainly focused on the daily press, especially regional dailies,[1] while in the mid 1990s it was focused on periodical reading: especially newly-launched weeklies and monthlies, which were more and more colourful, in accordance with the modernization of the printing industry, and which were introduced to the press market by major western publishers (especially German ones: Bauer, G+J, Axel Springer and to a smaller extent Burda and Swiss Marquard, and later Edipresse). This fact meant – in general – that the frequency of contact with the printed press as a medium decreased.[2]

Moreover, during this period, more and more Polish-language TV channels appeared on the market, as well as radio stations: commercial, Church, academic and even local-governmental. The latter was especially found in big cities, where the abundant advertising market allowed the broadcasters to maintain a few local TV channels simultaneously.[3] This meant that media other than printed press started to play a crucial role in the public debate.

This does not mean, however, that dailies (mainly paid regional and national information dailies), socio-political weeklies (opinion weeklies) and – to a certain extent, at a micro regional and small communities level – local (in particular county) and sub-local press do not play a critical role in the public debate. This part of the press market will be analysed first.

Print media in Poland

The prevailing majority of nation-wide information newspapers in Poland are *opinion dailies* which fulfil the standards of western so-called *quality papers* (*Gazeta Wyborcza, Dziennik, Rzeczpospolita* and *Polska*). Other titles – published with very modest[4] lay-out and content – represent the values of certain political or ideological milieus (*Nasz Dziennik, Trybuna*). On the nation-wide press market, almost the entire press offer are titles which were not in any way entangled in the communist regime. Numerous popular press titles in the People's Republic of Poland vanished from the market in the mid 1990s, despite the fact that they had been in the area of interest of commercial entrepreneurs or political forces[5] at the beginning of the 1990s.[6] So the present configuration of the press market was shaped only at the turn of the century. It is

Table 1: The hierarchy of national general-information dailies in 2001, 2004 and 2007 (according to average paid-distribution, data in thousand copies).

	2001		2004		2007	
Rank	Title	Thous copies	Title	%	Title	Thous copies
1.	Gazeta Wyborcza	459	Fakt	536	Fakt	515
2.	Super Express	335	Gazeta Wyborcza	436	Gazeta Wyborcza	448
3.	Rzeczpospolita	199	Super Express	231	Polska***	374
4.	Nasz Dziennik*	130	Rzeczpospolita	183	Super Express	198
5.	Trybuna	46	Nasz Dziennik*	110	Dziennik. Polska Europa Świat	190
6.	Życie	40	Życie**	20	Rzeczpospolita	164
7.			Trybuna	24	Nasz Dziennik*	90
8.					Trybuna**	18

Source: The data, based on the Press Circulation Audit Unit (ZKDP) except for * Nasz Dziennik (authors' estimation) and ** Życie (2004) and Trybuna in 2007 (publisher's information). *** Polska (launched on 15 Oct 2007) formally consists of 18 regional dailies which cover the whole country and which have the common central editorial office. The presented data (for a 2.5-month period of publishing) are just rough estimations.

worth adding that in 1996–2002 the right-wing daily *Życie* was an important element of the mentioned configuration because of its role in the process of integration of post-Solidarity and the AWS party, which was successful in the 1997 election.[7]

During the last two years (2006–7) some *opinion newspapers* evolved, in strength and polarized in terms of political sympathies. After the election of 2005, a national-Catholic newspaper published by Father Tadeusz Rydzyk – *Nasz Dziennik* – unexpectedly and, at first, one of a kind, became a propaganda instrument in the hands of the coalition government of 'Solidarity Poland' formed by Prawo i Sprawiedliwość, PiS (as the opposition to 'Liberal Poland', the term describing centre-right wing Platforma Obywatelska, PO). Later, for several months from the autumn of 2006 until the election in September of 2007, the pro-PiS sympathies (not including the PiS coalition partners, Samoobrona and LPR) were represented by the conservative *Dziennik Polska Europa Świat*, constructed on the model of German *Die Welt* as a conservative national quality newspaper, as well as by *Rzeczpospolita*, so far functioning as an independent and relatively neutral though conservative-liberal daily (Kowalczyk 2007a). The critics of *Rzeczpospolita* point out the fact that the newspaper is owned by the government.[8] Moreover, the new major shareholder, the Mecom group, came to an agreement with the PiS government in mid-2006 regarding the change of the newspaper's programme line and the appointments of *Rzeczpospolita* management. The new editor-in-chief, Paweł Lisicki, consequently implemented those provisions.[9] Conservative *Dziennik* had unexpectedly changed the orientation before the election in 2007:[10] The pro-PiS sympathy had been replaced by support for the election-winning party, conservative-liberal Platforma Obywatelska (PO).

These *political meanders* (Kowalczyk 2007b) were rather harmful to these two rivalry titles, especially because *Rzeczpospolita* and *Dziennik* competed for the favours of readers similar in terms of political sympathies and values. One can observe the effects of 'political cannibalism' on both newspapers. This can be seen in the decreasing sales results of both dailies. Moreover, the turn in the editorial line of *Dziennik* did not improve its reputation. The market position of *Rzeczpospolita* did not improve either, despite the implementation of the completely new, more handy and legible layout in October 2007.

Both titles, *Rzeczpospolita* and *Dziennik*, definitely try to combat the common enemy *Gazeta Wyborcza*. GW, a daily newspaper is criticized for its liberal left-wing orientation associated with the name of the long-term GW's editor-in-chief, Adam Michnik,[11] and also for the distance from the idea of the so-called Fourth Republic (IV Rzeczpospolita) and for general investigation and decommunisation.[12] Moreover, *Gazeta Wyborcza* is criticized for know-it-all elitism and willingness to overtake 'the rule of Poles' hearts and minds' (Bierzyński 2007). *Gazeta Wyborcza* has been present on the Polish press market for nineteen years. The daily was the fruit of the round table negotiations. Its GW's debut took place one month before the elections, which resulted in the appointment of Tadeusz Mazowiecki as the Prime Minister of the first non-communist government and the beginning of the Third Republic of Poland. *Gazeta Wyborcza* competently took advantage of its primacy over the free press market, shaped the idea of a modern daily on both national and regional scales (GW presently has 21 regional editions), used the 'opposition roots' of its management and gathered together famous journalists.[13] The publisher of *Gazeta Wyborcza* (Agora SA) had already developed into a big stock-exchange company by the end of the 1990s, investing in many segments of the Polish media market.[14] Until the end of 2003, GW had been the leader in the dailies market. Today *Gazeta Wyborcza* has lost the competition with *Fakt,* but still remains the leader in the quality papers sub-segment, keeping its sales at the same level (420–60 thousand copies) for years. Moreover, the niche post-communist[15] *Trybuna* has been fighting alone to survive on the national press market. Since the end of the 1990s the sales of *Trybuna* have decreased from 50 thousand to 18 thousand copies.

Until the autumn of 2003, the tabloid daily *Super Express (SE)* was placed at the forefront of the rank of sales results, second behind *Gazeta Wyborcza* among the quality information dailies (mentioned in Table 1). During this period, *SE* was politically neutral and since 1991 provided its readers mainly with entertainment and practical advice.

On 20 October 2003, Axel Springer Polska launched on the market a *new tabloid, Fakt,* (one used to say at that time it was the Polish *Bild Zeitung* after the only national tabloid in Germany, published by Axel Springer Verlag), which resulted in a fundamental change in the arrangement of forces on the press market in Poland. The tabloid, *Super Express* was also changed. After only three months, *Fakt* was successful: its average sales reached half a million copies, and *Fakt* gained the first position on the ranking list of dailies, gaining readers not only from *Super Express* but also from regional dailies and even sports publications (Filas 2005: 25–9).

Apart from tabloid content (for example covering the story of a whale that, allegedly, swam up the Vistula River, or getting involved in lawsuits with many show-business stars) *Fakt* turned out not to be a typical tabloid, but rather a noble version of the tabloid daily. Having a wide range of readers, *Fakt* successfully entered the public debate: with its everyday socio-political comments on pages 2–3, written by well-known experts, as well as its weekly supplement *Europa* (published until mid-2006) composed of articles by world-famous publicists and scientists.

Probably due to its populist publications, *Fakt* supported the election campaign of the winning parties in 2005 and it still remains the newspaper of considerable influence among the less-wealthy and less-educated social classes. Having such a dangerous rival, *Super Express* changed itself into a sharp, sensational, and to some extent erotic, tabloid for a few years, according to the rule: *if it bleeds, it leads.* On the other hand, *Super Express* did not avoid commenting current political events, doing it in a typically tabloid manner: from the perspective of an average man, distrustful of political elites, hunting for power abuse (or even provoking it) (Nalewajk 2003). Since the end of 2007, *Super Express* – empowered by a group of former employees of *Fakt* (for example the new editor-in-chief) – has become similar to *Fakt,* not only in terms of layout but also in terms of content (Światłowska 2008).

Generally speaking, the structure of the daily press market in Poland has been changing for the last few years. The total data on the sales results and free-of-charge distribution shows the strengthening of paid-for national dailies, which constitute over half of the total number of distributed copies of dailies. Free-of-charge dailies remained strong on the market until 2006. In contrast, regional dailies lost their position: the market-share of regional dailies decreased from 46.8 per cent in 2001 to 28.6 per cent in 2007. This process seems to be – to some extent – the effect of wrong policy on part of the publishers.

Since the middle of the 1990s, after the initial (1990–1) and so-called secondary (1992–4) privatization of newspapers which had been owned by the RSW concern, one can observe the continuing duopolization of the regional dailies market. Two western publishing groups divided the area of influences not by competing against each other but rather by co-operating on the

Table 2: The shares of different types of sold/distributed dailies in 2001–7

Total sales/distribution ...	2001	2002	2003	2004	2005	2006	2007
... of national paid-for dailies	48.1	46.6	48.0	56.2	51.7	48.9	55.0
... of regional and local paid-for dailies	46.8	47.4	44.8	35.5	31.4	28.5	28.6
... free dailies	5.1	6.0	7.2	8.3	16.9	22.6	16.4
TOTAL distribution/sales (%)	100.0	100.0	100.0	100.0	100.0	100.0	100.0
TOTAL distribution/sales (in mio. copies).	846.6	802.7	795.5	920.5	971.0	1050.6	1007.1

Source: Authors' estimations based on 'The rank list of publishers'. The special supplement to Press monthly, September 2006, p. 9 (data from the graph). Data for 2006 and 2007 based on Polish Chamber of Press Publishers' prepared for World Press Trends 2007 and 2006.

advertising market (due to a joint broker company Mediatak, until the end of 2007). Norwegian Orkla Media, which operated in Poland 1993–6, dominated the local market in eight regions (for example new provinces), whereas Polskapresse,[16] which is still in operation, has dominated the market in six regions.

Orkla's property was taken over in the middle of 2006 by the British group Mecom, along with the acquisition of controlling shares of the national daily *Rzeczpospolita*, and, in 2007, the regional *Życie Warszawy* as well. Each group had the rights to publish several titles, but as a result of many mergers since the beginning of the twenty-first century, Polskapresse has owned only seven titles before the launching of the *Polska* project. Media Regionalne (Mecom) has only ten titles in nine regions. At the beginning of this century, 32 regional dailies were published with the total single circulation of 1,315 million copies, whereas in autumn 2007 only 24 were left on the market (circulation: 892 thousand copies). At the same time, the number of so-called independent titles not possessed by either Polskapresse or Orkla/Mecom, decreased from twelve to eight and is, at present, seven. Dailies from this third group of independent publishers which survived in the market have a relatively strong position on their regional markets and – as a rule – they are the only titles which widen the information and opinion pluralism on the regional market. These titles more courageously express their attitude towards important social and political issues in the public debate.

This situation is completely different in comparison to the situation at the beginning of the 1990s – before the capital concentration – when three to five independent titles were published in a given region. At present, more than one regional daily is published in only six regions (voivodships) out of sixteen altogether, whereas in 1988 there were twelve such regions (out of seventeen).

The editorial policy of regional newspapers connected with Polskapresse and Orkla for over a decade was generally very careful. It was especially noticeable in the case of Polskapresse, caused by the Poles' (especially the political elites) oversensitivity to possible effects of German capital shares in the Polish media. In this duopolistic situation,[17] publishers try to realize a business model and not to get involved in political arguments at national or local levels. For a few years, Polskapresse and Orkla developed the model of a newspaper too much oriented towards regional and local matters. Since 2007 they have been limiting the number of local editions and supplements. Such a model would work well if their readers read, in addition, one more newspaper: a national one. Yet, such a situation is rather rare because of decreasing readership of the press. This explains why a regional daily should rather be a 'complete' newspaper.

Polskapresse has been trying to change this situation, for example by launching the project *Polska* in co-operation with *The Times* London on 15 October 2007. This project resulted in the appearance of a complicated newspaper construction: It is, in fact, a nationwide daily, but is registered as eighteen regional dailies, mostly edited centrally, and owned by one proprietor.[18] This project is responsible for the pages of Polish and world international news in common with the regional dailies. This explains why regional dailies seem to be complete in terms of content and are able to be more competitive in the confrontation with nationwide dailies, which have been developing their regional supplements, the best example being *Gazeta Wyborcza*.

Free-of-charge newspapers with their short, simple, and heavily illustrated texts, addressed to readers with a low level of communicative competence, are less valued. Moreover, the number of such newspapers significantly decreased after 2006 to one daily *Metro*, published five times per week, and one bi-daily *Echo Miasta*. These titles are supported by the logistic infrastructure of major media groups such as Agora SA or Polskapresse. The powerful international publisher Metro International (publishing daily *Metropol*) withdrew from Poland. At present, the publishers, especially if they own paid-for dailies in certain regions, launch free-of-charge weeklies distributed in bigger cities (for example Szczecin, Bydgoszcz, Toruń, Olsztyn) or they attach local county-level inserts to some editions of dailies.

Table 3: The hierarchy of opinion weeklies in 2001–7 according to average single paid distribution (data by ZKDP in thousand copies).

	2001		2004		2007	
Rank	Title	Thous copies	Title	Thous copies	Title	Thous copies
1.	Newsweek Polska	325	Angora	256	Angora	292
2.	Angora	270	Polityka	190	Polityka	165
3.	Nie	267	Newsweek Polska	185	Wprost	144
4.	Polityka	251	Wprost	168	Newsweek Polska	138
5.	Wprost	222	Nie	114	Gość Niedzielny	132
6.	Gość Niedzielny	126	Gość Niedzielny	113	Nie	91
7.	Przegląd	59	Przekrój	103	Przekrój	66
8.	Przekrój*	46	Przegląd	39	Przegląd	28

*Przekrój is an opinion weekly since 2003.

Opinion weeklies have a large potential for participation in the public debate. They represent a range of sub-types: general interest socio-political magazines, socio-Catholic re-print magazines, and humorous magazines. Their total single sales (excluding niche, low-circulation titles of narrow political orientation, not audited by ZKDP) were about 1.1 million copies in 2007 (five years earlier – 1.4 million copies).

This segment of the press market is diminishing from year to year (Filas 2007a: 36–7). In particular, the segment of 'general interest' magazines (creating opinions on a broad scope of issues – from politics, economy, social affairs to high culture and pop culture, media, arts and science) is diminishing. The weeklies *Polityka, Wprost* and *Newsweek Polska* are included in this group. Left-wing oriented *Przegląd* is a sort of outsider in this category.[19] Since 2002, several magazines that revealed their ambition to compete with these three titles have been present in this group: the best example is *Przekrój*.[20] In contrast, the episode with publishing *Ozon* turned out to be a failure.[21]

Apart from the mainstream of opinion weeklies, it is worth pointing to the stable position of Catholic opinion titles: *Gość Niedzielny* and *Tygodnik Powszechny*. At present, the latter is an example of a niche magazine with great traditions and is still perceived as valuable in intellectual milieus, especially owing to its vivid input in the discussion on culture, politics, religion and social life. In contrast to *Tygodnik Powszechny*, there is the publication *Nie*. This is a satirical weekly of tabloid character: provoking, shocking, with strong left-wing and anti-clerical orientation that has almost come to the end of its good times. The 'golden years' of success and popularity of weekly *Nie* were in the middle of the 1990s. The title of present success is, however, the weekly *Angora*. It is worth adding that its sales are increasing while the whole segment of opinion weeklies remains in crisis. Formally, *Angora* is a magazine which re-prints articles from the Polish and foreign press, but the weekly also includes many exclusive, editorial columns.

In the public debate, a significant role is played by *low-circulation socio-political titles*, varied in terms of political orientation. *Gazeta Polska,* an influential right-wing-oriented weekly, has the strongest market position. It offers a good representation of the sympathies of PiS supporters. In terms of sales (about 10 thousand copies each), the *Tygodnik Solidarność*, an honoured title of NSZZ Solidarność trade union, as well as the liberal-conservative *Najwyższy Czas* are in a worse situation. Several other titles which are valued in their milieus have a significantly smaller circulation, for example the leftist monthly *Dziś*. *Przegląd Społeczny*, the leftist-liberal *Krytyka Polityczna*, the 'common sense' centre-oriented magazine *Obywatel, Debata*, liberal quarterly *Przegląd Polityczny* and conservative right-wing oriented titles such as *Nowe Państwo, Opcja na Prawo, Fronda* and others. It is worth pointing out that there are two commonly valued, elitist Catholic monthlies which are 'beyond political divisions', *Znak* (published since 1946) and *Więź* (since 1958), and there is also the quarterly *ResPublika Nowa* (the title with an anti-Communist opposition and conspiracy origin) (Mielczarek 2007: 160–3).

The local and sub-local press[22] play an important role in local democracy. In general, despite fairly considerable fluidity of particular titles, their number has remained at 2.5 thousand.[23] However, their structure is changing. The number of local titles at the county or sub-regional level is increasing (about 1200 titles), while the number of sub-local ones is decreasing (1300 remaining). Three fifths of local magazines belong to the sector of the so-called independent press. More than half of them are published at least once per week and provide information at a local level with circulation of 2–3 thousand copies (the largest weeklies of that kind have sales of several thousand copies and five of them of 20 thousand copies). More than half of the sub-local papers represent local governments (Chorązki 2007: 87–91). There have been a number of publicized conflicts between both groups of papers. The editors of free-market papers have questioned the foundations of paid-for local government press – its credibility, the value of its information, funding from local government – although it operates in areas where there is no independent paper at all. The latter have great potential, based on the condition that they are fully professional. A few years ago the number of such titles was estimated at 100 (Chorązki 2007). These titles are published mainly in a single or with a few neighbouring counties.

A difficult situation in the media market has forced editors to carry out a number of cost-cutting actions, which have highly influenced the role of press in the public debate. One such action is re-allocation of their assets to the Internet and an attempt to gain higher income from network projects. That is why a number of social services, authors' blogs constructed among their editors, have appeared. A good example here is the re-construction of Agora – the publisher of *Gazeta Wyborcza* – portal. Another example of a rigid and visible cost-cutting policy is the redundancy of their employees. This affects not only the administrative and technical staff but often well-known journalists as well. Also noticeable, mainly in the regional press, is the idea of employing cheap trainees instead of professional, but expensive, journalists. Still another element of the cost-cutting policy is foregoing foreign correspondents or – on a local scale – not to send journalists to scenes, not to cover the expenses of their visits, limit the costs of phone calls at work, and so on.

The Polish radio system

In 1994, the fundament of the new order in the Polish radio system was established, a result of implementing the broadcasting law in Poland. However, since then its current shape has been formed in several phases.

Since the beginning – on the national level – the system of four public[24] and three private licensed[25] radio broadcasters has been established. Two stations of Polskie Radio (PR) are niche radios: Program II with a literature and art programme profile, and Radio Bis (Program IV), an educational programme addressed to the youth. Two other channels of public radio in Poland are quite strong in the national radio-listening market: Program I, a general interest programme with commentary and information profile, and Program III with commentary and entertainment. Both channels are losing more and more listeners, compared to the commercial stations: RMF FM (owned by the German Bauer group since the end of 2006) and Radio Zet (owned by the French Lagardere group). Both commercial market leaders play formatted music (*Adult Contemporary* format) and offer fast and reliable news services. Their several commentary broadcasts which are praised by politicians, who willingly appear in these broadcasts, as well as by listeners; especially young ones.

Apart from these four broadcasters, there is also Radio Maryja, the Catholic station founded by an influential and controversial Redemptorist from Toruń, Father Tadeusz Rydzyk – nowadays, probably the most influential representative of the Polish Catholic Church. Radio Maryja has a 'social broadcaster' status, which means that it cannot broadcast advertisements, and is basically prayer radio. In fact, Radio Maryja gives the floor to publicists and listeners who openly present their nationalist, fundamentally-Catholic and definitely Euro-sceptical opinions.

Table 4: The number of listeners of the largest national radio stations and over-regional* Radio Tok FM in 1997, 2002, 2007.

	1997		2002		2007	
Rank	Station	%	Station	%	Station	%
1.	Polskie Radio Program 1	19.2	RMF FM	22.4	RMF FM	22.5
2.	RMF FM	18.1	Polskie Radio Program 1	17.9	Radio Zet	19.3
3.	Radio Zet	13.6	Radio Zet	17.5	Polskie Radio Program 1	13.2
4.	Radio Maryja	6.3	Polskie Radio Program 3	4.6	Polskie Radio Program 3	6.1
5.	Polskie Radio Program 3	4.6	Radio Maryja	3.3	Radio Maryja	2.1
6.	–		Radio Tok FM	0.3	Radio Tok FM	1.0

*Such stations are the typical network. They broadcasted – using the low-powered radio transmitters – uniform programme in several of the biggest cities.
Source: Badania Radio Track Instytutu SMG/KRC.

Despite its decreasing number of listeners, Radio Maryja still has great power to influence millions of listeners, especially those gathered in the social movement 'The Family of Radio Maryja'. Father Rydzyk's radio is effective in organizing different kinds of actions, not only religious in character (for instance, annual pilgrimages with many thousand participants), but also social actions (mass protest actions) or even politically-oriented actions (more or less influencing election results since 1997).

The cross-regional level of Polish radio broadcasting has been shaped since 1998. Among three commercial stations – music Radiostacja, general interest and entertainment Wawa and news & talk formatted Radio Talk FM – the last plays an important role in public debate. Radio Talk FM offers many social and political commentaries which are prepared by well-known publicists of *Gazeta Wyborcza* and *Polityka*.

There are seventeen stations of public Polskie Radio operating at the *regional* level. Even though these public stations offer varied and valuable content, widely devoted to regional and local as well as ethnic themes, for many years they have been experiencing a decrease in the number of listeners and deep financial crisis.

At present, there are local radio broadcasters in Poland with about 25 – mostly commercial – licensed stations which operate on FM waves, and about twenty communal/municipal stations which broadcast about two hours per day on MW waves, rarely[26] used in Poland. Most of the twenty stations broadcasting on FM waves belong to the so-called networked radio stations, which means that they operate in one of four groups of stations (ZPR/Time, Agora, Eurozet and Broker FM). These are connected by capital (franchised), and co-operate in advertising, programme formatting, playing mostly music and limiting the talk on the radio (for example, news services). The number of so-called independent stations is still decreasing. There are about 40 at present, which are, to some extent, dependent on the Eurozet group owing to the advertising agreement 'Pakiet Niezależnych'. Other independent radio stations are non-networked Catholic (about 24), academic and so-called self-government[27] stations.

Public media

The status of Polish public radio and television (for example state treasury companies) results in the situation that the public media in Poland are an area of continuous competition of interests and struggle for influences. Maciej Mrozowski (2007: 156–7) claims that if we order the interests of the main 'players' according to their power of influence on the public media programme policy, it will turn out that the most influential are political groups, especially parliamentary and governmental. Consequently, one can clearly see the *politicization* of the public media. In Poland, the 'transmission belt' for political appointments at all levels of public media authorities came into being:[28] 'Undeveloped civil society is not able to create non-political and non-party ways of promoting people to public stands' – says Karol Jakubowicz – for instance,

> the National Broadcasting Council was projected to be a pluralistic mini-parliament where the decisions are made as a political compromise. But this idea led to irretrievable politicization of the Council and its domination by party interests which wanted to influence the appointment of supervisory boards and managements in the public media. To make matters worse, the Council turned out not to be a professional regulatory institution. (Jakubowicz 2007: 224–5)

The process of politicization of the public media in Poland is one of the results of the wrong state policy on the public media (Jakubowicz 2007: 248). But the most important factor of politicization is most likely omnipresent partiocracy (la partitocratie) in Poland: 'Political parties rule everything and public media are not the exception' (Jakubowicz 2007: 227). Low political culture of political elites cannot be forgotten, just as their lack of respect as far as the rules of democracy are concerned, and their own role in free media. What is more, they do not respect the position and mission of the public broadcaster. Their cynical attitude is based on the expectation that if they win the elections, the control over public TV is granted to them (Pokorna-Ignatowicz 2007: 237). In December 2005, it turned out that the 'omnipresent rule of spoils system (as opposed to merit system) was systematically introduced without equivocation, which means that the "winner (of the political election) takes all", including the public media' (Jakubowicz 2007: 228).

If we agree with T. Kowalski (2007) that something that might indicate the maturity of certain markets is progress in the distribution of new forms of communication such as HDTV and interactive or mobile TV, then one must admit that Poland, in comparison with developed western countries, looks very unfavourable. Poland has just taken the first steps in this domain. Additionally, as far as the configuration of influences on the new communication technology market is concerned, Poland seems to be different compared to mature western markets.

What seems to be a huge threat, especially for the public media, is technological backwardness. Radio and television in public service are 'traditional broadcasters oriented towards the production and transmission of linear broadcasts' (Jakubowicz 2007: 256). Developing websites is not enough. Moreover, such undertakings are at the margin of public broadcasters' activity. Launching interactive TV in 2007 (http://www.itvp.pl/) made the situation a little better. However, it comes down to the programmes already broadcast being presented via a new channel of communication, while the essence of the matter is to project a completely new television form, independent from traditional TV broadcasting (Jakubowicz 2007: 256).

The problem also has a more general dimension. The Polish state has still not worked out the policy concerning the development of public broadcasters in the new technologies domain. The plans for conducting digital conversion of terrestrial radio and television do not expect any support for the public broadcasters from the state. Yet, 'digitalization will end the time of a convenient balance and oligopoly of three broadcasters (TVP, Polsat and TVN)' – says Jakubowicz (2007: 256). He adds: 'if technological modernization of the Polish public media does not take place, these media will soon be found in a completely different world than viewers and listeners (especially young ones) live in' (Jakubowicz 2007: 257).

Advertising shares in the television market

Similar to most European countries, there is a mixed television market structure in Poland. However, Poland stands out owing to extremely high shares of public broadcasters in the TV audience market. Three terrestrial channels of Telewizja Polska (TVP): TVP1, TVP2 and TVP Info[29] had all together in 2007 about 46 per cent of the TV audience market; although in 2003–5 it had been over 50 per cent.

Not accidentally, observers notice that the Polish TV market has so far been the market of *three big players*, for example public television and two commercial groups: Polsat and ITI/TVN. There are four most popular channels in Poland: two public and two commercial ones. The fact that public channels dominate in terms of audience is very annoying for commercial broadcasters. TVP1 and TVP2 are still the most popular, despite the fact that their joint audience-share decreased from 47.1 per cent (2002) to 41.2 per cent (2007).[30] These public channels, which are additionally supported by money from licence fees, compete with commercial stations in the TV advertising market: public channels have a 30 per cent share. The two biggest commercial stations (TVN and Polsat) remained strong at the turn of the century because of the good position of Polsat, the leading commercial broadcaster on the TV ranking list, ahead of TVP2. Since 2003, commercial broadcasters have been increasing their market-share (from 30.2 per cent to 33.3 per cent) but this time due to the growing popularity of TVN (from 6.4 per cent in 1998 to 13.8 per cent in 2002 and 16.5 per cent in 2007), which is perceived as the most innovative on the Polish market. TVN is the leader, in introducing the world-trendy TV formats (starting with *Big Brother* in 2001). For two years, the shares of these commercial broadcasters in the market have been very similar: 16–17 per cent for each of them. Moreover, in 2007 Polsat re-gained the third place on the TV ranking list, the position it had lost in 2006. Both commercial stations have a similar share (25–6 per cent) in the income from the advertising market.

The 'big four' broadcasters treated en bloc are slowly losing market-share in favour of new competitors, which are appearing in great numbers: from 80 per cent (2001) to below

Table 5: The audience (shares in market) of information programmes in all-Poland and trans-regional terrestrial TV channels and satellite news TV channel TVN 24 in 1998, 2002, 2007.

	1998		2002		2007	
Rank	Channel	%	Channel	%	Channel	%
1.	TVP 1	30.0	TVP 1	26.5	TVP 1	23.2
2.	Polsat	25.2	TVP 2	20.6	TVP 2	18.0
3.	TVP 2	18.4	Polsat	18.5	Polsat	16.8
4.	TVN	6.4	TVN	13.8	TVN	16.5
5.	TVP 3*	5.0	TVP 3 Regionalna	4.4	TVP 3/TVP Info	4.9
6.	Nasza TV	1.7	TV 4	3.7	TVN 24	3.0
7.	–		TV Puls	0.5	TV 4	2.1
8.	–		TVN 24	?	TV Puls	0.5

*In 1998, total audience of programmes broadcast by twelve regional divisions of TVP
Source: AGB Polska (AGB Nielsen Media Research).

75 per cent (2007). Similarly, the shares of terrestrial stations are decreasing (from 88 per cent in 2002 to 82 per cent in 2007) for the benefit of satellite-cable channels, mostly special interest ones, their growth being from 11.6 per cent in 2001 to 17.8 per cent in 2007. It seems quite natural, however, that in comparison to developed media systems, like in Germany with 42 per cent or Great Britain with 25 per cent (see Kowalski 2007), one can notice a remarkable delay.

Nonetheless, overcoming this retardation is easier, due to an extremely fast development of satellite digital platforms even in comparison to other European countries: since 2005, the number of subscribers has increased from 1.4 million to 3.4 million in 2007. Since the end of 2006, two competing platforms, Cyfra+ (since 1998, at present with 1.1 million subscribers) and Cyfrowy Polsat (since 2002, 2.2 million subscribers), have had a third rival, for example N platform (300 thousand subscribers). The new platform has challenged its competitors in the area of technology: TV channels with HDTV, PVR, VoD standards.

According to the latest information (Gazeta Wyborcza, 21–2 May 2008: 28), 17 per cent of households in Poland are already connected to digital platforms. This is higher than the average for the five most advanced European markets, which is 12 per cent. In addition, at least 4.5 million Polish households are connected to cable networks. Several of the largest cable networks have been trying to introduce the digital TV service. The turning point is expected to happen by the end of 2008, because the biggest cable TV operator (UPC, 1 million subscribers) is planning to launch a digital TV service for its subscribers.[31]

The television audience in Poland

As far as the *TV offer* is concerned, Poland is significantly divided into two parts, these having been almost equal until 2005: the offer for privileged viewers, for example people having access to several dozens or hundreds of channels in cable or satellite television (at present these are about 8 million households) and the offer for underprivileged viewers (people having access to a maximum of seven, and usually four to five terrestrial broadcasting channels, about 5.5–6 million households). The acceleration of the development of digital platforms has significantly reduced the number of the underprivileged.[32]

The two biggest commercial broadcasters have been extending their main channels with additional entertainment channels: TV4, co-operating with Polsat (so-called pan-regional, a network of terrestrial transmitters in a few regions with 16 per cent of population) and satellite Polsat 2 International. TVN owns the satellite movie and entertainment channel TVN Siedem. Moreover, to broaden the TV offer, commercial broadcasters have developed numerous special interest satellite-cable channels. TVN has ten such channels and Polsat has six. Both broadcasters also have their own digital platforms. Polsat group owns Cyfrowy Polsat with 2.2 million subscribers, who tend to be non-wealthy inhabitants of provincial Poland. ITI/TVN group launched N platform and gained 320 thousand subscribers, who are mostly wealthy consumers willing to explore the possibilities of advanced digital technology, including paid-for programmes, movie subscription and HD television. The majority of the thematic channels (mostly in analogue technology) are available also in the cable TV network offer. The public broadcaster Telewizja Polska has accepted the challenge from commercial broadcasters and launched a few satellite channels (TVP Kultura, TVP Historia, TVP Sport), and is planning to start its own digital platform, which may happen in 2009.

There are a few channels which play an important role in the public debate at the national level: TVP1, TVP2, Polsat and TVN as well as two information channels: TVP Info and TVN24. Soon there will be another information channel – Polsat News. As far as informational TV channels are concerned, one fact should be underlined here: the outstanding popularity of commercial channel TVN24, which was patterned after CNN24. TVN24 was launched in 2001, but already in 2005 when the channel became part of the big cable networks' offer, the channel exceeded 1 per cent of TV audience share, and in 2007 reached 3 per cent, which is higher than pan-regional TV4. Among the many commentary programmes of TVN24, the greatest popularity and audience has been gained by 'Szkło kontaktowe', broadcast every evening. This programme is eagerly visited by many politicians of different orientations, even those who accuse TVN of representing 'liberal media', unfriendly toward populist parties. On the other hand, an 18-hour-long programme by public TVP Info (4.9 per cent of TV market shares in 2007) provides several information services, commentary programmes on national and international issues as well as transmission of parliamentary sessions and its select committees, apart from its four local versions.

The ranking list of TV audience of information programmes shows (Table 4) that two programmes of public TVP1 (*Wiadomości* and afternoon service *Teleexpress*) have the best results, but commercial broadcasters' programmes (TVN's *Fakty* and Polsat's *Wydarzenia*) successfully compete with them. In contrast, after being moved to a later hour (midnight), the formerly evening edition of *Panorama* (TVP2) lost its audience. Polsat had also broadcast a popular commentary programme *Co z tą Polską?* up until 2007, when its author and presenter Tomasz Lis quit Polsat and moved to TVP. TVN still attracts its audience with a popular political programme, *Teraz My*, with Tomasz Sekielski and Andrzej Morozowski, the prize-winners of many journalistic contests. Nevertheless, in public television (especially in TVP1) commentary programmes are broadcast more often, but the programming and authors change according to the changes of public television management which, in turn, is connected with every political change in Poland.

Table 6: The audience of information programmes in Polish TV channels as of April 2007 and 2008. The number of viewers and audience shares (in %)

Information programme	Channel	2007		2008	
		AMR	SHR (%)	AMR	SHR (%)
WIADOMOŚCI 19:30	TVP1	4 557 605	34.67	4 277 146	33.61
FAKTY 19:00	TVN	3 730 130	31.58	3 692 380	31.47
TELEEXPRESS 17:00	TVP1	3 819 996	43.55	3 648 584	41.84
WYDARZENIA 18:50	Polsat	2 361 658	20.65	2 308 888	20.23
PANORAMA 18:45/18:30	TVP2	1 509 715	13.67	1 322 413	12.21
PANORAMA 22:00/24:00	TVP2	1 536 347	13.55	418 102	10.07
PULS RAPORT 22:00	TV Puls	–	–	128 265	1.01
PULS RAPORT 19:30	TV Puls	–	–	57 453	0.45

Source: AGB Nielsen Media Research

Among other TV channels in Poland, trans-regional TV Puls has great developmental potential despite its limited market shares (so far 0.5 per cent). It is a Catholic channel which came into being on the basis of the religious station of the Franciscan Order. The changed licence allows broadcasting of more universal programming (including entertainment); as a result, Rupert Murdoch's News Corporation has been investing in TV Puls since 2006. Despite a preponderance of entertainment programmes, TV Puls introduced its own information programme (*Puls Raport*) in autumn 2007, and started to broadcast a few commentary programmes on social, political, philosophical and religious issues.

What seems to be an unfavourable phenomenon in Poland is some kind of underdevelopment of commercial terrestrial local stations. About ten local broadcasters were granted the licence in 1994. Until now, only six have survived in the market, but their activity is limited: they broadcast their own programmes for only two hours per day and the majority of broadcasting time is filled with retransmissions from TV4 (stations owned by Odra group) or TVN (NTL Radomsko). For the first time, one can observe the revival of broadcasters' interests in local markets this year. In March 2008, the Silesian satellite channel – TVS – was started, available in regional cable networks and satellite platforms; in autumn one can expect the launch of TVN Warszawa. Even TVP is planning to start its own local programme addressed to the inhabitants of the capital. Cable TV operators granted licences for their own local programmes; however the concentration into major groups led to a huge reduction of local programmes, which are often just static TV display panels containing information and advertising. At present, the medium cable operators mainly broadcast their own commentary and information programmes.

Progressive *centralization* is the factor which strongly limits public media abilities in fulfilling its social functions. At the beginning of the media system transformation in Poland, the idea decided upon was of bringing public media closer to the inhabitants of the whole country. The concept of structural regionalization was fully carried out in public radio, while in public television, structural integrity was preserved while programme regionalization was implemented. After some years, it turned out that the programme of public radio was becoming similar to that of commercial radio stations, despite the fact that the majority of public radio finances comes from license fees. In the case of public television, the history of regional programmes is a history of constant withdrawal from initial concepts and ambitions. TVP cannot completely resign from broadcasting regional programmes (because of statutory duties); moreover, a huge amount of money was spent on regional divisions. Nevertheless, public TV acts in a similar way to licensed broadcasters: regional programmes are not developed owing to high costs and low incomes from regional advertising markets (Jakubowicz 2007: 231–7).

More fundamental changes in the television offer in Poland are caused by the introduction of terrestrial digital TV. After a long period of stagnation, the implementation of the TV digitalization plan is presently being worked on: two out of six digital multiplexes (virtual sub-channels) are planned to be launched in 2009; in 2012 Poland will totally switch from analogue to digital television.

Working conditions for journalists in Poland

After 1989, the number of press titles and electronic media in Poland increased significantly. As a result, the large and open labour market for *journalists* came into being. During the last decade, the number of journalists in Poland doubled from 11 to 18–20 thousand. But after that period, as a result of phenomena such as economic depression (2001–2), a declining interest in the local press and formatting of radio stations, as well as reductions in the number of editorial offices and the number of their employees, took place. In 2006, according to rough estimates, the number of full-time journalists was about 15 thousand, with about 30 thousand media employees in general.[33] Journalists became younger: in 2000 the average age in this profession was about 35 years of age. The number of women employed in media – especially electronic media – significantly increased. Moreover, about 1,000 graduates of journalistic studies, mainly with Bachelor Degree from 30 universities, wish to enter the profession every year (Mielczarek 2007: 70–3).

At the beginning of the 1990s, an advanced exchange of journalistic staff took place. First, it was the result of moral-political vetting of journalists of the People's Republic of Poland. Second, it was driven by the market situation of many editors, for example the breakdown of many editorial offices because of political conflicts. And, third, it was caused by the influx of new students of journalism. All these processes caused deep disintegration of the journalistic milieu. A weak interest, and participation, in professional associations' activities is proof of this disintegration. According to rather optimistic estimations, only 30 per cent of journalists belonged to journalists associations, syndicates or different professional organizations at that time.

In Poland, two professional associations fiercely compete with each other: The Journalists' Association of the Republic of Poland (SDRP), with about 7.5 thousand members in 2000, who are older or mainly retired journalists, and the Polish Journalists' Association (SDP), with about 1.5 thousand members in 2000, which refers to the traditions of so-called first 'Solidarity' (1980–1), but has recently been quite resiliently active. The centre of interest of the SDP is the process of building a new democratic order and institutional guarantees of freedom of the media in Poland. SDP focuses on such issues as the relations between the media and public opinion, the protection of professional secrets of journalists, and the protection of privacy. There are also other journalists' organizations, such as the Catholic Journalists' Association (KSD) which is well integrated. For the protection of social rights of journalists, the Polish Syndicate of Journalists (with the nature of a trade union) has been established (Mielczarek 2007: 75–6).

One outcome of the journalists' activity is the Media Ethic Charter. This is the most important document of press deontology in Poland. In 1995 it was accepted by the Polish Media Conference, a gathering of journalist associations, representatives of press publishers and broadcasters' organizations.

Apart from the Charter, the members of Polish Media Conference agreed to respect the provisions of the Journalistic Moral Code of the Journalists' Association of the Republic of Poland, and the members of SDP have their Journalist Ethic Code. In the last few years, the Polish Chamber of Press Publishers have prepared a very important document: The Code for Good Practices for Press Publishers. It should be added here that public broadcasters have their own ethic codes (for example the principles of journalist ethics of TVP SA) and ethic commissions. Journalists and editors decided to establish the Polish Media Conference at the beginning of 1995. Soon after, the Media Ethic Council was established, which was authorized to make announcements and statements, especially in cases of violation of The Charter (Mielczarek 2007: 77–9).

What seems to be a fundamental threat is the *weakness of a public media journalistic milieu*, which makes it significantly difficult to solve the problem of media politicization. Deep crisis causes undesirable and sometimes cynical attitudes among journalists of the public media, who are mostly oriented towards their own interest. There is no debate about important problems of media and journalists, about threats to freedom of the media or about professional ethics. 'There is no professional solidarity', says K. Pokorna-Ignatowicz (2007: 239):

> 'even when the rights of a journalist are violated. The journalist milieu is deeply divided according to ideological, social, and generational differences. There is not a single effective professional association battling for journalists' rights, and existing professional institutions are disrespected (e.g. Media Ethics Council). (K. Pokorna-Ignatowicz 2007: 240)

Another factor that threatens public discourse in Poland, and seriously restricts the internal freedom of press, is Article 10 of the press law, according to which a journalist must obey and follow the general principles of his/her publisher. Thus, *journalists' internal freedom within editorial offices* is the *conditio sine qua non* for preserving pluralism of public discourse in Poland (Pisarek 2002: 16).

Conclusion

Tadeusz Kowalski (2006: 8) has recently stated that:

> ...in Poland the media market is stable and, moreover, it is just a system of mature and competitive market that has become a part of the European media system. The press market in Poland, despite possessing some specific features, does not differ essentially from the one of the developed European countries.

The situation on the TV market is also, as was pointed out, different and reveals many special features.

The press (media) market transformation from so-called real socialism to the market economy took place at least a decade ago. Since then, the free market mechanisms have challenged press and electronic media editors with economic barriers (for example input barriers). These barriers are hard to overcome for small economic entities of decent capital even on the local market. Therefore, ongoing concentration is taking place, which embraces firms operating at a regional and trans-national level. Apart from undisputable benefits, this development also brings about less favourable effects.

The phenomenon of European and global concerns entering the Polish market is accompanied by the conviction that '... media are a typical commodity that has to be under the same regulations as parsley or the nail market' (Żakowski 2008: 17). They are no longer treated as a serious source of information and ideas, and have become a source of emotional, mostly sensational, stimulation. Having entered the stock exchange, media and entertainment conglomerates, newspapers, magazines, radio and TV stations are more and more dependent on aggressive dividend-oriented investment funds, requiring the media only to be attractive to their consumers. As a result, the significance of media editors, publishers, journalists and authors is decreasing and the power of chief executives, who primarily care about other undertakings, commercials and good relations with political power, and managers and specialists in marketing, whose only mission is to provide satisfactory economic results, is increasing (Żakowski 2008: 18). Such a situation, for example, has led to the omnipresent phenomenon of the so-called 'Italian fashion' (newspaper advertisement inserts) which affect even serious opinion titles: the sales are built up on movies or cosmetics, while the press content is considered secondary.

These general remarks, under Polish circumstances, seem to be more fully justified in regard to the press market than to the TV market. Most of the former had been sold to Western media concerns much earlier, whereas, in the case of electronic media, foreign capital shares were limited until 2004. Among the biggest press publishers, one can find such companies as Axel Springer, Verlagsgruppe Passau, Mecom (originally – Orkla, Bonnier), while the magazine market belongs to the 'big four': Bauer, Axel Springer, G+J (indirectly Bertelsmann) and Edipresse, with growing shares by Marquard and Burda. Thanks to them, we are experiencing the inflow of 'leisure time' press, basically meeting entertaining needs. Tomasz Mielczarek (2007: 364) seems to be right when he writes that their expansion 'has objectively decreased interests in the opinion and Catholic press and commercialized the press addressed to the youth and kids.'

Thus, is there any space for plurality of opinions and information in the free market of dailies and opinion press? Undoubtedly, there are no other obstacles for the free market development apart from the above-mentioned economic input barriers and demand for specific content. For example, if rural inhabitants had wanted to read peasant press and if different peasant parties (ruling in coalitions for nearly two decades) had wanted to publish it, it would not have disappeared in the early 1990s. In fact, it is the only remaining uninfluenced space on the political map of newspapers and weeklies. All other political views are expressed in low-circulation magazines. The milieu of 'excluded', poor, elderly inhabitants from the countryside is supported by the media conglomerate of the controversial Redemptorist, Father Tadeusz Rydzyk (Nasz Dziennik, Radio Maryja, Telewizja Trwam). The tabloid press, in principle, supports populist views. The four biggest quality dailies often do not differ in views on the economy (liberal option), thus seeking their place on the market and attempting to distinguish themselves from the *Gazeta Wyborcza*. From time to time they follow socio-political trends, depending on the social situation in a given period of time and on the temper of leading journalists. Moreover, the three most popular opinion weeklies have a consensus on economic issues, seek their identity in relation to major socio-political disputes, positioning themselves on the left or on the right. Other titles, less popular, usually express more distinct views. Looking at press models in the European market, we can say that we are closer to the Anglo-Saxon than to the Mediterranean model.

In turn, the biggest commercial TV stations (TVN and Polsat) have a Polish origin and prevailingly Polish capital. While struggling for a wider audience, they follow the pattern of western[34] entertainment TV stations and chase after trendy formats; however, they still accept the position of the public giant (TVP), at least as long as it maintains its position on the market.

For the public media authorities, the interests of public media themselves seem to be most important. It leads to pathologization of 'corporate culture'. Mrozowski (2007: 156) says that 'the autonomy and independence – which in the case of the Polish media means lack of any control over the current activity of the public media – cause the situation in which the public media present their own benefits as public interests'. This situation was the effect of the lack of control over public media, not only from public authorities but from social institutions as well. Polish public broadcasters take only the interests of political principals and advertisers into account. Hence, the range of beneficiaries of public media activities is small: management, protégés of management and privileged deliverers of the programme (producers, performers, authors, and so on). As a result, Mrozowski says that the public institution is subordinated to oligarchic appropriation:

> The real control over the public media is in the hands of a narrow group of politicians and representatives of big corporations. The former decide about position appointments, the latter influence the income from advertising time sales...The interests of cultural institutions and civic society are marginalized...In this way the programme policy of the public media is a specific mixture of paternalistic and commercial model, while the civic model is totally ignored, says Mrozowski (2007: 156–7).

Another threat to the public media is the *crisis of identity*. The public media are torn between opposite values – declared vs. actually realized (Jakubowicz 2007: 250–1): independence, impartiality and public service vs. ideological engagement; non-commercial vs. dependence on advertising and commercialization; respect for audience and public service vs. objectification of the audience as an aim of ideological actions and 'audience-commodity'.

Public broadcasters in all countries must strive to confirm their existence and to gain public acceptance. In Poland, we also have to deal with the 'crisis of legitimization of existence of public broadcasters' (Jakubowicz 2007: 252). Some people refuse to support public broadcasters, especially if they do not meet public expectations. In Poland, commercial media (and also some politicians) excite social resistance to an obsolete model of the public media and especially to licence fees. Despite such an aggressive campaign, Poles still declare that they trust public media, though they also manifest their disappointment with how the public media function and operate. People commonly protest by not paying the license fee. Urgent and fundamental reforms are needed, otherwise – as Karol Jakubowicz (2007: 256) points out – 'progressive programme convergence between public and licensed broadcasters will finally deprive the former of the right to exist'.

Among many tendencies which push the public media away from the society, Maciej Mrozowski (2007: 158) lists the decline of the ethos of aspiring (original and valuable) creativity, the lack of concern about the quality of programme (attractive and valuable), and the lack of the sense of existence (caring about yourself, your own functioning, and employers' favour is more motivating than the idea of public service). Moreover, the public media in Poland thoughtlessly imitate their commercial rivals. Thus, commercialized and politicized public media do not respect their audience and are not pluralistic enough. What can be said about the public media as a kind of 'cultural industry' – according to Karol Jakubowicz (2007: 246) – is that they should be 'public in programme and commercial in management in order to be effective, which is necessary on the free competitive media market'. In Poland, however, 'the situation looks completely different: public media are commercialized in programme and definitely public in management (i.e. ineffective and poorly organized)'.

Obviously, a number of accusations about the commercialization of the TVP programme (mainly entertainment oriented TVP2) and its politicization (TVP1 and TVP Info) are justified, but all of these public and commercial stations are mutually checked and maintain a relatively high level of quality. The idea of a purposeful and determined weakening of public TV would probably open the way to even bigger 'primitivism' or 'tabloidization' of the offer of commercial broadcasters. Global giants, as is expected, are going to show up in a few years, when multiplexes of terrestrial TV are sold, and it is likely that Polish medium scale market players (TVN or Polsat Group) will not hold up against their competition.

Notes

1. The national dailies – except for Trybuna Ludu – were pre-dated, for example were printed in Warsaw and reached their readers in distant regions of Poland with outdated news (two days old).
2. Those titles were published once a week or month, so the readers' contact with the press was no longer everyday.
3. In 1994 the first radio (for seven years) and television (for ten years) broadcasting licences were granted according to the Broadcasting Act (29 December 1992). The second licence-granting process for radio stations began in 2001 and for television stations in 2004. According to the new broadcasting act (29 December 2005) licence validity periods for radio and TV were the same (ten years), so all licences for analogue terrestrial frequencies for TV broadcasters will have expired by 2014. However, obligatory analogue TV switch-off and conversion into digital terrestrial TV broadcasting is planned for 2012.
4. These titles consist of a smaller number of pages (twelve to sixteen) and they are printed on poorer quality paper. There are no supplements inside (which can be found every day in great numbers in quality papers), fewer illustrations and advertisements.
5. For instance, as a result of liquidation of the Communist press concern RWS, the right to publish *Express Wieczorny* was granted to the Press Foundation of 'Solidarity' trade union (Fundacja Prasowa 'Solidarności') related at that time to Porozumienie Centrum (PC), a party led by the

Kaczyński brothers. *Sztandar Młodych* was owned by another strong right-wing party of these times: Konfederacja Polski Niepodległej (KPN). Both titles, soon in crisis, were transferred to the portfolio of Swiss Marquard.

6. For instance, in 1995–9 high circulation dailies (during the People's Republic of Poland) vanished from the market: *Gromada-Rolnik Polski, Kurier Polski, Sztandar Młodych* (under the name *SM-Sztandar*), *Słowo Powszechne* (since 1993 as *Słowo-Dziennik Katolicki*), and additionally *Życie Warszawy* became a regional daily.

7. *Życie* was suspended at the time of the collapse of the stock exchange company 4Media (December 2002). The new investor re-launched the daily but published it for only one year (from January 2004 till January 2005). During this period its sales were about 20,000 copies.

8. 49 per cent of the shares of the publishing company Presspublika are owned by PW 'Rzeczpospolita' (a holding publishing a few other titles additionally possessing a book publishing house, music company and printing house). PW 'Rzeczpospolita' is state property (the Treasury). The new (since November 2007) government led by Donald Tusk announced the 'cleansing' of this ambiguous situation and selling the state treasury shares in the daily *Rzeczpospolita*. Other governments before 2006 did not interfere in the editorial programme line of *Rzeczpospolita*. The present government led by Donald Tusk wants to sell the shares. Currently the Treasury and Mecom are negotiating Mecom's purchase of the rest (49 per cent) of shares in Presspublica (see Makarenko 2008).

9. The president of Mecom Plc. Management, David Montgomery (2007), made a special announcement published in *Rzeczpospolita*, in which he supported the necessity of preserving the rule of not interfering in the press freedom of over 300 press titles (including *Rzeczpospolita*) owned by Mecom. The editors of *Gazeta Wyborcza* do not believe in such declarations (see Stasiński 2007).

10. The previous editorial line, oriented towards confrontation with that of *Gazeta Wyborcza* was broadly presented by editor-in-chief himself (see Gluza 2007).

11. Since the 1960s, Adam Michnik has been a well-known oppositionist and a political prisoner repeatedly.

12. Both papers – *Rzeczpospolita* and *Dziennik* – regard so-called 'Michnik-like-opinions' (in Polish *Michnikowszczyzna*, the term taken from the title of a famous book by a right-wing publicist, Rafał Ziemkiewicz) as the main evil in public life.

13. The right-wing milieu has made many accusations that the logo of Solidarity was appropriated and the funds used to develop a private company (see Remuszko 1999). The representatives of Agora denied these aspersions many times.

14. Agora SA owns (apart from *Gazeta Wyborcza* with 40 per cent of shares in daily press advertising market) the only free-of-charge daily *Metro*, several colourful magazines (with the leading, high-circulation women's monthly, *Poradnik Domowy*), the trans-regional radio TOK FM and about 25 local stations gathered in 'Złote Przeboje' network and Roxy FM, the Internet portal *Gazeta.pl* and other enterprises (for example, an outdoor advertising company).

15. The newspaper is a 'descendant' of *Trybuna Ludu*, which in the People's Republic of Poland was the official Communist party (PZPR) daily. After that time, and for many years, *Trybuna* has been published by a private company, but there is a popular belief that its editor-in-chief is still assigned by the authorities of social democratic party (SLD).

16. Since September 1994, Polskapresse has been a Polish branch of the Bavarian publishing house, Verlagsgruppe Passau.

17. In fact, there are seven dispersed 'independent' newspapers. But speaking about the 'duopolistic situation' on the regional dailies market makes sense, as in every region of Poland Polskapresse and Orkla own at least one title and very rarely is an 'independent' daily stronger (Kraków, Szczecin).

18. The regional daily, *Kuriel Lubelski* is still owned by Zbigniew Jakubas and only co-operates with the project Polska. In this case, contrary to other editions, the nation-wide part of *Polska* is just the supplement to the regional newspaper. The Polish Chamber of Press Publishers and Press Circulation Audit Unit do not let *Polska* be treated as the national newspaper competing on the same market with *Gazeta Wyborcza* or *Dziennik*. The situation is more complicated because in six biggest regions *Polska* is the nation-wide part of long-existing regional dailies. The editorial offices, though reduced in manpower, have remained in the regions and the front page is often filled with regional news mixed with national news. On the other hand, in most of the remaining regions – except for Warszawa, Opole and Lublin – there are no regional editorial offices so *Polska* is published in the version edited by the Warszawa headquarters. These editions have very low sales (about 700 to 2000 copies).

19. *Przegląd* has much smaller sales, limited content and simpler layout.

20. *Przekrój* – after the change of editorial formula into an opinion weekly – started to increase sales rapidly, and in 2004 exceeded 100 thousand copies, so it got close to the leading three (*Polityka*, *Wprost* and *Newsweek Polska*). Unfortunately, this result was not maintained.

21. The weekly *Ozon* – published from April 2005 until August 2006 – with its elegant layout and gathering of well-known, right-wing publicists, had difficulties with gaining satisfactory sales results (52 thousand copies in 2005, 31 thousand in 2006). Thus, for economic reasons, it stopped being published.

22. Sub-local titles, according to the Press Research Centre's methodology, are addressed to small communities in municipalities or in parts of big cities (quarters, districts, housing estates).

23. Other estimations: 2.6–3.1 thousand of sub-local titles in 2005 (Jarowiecki 2007: 29).

24. Since January 1994 Polskie Radio has been a public broadcaster. Before that, for a several dozen years it was a state institution.

25. According to the Broadcasting Act (1992), the status of 'public broadcaster' (Polskie Radio, Telewizja Polska) or the status of 'licensed broadcaster' was projected. Licensed broadcasters consist mainly of private ones, but also Church, academic and – initially – self-government ones. In 2001 the possibility of gaining the 'social broadcaster' status appeared and it was granted to some Church and academic stations. 'Social broadcasters' cannot gain profits from advertising. Other stations (without licence) are the pirate ones.

26. Several other MW stations, even though they have licences, have problems with broadcasting.

27. Since 2001 the licences of these stations have gradually been changed. Thus, they operate partially in commercial circumstances, indirectly financed by self-government funds (for example by cultural community centres).

28. Public television and radio remain under powerful political control. The National Broadcasting Council (Krajowa Rada Radiofonii i Telewizji – KRRiT), which has controlled the electronic broadcasting sector since April 1993, has broad rights as regards broadcasting supervision and administration of general viewer licence fees. The Council has powers in monitoring and regulating programming on radio and television, allocating broadcasting frequencies and licences, and apportioning subscription revenues to public media. In order to encourage KRRiT's apolitical character, the KRRiT members are legally obliged to suspend any membership in political parties or public associations. However, they are chosen for their political allegiances and nominated by the Sejm, the Senate, and the President

following political bargaining, thus raising potentially serious questions about the independence of broadcasting oversight from political influence. According to this principle, politically chosen members of the Council choose politically convenient members of the supervisory boards of the public television (TVP) as well as national and regional companies of Polish Radio (PR). Members of the boards, programming directors, and so on are appointed in the same way. Additionally, the Treasury (as the formal owner of TVP SA company and public radio companies) joins these 'party games' connected with appointing the public broadcasting authorities.

29. Until October 2007 TVP Info operated as TVP 3 Regionalna, gathering sixteen regional divisions of TVP, which in discrete time bands, broadcast their own programmes about four hours per day.

30. All quoted data about television viewing market shares come from AGB Nielsen Media Research telemetric surveys. There are also research results of TNS/OBOP available in Poland.

31. The number of cable TV subscribers has remained almost unchanged for a few years. Thus, one might say that cable TV broadcasters are not interested (for economic reasons) in spreading the networks in so-far not-cabled areas (suburban, parish). For the inhabitants of such areas, the only chance for a couple more years (until the digital terrestrial TV is launched) is to become a subscriber of a digital platform. Cyfrowy Polsat and platforma N offer cheap subscriptions (about 35–40 PLN) and many attractive sport channels which are entitled to transmit the most attractive sports events.

32. In 2005 the group of 'underprivileged' was about 2m higher.

33. After introducing the new labour code (1996), the phenomenon of encouraging journalists to become self-employed was observed in Poland (for example launching one-man companies). It has become easier to break an agreement with a journalist in such a situation than with a journalist as a full-time employee. (see Mielczarek 2007: 71).

34. TVN was launched in 1997 and employed many journalistic stars. TVN had an ambitious programme concept with information, commentary and entertainment programmes of 'high quality'. Unfortunately, at the beginning of 1998, under market pressure (and American shareholder CME and later SBS) the programme priorities were changed to more entertainment. The president of TVN, Mariusz Walter, admitted that in the clash with the market reality he had to resign from the dreams of perfect television. To some extent, these dreams were realized a few years later when TVN24 and special interest channels were launched.

References

Bierzyński, J. (2007), 'Szalony wyścig prasy', *Rzeczpospolita*, 17 December 2007, p. B10.

Dijk, T. van (1995), 'Discourse and Cognition in Society', in Crowley, David and Mitchell, David (eds.), *Communication Theory Today*, Cambridge, pp. 107–26.

Chorązki, W. (2007), 'Sytuacja mediów lokalnych w Polsce w III kwartale 2005 roku', *Polskie media lokalne na przełomie XX i XXI wieku: historia, teoria, zjawiska*, Kraków: BiblioTheca, pp. 83–98.

Filas, R. (2005), 'Rynek prasy codziennej w Polsce przed "Faktem" i z "Faktem"', *Zeszyty Prasoznawcze*, no. 3–4, pp. 7–32.

Filas, R. (2007a), 'Polskie czasopisma w XXI wieku – rozwój czy kryzys?', *Zeszyty Prasoznawcze*, no. 1–2, pp. 11–50.

Filas, R. (2007b), 'Prasa ogólnokrajowa po 1989 r', *Słownik wiedzy o mediach*, pod red. Chudzińskiego, E., Bielsko-Biała: Wyd. ParkEdukacja; Warszawa: Wydawnictwo Szkolne PWN, pp. 108–25.

Filas, R. (2007c), 'Sytuacja na polskim rynku prasowym a możliwości wpływu gazet i czasopism na debatę publiczną', *Media masowe w praktyce społecznej*, Redakcja naukowa Waniek, Danuta i Adamowski, Janusz. Warszawa: Oficyna Wydawnicza ASPRA-JR, pp. 255–70.

Gluza, R. (2007), 'Pępowina', Rozmowa z Robertem Krasowskim, redaktorem naczelnym 'Dziennika', Press, no. 3, pp. 34–9.

Jakubowicz, K. (2007), Media publiczne Początek końca czy nowy początek, Warszawa: WAIP.

Jarowiecki, J. (2007), Badania nad polską prasą lokalną. Studium przeglądowe, in Polskie media lokalne na przełomie XX i XXI wieku: historia, teoria, zjawiska, Krakó: BiblioTheca, pp. 11–36.

Kowalczyk, M. (2007a), 'Rząd dusz', Press, no. 2, p. 54.

Kowalczyk, M. (2007b), 'Reorientacja', Press, no. 11, pp. 50–2.

Kowalski, T. (2006), 'W kierunku rynku. Zmiany w prasie codziennej na tle tendencji europejskich', in Podstawowe czynniki przemian polskiego rynku prasowego w latach 1996–2006, materiały konferencyjne pod red. Jana Kani, Poznań.

Kowalski, T. (2007), 'Wizja bez granic', Ranking nadawców, Magazyn Extra no. 12, Press, listopad, pp. 4–5.

Makarenko, V. (2008), 'Trudne rozmowy Mecomu ze skarbem', Gazeta Wyborcza, 3 June 2008, p. 25.

Mielczarek, T. (2007), Monopol, pluralizm, koncentracja. Środki komunikowania masowego w Polsce w latach 1989–2006, Warszawa: Wyd. Akademickie i Profesjonalne.

Montgomery, D. (2007), 'Mecom gwarantuje niezależność redakcji', Rzeczpospolita, 16 November 2007.

Mrozowski, M. (2007), 'Media publiczne – władza publiczna – interes publiczny, czyli o poetyce trójkątów', in Danuta Waniek and Janusz Adamowski (eds.), Media masowe w praktyce społecznej, Warszawa: Oficyna Wydawnicza ASPRA-JR, pp. 137–58.

Nalewajk, A. (2003), 'Wzruszać, bulwersować', Press, no. 6, pp. 6–7.

Pisarek, W. (2002), 'Wolność słowa a wolność prasy', Zeszyty Prasoznawcze, no. 1–2, pp. 7–17.

Pokorna-Ignatowicz, K. (2007), 'Między misją a polityką. O politycznym uwikłaniu TVP w przeszłości i współcześnie', in Danuta Waniek and Janusz Adamowski (eds.), Media masowe w praktyce społecznej, Warszawa: Oficyna Wydawnicza ASPRA-JR, pp. 221–42.

Remuszko, S. (1999), Gazeta Wyborcza. Początki i okolice. Warszawa: Oficyna 'Rękodzieło'.

Stasiński, P. (2008), 'Kto wyrwie „Rzepę"?', Gazeta Wyborcza, 15 November 2007, p. 2.

Światłowska, U. (2008), 'Metamorfoza', Press, no. 1, p. 8.

Żakowski, J. (2008), 'Mea culpa', Polityka, no. 20, 17 November 2008, pp. 16–18.

Mass Media Developments in Bulgaria[1]

Lilia Raycheva

To understand the profound changes in the mass media system and its development trends in Bulgaria, one should go back to the roots of political upheaval after the fall of the Berlin wall.

The collapse of the totalitarian regime in the country brought about significant changes throughout its whole social system. For more than four decades the Communist Party dominated the functions of the State, curtailing the rights and liberties of the people. An atmosphere encouraging social obedience in line with propaganda requirements reigned in the country. Normal political life was practically non-existent in Bulgaria. Freedom of expression was limited. The public swam in an informational fog.

After 45 years of communism, Bulgaria held its first democratic elections in May 1990 following an inter-party coup that had ended the totalitarian rule in November 1989. A new Bulgarian Constitution was adopted in 1991. During the following years, a normal political environment was gradually established. The transition period of nearly twenty years witnessed four presidential elections (in 1992, 1996, 2001 and 2006), six parliamentary elections (in 1990, 1991, 1994, 1997, 2001 and 2005), five local elections (in 1991, 1995, 1999, 2003 and 2007), one EU parliamentary election (2007) and the appointment of ten governments. An encouraging sign is that the last two governments successfully completed their mandates.

However, as a result of the fierce political fights, all of the legislative and economic processes were crawling at low speed. This entailed new social and economic problems, and their solutions were nowhere in sight. Thus, the country lost the momentum generated by the quick start of the democratic reforms, missed the chance to become integrated with the Central European countries into the important European structures, and entered the twenty-first century under the already launched Currency Board.

In the meantime, important changes were taking place in the mass media system. In a very short time, without gate keeping or ideological control, the style and content of the press and the broadcasts departed very much from former patterns. Political pluralism brought about the establishmest of diversity of party organs, causing political marketing to boom in Bulgaria early in 1990. The same year marked the beginning of the political advertising telecasts in the country. The first live TV debate between presidential candidates was aired on 10 January 1992. The strong press, radio and TV involvement in defining the final choice of the voters played a significant role during the pre-election campaigns from the very beginning of the democratization of political life. Thus, mass media brought about a high polarization of the people in Bulgaria. Journalism in those first years of democratization operated as a mirror: frequently distorting the political processes in the country, and yet still exerting considerable influence over public opinion.

Nevertheless, the tendency towards democracy became irreversible. Among the major achievements during this period were the country joining NATO in 2004 and entering the European Union in 2007.

Prior to the democratic changes in 1989, the Bulgarian mass media system was centralized, state-owned and subordinated to the priorities of the Party-State system. Thus, for a good forty years, journalism was monotonous, instructive and politically controlled. The censoring institution prompted the development of self-censorship, the lack of information entailed misinformation, and the absence of pluralistic press and broadcasting resulted in newspapers, magazines, radio and television programmes of marginalized profile.

The democratization processes in society strongly influenced mass media developments in Bulgaria. The new Bulgarian Constitution guaranteed freedom of expression for any citizens. Article 40 (1) specifically defended freedom of mass media: 'The press and the other mass information media shall be free and shall not be subjected to censorship' (Constitution of the Republic of Bulgaria 1991).

Of all other institutions, it was the mass media which were the quickest and most flexible to react to the transformation of democracy after November 1989. It went through profound changes in structure, management and social functioning during the transition to a civil society and market economy.

The liberalization and deregulation of the whole mass media system led to its decentralization and to the emergence of pluralistic print and electronic media. Different patterns of media consumption and new advertising strategies were introduced. The establishment of a mass media market stimulated the development of new formats and styles of expression, thus fostering the higher selectivity standards of the audiences.

The spirit of pluralism and the understanding that the importance of each medium was bound to its contribution to social change became a pragmatic guideline for survival and development. Audiences forced journalists to assume the role of heralds of political, economic, cultural, and social change. Reality, however, proved quite different in style from 'wishful democracy' and the media world accordingly produced parallel pictures of reality in times of critical hardships, contests, and challenges.

Nevertheless, the media found themselves fulfilling the dual function of transmitters and catalysts of political change. This dual function was manifested in several critical situations, including: the TV attack against President Petar Mladenov in 1990 that compelled him to resign; the resignation of the Bulgarian Socialist Party Government headed by Andrey Loukanov in 1990; the mass media war launched by the Union of Democratic Forces Government of Filip Dimitrov, which led to its toppling in 1992; the exit of the Government of Lyuben Berov (under the Movement for Rights and Freedom mandate) in 1994; the withdrawal of the BSP government of Zhan Videnov in 1996; the siege of the House of the National Assembly during the governmental crisis of 1997, which led to a radical power shift; and the forced restructuring of the UDF government of Ivan Kostov in 1999, based on corruption allegations. In 2005, media pressure accompanied the ministerial shifts in the government of the National Movement Simeon the Second – the Centrist, leader-type party, with Simeon Sakskoburggotski (the former king of Bulgaria) as the sole leader. Following media attacks, some ministers in the current coalition government (BSP, NMSS and MRF) of Sergey Stanishev were forced to resign in 2007 as well as in 2008 due to corruption allegations and failure to fulfil the EU accession requirements.

Among the major challenges of the transition period were the general insufficiency of financial and technological resources and the lack of professional standards. Nevertheless, media competition stimulated the first dynamic open markets in the country, which established well-developed media consumption patterns.

However, although the public was offered a highly varied media menu, expectations that the media would aid the processes of democratization in a purposeful and effective manner proved unrealistically high. Media were in need of transformation themselves. Change of property and the departure from single-party control was not sufficient for rendering them professional. Although the guild had adopted its ethical code in 2004 (Ethical Code of Bulgarian Media 2004), it failed to build the mechanisms for sustaining it, and in many cases still reacts inadequately to important and publicly significant issues, as well as to a number of professional problems. In fact, in 2005 the Foundation National Council for Journalistic Ethics was registered with the major aim to establish a system for self-regulation of the media by implementing the Code of Ethics and resolving arguments between the media outlets and the audience. Co-founders of the foundation were the Association of the Bulgarian Radio and Television Operators ABRO, the Union of Publishers in Bulgaria, the Union of Bulgarian Journalists, the Bulgarian Media Coalition, and the foundation Media Development Centre. The foundation has two standing bodies – an Ethics Commission in the Print Media Sector and an Ethics Commission in the Electronic Media Sector, which deal with complaints lodged against infringement of the Ethics Code (National Council for Journalism Ethics 2004).

After two years of functioning, however, the Ethics Commission did not register significant results in encouraging the public debate on issues of journalistic ethics and professional standards.

Several journalistic unions were established, but they failed to defend basic professional rights and responsibilities. The activities of the civil society structures and professional organizations proved insufficient as well. Deprofessionalization and tabloidization trends accompanied the transformation period. Similar to the politicians, former and newly hatched, journalists were not ready to fully shoulder their new role and the subsequent responsibilities of a Fourth Estate in a society under transformation.

Although, according to the Reporters Without Borders third annual report, Bulgaria occupied the 36th place (among 167 countries in the world) in the freedom of expression index, freedom of speech and independent journalism provided convertible phraseology for many a non-governmental organization disbursing the funds of European and transatlantic institutions (Third Annual Worldwide Press Freedom Index 2006). Their activities, though, proved erratic, limited and ineffective in the long run. Thus, in the 2007 Reporters Without Borders annual report Bulgaria had dropped down to the 51st place (among 169 countries in the world) in the freedom of expression index. The report noted that '[a]ll of the European Union member countries made it into the top 50 except Bulgaria (51st) and Poland (56th). In Sofia, journalists can be physically attacked because of their work. The climate got even worse after charges were withdrawn against police officers who beat up a journalist in May' (Worldwide Press Freedom Index 2007).

While there is no law that regulates the print media in Bulgaria (slander and libel are enacted through the Penal Code), electronic media are regulated under the Radio and Television Act, adopted in 1998, and the Telecommunications Act, adopted the same year. Both of them have been amended frequently. Bulgaria joined the Television Without Frontiers Directive (1989) and later ratified the European Union's Convention on Transfrontier Television (1997). Current media regulations have been closely aligned with EU legislation.

Print media

The Bulgarian press dates back to 1844 when the country was still under Ottoman domination. Between then and World War II, the Bulgarian press went through a number of changes similar to that of other Balkan countries. After the establishment of the Eastern Bloc in the late 1940s, however, mass media developed along the lines of the party-state system. Censoring by the Party prompted the development of self-censorship in journalism. The lack of information and manipulation of the news, along with the absence of an alternative press, resulted in newspapers and magazines of marginal value.

Many challenges were encountered in the process of establishing the new press. By the early 1990s, state ownership of newspapers and magazines was abandoned and the first opposition daily newspapers *Svoboden Narod* [Free People] and *Demokratzia* [Democracy] appeared. In the post-1989 years many new publications came and went. The absence of any mass media regulations led to a boom in pornographic publications, virtually unheard of before 1989. Prices of newspapers soared in step with general inflation, and subscription, as had been the common practice before, was gradually abandoned.

Right after the political changes, extreme media partisanship was developed. Different parties established their own periodicals giving rise to a new, politically affiliated journalism. Newspapers of the then leading political parties became quite popular: *Duma* [Word], which was supported by the Bulgarian Socialist Party and *Democrazia*, the newspaper of the Union of Democratic Forces. The ideological heralds of the various political parties engaged in a newspaper war with no regard for the interests of public welfare. The broader public was often fed tailored information and interpretations. Superfluously, political media outlets seemed to offer an enormous quantity of information, but unfortunately the information was too biased and slanted to provide the reader with a consistent picture of on-going social change. In pursuit of daily stories, such partisanship segmented the audience reach. Thus, the process resulted in a steady decline in newspaper readership.

A wide range of highly varied editions quickly took shape: political, popular, quality, topical, and specialized publications. However, it was discouraging that people began to perceive and assess the processes of change via media models. Without being held politically or socially responsible, the mass media actually shaped the dynamics of public social and political space.

In the meantime, in the process of privatization, powerful forces consolidated the print media. A new press emerged which declared itself politically independent. These periodicals quickly gained the largest audience share. Their content corresponded to the pragmatic needs and attitudes of the economically active part of the general audience. They adopted a new, popular pattern of graphic layout styles in tabloid format, news presentation and new language and syntax, close to the everyday speech of the readers. These newspapers took over the expanding volume of advertising.

However, the general low credibility of the politically based and sensational independent tabloids posed a problem for trustworthy information sources. Newspaper readers lacked higher quality press – the serious broadsheets, presenting unvarnished hard news, interpretive and opinion journalism; a press which does not blur together the news and the interpretation. The first quality dailies, Continent and Pari [Money] were established in 1992, followed in 1993 by Cash and Capital. The general public, however, enjoyed the simple, hard and even sensational practices of the popular press. The quality press was not considered a serious competitive threat to the large-circulation papers, and therefore, it was difficult for it to gain regular, consistent readership.

Another group of independent publications encompassed a broad diversity of topically specialized periodicals; leisure, culture, fashion, feminine issues, health care, religion, entertainment, sports, eroticism, hobbies and so on. Today, most of them have a low circulation; some enjoy professional design and original content. The same holds true for the periodicals aimed at age and gender. World renowned titles, such as National Geographic, Business Week, Cosmopolitan, Playboy, are published in their Bulgarian version. Also, a special group of publications was established to target foreign information consumers with periodicals issued in English, French, German, Russian and Turkish.

Given the fact that the web versions of the printed periodicals are created mainly as a supplementary source of information, their layout is still simple, unsophisticated, and focused on the core information. Nevertheless, they enjoy a slow, but steadily growing readership.

Several main press groups were founded by professionals close to private banks, insurance companies, political and trade union establishments, thus starting the concentration process. The rigorously developing media market attracted foreign investors. In 1997, the German Westdeutsche Allgemeine Zeitung (WAZ) bought controlling interest in the two leading newspaper groups in Bulgaria: 168 Chassa and Media Holding.

The monopolist position of the state-owned Bulgarian Telegraph Agency (established in 1892) was broken by new private press agencies, such as Balkan Agency, BGNES and online agencies.

Currently, the public enjoys a rich print media milieu including 446 newspapers (63 dailies) with an annual circulation of 325,733,100 and 778 magazines and bulletins with annual circulation of 22,158,900 (NSI 2008a). The two dailies with largest circulation are Trud [Labor] and 24 Chassa [24 Hours], both owned by WAZ.

Professional development was encouraged by national nominations for high journalistic accomplishment. The annual ratings of the top newspapers in Bulgaria became a telling indicator of public and professional evaluations, as well as a significant index for the advertisers. Over 90 print media are represented by 28 members in the The Union of Publishers in Bulgaria (2000) – an independent, non-governmental association united by the principles of defending the freedom of the press, the independence of journalists and the encouragement of their work so that society is objectively informed. The Union of Publishers in Bulgaria is a member of the World Association of Newspapers (WAN) and of the European Newspaper Publishers' Association (ENPA) (The Union of Publishers in Bulgaria 2008).

The process of forming an independent, diversified and pluralistic press in Bulgaria after the political changes of 1989 demonstrates the following trends:

■ *Privatization* leading to establishment of a print media market at national, local and international levels.
■ *Proliferation* of press, accompanied by concentration of ownership.
■ *Diversification* of political, popular, quality and topical periodicals.
■ *Introduction* of new styles, formats and standards.
■ *Establishment* of Internet versions of the newspaper content.

Broadcasting media

In contrast to the turbulent transformation in the press, the changes in the broadcasting media were slower, incomplete and lacked general consistency. They started and were carried out in an atmosphere of deregulation – the Radio and Television Act was adopted only in 1998 (RTA 1998).

The new Bulgarian Constitution adopted on 12 July 1991, was the first legislative act that abolished the party-state monopoly in electronic media. Thus, along with the other East European countries, Bulgaria moved to regulate the licensing of private radio and TV stations. At first, The Parliamentary Commission for Radio and Television and the Provisional Council for Radio and Television became the controlling body of radio and television structure and functioning.

Although the former structures of the party-state in the state-owned electronic media were abandoned, the executive boards continued to be open to direct political pressure, causing overall personnel instability and a lack of continuity in programming policy. Problems regarding freedom of expression, agenda-setting issues, and journalistic investigative reporting gave rise to conflicts between professional managers and bureaucrats.

Nowadays, the two national institutions that regulate the electronic media are the Council for Electronic Media (CEM) and the Communications Regulation Commission (CRC). They issue radio and TV licenses and register cable and satellite broadcasters. CEM (formerly The National Council for Radio and Television) is the regulatory body that monitors compliance with the Radio and Television Act, including issues such as advertising, sponsorship, copyright and protection of minors. The Council also considers complaints by citizens and organizations. CRC (formerly The State Commission of Telecommunications) manages the radio spectrum. It also enforces the Electronic Communications Act, adopted in 2007, which lays the legal basis for the digital switchover (ECA 2007).

Radio

Radio broadcasting in Bulgaria was a state monopoly right from the very beginning of its existence in 1932. Until 1991 there was only one, Sofia-based, central broadcasting station (operating four channels) and five regional stations. The liberalization of radio broadcasting was a much slower process than that of the print media.

The liberalized rules for licensing of local radio and television stations stimulated a rapid development of private radio (Ordinance No 1 of the Committee for Postal Services and Telecommunications 1992). The first licenses for private radio stations were issued to several foreign radio broadcasters: Voice of America, BBC-World Service, Free Europe, France International, and Deutsche Welle. They were selected because of their sensitivity to the democratization process in Bulgaria. The first domestic private radio station, FM+, went on the air in October 1992. The first and the only license for a private radio broadcasting on a national level was issued in 1993 to Darik Radio. The new radio stations developed more flexible and attractive formats and styles, targeting different audience niches. They quickly gained popularity. The necessary conditions (financial, technological and personnel) for differentiation of the private broadcasting on a national scale were at hand. Nevertheless, the state-owned and operated radio network still holds a commanding lead in audience share.

Several telling trends in radio programme dynamics could be discerned during this period of transition. Radio broadcasting had displayed an enormous increase. In 1988, prior to the political changes, some 46,810 hours of programming were aired. In 1989 the number had increased to 48,498 hours; in 1993 the inclusion of private radio bounced the total number of on-air hours to 161,278. By 2006 the public was enjoying 591,834 hours of programming, more than twelve times the number of hours broadcast in 1988 (NSI 2008b). Programme supply had been strongly diversified. The local radio stations had developed a clear-cut public profile as well as introduced technological innovations, such as computer-run, RDS and online versions of the regular radio programmes. The introduction of new styles, formats and standards lead to steady segmentation of radio audiences. Foreign investments shaped the strongly developing concentration trends.

Television
Telecasts in Bulgaria first started in 1959 with three hours' programming twice a week. It took about ten years before the whole country was covered by a TV signal. Colour telecasting was introduced in 1972 and in 1975 a second national channel was launched. For years Soviet Television was retranslated and run on Fridays in place of the First National Channel. A correspondent's bureau in Moscow selected, translated and dubbed Soviet TV programmes. It also produced original programmes in Bulgarian.

In the mid-1970s a network of four local TV stations was established. County correspondents provided films and videotapes with local news. The TV news service was backed by foreign correspondents working in Berlin, Paris, Warsaw, Prague, the Middle East and Japan. Most of the foreign news coverage was supplied by Intervision (the former international TV organization of socialist countries) and Eurovision.

Compared to the other media, changes in television came much more slowly. Some major reasons for that included the state monopoly over national telecasting, political pressures resulting in frequent replacements of TV executives (in seventeen years, fourteen General Directors in succession headed the National Television), lack of research and development concepts and strategies, inefficient management, economic constraints and obsolete equipment.

If 1994 is remarkable for the development of the TV market, it is also regarded as a landmark in the liberalization of telecasts in Bulgaria.

The first private television station broadcasting locally, Nova Televizia (New Television) was launched in 1994. Because of the lack of financial, technological and personnel resources, it was limited to modest programming – primarily movies and imported popular entertainment programmes. The opening of the 7Dni (7 days) local TV station in 1995 signalled the beginning of competition in telecasting in Sofia. In December 1999 Rupert Murdoch's Balkan News Corporation was the successful bidder to become the first private TV operator functioning on a national scale. The emergence of alternative television encouraged programme diversification on the national TV landscape. Meanwhile, the almost uncontrolled reception of satellite, transborder and cable programmes exerted significant pressure on the domestic channels. Infiltration of foreign audio-visual products had an equally strong impact on national broadcasting policies.

The privately owned TV stations undoubtedly challenged the monopoly of the state-owned TV. A diverse TV market was gradually established in the country. Thus, recently bTV has taken the lead in audience share from BNT in a country where 98 per cent of households have a television set. According to June 2007 statistics, the national audience of bTV is 94.7 per cent; the corresponding numbers for Nova TV (the second private TV channel, broadcasting on a national scale) are 85.1 per cent and 81.6 per cent for Bulgarian National Television – Channel 1 (the public service broadcaster) (Alpha Research 2007). The same order is valid for the advertising revenues of the three broadcasters. However, the public service broadcasters still enjoy the highest audience credibility: BNT is approved by three-quarters of the population and BNR by two-thirds, compared to other institutions such as the police with 49 per cent and the army with 50 per cent (NCPO 2006). So far no tenders for analogue licensing of on-air TV broadcasters have been held in the country.

In 2007, following the Regional Telecommunications Conference RRC-06, the State Agency for Information Technologies and Communications completed a 'Plan for Introduction of Terrestrial Digital TV Broadcasting (DVB-T) in the Republic of Bulgaria'.

Currently, digital television in Bulgaria is offered via the following technologies:

- DVB-Terrestrial: experimental for the area of the capital city of Sofia.
- DVB-Satellite: by two major operators.
- DVB-Cable: provided by about 10 per cent of the registered cable operators for their subscribers with free-of-charge set top boxes for the contracted period.

The market of digital terrestrial, cable and satellite audio and video broadcasting in Bulgaria is liberalized but, nevertheless, no major progress has been marked in the development of terrestrial DAB and DVB.

Several important trends accompany the TV programme dynamics. TV broadcasting had displayed a significant increase. In 1988, prior to the political changes, 5,886 hours of TV programming were aired. A dramatic growth of 500 hours of telecasts was registered during the critical year of 1989. By 1994, when private television was officially introduced, audiences enjoyed 7,178 hours of TV programming, while in 2006 the number of hours reached 599,135 – more than a tenfold increase (NSI 2008c). The diversified programme supply encouraged higher audience selectivity. Digitizing, mobile- and web casting are the current technological challenges to the Bulgarian broadcasters.

In nearly nineteen years a highly saturated radio and TV landscape has been formed. In 2007 a total of 211 television and 154 radio channels were licensed or registered for delivery to the population by terrestrial broadcasting, by cable or via satellite.

The television market includes three national TV channels: BNT – the public service television broadcaster and the two commercial television stations: bTV, licensed in 2000 and owned by Rupert Murdoch's Balkan News Corporation and Nova Televisia, licensed in 2002 and owned by the Greek Antenna Group. Two national radio stations broadcast on-air: BNR – the public service broadcaster and the commercial Darik radio. All five of these national broadcasters are members of the Union of Bulgarian National Electronic Media (2005) – an independent non-government association, unified by the principles related to the assertion of the freedom of speech, the independence of journalists, and the promotion of their creative work aiming to provide objective information to the public.

The programmes of national channels and of other channels are additionally distributed by more than 1,800 cable networks and more than 23 nationwide satellite networks (Current Developments of Radio and Television Activities in Bulgaria 2007).

As of April 2007, over 160 radio and TV stations are members of the Association of Bulgarian Broadcasters (ABBRO), founded in 1997 as a voluntary, independent, non-political and non-profit organization, representing the broadcast industry in Bulgaria (ABBRO 2008).

The current radio- and TV landscape can be described with some important features:

- An established set of *legal regulations*.
- *Fundamental restructuring* of radio and TV systems at local, national and international levels.
- Establishment of *electronic media market* at national and local levels.
- *Segmentation of radio and TV audiences*, striving for a higher degree of credibility.
- *Introduction of new styles, formats and standards*, broadly using the new information technologies.
- Transfer to *digitalization*.

Online Media

The advent of new information technologies strongly influenced the media production cycle. The Internet was officially introduced in Bulgaria in 1997 and its market has expanded at encouraging rates ever since. Access to the Internet is provided mainly via telephone (dial-up) and via cable by specialized providers or as an additional service by the cable television operators. Satellite Internet is practically unused by end users. The Internet penetration in Bulgaria remains relatively low for private households – 19.0 per cent, compared to business companies – 88.1 per cent (NSI 2008d).

The use of new technologies is increasingly regarded as the key survival factor in an overcrowded media space. The newspapers with highest circulation maintain online editions, but some of the online versions require paid access: 24 Chassa (www.24chassa.bg), Trud (www.trud.bg), Standart News (www.standartnews.com), Monitor (www.zone168.com), and Sega Daily (www.segabg.com). National news agencies and broadcast media have also entered the online world: the Bulgarian Telegraph Agency (www.bta.bg), Bulgarian National Television (www.bnt.bg), bTV (www.btv.bg/home/), Nova TV (www.ntv.bg), Bulgarian National Radio (www.nationalradio.bg) and Darik Radio (www.netissat.bg/). Several web-based media exist: www.Mediapool.bg, www.novinite.com, www.news.bg and so on. A steady tendency towards increasing quantity and quality of electronic information and media sites has been observed.

In addition to traditional media and online-only news sites, some citizen-generated content has entered the World Wide Web. The Internet is beginning to be used for so-called 'citizens' journalism'. Even though this is a relatively new phenomenon, blogs on different social and political issues have multiplied. Another interesting phenomenon is a group of websites designed to facilitate public debate, where members of the public can write a story on a social, political or economic topic. These articles are published after approval of the site's staff and its most active users. A telling example of this is http://www.newsfactory.org/.

The increasing popularity of the Internet has definitely impacted the media system status quo. However, the online media business model is still problematic. The combination of content sales, subscription fees and advertising revenues can not bring sufficient income to assure content variety for attracting bigger audiences. Searching for their identity in the transforming social and market environment, the online and traditional media are serving more eagerly to advertisers rather than audiences.

Conclusion

Several main trends in the mass media development accompanied the democratization processes in Bulgaria:

- *Politically*, decentralization of the mass media system accompanied by the emergence of a pluralistic press and commercial broadcasters.
- *Legally*, liberalization and regulation of the mass media system, increasingly harmonizing with the mass media regulations in the European Union.
- *Technologically*, introduction of new information technologies in mass media production and dissemination.
- *Economically*, mass media market development in a highly competitive environment at local, regional and national levels.
- *Socially*, fragmentation of the audiences accompanied by higher selectivity standards and better social feedback.
- *Professionally*, departure from former media standards and introduction of new formats, styles and liberal journalistic ethics.

The growing roles of the mass media in the period of transition to democracy and market place economy have changed the status, rights and responsibilities of media professionals. The mass media power has become increasingly viable in social life. The changes have provided journalists with a strong hold on public opinion. Thus, the mass media system often operates as a Fourth Estate, influencing social attitudes, political opinions and decision-making on national priorities.

Note

1. The topic has been analyzed by the author in the following publications: *Television in Bulgaria on the Net*. A chapter in Nikos Leandros (ed.), *The Impact of Internet on the Mass Media in Europe* (2006), Bury St. Edmunds, Suffolk (UK and USA): Abramis, pp. 503–13; *Fifteen Years of Televised Political Advertising in Bulgaria*. A chapter in Lynda Lee Kaid & Christina Holtz-Bacha (eds.), *The Sage Handbook of Political Advertising* (2006), Thousand Oaks (Ca), USA: Sage Publications,

pp. 359–75; *Bulgaria: The Online Mirror Image of the Printed Newspapers*. A chapter in Richard van der Wurft & Edmund Laut (eds.), *Print and Online Newspapers in Europe. A Comparative Analysis in 16 countries* (2005), Amsterdam (The Netherlands): Her Sprinhuis Publishers, pp. 67–78; *Mass Media's Changing Landscape in Bulgaria*. Co-authored with Todor Petev. A chapter in David Paletz and Karol Jakubowicz (eds.), *Business as Usual. Continuity and Change in Central and Eastern Europe* (2003), Cresskill, New Jersey USA: Hampton Press, Inc., pp. 73–109; *Mass Media in Bulgaria. A Source Book* (2003), Dortmund: ENTIRE – Working Papers in International Journalism, p. 44; *The Challenges of Internet Media to Traditional Media System in Bulgaria*. A chapter in *Towards New Media Paradigms: Content, Producers, Organisations and Audiences* (2003), Pamplona (Spain), pp. 531–45; *Mass Media System in Bulgaria (1989-9)*. Co-authored with Todor Petev. (In English) A chapter in *The Global Network* (2000), Bucharest: No 13, pp. 7–17; *The Dynamics of the Electronic Mass Media System in Bulgaria (1989-9)*. A chapter in *The Global Network* (2000), Bucharest: No 13, pp. 37–57; *The Impact of Television on the Democratization Processes*. A chapter in Newman, B. (ed.), *Handbook of Political Marketing* (1999). Thousand Oaks, London, New Delhi: Sage Publications, pp. 485–505; *Turn-of-the-Century Challenges Facing the Mass Media in Bulgaria. Media Development* (1999), No 3, pp. 9–13; *Development of Alternative Broadcasting in Bulgaria*. A chapter in *Drustvo I Tehnologija'96* (1996). Rijeka, Croatia, pp. 154–61; *Mass Communication in Bulgaria during the Transitional Period (1989–93) – Points of Research*. A chapter in *Researching (Investigative) Journalism: A New Model for Public Communication* (1995), Zagreb: Croatian Communicologists Association, Nonacom, pp. 36–42.

References

Alpha Research (2007), 'TV Channels Rate: June 2007', http://www.aresearch.org/major_tv_channels.html. Accessed 10 August 2007.

Association of Bulgarian Broadcasters (ABBRO) (2008), http://www.abbro-bg.org/en/index.php. Accessed 22 April 2008.

Constitution of the Republic of Bulgaria (1991), http://www.Parliament.bg/?page=const&lng=en. Accessed 10 August 2007.

Current Developments of Radio and Television Activities in Bulgaria (2007), Sofia, Bulgaria: Council for Electronic Media Bulletin, No 5, 1–2.

Electronic Communications Act (ECA) (2007), http://www.crc.bg/v1/bul/index.htm. Accessed 10 August 2007.

Ethical Code of Bulgarian Media (2004), http://btv.bg/news/?magic=et_code_en. Accessed 10 August 2007.

National Centre for Public Opinion (NCPO) (2006), http://www.parliament.bg/?page=ns&lng=bg&nsid=9&aid=15. Accessed 31 January 2007.

National Council for Journalism Ethics (2004), 'Ethical Code and Ethics Councils', http://www.mediaethics-bg.org/?lan=EN2. Accessed 9 April 2007.

National Statistical Institute (NSI) (2008a), 'Publishing Activity', http://www.nsi.bg/SocialActivities_e/Culture_e.htm. Accessed 22 April 2008.

National Statistical Institute (NSI) (2008b), 'Radio Programme Activity', http://www.nsi.bg/SocialActivities/Culture.htm. Accessed 22 April 2008.

National Statistical Institute (NSI) (2008c), 'Television Programme Activity', http://www.nsi.bg/SocialActivities/Culture.htm. Accessed 22 April 2008.

National Statistical Institute (NSI) (2008d), 'Information Society', http://www.nsi.bg/IKT/IKT.htm. Accessed 22 April 2008.

Ordinance No 1 of the Committee for Postal Services and Telecommunications (June 18, 1992), Sofia: State Newspaper, p. 43.

Radio and Television Act (RTA) (1998), http://www.cem.bg/r.php?sitemap_id=142. Accessed 10 August 2007.

Reporters Without Borders (2006), Third Annual Worldwide Press Freedom Index http://www.rsf.org/article.php3?id_article=11715. Accessed 31 January 2007.

Reporters Without Borders (2007), Worldwide Press Freedom Index http://www.rsf.org/article.php3?id_article=24025. Accessed 31 January 2007.

The Union of Publishers in Bulgaria (2008), http://www.sib.bg/about.html. Accessed 22 April 2008.

Press Freedom and Media Pluralism in Romania: Facts, Myths and Paradoxes

Mihai Coman

The legal framework[1]

The Constitution

Two of the 152 articles of the Romanian Constitution directly address freedom of expression (Article 30) and the right of Romanian citizens to information (Article 31). The Romanian Constitution guarantees freedom of expression (Section 2, Chapter 2, Article 30) in 'The Fundamental Rights and Freedoms of the People' (see Camera Deputatilor 2007) which mandates that:

1. Freedom of expression, of thoughts, opinions, or beliefs, and freedom of any creation, by words, in writing, in pictures, by sounds or other means of public communication are inviolable.
2. Any censorship shall be prohibited.
3. Freedom of the press also involves the freedom to establish publications.
4. No publications may be suppressed.
5. The law may impose upon the mass media the obligation to make public their source of financing.
6. Freedom of expression shall not be prejudicial to the dignity, honour, and privacy of a person, and the right to one's own image.
7. Any defamation of the country and the nation, any instigation to a war of aggression, to national, racial, class or religious hatred, any incitement to discrimination, territorial separatism, or public violence, as well as any obscene conduct contrary to morality shall be prohibited by law.
8. Civil liability for any information or creation made public falls upon the publisher or producer, the author, the producer of the artistic performance, the owner of the copying

facilities, radio or television station, under the terms laid down by law. The law shall establish the indictable offences of the press.

Romania's post-communist media function within a legal framework that is defined by the audio-visual law, the public radio and television law, and the Penal Code, which addresses defamation, insults, false information and other real and imagined harms to individuals, the state, the government and their institutions. Furthermore, this legal framework includes dubious access to information laws and a copyright law, which elicited passionate debate before it was enacted in 1996. The law was modified in September 2005 by the government and was accepted by the Parliament in 2006. What is absent from the post-communist panoply of laws is a press law.

The access to information law
A law concerning classified information was passed by the Parliament in 2001, but rejected by the Constitutional Court in April 2001. Prime Minister Adrian Nastase called for EU arbitration on this law. The heated debates in Parliament over the proposed law continued several years. The problem, it seemed, was that the law had a very wide and vague definition of 'state secrets', in contradiction to international democratic standards. The proposed law provided no protection for journalists and did not make any provisions for state secrets that passed into the public domain, for example. The lack of clarity and accuracy, it was feared, would mean that the restrictions on freedom of expression and of the press could be used to protect interests that were purely political and not public or state interests. Finally 'The Law on Access to Public Interest Information' was accepted by the Parliament in 2006 (Media Monitoring Agency 2007).

The law concerning the Romanian press agency
In 2001, the Romanian Parliament promoted a law addressing the status of the national press agency, Rompres. Midyear, a government decision attempted to place the agency under the control of the Ministry of Public Information. In the wake of protests by journalists, however, the Parliament decided to create a specific law, Law 19/2003 (regarding the organization and the functioning of the National Press Agency/Rompres), that placed Rompres under parliamentary control. In May 2007, a new project was launched for the debate in the Parliament.

The audio-visual law
Romania's Audio-Visual Law, signed into law by the Romanian president on 20 May 1992, was the second such law to be enacted in post-communist East-Central Europe. The law outlined the parameters for the distribution and awarding of licences to private radio and television stations, established the National Audio-Visual Council (CNA), and regulated the functioning of public radio and television stations. The CNA, made up of eleven members appointed by the government, the Romanian president and by parliament, has engendered continuous controversy since its establishment, being seen as another avenue for politicians to attempt to control the broadcast media. The Audio-Visual Law forbids the assigning of broadcast licences to 'political parties or other political formations' or to 'public authorities' (Article 6, Paragraph 4) and calls for 'pluralism of opinions, equality of the participants' treatment, and the quality

and diversity of programmes' to be the basis for deciding who gets a licence (Article 12, Paragraph 4). The law also explicitly states:

> No public or private, natural or legal person shall be a direct or indirect majority investor or shareholder in more than one audio-visual communication company, and he/she shall not hold more than twenty per cent of the registered capital in other similar companies. (Article 6, Paragraph 1)

Furthermore, while allowing for foreign capital investments, inclusive of cable, the ownership of broadcast media has to be Romanian (Article 5, Paragraph 2 and 3; Article 7).

A new Audio-Visual Law enacted in 2002 and modelled after analogous European laws, relieved the CNA of the responsibility of assigning broadcast frequencies by establishing a new independent body, in charge of the technical issues (including frequency release). The law also introduced a unique provision for measuring radio and TV audiences, free of charge, for official use; the results of these surveys/polls are to be the basis for limitations on the maximum market share for broadcasters (30 per cent of the market at the national level, applicable to private broadcasters; 25 per cent at the regional or local levels, in order to avoid the control on the market by an individual owner or a media trust). Public tenders decide on the survey companies designated to measure the market shares for a period of four years, by means of a commission made up of five representatives of the Council, five from the audio-visual companies and five from advertising agencies.

Meanwhile, the audio-visual laws were trying to offer a solution for a paradoxical process: 're-regulate the media system in accordance with the new principles of a free market economy and political pluralism; de-regulate it in order to fit Western European trends' (Marinescu 2001: 84). In this respect, the indigenous legislative system and the evolution of the audio-visual phenomenon met both with 're-nationalization' and 'de-nationalization and privatization', phenomena considered by various analysts of post-communism as major trends during this period (Sparks and Reading 1998; Splichal 2001; Gross 2002). The preoccupation with a legislative solution for the relationship between the public and the commercial systems in the audio-visual area correlated with the failure to push a press law through Parliament and led to a special situation: the audio-visual is strictly regulated, while the written press is not restricted by a specific legal framework and functions according to 'permissive' rules.

In 2003, Romania ratified 'The European Convention on Transfrontier Television', making its provisions mandatory for public television.

The public radio and television law
Economic, political and even technical pressures demanded the rapid enactment of laws addressing commercial/private broadcasting. Only two years after the Audio-Visual Law had been accepted by the Parliament, 'The Law Concerning the Organization and Functioning of the Romanian Radio Society and the Romanian Television Society' was signed into law by President Ion Iliescu on 18 June 1994.

Romania's public radio and television are wrestling with the same problems that their brethren in the other post-Communist societies are facing. The public service institutions inhabit a nebulous space between the public and the state sphere, and enjoy only limited freedoms.

They are caught between the control and pressures exerted by the political institutions and the journalistic responsibility toward their public that is idealistically defined in their mandates. Ironically, in the strange twists of the transformation that is still in full swing, the regulations governing public broadcasting guarantee the right to correction and reply, whereas the commercial press and broadcast media are under no such legal obligations.

Defamation (libel and slander) and insults
In 1991, the Penal Code articles addressing defamation were 'changed only slightly to eliminate some of the more egregious communist-inspired elements' (Gross 1996: 82). After prolonged public debate, the Romanian Parliament made additional, major, revisions to the Penal Code, which retained articles that address defamation, insults and insults against individuals, particularly against government officials and parliamentarians. The provisions of the 1996 Penal Code, in a spirit reminiscent of the communist era, called for increased punishment of infractions committed through or by the mass media.

Journalists, representatives of Romanian civil society, and foreign journalism organizations have demanded that insult, slander and offence be treated as misdemeanours, not crimes. In 1998, following a proposal made by the Minister of Justice, a government order was issued to substitute the penal procedure with a civil one based on the payment of moral damages. However, it was vehemently attacked by the press because the amount of fines was very high: Journalists argued that it would be easier for a Court to pass a civil sentence against a journalist and that they would never have the resources to pay them. The project was withdrawn at the last minute to be replaced by a government decision concerning exemptions from judicial fees for certain legal processes, including those referring to defamation. This simply means that a new way of intimidating journalists was instituted, making it furthermore possible for a plaintiff to sue them in the civil court where damages ruinous to a journalist and a media outlet could be claimed. It generated numerous lawsuits, although there are no official statistics on the number of lawsuits and subsequent sentences. According to sources close to the Ministry of Justice, 400 defamation, offence and insult suits were initiated between 1996 and 2001. According to the Freedom of Expression (2007), the tabloid *Evenimentul Zilei* was hauled into court 318 times between 1997 and 2001; the daily *Ziua* was involved in 300 lawsuits and the daily *Adevarul* in 60.

The new draft of the Code was discussed with both civil society and the media community, and some important changes are being proposed. The amendments voted by the Parliaments in 2006 decriminalized insult, defamation and calumny; insults were no longer to be considered under criminal law, defamation was no longer to be punished with a prison sentence and the existing provisions regarding offence to state and nation, public officials and national symbols were to be dropped. Also noteworthy is that a journalist's defence against defamation was the notion of good faith, that is, that he/she had reasonable grounds to consider what is published to be true. However, in January 2007, the Constitutional Court rejected these changes and declared them to be 'unconstitutional'.

Other provisions of The Penal Code may affect the journalists' activities: (1) violation of privacy, interpreted to apply to entering public institutions (Article 276), (2) spreading false information that may start a war (Article 276); (3) hostile activities against another state that is a member of the North Atlantic Treaty Organization (NATO) and the European Union (EU)

(Article 279), (4) crimes against the dignity of people who enjoy international protection (for example, denying the Holocaust) (Article 280).

The numerous confrontations related to the Penal Code, both in Parliament and in the courts, reveal a paradoxical truth: when it comes to the battle against freedom of the press, the political class, whether on the right or left, in power or in opposition, bands together to maintain legal provisions perceived to benefit the political class. Investigative journalism can thus be curbed or minimized, either by harsh punishment mandated by law or just by the threat of such punishment.[2]

Professional body and self regulation mechanisms

Immediately after the fall of the communist regime, the number of journalists increased spectacularly: in 1989 there were 2,060 persons accredited as journalists and by 1992 The Romanian Society of Journalists' membership list, which did not include all journalists in the country, included 6,909 names; by 2000, there were an estimated 20,000 journalists (Petcu 2000: 20–1). This large professional group turns out to be generally heterogeneous in social origin, education, political beliefs and professional performance; between the dilettantism and quasi-professionalism exhibited by the journalists, the journalism practised is diverse, to say the least. The mechanism by which journalists are employed, the procedures for firing or promoting a journalist are not subject to transparent regulations; neither the professional associations nor media management did anything to institutionalize the mechanisms of access to or exclusion from journalism. There is no licensing requirement for journalists in Romania, a fact that is not surprising given the communist experience, and the membership in professional associations is not subject to actual journalistic work but is open to everybody interested.

Meanwhile various associations of owners have been established: the Association of Local Media Owners, the Association of Romanian Broadcasters (ARCA), the Association of Local Print Distributors, and the Romanian Press Club. The most active among these is the Romanian Press Club, which lobbies for owners' interests and attacks the Government every time a financial decision affects their interest, which also includes that of media leaders and journalists-managers. Professional associations are weak and display ambiguous missions: The Society of Journalists of Romania and the Association of Journalists of Romania functioned in the 1990s like unions and professional associations; the Union of Journalists of Romania, conceptualized as a trade union, did not arouse the interest of journalists and did not assert itself through any major union action; the numerous associations in the field (of journalists in sports, environment, tourism, photographers and so on) or of ethnic identity (of the ethnic Hungarian or German journalists) did not generate debates and neither did they produce any actions with a significant impact on the mass media. The Federation of Trade Unions of Journalists and Printers (see MediaSind 2007) was created in 2003; they claim to include 8,000 journalists. Starting in 2004, it has negotiated each year with the Association of Owners from Romania and press moguls a National Collective Labour Contract that formally guarantees the basic rights of journalists. When compared to other professions or occupations, journalism is characterized by a lack of solidarity; the ignoring of common professional interests can only be explained by the absence of an awareness of the joint objectives, of the adoption of a corporatist identity and especially of an inadequate professional culture.

Several attempts at establishing credible codes of ethics have been made public since 1989 – The Ethical Code of the Journalist, The Ethical Code of the National Radio and Television, The Ethical Code of the Romanian Press Club – but there is no sign that the provisions of these codes have been accepted, internalized, or respected by journalists or by editors. It is obvious that in such a fragmented environment there could be no homogeneous efforts or generally accepted codes of ethics; moreover, a common Code of Ethics would have increased the rights of journalists and would have reduced the capacity of control of the owners and managers.

In the first years of the twenty-first century, the profession has become increasingly split between the conception and practice of the media barons and that of the great mass of journalists. The euphoria and solidarity that marked the first moments of media freedom gradually disappeared and were replaced by battles to impose and assure control over resources – material, power and prestige – offered by the mass media system. The great majority of journalists came to depend on the decisions of the group of leaders without being protected by coherent legislation, professional rules, powerful associations and unions, or by cultural traditions that reinforce the respect for professional competencies. Most shocking is that the majority of those who have leadership positions – owners, majority shareholders, media managers – do not have a discourse that is consistent with the positions and strategies that they impose, with the values of a professional community, centred on the idea of belonging to this community and sharing its interests and ideals. In such circumstances, the concept of 'the freedom of the press' is very often used as just a slogan, behind which other interests are hiding.

Media landscape

The immediate post-communist evolution of the media is characterized by a rapid and chaotic increase in publications and circulations, in number of stations and audiences, followed by a slow stabilization from a quantitative point of view (the number of mass-media institutions) and from the qualitative point of view (clarifying the system of financing, defining the target audiences, separating the contents, organizing the editorial staff and making efforts to transform the journalists into professionals).

In the printed press, even though the number of titles grew, circulation dropped precipitously and has not rebounded to the levels held during the first few years of the post-communist era; by 2005 official data indicate a decrease in the number of dailies, and an upward development of magazines, testimony to a more specialized print media landscape that is still in flux (see Coman 2004; Coman and Gross 2006; Petcu 2000).

The local press also grew in numbers and circulation: 2,827 new local publications were launched after 1989, and of those, 400 were general interest publications. The ethnic minority

Table 1: Number of dailies and magazines in Romania 1989–2005.

	1989	1990	1993	1996	1999	2002	2005
Dailies	36	65	100	106	118	94	80
Magazines	459	1,379	987	1,313	1,868	1,853	2,044

Source: National Institute of Statistics 2006.

press in Romania followed the same pattern as the vernacular press, showing a rollercoaster evolution. The Romanian Statistical Yearbook (2004) reported 52 publications (eleven dailies and 41 magazines) in 1989 and 131 in 2005 (seven dailies and 124 magazines).

In 1989 the Romanian Radio Society broadcast 30,148 hours, by 1990 it reached 52,309 hours and 118,619 hours in 2002 (National Institute of Statistics 2006); it broadcasts on five channels: România Actualități (news), Radio Cultural and Radio Muzical (classical music) and Radio Tineret (youth), Antena satelor (rural programming, covers half of the southern part of the country) plus an international station; it has six territorial studios and had 2,301 employees in 2004. The dynamic of the private FM and AM broadcast stations is as follows:

Table 2: Number of private radio stations in Romania 1993–2006.

	1993	1996	1999	2002	2006
Radio stations	4	136	199	277	443

Source: National Institute of Statistics 2006.

The number of broadcast hours per one year grew from 96,033 in 1999 to 118,619 for the public radio and from 1,497,000 in 1999 to 1,585,875 in 2002 for the private stations (no data after 2002).

Public television, which in 1989 broadcast only 1,795 hours, gradually reached 8,541 hours in 1990, 9,997 hours in 1993, 13,095 hours in 1996, 14,197 hours in 1999, 25,111 hours in 2002 and 35,040 in 2005; it broadcasts on three national channels (the second covering only 60 per cent of the country and the third only 38 per cent), set up an international channel in 1997, and has around 2,700 employees. The number of commercial stations is growing rapidly:

Table 3: Number of commercial stations in Romania 1993–2006.

	1993	1996	1999	2002	2006
Commercial stations	2	53	88	106	158

Source: National Institute of Statistics 2006.

Only a few control the market: PRO-TV, Antena 1, and Prima (they broadcast both by ground and satellite relay and can be received directly with satellite dishes or through cable distributors). In 1999, public television channels broadcast a total of 14,197 hours, while private stations broadcast 512,247; three years later, in 2002 public television broadcast 25,111 hours and private stations 123,020 hours.

The development and growth of cable explains, to a large extent, the growth of commercial television stations in Romania because the small subscription costs have permitted large numbers of people to have access to the programmes offered by indigenous television. At the end of 2004, there were 653 licensed cable distributors. United PanEuropean Communication (UPC), which is part of American Liberty Global, dominated the cable television market with 37.5 per cent of all cable subscribers. Romanian Cable System (RCS) has 29.3 per cent of Romanian subscribers and the rest are divided among the small cable operators (*Ziarul Financiar* 2005).

Economical framework

Post-Communism brought a spontaneous privatization of the communist mass media and a rapid creation of new media enterprises. Control over almost all of the former communist print media – including the ownership of publication titles, facilities and equipment, and staffs – was quickly transferred from the state to private media companies, including domestic or international business groups, professional journalist associations, individual investors, banks and other entities. New print media enterprises were also created. Small local and regional private radio stations also sprouted up all over Romania in the immediate aftermath of communism's demise, operating illegally because the legal mechanisms for licensing them were not yet established. The state maintained its monopoly in the television field until the late 1990s when private, commercial television was, finally, given legal blessings (Coman 2003; Gross 1996). The income of the public radio station, for example, grew from $48.6 million in 1999 to $68.5 million in 2003, and its expenses in the same period went from $46.6 million to 67 million. Its 2003 financial report shows that $49 million came from advertising and $46.6 from the radio tax (*Capital* 2004a). Public television's financial pot grew from $60 million in 1999 to $112 million in 2003, at least $82.9 million of which came from the subscription tax and $9.2 million from advertising (*Capital* 2004b).

Arguably, the dominant media model in Romania is a liberal one. Since 1991, some have argued that the media system is closer to a 'libertarian' than to a liberal one, partly because of some aspects which violate the principles of a market economy: these include a lack of regulations; the race to make profits; political advocacy as the primary role and function; and the renunciation of the elementary responsibilities of the press as these are understood in the West (Gross 1996; O'Neil 1997). On the other hand, it is also argued that the complexity of the social and political transformations, and the manifold possibilities of establishing new media enterprises, resulted in no single media model becoming dominant. Instead, several models were concurrently operative (Aumente et al. 1999: 197; Coman 2003).

The Law on Competition (1996) attempted to regulate the commercial media and the tendencies toward monopolization by creating the Council on Competitiveness, which was to authorize media mergers and acquisitions. Ownership of media outlets is, however, often hidden. The pressure exerted by the Council on Competitiveness for full disclosure of ownership brought some results; Sorin Ovidiu Vantu, for example, one of the most controversial businessmen in Romania, came forward in February 2006 and admitted to being the owner of Realitatea TV, a news TV station that he controlled from behind several 'front-men'. Phantom companies or organizations in Cyprus or other countries are sometimes set up as media owners. Manuela Preoteasa (2004: 405) stated that:

as a rule, Romanian legislation forbids anonymous ownership; every [media] company is obliged to register [the name of the owner] in the Trade Register Office and to communicate changes [in ownership]. In practice, few companies meet this obligation because there are no sanctions in force.

Foreign capital was late in entering the Romanian media field, particularly when compared to Hungary, the Czech Republic and Poland, and was marginal at best when it finally arrived, being most visible in economic press (Ringier), women's press (Burda, Hachette, Ringier, Axel Springer and VNU-Hearst, which became Sanoma-Hearst), and the entertainment press (Gruner & Jahr, Playboy and Hustler). Ringier's history in Romania offers an excellent example of a strong development started after a discrete entrance in the Romanian market: in 1994, it launched the economic weekly *Capital* and its success subsequently led (five years later) to the purchase of the daily *Libertatea*, which was transformed from a newspaper for municipal information into a successful tabloid. Next, Ringier purchased the weekly *Lumea familiar* and the daily *Gazeta sporturilor*, which it sold in 2001 to the Intact group. In addition, it launched the monthlies *Unica* and *Bravo* and the weekly *TV Mania*; in 2003, it purchased the successful daily *Evenimentul zilei* and the sport daily *ProSport*, thus becoming one of the most important players in the Romanian press. According to one of its press releases, in 2004 Ringier earned €36 million, out of a total of €719 million profits in the Romanian press market (Ringier Romania 2007).

The main printed press groups are (by alphabetical order):

- Adevarul (Adevarul – daily, Adevarul economic – magazine).
- ARBO Media (23 local newspapers such as Renasterea Banateana, Crisana, Telegraful, Ziarul de Bacau, Obiectiv and so on, and 9 magazines – including Chip, AutoMotor, Disney, Tom si Jerry).
- Bluelink Comunicazioni/Fulcrum (Ziua, Gardianul – dailies, Averea, Ziua Turistica, Ziua TV – weeklies), plus Splendid Media Zece (Cotidianul, Bucharest Daily News – dailies; Academia Catavencu, Bucataria, Idei in Dialog, Ideal Marriage, Motor, Tabu – magazines).
- Burda (14 magazines – Auto catalog, Ioana, Gradina mea, Locuinta mea, Perfect and so on).
- Jurnalul (Jurnalul Naţional, Gazeta Sporturilor – national dailies; 'Jurnalul de...' – 2 local dailies; 5 local weeklies).
- MediaPro Group (Ziarul Financiar – national daily; Arădeanul, Bănăţeanul, Bihoreanul, Braşoveanul, Clujeanul, Hunedoreanul – local dailies; Acasa Magazin, Madame Figaro, Playboy, PRO TV Magazin, Interioare, Aventuri, Pro-Motor, Geo, Discovery, Cainele meu – magazines).
- Ringier (Libertatea, Evenimentul zilei, Pro-Sport – dailies; Capital, TV Mania, TV Satelit – weeklies; Unica, Bravo, Girl – monthlies).
- RPG (Romanian Publishing Group) – Avantaje, Elle, Viva, Estetica, 20 Ani, Look, Pop-Corn, Deco, Povestea mea, Olivia.
- Sanoma (VNU)-Hearst (Cosmopolitan, Easy PC, Mami, Beau Monde, National Geographic).
- WAZ (Romania Libera – daily; Magazin Internaţional – weekly).

The main Romanian groups in television are:[3]

■ Media PRO International (PRO TV, Acasa TV, MediaPro International, TV Sport, Pro Cinema, as well as 22 local stations; distributed by 416 cable operators; PRO TV reaches 88 per cent of urban households and 70 per cent of total households).
■ Intact (Antena 1, Antena 3, Euphoria, as well as 15 local stations; it is distributed by 350 cable operators; reaches 85 per cent of urban households and 65 per cent of total households).
■ SBS Broadcasting & UPC (Prima, cable network).
■ Bluelink Comunicazioni (Realitatea TV, Money Channel).

As of now, the most important private groups of radios are:

■ Europa FM (44 local stations, covers 85 per cent of the country).
■ PRO FM (15 local stations, 10 affiliated stations).
■ Kiss Radio (former Radio Contact, re-branded in 2003; 33 local stations, 23 affiliated stations).
■ Radio Guerila (former Radio 21, rebranded in 2003: 17 local stations and 6 affiliates).
■ Mix FM (35 stations in 17 towns).

Is media concentration an obstacle for press freedom?

This is not the place for a detailed exposition of the liberal theories which consider the association between freedom of speaking and financial independence of mass media institution as the core of democracy. Essentially, the main idea is that media support democracy by offering access to the public sphere and to the different 'voices' of the society. This means that the variety of media outlets ensures the variety of sources of information and opinions. In a classic text, Jürgen Habermas sustains that modernity brings a radical deformation of the public sphere, with the press integrally monopolizing the public sphere. Thus economical interest becomes the main source of mass media messages' production; the access to a greater and greater public (which has become a consumer), leads to distortion of the messages, adjustment of their content to meet the expectations and psychological level of those huge audiences, and thus a loss of the rational dimension which is typical to the public debates:

> The Big Press is based on the participation changing, for commercial purposes, of the main social classes in public sphere: it offers to the people the simple access to the public sphere. But this enlarged sphere loses its public feature as soon as the available instruments of 'psychological accessibility' could be transformed into a very purpose: sustaining the consumption to that level determined by the market laws. (Habermas 1978: 177)

In these conditions, concentration is a threat to freedom of expression and democracy by the reduction of the number of voices and by the bias of voices. Or in J. Keane's terms, concentration narrows the freedom of the press because it triggers 'access limitations, monopoly and also the restriction of the options number' (2000: 81).

In the period of maximal development of the post-communist press, 'financial independence' did not seem to be an important topic for public debate. Nobody considered such issues as financing sources, production costs, tax payment, unverifiable circulation, and an underdeveloped advertising market to be important in comparison to the spectacular increase in the population's purchasing enthusiasm. After that initial momentum, when the public interest in the press offer diminished, the economical problems became more visible and were transformed into major topics of public debates. Now, the issue of the freedom of the press clears itself and is framed as the subject of press economical liberty (or, from another point of view, the issue of political influence starts to be treated as the issue of political influence by economical control). Two major processes dominate this period: (1) the growth and development of the mass media market; (2) the fight for economical control of mass media trusts.

(1) The media market

During the last few years we have witnessed a paradoxical phenomenon: an increase of the investments in advertising parallel with a decrease in the audience of the major radio and TV stations, as well as of the most important weekly and monthly journals. According to Alfa Cont Mediawatch, advertising expenditure rose from $26.6 million in 1993 to $105.4 million in 1996, $287 million in 1999, $1,064 million in 2002, €1,299 million in 2003, €1,499 in 2004, to €2,827 in 2005. In 2006, advertising revenues were estimated to have increased by 40 per cent (Campaign 2007). The distribution of advertising revenues by medium is as follows:

Table 4: Media spending development – rate card.

1995–2001 m USD; 2001–5 m EURO	TV	Radio	Print	Cinema	Outdoor	Total
1995	24.5	3	5	0.1	2.5	35.1
1996	57.6	4.8	13	0.3	5.6	81.3
1997	73.5	5.5	26	0.5	11.3	116.8
1998	132.2	7	44	1.3	15	199.5
1999	192.8	8.8	63.4	1	19	285
2000	326.3	12.1	105.8	1	30	475.2
2001	481.3	18.8	113.2	1	23.9	638.2
2002	1,044	25	145	1	18.9	1,214
2003	1,299	29	165	No data	No data	1,492
2004	1,799	43	255	No data	No data	2,067
2005	2,554	55	272	No data	No data	2,827

It is obvious that television is the major beneficiary of this advertising expenditure and receives a much greater portion of advertising money than its counterparts in Western European countries. In 1999, television received 61 per cent of the advertising expenditure, compared to the printed press which received 23 per cent, radio 5 per cent, movie theatres 1 per cent, and outdoor advertising 10 per cent. These disparities continued to grow. According to Alfa Cont Mediawatch, in 2000 television received 73 per cent of total advertising expenditure, daily newspapers 16 per cent, magazines 8 per cent and radio 3 per cent. By 2004, television garnered 87 per cent of advertising expenditure, the print media 11 per cent and radio held steady at 3 per cent.

The interest of advertisers in television, the medium that reaches over 80 per cent of the public, explains the low level of investments in the other media and their dependence on revenues from sources other than advertising. In this context, one can understand the print media's desperate search for revenues; and that in 2001–4 the advertising expenditure of the Nastase government amounted to €64.7 million of public money (Hotnews 2005). In 2003, among public institutions, Petrom spent $1.5 million on advertising, The National Authority for Privatization $926,000, the Government $922,000, Posta Romana $858,000 and Romtelecom $802,000. The amounts spent on advertising by public institutions such as Petrom, Posta Romana, Romtelecom, and the National Authority for Privatization, represented almost 50 per cent of the total advertising expenditure in the printed press. Alfa Cont Mediawatch's research (Capital 2004c) shows that in the first six months of 2004 public institutions spent 4.7 million Euros, 1.8 million of which went to seventeen national dailies. The biggest beneficiaries were Adevarul (479,000), Ziua (360,000), Jurnalul National (310,000), Curentul (115,500), and Gardianul (75,000).

(2) The mass media control

Following a pattern evidenced in other Eastern European post-communist nations, by the turn of the century an increasing number of local political and business leaders entered the press world, joining those who already owned or controlled the national and local media. The former mayor of Bacau, Dumitru Sechelariu, who was also a local businessman, purchased the local 12,000-circulation daily Desteptarea and the local Radio Alpha and Alpha TV stations. Other examples abound: in the Oltenia region, the media group Media Sud-Est, led by Constantin Paunescu, owns the 30,000-circulation Gazeta de Sud and the station Radio Sud; in Brasov, the president of the County Council, ex-Democratic Party Senator Aristotel Cancescu, is the owner of the powerful radio and TV network Mix-FM (taken over by SBS Broadcasting Media in 2007); controversial businessman and Constanta Mayor, Radu Mazare, controls the daily Telegraf and Soti-TV; the mayor of the fifth Sector in Bucharest, Marin Vanghelie, purchased the daily Monitorul de Bucuresti in 2002. The mayor of Piatra Neamt, Gheorghe Stefan, is the owner of Radio Unu and Unu TV; parliamentarians also control media enterprises, for example, Victor Ponta controls Radio 21, Verestoy Attila, local print media in Harghita, and Gyorgy Frunda, Radio Gaga. In 2004, Liviu Luca, the leader of the syndicates from Petrom who owns Petrom Service, took ownership of the dailies Ziua and Gardianul, of Realitatea TV and Radio Total; in 2005, he sold his media holdings to the controversial businessman Sorin Ovidiu Vântu. Politicians owning media outlets raise a question regarding the independence of the press: What is the possibility of an independent editorial policy when the press is controlled or influenced by individuals with political interests and aspirations? However, the political people who have invested in mass media were not able to receive representative positions. With one exception, the big mass media groups are controlled by Romanian or foreign businessmen.

Adrian Sârbu controls PubliMedia (journals, magazines, press agency), Pro Cinema and, with Central Media Entreprises, Media Pro International (with radio and TV divisions). Sorin Ovidiu Vântu recently created a media empire, which includes radio and TV stations, one press agency, and journals and magazines. At the same time, Dinu Patriciu (owner of Rompetrol group) is beginning to construct a similar trust, including dailies and magazines. Dan Voiculescu, who controls televisions and radio stations and publications press through the Intact group, is involved in both economic and political life (he is the leader of the conservative party and member of Parlament). His media group has developed slowly since 1995 (unlike the rapid acquisition made by Vântu and Dinu Patriciu). Officially, he isn't involved in media activities any more because he has yielded the management of the group to his daughter. Besides these moguls, the media market is owned by groups such as Ringier (Switzerland), WAZ (Germany), Lagardère (France). Essentially speaking, the landscape of media institutions in Romania is controlled by what the journalist Iulian Comănescu calls the five 'Bigs' (Ringier, Voiculescu, Sarbu, Vântu and Patriciu for printed press; and public radio and television, Sarbu, SBS, Voiculescu, Vântu for audio-visual). Comparing the concentration degree in 2006 with the situation in 2004, he writes: 'The number of the national newspapers whose owners are others than the 5 "Bigs" decreased from 8 to 3. The situation is similar in other markets, such as TV niches or economical publications' (Comănescu 2007: 21). Even if Comănescu exaggerates the idea of concentration including public service institutions together with private ones, Comănescu's figures in the following table illustrate a definite trend:

Table 5: Audience market share of the five big media companies in Romania.

Market shares in	Ringier	Voiculescu	Sarbu	Vantu	Patriciu	SBS	Public service	Others
National printed press	54%	20%	6%	4%	6%	–	–	10%
National commercial television	–	5.1%	26%	3.7%	–	4.7%	22.1%	28.4%
National commercial radio	–	1.6%	7.1%	–	–	14.8%	36.9%	39.5%

Source: Comănescu 2007: 21.

This evolution clearly shows not only that we are in the middle of a slow, but irreversible process of trust formation, but also that the major actors on the stage of the press have acquired power and stability: Consequently, they do not depend on the political sector, but they negotiate their position from the same level as the political actors. Such a position of power is not damaging to the freedom of the press because economic consolidation make them less dependent on political interest. Thus the annual actions of monitoring the press that take place within the programme 'The Freedom of Expression – FreeEx' (an USA based foundation) show a significant change between the moments of economical weakness of the press and those of trust formation and acquiring an economical stability. With reference to 2003, the Report shows that the monitoring of the news programmes belonging to four TV stations (27 June 2003 - 6 July 2003) resulted as follows:

> [T]he representatives of the governing party benefited of 71% of TV showing 'while' according to the data published by the Ministry of Finance at 1st October 2003 the most important private TV stations in Romania had debts of about 20 million dollars to the national budget. (Programul FreeEx 2003, 2005: 8–9).

On the other hand, referring to 2005, the Report shows that the political pressure diminished and 'there appeared critical news on the political power in the news bulletins broadcasted by the TV stations' (Programul FreeEx 2003, 2005: 4). Even if the beginning of transformation into trusts and the economical consolidation are not exclusive factors in this process of change, we cannot fail to notice this significant correlation, which is also confirmed by the history of the press in the capitalist countries and the evolution of other post-communist countries. Undoubtedly, the problem of the freedom of expression is not entirely solved, because the weakening of the political pressure is compensated by the increasing role of the economic pressures. But this is another story ...!

Freedom of expression as an alibi for non-professionalism

It is a frequent practice of journalists to use the freedom of expression in order to legitimate different journalistic initiatives, or to defend themselves against the accusations of the representatives of power, or to justify different acts considered to be almost illegal or unethical. But in the Romanian post-communist press, freedom of expression was also used to mask utter mistakes or to hide immoral interests. In order to support my previous point, I am going to take two examples into consideration: (1) the so-called 'scandals' of Evenimentul Zilei, România Liber and Adevărul in 2004 and (2) the case of corruption at 'Gazeta de Cluj'.

The three 'scandals'[4]

At the beginning of September 2004, a group of 40 journalists at Evenimentul Zilei published a protest, disseminated in all national newspapers, claiming that 'under the guise of organizational changes, interference with editorial policy grew,...endangering the independence' (Hotnews 2005) of the newspaper. In his answer to the protest letter, Thomas Landolt, Ringier representative in Romania (Ringier is the owner of Evenimentul Zilei) denied involvement in editorial policy and reaffirmed the intent of transforming Evenimentul Zilei into a newspaper 'of record'. He claimed that the corporate owner wanted simply to improve the management of the newspaper, to raise the responsibility of the journalists, to improve the look of the newspaper, and the improvement of the work flow (Hotnews 2005). The reactions of one journalist, Andreea Pora, were significant in articulating the notion that journalists also have to have a stake in the newspaper management. She told Radio Free Europe that the organizational structure of the newspaper was changed without consultation with the journalists (Hotnews 2005). In an interview on BBC (Hotnews 2005) another striker, Dan Turturica explained, 'I think that Ringier simply cannot tolerate having a newspaper whose leadership does not follow its orders' (Hotnews 2005). And the columnist Cristian Tudor Popescu, the director of the daily Adevarul wrote that:

We journalists lived for too long with the idea that the West is a better *boier* (the old landowners) that it will not step on our toes as was the custom of Romanian [press] magnates who purchase a newspaper or [get] a television [station] for personal use. See, however, that even the refined European owners do not shy away from [using] a fist or a boot in a newspaper. (*Adevarul* 2004)

On 13 September 2004, two announcements appeared on the front page of *Romania Libera*, a prestigious daily that was, however, steadily losing readers. In the first announcement, the editorial staff accused Klaus Overbeck, the representative of the German media conglomerate WAZ, of interfering with the editorial policy of the newspaper. In the second press release, the journalists' union at *Romania libera* announced that it had asked the police in Essen, Germany, the headquarters of WAZ, for a permit to demonstrate in front of WAZ. The director of *Romania libera*, Bacanu, declared that WAZ proposed quadrupling the price of the daily from 5,000 lei to 20,000 lei and that they suggested changing the nature of the articles published to make the newspaper more entertaining and relaxing for readers. In their statement, the journalists claimed that WAZ reproached them for publishing too many articles that were critical of the powers-that-be. They insinuated that the representative of WAZ in Bucharest, Klaus Overbeck, 'from the beginning [wished] to distance the paper from the political arena, suggesting that large, positive pictures be published and that as many fashionable items be introduced in the pages of the paper as possible' (*Romania Libera* 2004). The meeting between Bacanu and Bodo Hombach, the representative of WAZ in Bucharest, took place in May 2004 and, according to journalists loyal to Bacanu, the owners:

> began to demand that we renounce publishing thematic supplements, that we increase the number of pages dedicated to advertisements, to find positive subjects we could investigate, and that we accentuate lifestyle articles; Saturday, for example, he wanted to offer eight pages covering celebrities, sports, and other entertainment oriented fare. (*Romania Libera* 2004)

In essence, from the perspective of the journalists, the motives for the conflict at *Romania Libera* were (1) injecting WAZ into the editorial activities, (2) modifying the editorial contents by reducing the space assigned to politics in favour of human interest items, or the translation of some articles from the foreign tabloids, and (3) pushing the paper into the tabloid genre. The pressures and changes evoked by journalists were never proved with specific evidence.

Klaus Overbeck addressed a letter to *Romania Libera*'s staff that was published on 15 September 2004 on the front page under the rubric 'The Right to Reply'. Overbeck claimed that WAZ, in accordance with its own policy that it applies to all the newspapers it owns in Southeast Europe, did not interfere in the editorial policy. WAZ's basic argument was buttressed by the fact that, during its three year ownership of *Romania Libera*, the editorial staff had the freedom to publish any materials, including the protest signed by the editorial staff, which was published on the front page of the 13 September 2004 issue. The representative of the German company claimed that he had no desire to change the newspaper into a tabloid. The publication, he stated, should remain a newspaper of quality, which should offer relevant information to its readers. He was in full accord with the principles of a free press. Subsequently, in an interview with *Jurnalul National* (2004), Overbeck stressed that the data from the National Audience Study (Studiului National de Audienta – SNA) demonstrated that *Romania Libera* had lost 32 per cent of its readers between October 2002 and July 2004. Overbeck stated that he 'did not come to Romania to change the [editorial] line of the newspaper or to impose German standards but to place a daily newspaper on the market that can be competitive'. At the same time, he attempted to prove that Bacanu had great personal interest in the scandal because he had a salary of hundreds of millions of lei and income from commissions paid by companies associated with *Romania Libera*. In other words, Overbeck suggested that he had no connection with Romania's political world and that the attacks directed at WAZ were also attacks against all foreign owners of media in the country, and furthermore, that it was a conspiracy of sorts hatched before the elections in November 2004.

The leadership of *Adevarul* – Cristian Tudor Popescu, Adrian Ursu, Lelia Munteanu, Bogdan Chireac – resigned at the end of the newspaper's Administrative Council meeting on 20 March 2005. The reason for the resignation was that the majority owner, Ana Maria Tinu, together with the members of the Administrative Council, decided that it was not appropriate that those responsible for the editorial policy of the newspapers also be responsible for its economic policies. Thus they wanted to replace Popescu, Ursu, Munteanu and Chireac in the Administrative Council but leave them on the Editorial Board. The four resigned from both and maintained that they were leaving *Adevarul*, because:

there is no justification for replacing us...It is natural that we have a say in the Administrative Council. We have done our duty on the Council to the very end and were replaced and we no longer feel secure. We cannot guarantee the quality of the newspaper. (Cotidinul 2005)

Commenting on the situation, Mircea Toma, the director of the weekly *Academia Catavencu*, observed that the matter concerned a 'profit (of 22 million Euros in 2004) [that] was pretty well [lessened] because of the salaries of the "barons" and by their personal publicity agencies, which melted away a good deal of the newspaper's share holder profits' (*Academia Catavencu* 2005). Toma also claimed that at a time when shareholders who were also in the Administrative Council of the newspaper received insignificant amounts of money, Popescu had a monthly income of 10,000 Euros. This is the background for the decision by the owner of *Adevarul*, who inherited his shares in the newspaper, to change things at *Adevarul*: that is, to separate the business from the editorial and to identify strategies to make the newspaper financially competitive and profitable.

On the other hand, commenting on the decision to separate the commercial from the editorial leadership, Andrei Postelnicu, a journalist at the *Financial Times*, wrote in an issue of *Evenimentul Zilei* (2005):

The fact that this was not yet taken puts into question the editorial integrity of Adevarul from its very beginning. The wide-spread practice of encouraging journalists to conclude contracts for advertising, earning a commission and supplementing their salaries, discredits the reputation of the newspaper and of those who are leading it (it must be noted that this strategy is applied at other newspapers, including *Romania Libera*, a fact confirmed in one of Bacanu's declarations on Realitatea TV).

Corruption and blackmail

In October 2006 the Prosecutor's Office finalised the indictment against a group of journalists from the trust 'Gazeta' that held ten journals and magazines in different towns in Transylvania (the central unit being *Gazeta de Cluj*). Seven leading journalists were charged, accused of qualified blackmail and being part of a criminal organization. The indictment showed that, starting in 2004, these journalists had begun to gather information about different businessmen, and then, by threatening them with publishing disreputable information, the journalists signed numerous advertising contracts (using blackmail). In many cases, instead of these contracts (from which the journalists took substantial favours) sums of money were also obtained for personal use:

> According to the evidences the culprits, the accused and the other members of the group took advantage of being journalists for blackmailing both private and public persons by using press information in a tendentious and malicious way; by doing so their activity lacked the purpose of informing the public correctly and thus they broke the provisions in art. 10 para. 1 and 2 from The European Convention of The Human Rights of which Romania is a part as well. (Hotnews 2007)

At the moment these accusations were uttered, the leaders from the newspaper *Gazeta de Cluj* published a press release in which they stated that the prosecutors' accusations were violating the freedom of expression:

> In Romania hunting journalists has become a national sport. In today's Romania attacking journalists and looking for their relatives so that one hurts journalists through them, has become part of some agreements up to a level much more than high. Today, our friends, fellows for over 15 years in a battle long before lost against the political-economical crap, were kept in Cluj in a very disdainful and revanchistic manner…We know for sure that a clear and fair examination of our colleagues, who for years are fighting alone against the flaws of Romanian society, will prove that everything reduces to some people that afford buying human and material resources of the state just for their personal revenge. (Hotnews 2006)

This was the sole document that explained the case of the journalists from *Gazeta de Cluj*. In December 2006, three more journalists were charged; the trial started in January 2007. Beside the accusatory statements of businessmen, politicians and members of the local administration, the press showed that two of the accused admitted during the hearings that these practices were means of the company for acquiring its own or other personal financial interests. The professional association did not support the journalists and took distance:

> The Romanian Press Club considers that the searches, hearings and detains carried out by the legal authorities in Cluj upon the editorial staff of 'Buna ziua, Ardeal!' and 'The Cluj Gazzette' do not represent attacks against the freedom of the press. The accused journalists must answer legally to the multiple accusations of blackmail. (See Ghinea and Fotiade 2007)

And The MediaSind union:

> The arrest of the journalists...casts blame on being a journalist in Romania. It is obvious that the journalists in Cluj must give an answer before the law for what they did like any other citizen as the judicial resort is the only one capable of deciding whether the law was broken. Even if they are not members of our union, as it is about involving other journalists as well, US MediaSind will monitor this case attentively. But what is particularly serious is that some employers offer the permit of being a journalist to any person who has or not any connection to the press, without following the minimal provisions for this, and by doing so their actions lead to compromising the profession of a journalist... (See Ghinea and Fotiade 2007)

While commenting upon the way this case was presented in Romanian media, the authors of the report on media corruption remarked, not without some irony:

> Still, the journalistic guild did not look too surprised by the possibility that the accusations may be true. The event seems to have appeared against the background of some scepticism among the journalists: they knew that blackmail by press was taking place in Romania. The real surprise seems to be that the Prosecutor's Office took a position in this case. (Ghinea and Fotiade 2006: 38)

Indeed, blackmailing by press has had a long history in Romania, before, during and after the communist period (see Petcu 2007; Coman 2004). But, from the perspective of the present discussion, beyond the facts themselves, what is significant is the discourse of the accused who used the freedom of expression as a magic shield meant to intimidate the prosecution and exculpate the convicted journalists.

Notes

1. For more information of these issues see Coman 2003; Coman and Gross 2006.
2. For more information see Press Freedom Reports on Media Monitoring Agency (2007).
3. See also CNA 2007.
4. This a short version of my analysis in Coman and Gross 2006.

References

Academia Catavencu (2005), 'Care a fost baiul si malaiul la Adevarul?' (Who was the owner of Adevarul?), no. 11. Accessed March 2005.

Adevarul (2004), 'Presa sub presiune' (Media under pressure). Accessed 14 September 2004.

Adevarul (2008) '8 milioane de reclame au atacat Romania, zi de zi, in ultimii sapte ani' (8 millions advertisements have aggressed Romania in the last six years). Accessed August 2008.

Aumente, J. et al. (1999), 'Lessons Learned and Predictions for the Future', in J. Aumente, P. Gross, R. Hiebert, O.W. Johnson and D. Mills (eds.), Eastern European Journalism: Before, During, and After Communism, Cresskill (New Jersey): Hampton Press Inc, pp. 41–78.

Camera Deputatilor (Deputies Chamber) (2007), http://www.cdep.ro. Accessed 11 June 2007.

Campaign (2007), 'Piata publicitatii in crestere' (Advertising market is still growing), no. 1, 2007.

Capital (2004a), 'Radioul public vrajeste pe parlamentari' (Public radio bewitched [or – put a spell on] the parliament), no. 19. Accessed 6 May 2004.

Capital (2004b), 'Taxa Tv a umflat veniturile televiziunii publice' (The taxes for television increased the budget of public television), no. 18. Accessed 29 April 2004.

Capital (2004c), 'Reclamele tin presa sub presiune' (Advertisers keep media under pression), no. 33. Accessed 12 August 2004.

CNA (2007), 'Consiliul National al Audiovizualului' (National Council of Audiovisual), http://www.cna. ro. Accessed 15 January 2007.

Coman, Mihai (2003), Mass media in Romania post-comunista, Iasi (Romania): Polirom.

Coman, Mihai (2004), 'Media Bourgeoisie and Media Proletariat in Post-Communist Romania', Journalism Studies, 5:1, pp. 45–58.

Coman, Mihai and Gross, Peter (2006), Media and Journalism in Romania, Berlin: Vistas.

Comănescu, Iulian (2007), Tendinţe despre reflectarea presei în presă III: Studiu de caz – concentrarea proprietăţii de media, Bucharest: Centrul pentru Jurnalism Independent.

Cotidinul (2005), 'Nu putem garanta un ziar de calitate' (We cannot guarantee the quality of the newspaper). Accessed 21 March 2005.

Evenimentul Zilei (2005), 'Dictatura conspiratiei peste adevaruri care dor' (The dictatorship of conspiracy hide truths that hurts). Accessed 28 March 2005.

Freedom of Expression (2007), http://www.freeex.ro. Accessed 11 June 2007.

Gross, Peter (1996), Mass Media in Revolution and National Development: The Romanian Laboratory, Ames: Iowa State University Press.

Gross, Peter (2002), Entangled Evolutions: Media and Democratization in Eastern Europe, Washington DC: Woodrow Wilson Center Press.

Ghinea, Cristian and Fotiade, Nicoleta (2006), Tendinţe în reflectarea presei în presă. II: Studiu de caz: Corupţia în presă, Bucharest: Centrul pentru Jurnalism Independent.

Habermas, Jürgen (1978), L'espace public, Paris: Payot.

Hotnews (2005), 'Adevarata miza a cazului Evenimentul zilei' (What is at stake in Evenimentul Zilei scandal), http://www.hotnews.ro/articol_30537. Accessed 21 September 2005.

Hotnews (2006), 'Ne-au ucis' (They killed us), http://www.hotnews.ro/stiri-presa_regionala_arhiva-1713736. Accessed 15 January 2007.

Hotnews (2007), 'Mecanismul gazetei descries de procurori' (The mechanism of Gazeta as the prosecutors describe it), http://www.hotnews.ro/stiri-presa_regionala_arhiva-1710718. Accessed 15 January 2007.

Jurnalul National (2004), 'Romania Libera nu va fi un ziar bulevardier' (Romania Libera will not become a tabloid newspaper). Accessed 21 September 2004.

Keane, John (2000): Mass media si democratia (The Media and Democracy), Iasi, Institutul European

Marinescu, Valentina (2001), 'Normative Changes of the Romanian Media after 1990', The Global Network, no. 17, pp. 83–102.

Media Monitoring Agency (2007), 'Agentia de Monitorizare a Presei', http://www.mma.ro. Accessed 15 January 2007.

MediaSind (2007), 'Uniunea Sindicala MediaSind' (MediaSind Trade Union), http://www.mediasind. ro. Accessed 11 June 2007.

National Institute of Statistics (2006), The Romanian Statistical Yearbook, Bucharest: INS.

O'Neil, P. (1997), 'Introduction: Media Reform and Democratization in Eastern Europe', in Patrick O'Neil (ed.), *Post-Communism and Media in Eastern Europe,* London: Frank Cass.

Petcu, Marian (2000), *Tipologia presei romanesti,* Iasi: Institutul european.

Petcu, Marian (2007), *Istoria jurnalismului şi a publicităţii în România,* Iasi: Polirom.

Preoteasa, Manuela (2004), *Media Ownership and its Impact on Media Independence and Pluralism* [editor Brankica Petkovic], Ljubljana: Peace Institute; Institute for Contemporary Social and Political Studies, available online at http://www.mirovni-institut.si/media_ownership/pdf/preface.pdf. Accessed 14 October 2007.

Programul FreeEx (2003, 2005), *Libertatea presei în România,* Bucharest: Agenţia de Monitorizare a Presei.

Ringier Romania (2007), http://www.ringier.ro. Accessed 12 April 2007.

Romania Libera (2004), 'Comunicat' (Press release). Accessed 13 September 2004.

Sparks, Colin and Reading, Anna (1998), *Communism, Capitalism and the Mass Media,* London; Thousand Oaks and New Delhi: Sage Publications.

Splichal, Slavko (2001), 'Imitative Revolutions: Changes in the Media and Journalism in East-Central Europe', *Javnost – The Public,* 8:4, pp. 31–58.

Ziarul Financiar (2005), 'Cum schimba piata de cablu preluarea Astral de catre Liberty Global' (Liberty Global took over Astral: changes on the cable operators market). Accessed 25 July 2005.

MEDIA FREEDOM AND PLURALISM IN THE UNITED KINGDOM (UK)

Peter Humphreys

Key political systemic and media systemic features

According to Hallin and Mancini's (2004) much-cited typology of models of media and politics, the UK media system corresponds to the 'North Atlantic/Liberal' model, which is characterized by:

- Market-domination (however, they note, except the BBC).
- A neutral commercial press characterized by internally pluralistic journalism (again, except that in Britain they acknowledge that there is external pluralism, namely party political 'parallelism'), and
- Professionalization and non-institutionalized self-regulation.

In fact, as the exceptions noted by Hallin and Mancini already suggest, the UK media system is far from bearing any close resemblance to that of the United States. Like the media system of France, or that of Germany, or Italy, it is in many respects *sui generis* (see Humphreys 1996). It functions in a very different cultural and socio-political context from the United States, or indeed from other 'North Atlantic' (taken to mean 'Anglo-Saxon') countries.

Politically, following Lijphart's (1984) well-known models of democracy, the United Kingdom is institutionally 'majoritarian' in significantly more respects than the United States, which has important consensual features such as federalism, strong judicial review and the separation of powers. None of the latter have featured in the United Kingdom as key restraints on the exercise of majoritarian power by the single party governments that typically win elections, making all the more remarkable the consensual approach to broadcasting in the United Kingdom (see below). In terms of political and economic development, the two countries may have shared a 'weak state' tradition compared to many countries of Continental Europe, making historically for less extensive or intrusive regulation of the press, but in the United Kingdom's case this too has to be qualified. With regard to freedom of information and the reporting of matters deemed sensitive for national security, the United Kingdom has – at least, until recently – featured as a rather strong, quite 'secretive' state, again in considerable contrast to the United States.

Key, one might say 'striking', characteristic features of the UK media system, some of which contrast strikingly with the United States (and other 'Anglo-Saxon' countries) as well as with other European countries, have been:

- Strong public service broadcasting (in contrast to the other 'Anglo-Saxon' countries: United States, Canada and Australia)
- Relatively politically independent public service broadcasting (in comparison to many countries in the rest of Europe)
- High professional standards in the 'quality press' (like Hallin and Mancini's 'North Atlantic' model and also like their 'Northern European' model), but a particularly strong and vibrant 'tabloid' press (compared to the United States and much of the rest of Europe)
- A tradition of weak freedom of information and strong state secrecy (compared to the United States and much of Europe).

In common with other Anglo-Saxon countries, there is a strong tradition of relatively independent journalism in the United Kingdom. The press sector has been by international standards relatively free from state regulation. Issues of state security (and criminal law) aside, the limits of journalistic autonomy are largely set by proprietorial power. UK national newspapers pursue a distinct editorial politico-philosophical line, generally determined by their owners, with regard to issues of politics and society. Though much more closely regulated by the state, UK television has been remarkably free from politicisation. All holders of a UK licence to broadcast are bound by law and regulation to be impartial. Further, unlike public service broadcasting in much of the rest of Europe, the UK broadcasters have benefitted from a political consensus that has long existed in favour of non-politicisation of broadcasting. Media policy, too, has generally been comparatively consensual (except during the Thatcher premiership), with government generally respecting the advice of regulatory bodies, cross-party committees and periodic non-partisan commissions that have informed broadcasting and press policy (Humphreys 1996: 111–58).

Thus, the latest Freedom House survey of global press freedom (Freedom House 2007) notes that the UK media are: 'free and largely independent from government interference. The United Kingdom has a strong tradition of public broadcasting, and the British Broadcasting Corporation, although funded by the government [through levying a household TV licence fee], is editorially independent.' While press ownership is 'concentrated in the hands of a few large companies', the Freedom House report goes on to note that '[t]he law provides for freedom of the press, and the government generally respects this right in practice'. The United Kingdom ranked as 'free' and 32nd in the global ranking. However, it only ranked eighteenth out of the 25 West European countries in the Freedom House survey (Freedom House 2007). The reason for the United Kingdom's comparatively low ranking in Western Europe would appear to be the unlawful intimidation encountered by journalists in reporting Northern Ireland and, from the side of the state, the existence of exemptions from freedom of information, limitations on freedom of expression relating to encouragement of terrorism and also incitement to religious hatred, and restrictions with regard to national security and the combatting of terrorism. Reporters Without Borders' (2007) latest worldwide index of press freedom similarly placed the United Kingdom at 27th, behind nineteen other European countries, mainly because of the hostile nature of Northern Ireland for journalists despite the peace process (because of the murder of the *Sunday World* reporter Martin O'Hagan, the failure of the police investigation, other death threats and so on).

Press freedom in the United Kingdom: Legal provisions

Having no written Constitution as such, the United Kingdom lacks any explicit constitutional guarantee of press freedom. Nonetheless, the principle of press freedom is an important element of Britain's 'unwritten constitution'. Courts often refer to 'constitutional principles', including freedom of speech and press freedom. Moreover, the United Kingdom has always been party to the European Convention of Human Rights (ECHR) and in 1996 the United Kingdom accepted the right of its citizens to individual petition, since which time applications to the European Commission and Court of Human Rights have struck down several aspects of UK law deemed incompatible with freedom of expression (Nicol and Bowman 1993: 167). New Labour's 1998 Human Rights Act went much further, by actually incorporating the ECHR into UK law, thereby strengthening freedom of expression (therefore press freedom). It also strengthened protection of individuals' rights to privacy, but in such cases UK judges are required to pay particular regard to freedom of expression (Humphreys 2000: 233).

Governments have been generally non-interventionist *vis-à-vis* the press. Ever since the licensing of the press was abolished in 1684, there has existed a general right to publish newspapers, books or magazines without state authorization; no licence has been required. Moreover, since becoming a highly commercial industry – from the early twentieth century onwards – the independence of the press has been underpinned by its commercial freedom. The UK press is not subsidized (apart from VAT exemption), so governments have never had this particular lever of potential influence. As is generally the case among liberal democracies, newspapers and magazines have been free to pursue their own politico-philosophical editorial line, a freedom that UK proprietors of national newspapers have taken advantage of, aligning their titles with various moral stances on socio-political and politico-economic issues, and indeed producing newspaper/political party system 'parallelism'. Unlike broadcasting (see below), there is no statutory duty of impartial reporting.

Unlike many European countries with their own bodies of specific press law, newspapers and magazines in Britain have been subject to little sector-specific regulation; the press is subject only to the general laws of the land, such as the anti-defamation and anti-obscenity laws, the law against incitement to racial hatred, or the law of trespass (for example in the pursuit of information). Otherwise, the press has regulated itself (see below). As Gibbons (1998: 26) notes, the formal approach in the United Kingdom is libertarian: 'there being no prior restraint on speech,...an individual may communicate without first seeking official approval and thereby risking unpredictable, possibly ill-motivated and bureaucratic exercises of discretion'. However, as Gibbons explains, the law does provide certain significant restraints; it 'effectively inhibits speech [and press freedom in the absolute sense] in the interests of preserving reputations, official secrets and confidences, and safeguarding intellectual property'.

One of the main restrictions on what the press have been able to publish has undoubtedly been presented by Britain's comparatively strict libel laws. UK libel laws place the onus of proof on the defendant, a state of affairs which has traditionally generally favoured the plaintiff. Unsurprisingly, many have observed that this has had a 'chilling effect' on the media's freedom of expression. However, in 2006 UK libel laws were reformed following a key Law Lords ruling in favour of the defendant – the *Wall Street Journal Europe* – despite the paper's lack of evidence in its defence, on the grounds that the article was in the public interest. As Freedom House (2007) reports, this latest ruling 'should afford journalists greater freedom to report allegations against public figures without fear of reprisal'.

As suggested already, state restrictions on press freedom have largely been limited to issues of 'national security', though as the (above mentioned) Freedom House ranking of the United Kingdom suggests, the United Kingdom has resorted to such measures rather more than a considerable number of other European countries. Indeed, one academic cross-national study of censorship, looking at nine liberal democracies, six of which were West European, found that the United Kingdom censored the most over the period 1970–90, particularly during the (Thatcherite) 1980s. The study concluded that key features of the United Kingdom's political system presented 'the opportunity to censor': notably, the absence of a written constitution and Bill of Rights, the country's 'majoritarian' political institutions, the weakness of freedom of information, and the draconian nature of the United Kingdom's secrecy laws (Newton and Artingstall 1994). Only since 2000 has the United Kingdom actually had a Freedom of Information Act (introduced by New Labour). The Official Secrets Act has used criminal law to guard against disclosure of state secrets. In the United Kingdom, civil servants are bound by confidentiality; there is no protection for 'whistleblowers'. The Contempt of Court Act provides for protection of the confidentiality of journalistic sources, but also provides for disclosure in the interests of justice, national security, or the prevention of disorder or crime (Nicol and Bowman 1993; Humphreys 1996: 53–6).

Two other features set the United Kingdom apart from the European norm. Firstly, in the United Kingdom, privacy of the individual citizen has been exceptionally weakly protected from the press; there is no special statute on privacy. On the positive side, this has worked to the advantage of investigative journalism, which has undoubtedly flourished in the United Kingdom rather more than in a number of other European countries. On the negative side, however, it has also encouraged a characteristically prurient culture of intrusive 'tabloid journalism', and there have been periodic calls for stricter regulation (see below). Equally unusual for a European country is the fact that UK law provides for no statutory Right of Reply. As with press standards and privacy (largely), this matter has been left to the press's self-regulatory instruments (self-regulatory bodies, codes and so on).

The regulatory structure of the UK press sector: Self-regulation

Reflecting a perhaps surprisingly consensual approach to media policy for a 'majoritarian' polity, policy innovations regarding the press have generally occurred following the recommendations of Royal Commissions (of inquiry). Thus, in 1947 the first Royal Commission on the UK press (the Ross Commission) recommended the establishment of a self-regulatory institution, the Press Council. The reason was mounting public and political concern about declining press standards and also about press concentration, though nothing was actually done about the latter (which remains a key feature of the UK press – see later). The Press Council proved to be a weak regulatory institution regarding press behaviour. This was unsurprising; its entire membership was drawn from the press itself and it had no real sanctions other than criticism. Following a second Royal Commission (the Shawcross Commission), the Press Council's membership was extended to some representatives of the public and following a third Royal Commission in 1974 (the McGregor Commission) the public's representation was increased to half of its membership, though these members were actually chosen by the Council itself and it continued to lack authority and was perceived to lack independence from its regulatees, the press. By now there was serious concern about the issue of tabloid newspapers' intrusions into citizens' privacy, a matter addressed by a parliamentary private members' Bill, and the government established a special committee of inquiry (the Calcutt Committee) to address the issue. The Committee's first report (Calcutt 1990) recommended improving self-regulation, and the Press Council was duly replaced by a new institution called the Press Complaints Commission (PCC). However, it was mainly composed of newspaper editors. A second report (Calcutt 1993: xi) famously deemed it to be a 'body set up by the industry, financed by the industry, dominated by the industry and which [was] over-favourable to the industry' and recommended the introduction of a statutory regulatory regime for the press (Humphreys 1996: 60–1).

Despite persisting criticism of the PCC's alleged weakness, successive governments – Conservative and New Labour – have continued to favour self-regulation of the press over statutory regulation, though – in the wake of calls for privacy legislation following Princess Diana's death and alleged hounding by newspaper reporters – newspaper editors did tighten up the PCC's code of conduct with effect from 1998 onwards (Humphreys 2000: 232–3).

Press pluralism in the United Kingdom

The UK national press is generally characterized as consisting of three categories of newspaper. 'Quality' papers – notably, The Guardian, the Independent, the Daily Telegraph, and The Times, and their Sunday namesakes (in the Guardian's case, the Observer), and also the Financial Times, have catered to an 'upmarket' educated middle class readership. (Until recently these papers appeared in broadsheet format, though they now all appear in tabloid format). In 2006, these titles accounted for between a quarter and a fifth (22.6 per cent) of the total circulation of national newspapers. The popular 'midmarket' tabloids – notably, the Daily Mail and the Daily Express, and their Sunday editions – have appealed to a mainly white-collar middle class readership. In 2006, they accounted for over a quarter (26.9 per cent) of the circulation of national newspapers. Finally the 'downmarket' tabloids – the dailies being the Sun, the Daily Mirror and the Daily Star, the Sunday papers being the News of the World, the Sunday Mirror, the Daily Star Sunday, the People and the Sunday Sport – have served a largely working class and lower middle class readership with their content heavily orientated towards celebrity, sport, sex and crime. In 2006, they accounted for half of the circulation of the national newspapers.[1] In addition, 1,313 local and regional newpapers registered a total weekly circulation of 64.3 million (Mediaguardian/Gibson 2007: 26). The national press is without any question the much more important source of national and international news and information, and also of celebrity gossip, national sports news and suchlike; with the significant exception of several titles (notably the Scottish national press and a few English titles such as the Yorkshire Post) the local and regional press serves more local communication needs.

Table 1: National newspaper ownership in 2006.

Group	Market share	Titles	Executive Control
News International	34.4%	Sun, Times, Sunday Times, News of the World.	Rupert Murdoch (News International)
Daily Mail and General Trust	20.5%	Daily Mail, Mail on Sunday	Viscount Rothermere
Trinity Mirror	15.1%	Daily Mirror, Sunday Mirror, People	Victor Blank
Northern and Shell	13.6%	Daily Express, Daily Star, Sunday Express, Daily Star Sunday	Richard Desmond
Telegraph Group	7.5%	Daily Telegraph, Sunday Telegraph	Barclay brothers
Guardian Media Group	3.4%	Guardian, Observer	Scott Trust
Pearson	3.3%	Financial Times	Pearson board
Independent Newspapers	2.2%	Independent, Independent on Sunday	Anthony O'Reilly

Source: Adapted from Table in Mediaguardian/Gibson (2007: 24). The data is for the period January–June 2006.

Both of these markets are highly concentrated in terms of newspaper ownership and/or control. As Table 1 illustrates, in 2006 the leading two national newspaper groups controlled over half of national newspaper circulation (54.9 per cent), and the leading four groups accounted for over four fifths (83.6 per cent).

Control of the United Kingdom's 1,313 local and regional titles was similarly highly concentrated. Trinity Mirror, with the United Kingdom's third largest circulation of national titles (see above), also owned 234 local/regional titles with a weekly total circulation of 13.8 million, representing a market share of 21.5 per cent. Next came Newsquest Media Group with a market share of 15.4 per cent, (219 titles, weekly total circulation of 9.9 million); followed by Johnston Press with a market share of 14.1 per cent (282 titles, weekly total circulation of 9.1 million). The Northcliffe Newspapers Group had a market share of 11.7 per cent (111 titles, weekly total circulation of 7.5 million). Associated Newspapers, part of the national Daily Mail group, with eleven local titles accounting for a total weekly circulation of 6.7

million, had a market share of 10.4 per cent. As of July 2006, these five newspaper groups between them accounted for nearly three quarters (73.1 per cent) of the readership market (Mediaguardian/Gibson 2007: 26). Furthermore, most UK regional markets are characterized by local monopolies, even in the largest cities. Thus, the *Evening Standard* (owned by Daily Mail and General Trust) controlled the London market, the *Manchester Evening Post* (owned by Guardian Media Group) the Manchester market, and the *Evening Times* (Newsquest) the Glasgow market. Press pluralism has been increased somewhat by the ubiquitous appearance of free newspapers. The big-city *Metro* free newspapers, however, were owned by one of the largest press groups, the Daily Mail and General Trust (Humphreys 2006: 321–2).

Public service broadcasting in the United Kingdom and the 'paradigm shift' towards 'lighter touch' regulation for commercial broadcasting

Whereas the newspaper sector has supplied (a degree of) 'external pluralism' through a multiplicity of outlets, the broadcasting sector – characterized until fairly recently by a 'scarcity of frequencies' – has needed to be regulated to provide 'internal pluralism' within licensed programme services. Indeed, until 1954, broadcasting in the United Kingdom was a public service monopoly of the British Broadcasting Corporation (BBC), which – according to the formula of its first Director General Lord John Reith – had a remit to inform, educate and entertain. Over the years, the BBC's programme remit evolved considerably in step with societal changes, but the core principle remained that the Corporation should provide a ('internally pluralistic') range of high quality programmes. This principle was to serve as a model when additional broadcasters, with varying degrees of public service remits, were licensed (see below).

After the Second World War, the BBC quickly acquired a world-wide reputation for political independence. Several factors help explain this feature, which was (as with media policy generally) perhaps rather surprising given the scope for politicisation that a 'majoritarian' political system obviously presents for government control or interference. As Tunstall and Machin (1999: 91–2) explain, the origins of the BBC's independence can be traced to the deeply embedded notions of the 'public good' in the United Kingdom (as in the United States), to the role played by Post Office civil servants in its establishment, which led it to adopt the non-partisan principles of the British civil service, and also to the fact that during its early decades the BBC relied heavily on British news agencies (the most famous of which was Reuters) which had a tradition of political neutrality. Some other factors should also be acknowledged. Certainly, the BBC's relative autonomy from the state owes much, too, to the independent ethos of its management and journalists. Moreover, although government determines the level of the household licence-fee which funds it, which has presented some scope for political pressure, the BBC has always been left discretion as to how it allocates its licence-fee so long as it respects the broad public service guidelines which are established by its Royal Charter and Agreement. Importantly, the BBC has benefitted from a large degree of self-regulation in that, until very recently, it has been internally regulated by its own Board of Governors. Though appointed directly by the relevant government ministry, the Governors always functioned as 'trustees of the public interest', rather than as political place-men, to the extent that they soon became seen as guardians of the Corporation's independence, as much as its regulators. However, the criticism that the Governors too closely identified with BBC and were not sufficiently detached in fulfilling their regulatory duties was the principal reason why the government decided that the BBC's new Charter (entering effect in 2007) should replace the Board with the supposedly more critical BBC Trust.

In 1954, following a particularly vigorous political campaign largely on behalf of the advertising industry lobby, Independent Television (ITV) was introduced, as a system of fifteen regional private television franchises (later joined by a breakfast TV franchise) for 'programme contractor' companies, namely the privately owned 'ITV' companies. The franchises were allocated by the regulator, the Independent Television Authority (ITA), in 1973 renamed the Independent Broadcasting Authority (IBA), which was a public corporation. A unique feature of ITV was that, apart from exercising licensing and supervision powers, it was the regulator, rather than the ITV companies, which actually owned and operated the ITV transmission network. The ITV contractors provided programme services, which were funded by attracting advertisers. ITV was subject to a strict regulatory regime, to the extent that it came to be considered as one part of a public service 'duopoly', the other being the BBC.

In 1982, this duopoly structure was broken by the introduction of Channel Four, a non-private, but advertising-funded, public service broadcaster. Until 1990, the IBA allocated Channel Four a share of ITV's advertising revenue. Since 1990, Channel Four has been entirely independent of the ITV sector, responsible for its own commercial success, but still a non-private public service broadcaster. It has always had a special remit to be innovative and to serve minority interests and tastes. At the same time as Channel Four, a Welsh public service channel called S4C was also introduced. In 1997, a fifth terrestrial broadcaster was introduced, namely Channel Five, a privately owned and advertising-funded channel with only light public service obligations.

By this time, a series of Conservative government legislation – the Cable and Broadcasting Act 1984, the Broadcasting Act 1990, and the Broadcasting Act 1996 – had introduced 'lighter touch' regulation for private commercial broadcasting in the United Kingdom. For the terrestrial broadcasters, which are still all regarded officially as public service broadcasters, this meant significantly lighter public service programme content obligations and expectations regarding standards for ITV (now termed Channel Three) and Channel Five than for the BBC and Channel Four. By the end of the 1990s, there was also a well-established private commercial cable and satellite sector, which was subject to minimal – but still important – regulatory obligations such as the political impartiality rule, and rules governing taste, decency and advertising standards. The Broadcasting Act 1990 replaced the IBA with the Independent Television Commission (and the Independent Radio Authority), which no longer owned the ITV network (sold to a private transmission company) and which now served as regulator for all commercial broadcasting in the United Kingdom.

The regulatory paradigm shift towards 'lighter touch' regulation was justified largely by reference to new technological realities. While there continued to exist good grounds for retaining strong public service broadcasters (Graham and Davies 1997), the principal justification for across-the-board strict regulation for all operators had fallen away when 'scarcity of frequencies' was replaced by technologies which made possible an increasing abundance of new programme services. A few statistics illustrate the huge scale of the transformation. In a single week in 1980 British viewers could choose from 300 hours of television provided by three channels (BBC 1, BBC 2 and ITV). By the turn of the new century, UK households with multi-channel television could choose from over 40,000 hours provided by over 250 channels and the number of UK (analogue) terrestrial channels had grown to five with the arrival of Channel 4 in 1982 and Channel 5 in 1997 (DTI/DCMS 2000: 1.1.2). The expansion has continued, with the take-off of digital TV. According to the latest report produced by Ofcom, the new regulator and competition authority for the converging electronics communications sector established in 2002, (Ofcom 2006a: 208), the year 2005 saw 1.4 million hours of output broadcast on all UK television channels. By now three quarters of UK homes could receive digital television whether by satellite (BSkyB's pay-TV platform), by cable (Virgin Media's pay-TV platform) or by the terrestrial 'Freeview' service (a joint venture of the BBC and BSkyB). A number of operators (including the BBC) were developing on-demand content and TV-over-broadband services. TV-over-mobile was also being developed.

The impact on television audience shares

These changes have inevitably impacted on the audience shares of the traditional mainstream broadcasters, who have responded to the multi-channel challenge by expanding their channel portfolios beyond the supply of 'generalist' services to include new 'niche' services for distinct audiences. Thus the BBC has launched channels for youth (BBC 3) and for children (CBBC, CBeebies), in order to provide an alternative to a diet of US children's channels provided by cable and satellite. It has also launched a cultural and educational channel (BBC 4), a political channel (BBC Parliament) and a 24-hour news service (BBC News 24). Other mainstream broadcasters – ITV and Channel 4 – have also developed new channels – respectively, ITV2 and ITV3; and E4, FilmFour and FilmFour Weekly – to meet the competition. Table 2 illustrates the inexorable nature of the downward trend in the mainstream channels' audience shares. On the other hand, the 2007 figures showed that with by now over three quarters of UK homes viewing multi-channel TV, their audience shares remained impressive.

The Communications Act 2003; the new regulatory framework

As a result of new technologies and governmental 'de-regulation', by the end of the 1990s the duopoly structure had effectively been replaced by a distinct three-way regulatory structure: (1) the internally self-regulating, licence-fee funded BBC; (2) the advertising-funded 'public service' broadcasters, externally regulated by the ITC (with C4 retaining the most clear public

Table 2: TV Percentage Annual Share of the Audience 1981–2006.

Channel	1981	1985	1990	1995	2000	2004	2006
BBC1	39	36	37	32	27.2	24.7	22.8
BBC2	12	11	10	11	10.8	10	8.8
ITV	49	46	44	37	29.3	22.8	19.6
C4		7	9	11	10.5	9.7	9.8
C5					5.7	6.6	5.7
Others					16.6	26.2	33.3

Source: The data is from Broadcasting Audience Research Board Ltd (BARB) (2007).

service character, and C5 the least); and (3) a third pillar of externally (ITC) but very lightly regulated satellite and cable TV channels, largely funded by subscription, but also some advertising. This '3-tier' regulatory situation has now been institutionally rationalized by the single regulatory framework provided by New Labour's 2003 Communications Act. This legislation merged into a single Office of Communication (Ofcom) all the different pre-existing electronic communications regulatory bodies (for TV, radio, broadcasting standards, spectrum management, and telecoms). Ofcom now presides over the entire 'converging' electronic communications sector (though not the Internet), with the notable exception being that the BBC continues largely to regulate itself, though Ofcom exercises authority over issues of economic competition.

Essentially, the Act subjects all UK-licensed broadcasters to a basic tier of regulatory obligations, regarding such matters as taste and decency, rules on advertising and sponsorship, the requirement for impartiality and accuracy, and the European Union's 'Television Without Frontiers' television quotas that specify that a majority of the programming should be European in origin. The new regulatory framework subjects the 'public service broadcasters' – which are still officially held to include ITV (Channel 3) and Channel 5 – to Ofcom's regulatory oversight of their delivery of a number easily quantifiable and measurable content obligations, such as quotas for independent and original productions, targets for regional productions and regional programming, and the availability of peak time news and current affairs programmes. Here, the BBC and Channel 4 are subject to the heaviest degree of these programming obligations and Channel 5 the lightest. Finally, these mainstream broadcasters are all required to draw up programme statements consistent with their varying degrees of public service remit and they are required to report annually on how they achieve them, with Ofcom – or in the BBC's case, the BBC Trust – ensuring compliance. Ofcom is required to review the broadcasters' self-evaluations of their perfomance and also periodically to produce reports on the state of public service broadcasting. Reflecting the government's concern that regulators respond equally to the needs of consumers (in the market) and citizens (in society), the legislation required Ofcom to establish an internal Consumer Panel and a Content Board to help determine the regulation of broadcasting content.

The deregulation of media ownership rules

Controversially, the Act completed the incremental deregulation of media ownership rules conducted by the Conservatives through the 1990s. In particular, their 1996 Broadcasting Act, following a 1994–5 review of cross-media ownership, replaced the traditional approach of placing quite strict limits on accumulations of interests within and between licensed television services with a new scheme based on a measurement of audience share that allowed for a considerable consolidation of the ITV sector. Over the next few years, ITV effectively became dominated by two companies in England and Wales (Carlton and Granada) and one company (Scottish) in Scotland. The reason for this policy turn appeared 'to lie in the "economic" arguments submitted to the [government] by...large UK media firms and...the Government's receptiveness to these arguments' (Doyle 2002: 85–103, 102). These arguments centred on the perceived need to promote economic efficiency and to establish 'a framework which would strengthen the economic performance of the UK media industry' (Doyle 2002: 104–21, 113). Essentially, the same argument was a major motive for New Labour's 2003 Communications

Act. According to the White Paper, preceding the Act, regulatory reform was intended to '... help make the UK home to the most dynamic and competitive communications market in the world' (DTI/DCMS 2000: 10).

In particular, New Labour's Act opened up the way for the creation of a single ITV by abolishing audience share restrictions on mergers of ITV companies. The Act retained the cross-ownership rule that prevented a national newspaper proprietor with a market share of more than twenty per cent from holding an ITV licence or owning more than twenty per cent of a licensee. However, the Act removed this cross-media restriction for ownership of Channel 5. It lifted the disqualification of non-European Economic Area companies' ownership of UK terrestrial broadcasting licences. It also liberalized the ownership rules governing radio, significantly increasing the scope for radio mergers, and removed the ban on common ownership of national TV and national radio licences. All in all, the Act left little left in the way of media-specific rules for controlling UK media concentration. Instead, general competition law would play the main role.

However, an important new element of media-specific regulation was introduced in recognition of the importance of the media for pluralism as well as simply economic competition. The Act now made provision for a 'plurality test', whereby the Secretary of State (Minister) has been given powers to intervene in the case of media mergers that raise issues of media plurality. Accordingly, the grounds on which a broadcasting or cross-media merger or acquisition might be blocked by the 'plurality test' will depend on whether there is sufficient plurality of persons with control of media outlets and the availability of a wide range of quality television and radio. This measure had been introduced at the Communications Bill's third reading in response to House of Lords protests about the extent of media ownership deregulation. Moreover, in recognition of the possibility that the extensive deregulation may not provide adequate protection against media concentration, Ofcom is required to review ownership patterns in the United Kingdom at three year intervals and to report on key issues. It falls to the government to decide what action, if any, to take (for detail see Gibbons and Humphreys 2008).

The market structure of broadcasting and industry concentration

What are the implications of the new regulatory framework for pluralism and diversity in UK broadcasting? Clearly, the first thing to note from the above account is that the preservation of an important role for public service broadcasting marks an important point of continuity with the past. The five free-to-air terrestrial broadcasters all carry varying degrees of public service content regulation, though it is fair to question whether ITV and Channel Five should continue to be seen as public service broadcasters *per se*. What about plurality and diversity of channels/platforms, and their ownership (or control)?

As is clear from what has been said already, the two dominant free-to-air operators are the publicly owned BBC, with a 2006 audience share of 31.6 per cent, and privately owned ITV, with 19.6 per cent (see Table 2 above). Until the 1990s, the decentralized ITV structure, with fifteen separate regional franchises (plus a breakfast TV franchise), was characterized by a remarkable plurality of ownership. Reflecting its policy on regionalism and its public service concern for pluralism, the then regulator, the IBA, had ensured that the ITV franchises were operated by different companies with generally diverse internal ownership structures. However, as suggested above, starting with the Conservatives' Broadcasting Act 1990, which replaced regulator-discretion with statutory regulation, there occurred an incremental deregulation of the ITV ownership rules, culminating in New Labour's 2003 Communications Act abolishing altogether any obstacle to the single ownership of ITV. This allowed the (by then) two remaining ITV players in England, namely Carlton and Granada, to merge into a single 'ITV plc' for England and Wales, and the Scottish Media Group to gain control of the main Scottish franchises (Grampian and Scottish). While the ITV licences retain positive requirements to regional programming and production, most of the regional identity of ITV has therefore disappeared (Humphreys 2006: 334). The two smaller terrestrial broadcasters are the publicly owned Channel Four, with a 2006 audience share of 9.8 per cent, and privately owned Channel Five, with 5.7 per cent (see Table 2). In 2000, Channel Five came under the majority ownership (66.6 per cent) of the major European RTL group, owned by Bertelsmann, one of the world's largest media companies.

The UK pay-TV market, too, is concentrated. The leading provider of pay-TV in the United Kingdom is BSkyB, whose only large shareholder (35 per cent) and effective controller is News Corporation (Rupert Murdoch). As seen in Table 1, Rupert Murdoch's News International, the UK subsidiary of his global News Corporation, also owns a number of UK national newspapers, accounting for 34.4 per cent of the latter market in (Jan–June) 2006. News Corporation itself was one of the largest global media companies, with operations in film, broadcasting, newspapers and book publishing. According to figures from Ofcom's latest market report (2006a: 199), in the year ending on the 31st March 2006 BSkyB had a UK subscriber base of 7.7 million, which represented over two thirds of the UK pay-TV market. The rest of the market was dominated by Virgin Media, the rebranded name of the recently merged cable television company NTL/Telewest (previously separate companies), with around 3.32 million subscribers. As Ward et al. (2004: 206–7) note, this dominance of UK cable TV by a single company followed an intense concentration process – in 1992, there had been as many as 29 cable companies – in a sector marked by high sunk costs and daunting competition from BSkyB, while the combination of high sunk costs and the considerable market power of BSkyB made it highly unlikely that the latter would ever face a competitor in the satellite TV field.

However, these two pay-TV platforms did face competition from a new 'third force' in UK broadcasting, namely Freeview, which offered a free-to-air alternative source for a basic package of multi-channel viewing. Freeview, a BBC-led joint venture involving BSkyB (which also supplied some channels), was granted a digital terrestrial TV licence by the then regulator, the ITC, following the closure of ITV's digital terrestrial pay-TV venture, ITV Digital, in 2002. Since then, Freeview has become a major part of the UK government's plans to switchover from (and switch off) analogue to digital broadcasting. According to Ofcom (2006a: 199), at the end of March 2006 Freeview's subscribers numbered 7.1 million, making it the United Kingdom's second most popular choice of platform for multi-channel viewing, very close behind BSkyB. Freeview is without any question an important support for public service broadcasting in that it has provided the UK public with a low-cost alternative (the only cost being the one-off expenditure on the digital set-top box) multi-channel platform to the two aforementioned pay-TV operators. Also, as Ofcom (2006a: 184) notes, it has provided 'some protection to the five main channels [with their varying degrees of public service obligations] from the steep falls in audience share typically associated with analogue terrestrial homes moving to satellite or cable, [though] this protection is diminishing'.

Alongside plurality of market players and diversity of channels, the diversity of commissioning within channels as a means to meet the needs and interests of viewers is held to be an important part of the regulator's approach to UK programming diversity (see Ofcom 2006b: 13). Traditionally, the BBC and ITV were vertically integrated broadcasters, producing most of their own programmes. However, from the 1980s the picture began to change. Channel Four introduced a new 'publisher broadcaster' model to UK broadcasting, by commissioning or buying in all its programmes. This model was imitated by Carlton, one of the leading ITV companies, and also by Channel 5. Moreover, the BBC also opened itself up to commissioning from external production units, partly because the Conservatives' Broadcasting Act 1990 introduced a positive requirement that the terrestrial broadcasters each devote at least 25 per cent of their air-time (excluding non-news programmes) each year to the transmission of a range and diversity of productions from the independent production sector. Although the main terrestrial broadcasters are the main buyers, demand from commercial digital channels as well has grown. As a result, the United Kingdom has a large and thriving independent production sector. Ofcom's latest survey evidence (2006b: 19) suggests that in 2006 the independent production sector accounted for 44 per cent of the market for UK-originated programmes (the remaining 56 per cent being 'in-house' production by the broadcasters). However, concentration in the sector is significant. Ofcom (2006b: 19) points to the concentration of UK production (both in-house and independent) in the London area; hence the need for continuing regulatory requirements for programming from beyond the metropolis. Moreover, larger production companies accounted for much of the programming commissioned by the BBC and ITV. Also, concentration in the independent production sector was considerable. Four 'super-indies' (Hi Entertainment, All3Media Group, Talkback Thames and Endemol UK) had 2004 revenues of £100 million or over, and three (TWI, Television Corporation and RDF Media) had revenues of between £50 million and £100 million. It was estimated that these top seven firms accounted for nearly half of the combined independents' revenues (Ofcom 2005: 202–4; Humphreys 2006: 333).

As regards radio, as Ward et al. (2004: 208–9) have noted, the BBC is the 'major player in the overall radio sector and far surpasses the market share of any individual commercial group'. The BBC offers five national radio channels (Radio 1, 2, 3, 4 and 5), two national digital channels, 5 Live Sports Extra und 6 Music, and operates 40 local radio stations (and the World Service). In 2006 there were 320 local commercial stations broadcasting on analogue and/or digital radio. In addition, there were seven UK-wide commercial radio stations (Ofcom 2006a: 54). However, six groups owned 65 per cent of the commercial stations: GCap Media, The Local Radio Company (TLRC), Classic Gold Digital, UTV Radio, Emap and the UKRD Group. Three other groups, with fewer stations, were also important by virtue of their significant shares of listening. They were: Chrysalis, the Guardian Media Group and the Scottish Media Group, which owns Virgin Radio (Ofcom 2006a: 62–3).

The Internet, regulation and public service

According to UK government statistics (see UK Statistics Authority 2008) an estimated 14.3 million UK households could access the Internet from home in 2006 and 69 per cent of these had a broadband connection. The 2003 Communications Act did not provide for any regulation of Internet content. While content posted on the Internet falls under all the general laws of the land, given the nature of the medium, practical regulation and enforcement can clearly pose a problem. UK Internet regulation combines features of 'self' and 'co'-regulation. On the one hand, the Internet Service Providers (ISPs) practice a degree of self-regulation, while 'co-regulation' is provided by a non-governmental organization, the Internet Watch Foundation (IWF). Funded mainly by the industry stakeholders (the ISPs and so on), it works in partnership with Government, ISPs, telecommunication companies, mobile operators, software providers and the police to minimize the availability of illegal Internet content. It operates a hotline allowing the public to report illegal material, which it then passes on to the police if the material was posted in the United Kingdom, or if not, then it notifies the National Criminal Intelligence Service who in turn notify Interpol.

Of course, by its very nature, the Internet allows freedom of expression and external pluralism on a tremendous scale. However, from the point of view of democratic pluralism, notably with regard to fulfilling the information needs of an informed public, it is not entirely unproblematic. Although the Internet has certainly the positive potential to improve the citizenry's media access and usage, there exists clearly the danger that citizens may be overwhelmed by a superabundance of poorly edited or downright unreliable information. A strong case can therefore be made for public policy intervention to ensure a strong 'public service communications' presence on the Internet not least in order to provide a reliable and trustworthy source of information. Accordingly, with the Government's blessing, the BBC has developed an extensive web service (http://www.bbc.co.uk), with the aim to provide a universal service of innovative and distinctive content, spanning a wide range of themes, including news, sport, art and education, in line with its overall remit. According to the latest BBC Annual Report (BBC 2006: 42), by the end of the reporting period 2005/2006 the average monthly reach of bbb.co.uk had reached 56 per cent of the UK online audience. According to the Guardian Media Directory (MediaGuardian/ Gibson 2007: 234) it was the United Kingdom's fifth most popular website.

Note

1. These calculations are based on ABC figures for the period January–June 2006 (see Mediaguardian/ Gibson 2007: 20).

References

BBC, Annual Report and Accounts 2005/2006.

Broadcasting Audience Research Board Ltd (BARB) (2008), 'TV Facts – Annual % Shares of Viewing (Individuals) 1981–2007', http://www.barb.co.uk. Accessed 16 May 2008.

Calcutt, David (1990), Report of the Committee on Privacy and Related Matters, London: HMSO, Cm. 1102.

Calcutt, David (1993), Review of Press Self-Regulation, London: HMSO, Cm. 2135.

Department of Trade and Industry/Department for Culture, Media and Sport (2000), A New Future for Communications, The White Paper.

Doyle, Gillian (2002), Media Ownership. The Economics and Politics of Convergence and Concentration in the UK and European Media, London/Thousand Oaks/New Delhi: Sage.

Freedom House (2007), 'Global Press Freedom 2007', http://www.freedomhouse.org. Accessed 20 June 2007.

Gibbons, Thomas (1998), Regulating the Media, London: Sweet & Maxwell.

Gibbons, Thomas and Humphreys, Peter (2008), Media Ownership Rules in the United Kingdom and Germany, http://www.socialsciences.manchester.ac.uk/politics/research/avregulation/media_ownership.htm. Accessed 28 May 2008.

Graham, Andrew and Davies, Gavyn (1997), Broadcasting, Society and Policy in the Multimedia Age, Luton: John Libbey Media.

Hallin, Daniel C. and Mancini, Paolo (2004), Comparing Media Systems: Three Models of Media and Politics, Cambridge: Cambridge University Press.

Humphreys, Peter (1996), Mass Media and Media Policy in Western Europe, Manchester: Manchester University Press.

Humphreys, Peter (2000), 'New Labour Policies for the Media and Arts', in David Coates and Peter Lawler (eds.), New Labour in Power, Manchester: Manchester University Press, pp. 221–39.

Humphreys, Peter (2006), 'Medien und Medienpolitik', in Hans Kastendiek and Roland Sturm (eds.), Länderbericht Gro britannien, Bonn: Bundeszentrale für politische Bildung, pp. 316–39.

Lijphart, Arend (1984), Democracies: Patterns of Majoritarian and Consensus Government in Twenty-One Countries, New Haven: Yale University Press.

Mediaguardian/Gibson, Janine (2007), Media Directory 2007, published by Guardian News and Media.

Nicol, Andrew and Bowman, Caroline (1993), 'Press Law in the United Kingdom', in Article 19, Press Law and Practice: A Comparative Study of Press Freedom in European and Other Democracies, published by Article 19 for the United Nations Educational, Scientific and Cultural Organisation (UNESCO), pp. 167–91.

Newton, Kenneth and Artingstall, Nigel (1994), 'Government and Private Censorship in Nine Western Democracies in the 1970s and 1980s', in Ian Budge and David McKay (eds.), Developing Democracy, London: Sage, pp. 297–321.

Ofcom (2005), The Communications Market 2005, published by Ofcom.

Ofcom (2006a), The Communications Market 2006, published by Ofcom.

Ofcom (2006b), Review of the Television Production Sector: Statement, published by Ofcom.

Reporters Without Borders (2007), 'Freedom of the Press Worldwide in 2007: 2007 Annual Report', http://www.rsf.org. Accessed 20 June 2007.

Tunstall, Jeremy and Machin, David (1999), The Anglo-American Media Connection, Oxford: Oxford University Press.

UK Statistics Authority (2008), http://www.statistics.gov.uk/cci/nugget.asp?id=8. Accessed 4 June 2008.

Ward, David; Fueg, Oliver Carsten and D'Armo, Alessandro (2004), A Mapping Study of Media Concentration and Ownership in Ten European Countries, Commissariat voor de Media (Netherlands) and David Ward.

Mind the Gap? Press Freedom and Pluralism in Finland

Inka Salovaara-Moring

Introduction

Freedom of expression and freedom of the press are basic pillars of western democracy. The contemporary theoretical framework that gives support to these rights was generated in the wake of the liberal revolutions, which took place in Western Europe and in North America from the second half of the seventeenth century onwards. Since then, both external and internal conditions of press freedom and pluralism have changed considerably in both European and other western societies.

Although Finland today regularly takes the top position in the worldwide press freedom index conducted by the International Press Institute, both external determinants (market forces, technological convergence, concentration of ownership) as well as internal preconditions (professionalization, digitalization, media management) have affected the diversity of media and freedom of expression in Finland. The effects of market forces on journalistic practices and a toughening of competition for audience shares create tightening conditions for the media and through that create new challenges for press freedom.

This chapter explores the possible gap between normative ideals of press freedom, legal provisions, and the empirical reality of the Finnish media system. It aims to highlight press freedom and changing relations between market(s), governmental policies, and regulatory bodies in the Finnish context. An important part of understanding any media system is also to know the historical and cultural conditions under which the current modus operandi of press freedom has been achieved. Thus, the first part focuses on the historical development of the media and freedom of expression in Finland. The second part explores the current situation of the media system and the new tendencies that modify the press freedom of the EU-era. The third part presents the legal provisions that guarantee the freedom of expression, the main emphases of the Government's media policy, and how the self-accountability of Finnish journalism is conducted. The last chapter summarizes the main modifiers of the Finnish media system and discusses how challenges to the diversity of media and press freedom have changed during the last decades.

Press freedom and the historical conditions of the Finnish media

Alongside other Nordic media systems, the Finnish media system has often been considered to guarantee the ideal conditions for press freedom. The media system fits within the Nordic tradition, where the basic objective of media policy is freedom of speech supported by legislation, public subsidy, taxation and reductions in fees. However, it is not easy to locate Finland within European media systems. In the light of the three models of media and politics coined by Hallin and Mancini (2004), Finland is indeed historically closest to the 'Democratic-Corporatist Model' or 'Northern European Model'. Thus the Finnish system meets some of the 'three coexistences' characterizing this model, such as strong mass-circulation of privately owned print media, media partially tied to political and civil groups, weakening political parallelism, journalistic professionalism, and the coexistence of liberal traditions of media freedom and strong state intervention. Through these co-existences, the media has also been seen traditionally as a social institution (Moring 2008: 144–5; Hallin and Mancini 2005: 195–6).

Economically, the Finnish media system can be characterized as a mixed system including privately owned as well as state-funded companies. Like Scandinavian countries, Finland has a strong tradition of public service broadcasting. Television in Finland is based on the public service company Yleisradio Oy (the Finnish Broadcasting Company YLE), and privately owned commercial channels, which are financed by advertising revenues. Seen in a Nordic context, the publicly owned radio and television sector in Finland turned into a dual system remarkably early when a commercial operator was accepted as a co-operator under the broadcasting license of the Finnish Broadcasting Company in 1956. From 1985 onwards, private operators have been granted licence to broadcast on radio, and from 1993 onwards, also on television.

Historically, the specific feature of the Finnish media system is an extraordinarily strong position of print media. Avid newspaper reading lies partly in the main values of Finnish culture: education, literary culture and self-improvement. The 'good citizen' was traditionally expected to be informed, not only about facts concerning domestic issues but also about foreign issues. Partly because of these tendencies, the circulation figures for daily newspapers have remained very high throughout the history. The increased number of online newspaper hits along with strong reader coverage demonstrates that newspapers have more readers and customers than ever.

Press freedom in Finland is closely intertwined historically with the country's geographical position between east and west, including its long land-border with Russia. The first newspapers in Sweden and in the Baltic countries, which then, like Finland, formed part of the Swedish Kingdom, appeared in the mid-seventeenth century. Finland, however, received its first newspaper only in the late eighteenth century. The first Finnish newspaper was founded in 1771 by the learned Aurora Society in Turku, under the title *Tidningar utgifne af et Sällskap i Åbo* ['News published by a society in Turku']. In the 1790s the paper became the chief source of foreign and domestic news (Salokangas 1996; Jyrkiäinen 2004).

The first newspaper had a special role and remained in circulation for over 90 years. It was the official organ of the national government when Finland gained autonomous status as a Grand Duchy of Russia in 1809.[1] In 1850 a decree was passed according to which only religious and economic literature could be published in Finnish. At that time the Russian model censorship board was established with local censors in Finland. This strictly constrained newspaper content, permission was required for the publication of newspapers and periodicals, and all were examined in advance (Ekholm 1997: 46).

After the period of strident Russification, it was announced in 1905 that advance censorship would be lifted. In reality, freedom of the press was fully achieved only after Finland gained its independence in 1917.[2] Since then matters concerning press freedom have been scrutinized by the Ministry of Justice, with a law guaranteeing freedom of the press being passed in 1919. According to Ekholm (1997: 47), however, writers during the early years of independence had to be careful of what they wrote, with leftist, atheist and anti-ecclesiastical articles considered the most dangerous. Communist newspapers were suspended during the time of the Lapua Movement.[3] Extreme right-wing newspapers were also under threat of suspension for their actions in 1938 and the final kiss of death was given when Finland signed the armistice agreement with the Soviet Union in 1940.

War censorship prevailed between 1939 and 1947 and was based on retrospective surveillance, imposed first by the Military Headquarters, subsequently by the Minister of Interior, and during the Continuation War (1941–4), by the Finnish State Centre for Information. During the early years of the war, censorship was clear and apolitical. The State provided instructions to the press that advised them to forestall all information that might endanger the Armed Forces or overall security of the country. The aims of official censorship were modified and politicised between 1940 and 1941, and then 'national unanimity, belief in future and increasing the self-discipline of the people' were seen as the main task of the censors. During the Continuation War, the Finns learned to know both their German colleagues and what was meant by extremely strict censorship. This was conducted by seventy specifically recruited censors who were located in different newspapers and who were often collocated with the editors-in-chief to monitor the printed material on the spot. After losing the Second World War to the Soviet Union, the Finns had to obey an obligation to remove so-called politically dubious books and printed materials from bookshops. The rigours of wartime had served to educate Finns on the need for caution in public discussion concerning foreign policy (so called 'self-censorship') and this was to continue for the next forty years (Salminen 2003; Ekholm 1997).

The concept of self-censorship arose in the atmosphere of the post-war years that saw Finland in the shadow of strong Stalinist foreign policies. The Finnish political leadership vehemently urged the Finnish media and journalists to be restrained in their critiques of the Soviet Union, and this modified what could be said in public discussion. Finnish media had to learn to take heed of their eastern neighbour's warning signs to avoid encouraging a stronger grip on the sovereign but fledgling nation-state. The death of Stalin in 1953 was followed by even stricter surveillance as Soviet diplomats followed developments in Finland closely. It was against this background that broadcasting in Finland started to develop. Like radio, commercial participation in television was notable in Finland almost from the start and this was early compared to other Nordic countries. Commercially funded programme operations were initiated by the Foundation for the Promotion of Technology (Tekniikan edistämissäätiö) in 1956. In 1960 this became organized as the commercial company Tesvision. The Finnish

Broadcasting service began television test transmissions in 1957 and regular service started in 1958 when television licences also became compulsory in Finland.

During the late 1960s and 1970s the term 'Finnlandisierung' in English 'Finlandization', was coined as a cautionary term in the commentaries of West German political scientists and conservative politicians. On a general level it referred to a political configuration where a small state is too weak to challenge or resist the influence of a more powerful neighbour and consequently has to give up portions of its sovereignty and neutrality. The famous Finnish political cartoonist, Kari Suomalainen, for example, defined Finlandization as 'the art of bowing to the East so carefully that it could not be considered as mooning', that is displaying your bare buttocks 'to the West' (Jokisipilä 2007). The Finnish experience of self-subordination is aptly described by the Finnish columnist Jukka Tarkka: 'The essential nature of Finlandization was an emotional fancy, that by pleasing the superpower and overemphasising one's humility, the superpower could be made to do something that it would not do on rational grounds.'

The most integral part of Finlandization was the self-censorship exercised by the Finns themselves. It became everyday practice for participants in public discussions to take particular caution when they expressed views on the Soviet Union or Finnish-Soviet relations. That was understood as the wise practice of a small country keen not to irritate a bigger, unpredictable neighbour. Historian Esko Salminen (2003) divides Finnish self-censorship into two categories: exaggerated cautiousness and fear in terms of the threat of the Soviet Union, and tactical silence and regulation of media motivated by domestic politics and political tactics. The political elite and the President, in particular, often used the 'East card' when the media started to act in an unruly fashion and question foreign policy too loudly.

News journalists were especially cautious in their line concerning the Soviet Union or its satellites; indexed countries. Finnish authorities closely monitored the media in order to keep any criticism of the Soviet Union out of the public eye and made specific requests to publishers to abstain from giving voice to opinions that could be detrimental from the point of view of Finnish-Soviet relations. To make the compliance with these requests more attractive, this principle of foreign political reserve was even sanctioned within criminal law. Eventually, it became customary for the journalists themselves to, voluntarily and on their own initiative, omit parts of their stories and articles that could be interpreted as anti-Soviet either by the Soviet Union or by the President, who, according to the Finnish historian Markku Jokisipilä (2007; see also Salminen 2003), kept a close eye on Finnish public opinion.

The policy-line of news service of YLE was aiming at 'impartiality' and 'even-handedness' in its foreign news reporting. Major crises on the world arena, like the occupation of Czechoslovakia in 1968, put the infant news service to the test. Ralf Friberg, Head of News services during the late 1960s was hired to reorganize YLE's news services. After study-trips to approach and study BBC instructions and US news journalism manuals on the style of broadcasting, YLE's own current-affairs programmes and news were raised to Western standards in terms of professional skills and concepts (Salokangas 1996: 117).

Cautiousness in terms of the Soviet Union lasted until the collapse of communism in 1991. At the time of the collapse of the Soviet Union, preventive censorship in Finland applied only to films and videos and the censorship was not affected by Finland's relationship with the Soviet Union. In the late 1990s, preventive censorship of films was justified primarily by the protection of children.

During the 1990s many things in the Finnish foreign policy and economy changed. During the years 1991–6 the national economy of Finland drifted into an economic crisis. When the Soviet system collapsed in 1989 and Finland joined the European Union in 1995, the contextual conditions for the economy and politics changed. Not only did the era, sometimes called Finlandization in the West, come to an end, but a deep economic crisis followed. This was caused in part by the collapse of trade with the Soviet Union and the rapid internationalization of the Finnish economy, which also affected the media industry by tightening the competition.

During the EU accession period, Finland experienced a new type of media-influence, reminiscent of earlier mechanisms of self-censorship. In Finland the media actively promoted the benefits of EU membership in the months leading up to their respective referendums. In particular, domination of the media by an almost unanimous but narrow band of pro-EU elites was striking. According to the study of EU journalism, the ideological atmosphere inside news rooms, editorial policy-line and editors-in-chiefs of the big media houses often publicly announced the integration as 'not only necessary and wise but the only realistic solution for a small country' bordering Russia (Mörä 1999). Critical journalistic voices were not considered reliable and the overall atmosphere favoured EU-integration. During the mainstream media campaign, however, the public remained stubbornly sceptical. According to polls, the Finns were among the most Euro-sceptical of all countries during the time of referendum. Although the 'Russia-card' wasn't actively used, according to President Koivisto it was a decisive factor when the decision was made. Eventually the European Union was chosen in many cases in order to make a clean break with the 'East' (see Salminen 1999; Forsberg, Kekäle and Ekholm 2001: 129–38).

As has been described above, the fields of press and media freedoms have also been particular in Finnish history. Whilst Finland has hosted a system that is based on the right of access to official documents, typical to Nordic states, and also based on respect for freedom of the press, Finnish politicians as well as the media have been exercising a temperate policy in using these freedoms (Moring 2008). This has been particularly visible in the way that the political elite and the media have behaved with regard to relations with the Soviet Union, later Russia and in the early years towards the European Union. In recent years, a more open debate on foreign policy issues has also emerged and the role and performance of the President has been openly challenged. There is still, however, a clear tendency within the political elite to try to maintain this sector within a sphere of national consensus, and the media have not done very much to challenge this consensus whether in regard to the possible NATO membership or political upheavals among the Baltic neighbours.

New challenges: Media system, press freedom and commercialization

The contemporary Finnish media landscape can be described as vivid, commercial and highly competitive. Finland's per capita consumption of print media has traditionally been one of the highest in the world. The circulation figures for daily newspapers have remained fairly stable, although with the onset of the deep recession in the early 1990s the total circulation of Finnish newspapers showed symptoms of decline for the first time since World War Two. Despite market changes newspapers are doing comparatively well.

Print media reach over 80 per cent of Finns daily, making it the medium with the second best coverage after television. In addition, Finland ranks first in the European Union and third in the world, after Japan and Norway, with 518 copies sold per 1,000 inhabitants in 2005. Economic statistics lend support to this image: newspapers' shares of mass media turnover (30 per cent) and advertising revenue (55 per cent) remain very high. Newspapers are also widely read with 87 per cent of the population aged 12 years and over reading a newspaper every day. A total of 205 newspaper titles were published in 2005. Of these, 53 were dailies appearing four to seven times a week, whilst 29 were published every day of the week, more than in any other Nordic country.

In terms of party-parallelism, the overall trend since the Second World War has been for party newspapers to declare themselves politically unaffiliated, resulting in a gradual decline of the party-political press.[4] Today, more than 95 per cent of Finnish newspapers declare that they are politically unaffiliated. Among the main parties, the National Coalition Party is the only one with no daily organ. Remaining party papers have limited circulation, appear less frequently than they used to, and have fewer pages than a standard newspaper (Jyrkiäinen 2004). Finns are also becoming more and more active in using online services, and newspapers, along with other traditional media, are getting a significant share of online visitors. Three newspapers and two television channels are in the top ten of the most visited online services. Content providers that hold positions of trust in traditional publishing channels appear to enjoy similar levels of trust online.

Television in Finland is based on the public service company Yleisradio Oy (Finnish Broadcasting Company YLE), privately owned MTV3 (MTV Finland) and Nelonen (Channel Four Finland). YLE is financed by a television fee that is compulsory to all households that possess a television set. The latter two companies are both financed by advertising revenues. In 2005, YLE's aggregate share of daily television viewing was 44 per cent, split between its two channels TV1 (25 per cent) and TV 2 (19 per cent). Commercial MTV3 has a 33 per cent share whilst Nelonen (Channel Four) has a 19 per cent audience share. The domestic production rate is high in the nationwide television channels. Two thirds of YLE's, half of the MTV's programmes and a little over 30 per cent of the Channel Four's programmes are produced domestically. This has increased the share of the independent production companies as content providers in all channels.

Table 1: Dailies: Circulation per 1000 Persons in 1991–2005.

	1990 Total population	2000 Total population	2005 Adult population
EU	179	153	170
Finland	558	445	518
United Kingdom	390	319	348
Germany	333	291	305
Italy	118	105	114
Spain	76	108	113
Estonia	523	191	225

Source: World Press Trends, Statistics Finland 2006.

During the development of digital television in Finland, YLE has taken the role of innovator and has been the driving force of the digitalization process, with commercial media companies largely following their lead. A milestone for the introduction of regular digital television to Finland was August 2001. The target date for the switchover from analogue to digital national television was in September 2007, resulting in Finland being among the first to digitize its television broadcast network. In contrast to, for example, Sweden and Germany, the whole of Finland switched over to digital television at the same time, and not by region. However, cable television service providers have until the end of February 2008 to convert to digital signal from analogue. After that, cable households will also need a digital receiver to watch television broadcasts. As part of the digitalization process, private broadcasters were freed from an earlier obligation to contribute to the financing of public service broadcasting.

Since the switch-over to digital television, the commercial television companies in Finland have increased their investments in and marketing of pay-TV niche channels, which are expected to be a growing business.

There is no special legislation on media concentration in Finland and this has facilitated an accelerating trend towards newspaper chains in the ownership structure. In 2004, there were 22 newspaper chains, three of which publish Swedish-language newspapers. Through take-overs and mergers, the market share of the biggest media houses has also grown. The publishing of dailies has been concentrated into five newspaper chains that control half of the dailies' net sales in Finland: SanomaWSOY, Alma Media, Keskisuomalainen, Turun Sanomat Group and Ilkka Group.

The concentration of newspapers into chains is expected to continue at both a national and Nordic level. The two major newspaper houses account for 56 per cent of the aggregate circulation of dailies. From net sales (that is to say newspaper sales and advertising sales combined) SanomaWSOY accounts for 24 per cent and Alma Media 18 per cent. MTV3 and the new digital channels MTV Max and Subtv (the latter also broadcast over the cable network) were taken over by Nordic Broadcasting in 2005. Nordic Broadcasting is half-owned by Sweden's biggest media company Bonnier and the investment company Proventus Industrier (Sauri 2007: 109).

The big newspaper publishing houses have diversified and expanded since the 1980s from print houses into electronic media, online services, mobile services, and multimedia products, thus becoming real multimedia corporations. The leading book publisher WSOY (Werner Söderström Oy, founded in 1878), the Sanoma Corporation (1889), and the Helsinki Media Company merged in 1998 to become SanomaWSOY. Today SanomaWSOY is the biggest media corporation in the Nordic countries. SWelcom, the electronic media division of the SanomaWSOY also owns the television channel Nelonen (Channel Four) and a radio channel (Radio Helsinki).

Sanoma Magazines publishes over 200 magazine titles in nine countries and is among the top five magazine publishers in Europe. All in all, SanomaWSOY has operations in sixteen European countries including magazine and press publishing, book publishing, kiosk operations, press distribution, book and movie stores, and restaurant operations. SanomaWSOY acquired local publishing rights to Metro in 2006 and is also strongly represented in the rapidly growing free-distribution newspaper market.

YLE is the second largest media company in economic terms after SanomaWSOY and Alma Media. Its turnover was over 383.5 million Euros in 2006 and it is a public service limited company owned by the state, with five national television channels and thirteen radio channels.

Broadcast-news institutions are responding in unprecedented ways to a public that increasingly produces and consumes its own journalism. These trends challenge traditional notions of citizenship and the role of broadcasters. Traditional mass media companies have been working actively to develop integrated communication products and services. In the Finnish context, commercial companies have increasingly questioned YLE's monopoly, especially with regards to online services. The public broadcaster is able to build online services that are not under the same financial constraints to create economic revenue as the online services of commercial competitors, in an era when the toughest competition is the fight for these new channels and their audience. Due to the financially tight situation created by digitalization, YLE is going through heavy streamlining and re-organization. In particular, radio services are being dismantled and converted into Internet services. The move to digitalization challenges the ability of the market to sustain more channels for general broadcasting. According to plans, the future of the Finnish public service system, which is presently financed through licence fees, will be discussed in a parliamentary committee due to commence in 2010.

New media innovations, like blogs, websites and other user-generated media content have driven the media landscape to seek new openings, causing the big media companies to embrace these new types of 'media'.[5] This reflects the change in the market in more general terms. Media companies have realized that the whole concept of 'media' may look totally different than the traditional model. Media has no monopoly of media, nor can journalists monopolize journalism. The blogosphere is part of the media landscape but its real significance has yet to be defined and it is still in a state of development. In addition, other user-generated services such as different types of lists, chat-sites and social media-sites are part of the new strategy of the media houses to adjust to the changing market situation.

Freedom of expression, transparency and ethical codes

Legal provisions

A legally established freedom of speech is the foundation of any democratic society. The basic objective of the Finnish government's media policy has been the promotion of freedom of speech supported by legislation, public subsidy, taxation, and reductions in fees. In Finland, freedom of expression stands on two pillars: The Constitution of Finland guarantees freedom of speech, and access to official documents is guaranteed by the Openness of Government Activities Act. The first principle, designated as 'freedom of expression', is included in the Finnish Constitution (revised 2000) and in the Exercise of Freedom of Expression in Mass Media Act, which provides medium-neutral regulation of freedom of speech (revised 2004). Complementing the aforementioned section of the Constitution is the Exercise of Freedom of Expression in Mass Media Act (460/2003). It contains more detailed provisions as to the practice, in the media, of the freedom of expression as enshrined in the Constitution.

In the application of the Act, interference with the activities of the media are legitimate only insofar as it is unavoidable, taking due note of the importance of the freedom of expression in a democracy, subject to the rule of law. One of the main aims of the new law is to regulate all media regardless of their technology.

The second principle, designated as 'open access to public documents' (Openness of Government Activities Act, 621/1999; amendments up to 1060/2002 included) guarantees that official documents shall be in the public domain unless specifically otherwise determined. The Openness of Government Activities Act, that is, the principle of transparency in public issues, is a specifically Nordic feature and obliges the government and public administration to embrace openness and freedom of information in all administrative activity. Civil servants have to give information and copies of documentation to journalists on any projects they are handling, unless the matter has been specifically declared to be secret. For example, taxation, including the income of the citizens, is public information. In the case of restraining access to information, journalists have been able to appeal to the courts, and many have successfully done so. However, when it comes to private companies, obtaining accurate information is increasingly difficult, though account and balance-sheets are public knowledge.

The Ministry of Transport and Communications oversees telecommunications, the operating licences for local radio and television, and the press subsidy system. The Ministry of Education promotes the content production for TV, video and motion pictures, copyright matters, education, archiving and research. The Telecommunications Administration Centre inspects technical infrastructures, equipment, frequencies and technical licences. The Government grants operating licences for commercial radio and television, and also decides the size of the annual television fee for viewers.

The operations of the Finnish Broadcasting Company (Yleisradio Oy or YLE) are regulated through the Finnish Broadcasting Company Act.[6] The financing of YLE is regulated through the State Television and Radio Fund Act (Act No. 745/1998). Private radio and television operations over the air are regulated by separate legislation. Private, non-public service broadcasting can be pursued only by those who have been granted an operating licence by the government under legislation issued in 1998. This comprised the Television and Radio Operations Act.[7]

YLE does not require an operating licence for broadcasting because its operations are based on the conditions of the aforementioned Act on Yleisradio Oy. The national government submits proposals concerning electronic communications to Parliament and grants operating licences for local radio and local television. Operating licences are not required for cable broadcasting, but an announcement of operation has to be made to the Telecommunications Administration Centre.

In November 2001 a new Radio Act was approved before coming into force on 1 January 2002. Changes related to the reform of the entire legislation concerning the communication market were made to several pieces of this legislation in two stages. The Act on Yleisradio prohibits radio and television advertising on YLE's channels, and sponsored programmes are not permitted on YLE. YLE's operations are financed mainly by television licence fees. In 2004, a television licence cost €186 per year. In practice, YLE's final accounts are approved by the Ministry of Transport and Communications.

For the printed press, there have been various forms of public subsidy systems since the 1970s. Government subsidies for the printed press, cultural and opinion papers, and for political party publications, have been granted according to a proposal made by a state committee (Jyrkiäinen 2004). Diversity of content is granted by press subsidies and the state has granted subventions to both the party press and to so-called second newspapers (regional or national). Support of the party press (parliamentarian support) is divided in proportion to the parliamentary representation of the parties. Support of other newspapers (selective support) has been determined through a selection committee. Until 2007, the division of parliamentary and selective support has been of an approximately similar size. From 2008 onwards, the press subsidy system has shifted to predominantly focus on parliamentary support (€90,000 for each Member of Parliament). At the same time, the Support Budget was raised from €14.3 million to €18.5 million. A smaller sum of €0.5 million will remain for selective support and this provides funding for national minority language newspapers, including provision for a Swedish news service.

The new Communications Market Act (2003) – covering all communication networks from mobile to digital terrestrial broadcasting networks – aims to ensure that networks and services are available to all telecommunication operators and users throughout the country, and that they are technologically advanced, of a high quality, reliable, safe and inexpensive. In July 2002 the first phase of the reform entered into force through changes in the Telecommunications Market Act, the Television and Radio Operations Act, the State Television and Radio Fund Act, the Finnish Broadcasting Company Act, and the Communications Administration Act. These changes included, among others, regulations concerning digital television and radio distribution, as well as an increase from ten per cent to fifteen per cent for the percentage of transmission time required to be reserved for programmes produced by independent production companies. On 25 July 2003 the second phase of the reform came into effect. The new Communications Market Act (Act No. 393/2003) replaced the Telecommunications Market Act and changes were made through amendments to the Television and Radio Operations Act, the State Television and Radio Fund Act and Finnish Broadcasting Company Act. With these changes, the EU regulatory framework for all electronic communication was reflected by Finnish legislation.

In addition, Finnish media policy is affected by recurrent calls in Brussels for support for the Union's internal Single Market in order to achieve economies of scale and develop new, cross-border services capable of competing in the global economy. The present policy line of the Government promotes the single communications market and a simultaneous enactment of the Communications Directive across the Union. Active measures are taken to support the competitiveness and productivity of the communications industry and to look after the interests of European consumers, that is to say market-based competition among all actors within the field. When communications laws are harmonized, steps will be taken to ensure that due consideration is given to technological advancement. General laws will continue to regulate the communications market when no valid grounds for any special regulation exist.

The current goals, however, emphasize support of an efficiently functioning market. The present government programme (2007–11) sets as its goal the boosting of competitiveness and productivity. The aim is to maintain Finland's position as one of the world's leading producers and users of information and communications technology. More citizen-focused aims are to promote social and regional equality, and to improve citizens' well-being and quality of life through the effective utilization of information and communications technologies. Public service structures will be renewed by making use of information and communication technology. The Government will prepare a communications policy programme aimed at encouraging investment and innovation in the communications sector. The communications infrastructure will primarily be developed on commercial terms using competitive technologies. At a policy level, Finland currently invests more in technology rather than in the use of the new innovations for enhancing diversity and civil society.[8]

Self-regulation and new ethical codes
Good journalistic practice is based both on legal provisions that guarantee the public's right to have access to facts and opinions, and the self-accountability of journalists. In Finland, publishers and journalist organizations have accepted a voluntary ethical code of 'good journalistic practice' that should be known to all journalists. The aim of this code is to support the responsible use of freedom of speech in mass communication and encourage discourse on professional ethics. The code concerns all journalistic work and was drafted with self-regulation in the field specifically in mind. However, the code is not intended to be used as grounds for criminal or indemnification liability. The code concerns professional status, obtaining and publishing information, the rights of interviewer and interviewee, corrections and the right of reply, as well as what can be defined as private and public.

A revision of the ethical code (from 1992) came into force in 2005 and it places less stress on generally formulated principles and values but gives greater prominence to the right to publish. In addition, it includes a clause on transparency when reporting on issues that pertain to the owners of the media in question. YLE maintains a separate ethical code with a complementary function vis -à -vis this code, including, for example, principles on political programming prior to elections.

The Council for Mass Media monitors good journalistic practice on the basis of the ethical code and operates on a self-regulatory basis, agreed on by the parties involved, without special legislation. The Council was founded in 1968 by organizations of journalists and press publishers. The Council receives approximately 50 to 70 complaints annually. In 2007 there were 64 complaints, 50 of which led to an acquittal. The latest complaints have concerned the blurred line between privacy and the right to publish, online journalism and incorrect information.

In the revised Exercise of Freedom of Expression in Mass Media Act, responsibility has shifted from the editor-in-charge towards the journalist and other editorial staff involved in the practical crafting of published material. In the case of defamatory reporting, liability lies with the offender in penal cases. The publicist has to define the editor-in-charge of a publication, who supervises and makes decisions regarding the content of the publication. If the editor-in-charge is guilty of dereliction of duty and that, in turn, causes defamatory or flawed reporting, then s/he can be sentenced to pay a fine. The editor-in-charge doesn't necessarily have to be the editor-in-chief; s/he can come from middle management or be a general journalist.

According to district prosecutor Heikki Poukka, the new Press Freedom Act (revised 2004) has also changed the prosecution process (Ranta 2007). Currently, the investigation pays more attention to issues such as how a headline has been created as part of the edition process, 'in headline-driven news'. The starting point is to find the offenders and demonstrate culpability. In this case, according to Poukka, organizational arrangements should allow the journalists to consult the editor-in-charge in case the news piece is significant and needs checking.

Moving responsibility downwards has been especially popular with editors-in-chiefs but this revision of responsibility has been also criticized. Earlier, the practice gave prominence to editors-in-chief who were also forced to take responsibility when their subordinates made blunders. 'In the history of the Finnish mass media the change is radical if the power and responsibility starts now to flow downwards' according to Professor Raimo Salokangas:

> The newly revisited Act has an American flavour – everyone can be summoned and claim compensation for damage. The Act can also make it easier to apply pressure on the media and make journalists too careful. It is easier for mighty editors-in-chief to resist intimidation. An ordinary journalist is more vulnerable. (Salokangas in Ranta 2007)

Online competition between news media complicates the decision-making process although an editor-in-charge should always be reachable by telephone. In practice, the issue proceeds from a journalist, to a news producer and then to the vice editor-in-chief and finally to the editor-in-chief. This process was clearly demonstrated during coverage of the Jokela school-shooting when the news media were accused of intrusion and inappropriate means of acquisition of information.[9] This process is especially important in crisis situations where the online journalist, the news producer and graphic producer must be in the position to reach a quick decision, particularly when it comes to interviewing young people or people in shock, or using still pictures and video footage.

Mind the gap: Conclusions

The Finnish media system still has a rather traditional outlook: the role of the print media is strong; people watch television relatively infrequently; and much of their viewing is focused on public service channels. Traditional news is both heavily produced and consumed, journalism has retained its flavour of social responsibility and ethical codes are respected. However, new global and European tendencies modify the Finnish system as well.

Technological convergence, for example, is profoundly changing the market conditions and social conditions under which the journalists conduct their daily work. Economic constraints have forced many media companies to 'outsource' their 'content producers', creating a new situation whereby a new generation of journalists are only offered short-term contracts.

During the last decade, user-generated content and social media have revolutionized the field. In the current situation, traditional tasks, such as informing citizens and scrutinizing those who govern, may sometimes be in contradiction to the demands of the market. Small societies also have their own specific problems in comparison to larger media systems. These can sometimes include closely-knit power cliques of political, economic, and journalistic elites, the intertwined interests of different actors, and self-censorship of journalists in an uncertain labour market situation.

Debate on the erosion of journalistic culture and commercialization is notable in Finland. Ari-Pekka Pietilä, the former editor-in-chief of the largest Finnish tabloid paper claims that news media is turning into a news industry that is governed by investors. This perspective sees journalism as increasingly standardized and cost-efficient. The worst scenario is a future media landscape divided into a multitude of different channels that on the one hand deliver cheap, commercialized, bulk-produced entertainment for the masses, and on the other hand elite-based, solvent and refined knowledge sources. This division is not driven by the channel but by the content. Pietilä sees the interest groups of the field as rescuers of the public's declining faith in media. The field should create tighter regulations and restore the faith of readers and viewers before unchecked competition erodes whatever faith remains (Hakkarainen 2007).

As described earlier, Finland has a very particular history of press freedom and thus journalists are aware of the lures of being overly cautious of self-censorship. Although taboos concerning Finland's eastern neighbour and foreign politics have disappeared, new taboos for press freedom are always on offer. Self-censorship mostly functions at a subconscious level and is, therefore, difficult to detect. Press freedom and its restrictions require constant observation and its infringement has to be given serious consideration.

Obviously, the media's social function within Finnish society will remain strong despite ever-multiplying channels and the growing volume of mass media. However, the gatekeeper role of journalism is being eroded. The main reasons for ailing journalism are the proliferation of user-generated content and blogs through which politicians can communicate without the journalistic echelon. This removes processes of editing and control of messages, and multiplies the audience in an unequalled way. At times, this has lead to something of a free card with respect to critical surveillance of the political elite.

Today, self-censorship may arise, for example, in situations where young journalists feel that their short-term contracts with the media houses may be in danger. When, earlier, there were 'official silences' in Finnish public discussion, now the problem seems to be 'to find someone who would have something new to say', as tabloid newspaper journalists claim from time to time. Thus headline-driven news, various entertainment materials and new types of commercial services for the audience are in demand. At the same time, new types of challenges to press freedom are appearing driven by market economics.

Media policies also follow the tendency of market primacy. During the last decade most basic legislation has been revised in order to accommodate the situation created by an open-market environment, the convergence of technologies, and the single-market requirements of the European Union. At the European regulatory level, there are certain public-interest objectives that are attached to single-market development. In general, national regulatory models should not disturb the development and functioning of the European single market by fragmenting markets. This can be seen as a positive approach to market freedom but certain potential effects may endanger national media policies.

When describing the Commission's recently proposed reform of EU telecom legislation, Commissioner Viviane Reding explained: 'We need a means to break away from a national mindset, so that the full potential of a market of 500 million consumers can be realised.' Such thoughts lie behind the Commission's criticism of the fragmented regulatory environment in Europe and its insistence on establishing a simpler, more harmonized set of rules (Celsing 2007).

Across Europe, press freedom and pluralism may find itself between a rock and a hard place, where an overall policy approach that favours a competitive edge and an earlier attachment to social responsibility are at loggerheads. In addition, the neo-liberal single market approach of European media policy may create conditions that encourage a concentration of ownership that diminishes the internal diversity of media sources. Media houses may also seek new ways of increasing their revenues. Often this comes from 'economies of scale and scope', that is to say reaching larger audiences through bigger conglomerates that can generate a larger turnover. This type of economic logic rarely follows the ideals of socially responsible journalism. The gap between vital ideals of press freedom and the empirical reality between many European countries may be bridged by supporting legislation that harnesses these new challenges. Most of all, the new situation requires tireless monitoring and research of the challenges to press freedom that may endanger the democratic processes where critical journalism plays a fundamental role.

Notes

1. Finland has had a newspaper published continuously at least once a week ever since 1791. The first Finnish-language newspaper in Finland was the educational *Suomenkieliset Tieto-Sanomat*, published by Antti Lizelius in 1775. Finnish did not become the majority language of Finland until the 1820s. Finnish-language newspapers have been published regularly since 1844 (Jyrkiäinen 2004).

2. The *New York Times* reported on 20 March 1917: 'Home rule for Finland is one of the policies of the new Russian Government according to a Reuter dispatch from Tammerfors, Finland's greatest manufacturing city. The correspondent says that the Finnish Diet will be convened soon and asked to establish a Government possessing the full confidence of the people.'

3. The Lapua Movement (*Lapuan liike*), sometimes referred to as 'Lapua Fascism', named after the then municipality and present day town of Lapua, was an influential political movement in Finland. It started in 1929 and was initially dominated by ardent anti-communist nationalists, emphasizing the legacy of the nationalist activism, the White Guards and the Civil War in Finland.

4. This trend towards unaffiliated newspapers has strengthened since the 1950s with the increasing number of local papers (though *Helsingin Sanomat*, the biggest nationally daily, became politically independent already in 1932).

5. For example SanomaWSOY, the biggest media house in Finland bought a Bloglist-site that offers listing of the blogs maintained by private people.

6. Act No. 1380/1993 amendments up to 635/2005 included, which came into effect on 1 January 1994.

7. Act No. 744/1998; and certain technical amendments to the Telecommunications Administration Act and the Copyright Act (Acts No. 747/1998 and 748/1998).

8. On 29 January 2004 the Government adopted a resolution on the national broadband strategy that included a fifty-point action plan. On 3 February 2005 it adopted a new resolution specifying the objectives of the strategy and complementing the original resolution with nine new action points. These included the following: the promotion of the development of wireless broadband; the promotion of new content and services; and removal of remaining obstacles to competition. According to the strategy, Finland should have had 1,000,000 broadband subscriptions by the end of 2005. In January 2007 the number had already amounted to 1,500,000. Broadband services through a fixed network, which were to be available to at least 95 per cent of the population, were, in January 2007, available to 96.1 per cent.

9. According to the latest EVA report (Haavisto and Kiljunen 2008), Finns are fairly critical towards media. When asked whether people consider the 'power of media' too large, 64 per cent agreed. The follow-up question on media's power – 'Do journalists govern public opinion too much in Finland?' – produced almost as critical an outcome. Almost two thirds of the population agreed with the claim (63 per cent).

References

Celsing, Anna (2007), 'European Media Policy 2007', *Nordicom*, http://www.nordicom.gu.se/mt/letter. php. Accessed 21 December 2007.

Ekholm, Kai (1997), 'Censorship', in Olli Alho (ed.), *Finland: Cultural Encyclopedia*, Helsinki: Finnish Literature Society, Vammalan Kirjapaino.

FINLEX (Finnish legislation) (2008), http://www.finlex.fi/en/. Accessed 3 January 2008.

Forsberg, T.; Kekäle, P. and Ekholm, P. (2001), 'Yleinen mielipide ja ulkopolitiikka. Hyvä renki muttei niin huono isäntäkään?' *Ulkopolitiikka*, 3, pp. 129–38.

Haavisto, Ilkka and Kiljunen, Pentti (2008), *Kenen joukoissa seisot? EVAn Suomi, EU ja maailma -asennetutkimus 2008*, Helsinki: Yliopistopaino.

Hakkarainen, Timo (2007), 'Bulkkiviihde tuo voittoa', *Journalisti*, 21 December 2007, http://www.journalistilehti.fi/tuotteet.html?id=53/192. Accessed 21 December 2007.

Hallin, Daniel C. and Mancini, Paolo (2004), *Comparing Media Systems: Three Models of Media and Politics*, Cambridge: Cambridge University Press.

Jokisipilä, Markku (2007), 'Finlandization', http://jokisipila.blogspot.com/2007/10/finlandization.html. Accessed 17 December 2007.

Jyrkiäinen, Jyrki (2004), 'The Finnish Media: outlets increase, audiences diversify', http://virtual.finland.fi/netcomm/news/showarticle.asp?intNWSAID=27113. Accessed 21 December 2007.

Moring, Tom (2008) The Political Communication System in Finland in *Communicating Politics: Political communication in the Nordic countries* (ed.) Jesper Strömbäck & Toril Aalberg & Mark Ørsten. Nordicom: Göteborg.

Mörä, Tuomo (1999), *EU-journalismin anatomia*, Helsinki: Yliopistopaino.

Ranta, Elina (2007), 'Sananvapauslaki testataan pian tuomioistuimissa', *Journalisti*, http://www.journalistilehti.fi/tuotteet.html?id=48/174. Accessed 7 January 2008.

Salminen, Esko (1999), *The Silenced Media: The Propaganda War between Russia and the West in Northern Europe*, New York: St. Martin's Press.

Salminen, Esko (2003), 'Suomalaisen sensuurin läpileikkaus' (The cross-section of the Finnish censorship), in Inkeri Salonharju (ed.), *Kirja tietoverkkojen maailmassa*, Verkkojulkaisu, Helsinki: Helsingin yliopiston kirjasto, http://www.lib.helsinki.fi/julkaisut/kirjatietoverkkojenmaailmassa/. Accessed 7 January 2008.

Salokangas, Raimo (1996), 'The Finnish broadcasting company and the changing Finish society, 1949–66', in Rauno Endén (ed.), *A History of Broadcasting in Finland*, Yleisradio: WSOY.

Salovaara-Moring, Inka (2004), *Media Geographies*, Helsinki: Gummerus.

Sauri, Tuomo (2007), 'Introduction: the changing mass media scene in Finland', in *Joukkoviestimet 2006 (Finnish Mass Media 2006) Culture and the media*, Helsinki: Statistics Finland.

Tarkka, Jukka (2002) Uhan alta unioniin. Asennemuutos ja sen unilukkari, Eva. Otava.

Union of Journalists in Finland (2007), https://www.journalistiliitto.fi/Resource.phx/sivut/sivut-journalistiliitto/index.htx. Accessed 20 December 2007.

Ylönen, Olli; Nordenstreng, Kaarle and Heinonen, Ari with Österlund-Karinkanta, Marina and Alanen, Antti (2004), 'Media System of Finland', for the Study on Co-Regulation Measures in the Media Sector Study commissioned by the European Commission, Directorate Information Society Unit A1 Audiovisual and Media Policies, Digital Rights, Task Force on Coordination of Media Affairs DG EAC 03/04, http://www.hans-bredow-institut.de/forschung/recht/co-reg/reports/1/Finland.pdf. Accessed 15 December 2007.

Pre-Conditions for Press Freedom in Germany

Andrea Czepek, Melanie Hellwig and Eva Nowak

Freedom House placed press freedom in Germany at position sixteen in its 2007 index, behind Jamaica (position fifteen), but still very high on the list of 195 countries (Freedom House 2008). On the index compiled by Reporters Without Borders (RSF), German press freedom comes in twentieth in the world (just behind Trinidad and Tobago at position nineteen) with quite a positive score (5.75 – Eritrea, the last country on the list, has a score of 114.75. See Reporters Without Borders 2008). Hence, all is well and nothing to worry about? Of course, compared to media in other regions of the world, the German media enjoy high independence from state and government influence, and journalists work mostly without fear of harassment. However, we do think that even in Germany there is cause for some concern regarding press freedom, especially when looking at structural factors, not just independence from state interference.

There have been some recent improvements regarding legislation (in 2006, a freedom of information act was implemented), but also drawbacks regarding jurisdiction (courts have increasingly placed privacy rights above the right to publish certain information, not just with regard to celebrities' gossip) and law enforcement (in recent years and in several cases, newsrooms have been searched for journalists' materials and sources, and the German secret service has monitored e-mails and journalists' telephone connections). An increasing concern is the dominance of economic objectives in media organizations (cost reduction and profit maximization) which result in an orientation towards mass markets, a lack of resources for journalistic work, and a growing dependence of media outlets and journalists on commercial considerations.

Regarding the structural conditions for press freedom in Germany, the Second World War was an important break for the German media system. Up until then, journalism was dominated by an opinionated press with newspapers owned by parties, unions and churches. Censorship had been the rule, off and on, for most of the time, except for the years of the Weimar Republic between 1918 and 1932. After World War II, the West German media system was completely re-organized with an independent press system and a public service broadcasting system. In former East Germany, the media remained under state and ruling party control until 1989. Today, the overarching political paradigm regarding the media in Germany is still a corporatist approach with the ideal that media content should reflect the diversity of society. But the political sphere is losing ground in comparison to the economic objectives, and market oriented approaches tend to prevail. Concentration processes are ubiquitous and the broadcasting market is about to change fundamentally.

Historical Development

The current structure of the German information media system has been formed by several distinct historical events (see for example Stöber 2005). Based on technical advancements (Gutenberg's invention of the printing press and the inauguration of the postal service) as well as social achievements (discovery of new continents, increase of trade relations) in the early modern era, newspapers were established (Braudel 1990: 122–67, 223–39, 390–428). In the aftermath of the 30-year-war in the seventeenth century, periodicals started to become available for a wider public, the so-called *Avisen* or *Relationen*. In these times, publication intervals were reduced from half-yearly to four times a week until the eighteenth century.

In the seventeenth and eighteenth century, the emergence of international trade and a citizen class that was better educated furthered the culture of newspaper reading. Enlightenment emphasized educational information and the 'coffeehouse' and 'salon' traditions made political exchange popular. At the same time, censorship by church and state was established. The main intention of the state was to not cause trouble in foreign politics with any statements in the newspapers. Further objectives of censorship were maintaining the reputation of the state and the inner freedom of states or cities (Stöber 2005: 108–10). The interest of the church was to guarantee that only the opinion of the church was published. In the nineteenth century (1819), the 'Bundespressegesetz' (German law for the press) was enacted. It stated that any publication of less than twenty sheets (320 pages) had to be approved before publication, which meant a massive repression of press freedom. An indirect inhibition of a free press market was the so-called 'Intelligenzblätter' (public advertisers). These state-owned newspapers had, by law, a monopoly on advertising in each region they were published, and civil servants had to subscribe to them.

In the following one and a half centuries, press freedom and censorship had a checkered history. With the new press law of 3 March 1848, in the context of the 'Märzrevolution', some important changes came about: press freedom was guaranteed. Newspapers, journals, booklets, wall newspapers and caricatures were no longer censored. But the revolution failed and in 1854 the press law was changed again. The central component was that publishers and printers needed to apply for a licence. They had to deposit a bond, publish the name of the responsible editor in the flag, and deposit a copy with the authorities. In 1874 the law was liberalized (press law) (Stöber 2005: 143–7). In World War I, under the state of war, censorship and instructions for the press were yet again installed. The basis for the restrictions was the declaration of the war. After the war in 1918, the law of 1874 was applied again.

In the Weimar Republic (1918–32), a strong tradition of the party press developed. There were three types:

1. Newspapers which sided with one party
2. Newspapers which founded a party
3. Newspapers which belonged to a party – political parties, unions, church and so on.

In the time of the Nazis (1933–45), newspapers had to publish so called government announcements; the 'Ermächtigungsgesetz' abolished the freedom of the press and expression (Stöber: 149–52).

In the years 1946–9, the press was licensed by the Allied Forces. During national-socialism, Jewish and Communist publishers were murdered or left the country, while others struggled to regain their publication rights. On the other hand, publishers who had sided with the Nazis, or at least continued to publish newspapers under them, were not granted printing licenses by the Allied Forces. Thus, in this vacuum, new publishers emerged. The Allied Forces (especially the British Government) (see Stöber 2005: 255 and Koszyk 1999: 44–6) tried to implement a party press again, but in fact since 1949 the party press has not recovered in West Germany. Instead, the press (officially) followed the Anglo-Saxon model of neutrality and separation of fact and opinion. In East Germany, on the contrary, there was a continuance of the party press. In the 1950s, 60 per cent of the press in the GDR was held by the ruling party SED. That increased in 1988 to 91 per cent (Stöber 2005: 255; Dussel 2004: 198–205; Holzweissig 1999: 574–99).

After the reunification in 1990 and 1991, the 'Treuhandanstalt' (governmental privatization fund) maintained the East German press structure with its large district party newspapers and sold thirteen of the fourteen regional SED-newspapers to West German press companies. One effect of that is that there are still, today, regional monopolies in the East German newspaper market mostly run by West German publishing companies.

Legal Regulations

Press freedom, freedom of expression and the right to publish any opinion are guaranteed today by the German constitution. However, there are legal exceptions that limit press freedom. Restrictions apply especially to reporting about current criminal investigations, endangering national security, protection of children and youth, and agitating for violence and Naziism. Furthermore, privacy rights and commercial laws can be weighed against press freedom in civil lawsuits. In principle, the constitutional rights are weighed against each other. Usually, freedom of expression is held highly by German courts, but rulings of the Constitutional Court tend to favour privacy rights over press freedom, especially when there is no 'public relevance' to the reported information, such as private information about non-political celebrities. Defining the line of when an item is of public interest or not is an ongoing debate.

A clear exception to freedom of expression unique to German law is the prohibition of using or publishing Nazi propaganda and Nazi symbols. Constructed in the aftermath of the Second World War, this prohibition has been strictly implemented by German courts and has never been seriously questioned.

A positive development towards widening the legal provisions for press freedom has been the enactment of the 'Freedom of Information Act' in January 2006 (Bundesministerium der Justiz 2006). For the first time in Germany, this law awards all citizens (not just journalists, as was the case until 2006) the right to access information from administrative authorities on the

German federal level. However, only nine of the sixteen German states have so far adopted similar laws regarding the *state* authorities. Large states such as Lower Saxony, Bavaria, Baden-Württemberg and Saxony have no Freedom of Information law yet; the Saxony state parliament has even voted against it.

There are some regulatory measures which are supposed to enhance plurality and media freedom. One is the subsidy for periodical print media distribution (newspapers and periodical magazines with a majority of editorial content, regardless of their views, are granted lower distribution prices by the postal service; since privatization of the postal service in 1995, the state subsidizes the cost with tax revenues, see Bundesministerium der Finanzen 2007). Another measure is the reduced value added tax, which is applied to printed periodicals.

A further legal measure is the law on fixed prices for print products (books, newspapers, magazines) which was enacted in 2002 and which replaced the contractual arrangements between publishers and booksellers that had existed earlier (Buchpreisbindungsgesetz 2002). The law determines that printed products have to be sold to final customers at the copy price fixed by the publishers; rebates for intermediate dealers are also restricted. The law is supposed to facilitate the publication of books with small circulations by guaranteeing a certain margin to the publisher and thus allowing for a 'mixed calculation' of co-financing low-circulation books with bestsellers. In addition, the law is supposed to preserve smaller bookstores and newspaper vendors (thus ensuring availability and access to print media even in rural areas) by guaranteeing that they can sell books at the same price as a large competitor. Indeed, these measures have preserved to some degree a very disperse structure of small bookstores until recently. Nevertheless, large bookstore chains have in recent years expanded drastically and dominate the market with their advantage of better buying prices and larger selections. The fixed book price law alone could not prevent the rapid concentration of ownership among bookstores as well as book-, magazine- and newspaper publishers. In any case, the law has been contested by the Commission of the European Union and is repeatedly under scrutiny for deterring competition, especially since the fixed book price regulation was abolished in Switzerland in 2007.

A popular demand when discussing freedom of the press is that journalists or 'the media' should use their freedom more responsibly. Therefore, in order to avoid legislation interfering with the independence of media organizations, German print media founded a self-regulatory body in 1956, the Deutsche Presserat (press council). It has no legislative powers and is a voluntary, independent council comprised of 28 members representing publishers associations and journalists' unions. The council has established a code of conduct which lists ethical standards journalists should adopt (Deutscher Presserat 2006). Anyone can submit complaints regarding perceived breaches of this code. The council discusses these complaints and, in case they are considered justified, can issue either a 'disapproval' or a 'rebuke'. Most German newspapers have committed to publishing rebukes concerning their reporting, but the newspaper which is most often reprimanded, Springer's tabloid *Bild,* never publishes its rebukes, and there are no other consequences, since self-regulation is voluntary. In 2007, the German press council discussed 328 complaints, of which it dismissed 135; the rest were sanctioned with disapprovals and rebukes. The complaints most often involved 'lack of care in research', followed by 'lack of respect for privacy' (Deutscher Presserat 2008). Recently, the German press council's structure has been criticized, especially the fact that it consists of media representatives (publishers and journalists) only and that its hearings are not public. A different council including citizens and scientists has been demanded (see Desgranges and Wassink in Baum et al. 2005: 79–88), but there are no concrete plans yet for such an alternative council.

Criminal investigations and surveillance
A current issue of some concern to publishers and journalists is the increasing use of investigations and surveillances by authorities and private companies, mainly with the aim of uncovering sources who revealed secret information to journalists, and thus hindering investigative and critical reporting.

Editing rooms can be searched when journalists or editors are sued for 'disclosing secrets'. In 2006 and 2007 there were two cases (see for example epd Medien 2007; Schmitz 2006) in which this was done; both cases involved renowned journals (*Cicero, Stern*) and were, in different ways, related to Islamist terrorist investigations and the actions of the government in this context.

The question was whether publishing those secrets constitutes a crime. According to German law, 'disclosing secret information' is an offence which, however, is completed the moment a person discloses this secret to another person, for example a journalist. The courts do not agree on the question of whether the journalist who then publishes the information is attributing to the crime since he himself is not actually disclosing the secret. The authorities who ordered that the editing rooms be searched on these grounds were accused of having used this legal 'loophole' to make the searches possible, and that the true reason was to find out who the sources were – which, under German law, the journalists do not have to disclose (protection of sources is guaranteed in the constitution). In both cases, the final decisions by the Constitutional Court are still pending.

In addition to those cases of actual investigations in newsrooms, a number of cases of illegal monitoring of telecommunications data have recently become public. The German secret service (Bundesnachrichtendienst, BND) has continuously monitored e-mails of journalists in order to uncover their sources in the context of conflict and terrorism. In 2006, a parliamentary commission was established which investigated these actions by the secret service and which published a report confirming that these illegal data evaluations had actually taken place (Schäfer 2006). Despite the public stir and promises by the President of the secret service, Ernst Uhrlau, to abstain from the practice of observing journalists' e-mails and other communications, in April 2008 it was revealed that a department of the BND had continued to do so all along. After the report in 2006, the BND monitored the e-mails of a German Afghanistan correspondent, including her private e-mails and her communication with the Afghan trade minister Amin Farhang, which was especially criticized since Farhang was considered a friend to Germany and there was no suspicion of contacts with terrorists (Richter 2008; Müller-Neuhof 2008; Hanfeld 2008; Schuler 2008).

Commercial companies apparently also use modern communication technologies to observe their employees – and their contacts with journalists. In May 2008, it was revealed that top managers of the formerly state-owned, now privatized telecommunications provider Deutsche Telekom[1] had allegedly monitored their managers' communications, including e-mail and mobile phone contacts for years, especially contact with journalists, in order to find 'leaks' that revealed internal information about the company to journalists and the public (Heuzeroth

2008; spiegel online 2008; zdf heute.de 2008). At the time this chapter was written, the cases were still pending. This case is especially worrisome because, since January 2008, Telekom has been officially ordered by the German government to store all telecommunications data (e-mail, telephone, mobile phone connections) for six months for potential criminal investigations.[2]

With regard to press freedom, there are concerns that the current laws regarding disclosure of secrets and treason and security and surveillance have increasingly been used by authorities to hinder investigative and critical reporting. In addition, there has been illegal abuse of modern technologies to observe journalists and their sources, by both the state secret service and private companies. Mainly, the protection of sources has been made more difficult and thus the chances of finding out about grievances have been reduced. In this context, it may appear worrisome that the German federal ministers agreed in June 2008 on a law to allow the police to search computers online without the 'target' knowing (tagesschau.de 2008; Decker 2008).[3]

These decisions raise fears that, despite its being guaranteed in the constitution, press freedom is endangered by the political situation and economic interests. A lively public debate on this topic, however, shows that press freedom is a highly regarded value in Germany. This was not always the case, as the development of broadcasting in Germany shows.

Economic structures
The dual broadcasting system: Public service in the age of marketization

Broadcasting in the aftermath of World War II
The German broadcasting system has been shaped until today by the decisions of the Allied Forces in post-war Germany as a reaction to the Nazi experience. The idea of state distance and support of pluralism regarding ownership as well as content have been influencing German media policy until today.

When Germany capitulated in 1945 and the Allied Forces had taken over power, they made a clear cut in the German media system. The Allies took over all media and only journalists who were not suspect regarding National Socialism were allowed to publish under the Allies' censorship. During the first years after World War II, radio played a special role as this was the easiest way for the Allies to disseminate information and anti-Nazi re-education during the occupation. Paper was not always available and the distribution of newspapers was a great problem in destroyed Germany. But there were 'Volksempfänger' in many German households, the relatively cheap radio receivers with a low range of frequencies which Goebbels' Nazi propaganda officials had implemented to agitate Germans, especially during the war. The Nazis had treated as treason the listening to foreign radio stations like the BBC World Service in order to increase the efficiency of their radio propaganda and lies about the situation at the war front.

After this experience, the victorious powers in the three western zones decided to restructure the German broadcasting (= radio) system in a way that guaranteed decentralization and freedom of direct state influence. This was, of course, different in the Soviet zone, where broadcasting was also denazified, but where the state kept broadcasting centralized and exerted direct influence. In the western zones, the US-Army founded Radio Frankfurt, Radio Stuttgart, Radio München and Radio Bremen in their sector, the French founded Südwestfunk in Baden-Baden and the British the Nordwestdeutscher Rundfunk in Hamburg and Cologne for the British sector. In 1948 and 1949 the Allies handed over the radio stations to German authorities after having imposed a new broadcasting system.[4] The discussion about the best system had a clear result: The French model was considered inappropriate because of its state influence and centralization. The US-American radio system with its commercial stations did not have a chance because the German economy was too weak to finance radio by advertising and it was doubtful if this would be changing in the near future. Thus the British BBC became the model for post-war German radio and later TV: a public service broadcasting system, financed by mandatory fees but, unlike the BBC, decentralized. There was no central radio station broadcasting to the whole country at that time.

Public service broadcasting
The public service stations (*Rundfunkanstalten*) were established in regions, broadcasting from and for these regions, mainly oriented on the federal states (*Bundesländer*).[5] Today, the states are still in charge of the broadcasting policy, not the federal German government. The one exception was in 1953, when the federal German government founded the Deutsche Welle (DW) as the German world service. The only national radio station followed in 1962: The Deutschlandfunk (DLF) was supposed to inform German speaking people in Eastern Europe about politics and culture in Western Germany, especially focusing on East Germany, the *DDR* ('Deutsche Demokratische Republik'/'German Democratic Republic'). In 1950 the public service stations (PSBs) founded a common body, the Arbeitsgemeinschaft öffentlich-rechtlicher Rundfunkanstalten der Bundesrepublik Deutschland (ARD), which became relevant when the first PSB TV channel Deutsches Fernsehen (later Erstes Deutsches Fernsehen/Das Erste) started broadcasting in 1953. ARD and Das Erste were and still are a co-operation of the regional PSB-stations.

The public service broadcasting stations are regulated by two bodies: The broadcasting council (Rundfunkrat), which consists of relevant groups of the German society (*gesellschaftlich relevante Gruppen*), representing the public and supervising programming and content, and the administrative council (Verwaltungsrat), which is elected by the broadcasting council and supervises finances. The Chief Executive of the public service broadcaster, the *Intendant*, is elected and controlled by the broadcasting council together with the administrative council.[6]

A law on the level of the states appoints the representatives of the relevant groups of society. These groups are, for example, unions, employer organizations, religious groups (Christian and Jewish), farmers, artists, migrants, disabled, cultural groups, youth and sports organizations but also political parties represented in the federal state governments. This is often criticized not only for the political party appointments but also as the representatives of other groups are often related to political parties. Thus the ruling party (or parties) in a federal state often dominates the broadcasting council as well as the administrative council (see Schrag 2007: 187).

The idea of nominating representatives of relevant groups of society for the regulative bodies of public service broadcasting reflects the demand for internal pluralism within the PSB stations, which is considered important not only on the organizational level but also on the content level. This is secured in the Federal Law on Public and Private Broadcasting (Rundfunkstaatsvertrag 2006: §11), which defines the mandate of public broadcasters as follows:

(2) Public Service Broadcasting has to give a comprehensive overview on international, European, national and regional events in all relevant areas of life within its services...Its programme has to serve information, education, advice and entertainment. It has to offer contributions especially on culture.

(3) In fulfilling its task Public Service Broadcasting has to account for the principles of objectivity and impartiality in reporting, for the plurality of opinions as well as the fair balance of offers and channels.[7]

The 'fair balance of offers and channels' was discussed only a few years after the ARD had started the first German TV channel. Konrad Adenauer, of the conservative party CDU (Christian Democratic Union) and chancellor since 1949 was not satisfied with the TV channel, particularly the way they reported about German politics (see Schrag 2007: 177). Thus he intended to found a second TV channel which would be, however, privately organized. The federal German government was to hold 51 per cent, the federal states 49 per cent of the Deutschland Fernsehen GmbH (German TV Ltd.). The federal states refused to take part in the project and the opposition party, the SPD (*Social Democrates*) took legal action at the Constitutional Court. In a fundamental decision in 1961, the first of nine decisions, the constitutional court pointed out that broadcasting has to be organized without direct state influence[8] or a majority influence of one societal group because of its societal task as opinion former and that broadcasting is a matter of culture. The latter is relevant as the states are in charge of cultural policy. 'Adenauer-TV' was thus incompatible with the German constitution in regard to two criteria: absence of state influence and regional organization. Private broadcasting, the Constitutional Court said, is currently impossible because of a shortage of frequencies and other means of distribution. The reaction of the federal states was to found another national public service television channel, the Zweites Deutsches Fernsehen (ZDF), which started broadcasting in 1963.

The dual system of public and private broadcasting
It was again conservative politicians who in the late 1970s started a discussion on whether the public service broadcasters were sufficiently politically balanced. The ARD, especially, was blamed for left-wing oriented reporting. At that time, the nine ARD stations offered numerous radio channels, usually three or four per station, a co-operative national TV channel, as well as regional TV channels from most state-based stations (*Das Dritte*/'The Third'). The ZDF still offered one national TV channel.

The conflict led to another fundamental decision on broadcasting by the Constitutional Court. In 1981, the judges decided that broadcasting was an individual right. This meant that everybody would have the right to offer broadcasting, to have a radio or TV station. With the new technologies – cable and satellite – there was no reason left to prohibit private broadcasting as there was no more shortage of frequencies. Starting in 1982 in Mannheim-Ludwigshafen, then in Berlin, Munich and Dortmund, a new kind of technical distribution was tested in small pilot projects: cable TV, for the first time with the participation of private broadcasters. In 1984 RTLplus started to broadcast from Luxemburg, the home of RTL Radio, but for the German TV market.[9] One year later SAT.1, the former cable pilot project participant PKS from Mannheim-Ludwigshafen, started to broadcast with new investments from several newspaper publishers.[10] RTL and SAT.1 are now the core channels of the two big families of private TV stations in Germany. Today RTL is part of the RTL Group, the majority of which is owned by Bertelsmann. In Germany, the RTL Group operates three comprehensive channels (RTL, VOX, RTLII), a news channel (n-tv), a children's channel (superRTL), four special interest channels (RTLshop, RTLcrime, RTL Living, Passion) and the Internet operator RTLinteractive.[11] Today, Sat.1 is part of the ProSiebenSat.1 Group, which operates free and pay TV in thirteen countries. In Germany, it operates the comprehensive channels Sat.1, ProSieben and Kabel 1 as well as the news channel N24, the call TV channel 9Live and the video-on-demand portal Maxdome.[12]

In the early 1980s, the states with conservative governments started to found regulatory bodies (*Landesmedienanstalten*) for private broadcasting that are in charge of licensing and controlling private broadcasting, as well as designing broadcasting laws, which differ in each state. The SPD-opposition in Lower Saxony rejected the new broadcasting law and went to the Constitutional Court, which in 1986 established private and public broadcasting with different tasks in the media system. Public broadcasters are now still financed by obligatory fees in addition to having limited opportunities to sell advertising time, sponsoring and syndication.[13] In return for the fees, PSB-stations have to fulfil the criteria of internal pluralism, guarantee the basic supply of information ('*Grundversorgung*[14]'), cover minority topics and report in a balanced way and pluralistically.

The fees are collected by the *Gebühreneinzugszentrale* (GEZ), a collection agency owned by the PSBs, in order to guarantee the absence of state intervention. From €17.03 the ARD receives €5.04 for radio and €6.90 for TV, the ZDF gets €4.39, DeutschlandRadio (the former Deutschlandfunk) gets €0.37 and the private broadcasting authorities *Landesmedienanstalten* get €0.32 per month and household.[15]

Private broadcasters are, however, according to the Constitutional Court, part of the concept of external pluralism. Not a single station alone has to guarantee the pluralism of voices and content but all private broadcasters together. Nevertheless, the Constitutional Court did not leave external pluralism to a free market but demanded a control of monopolies for the private broadcasting market, which led to the founding of KEK, *Kommission zur Ermittlung der Konzentration im Medienbereich* (Commission for the Investigation of Concentration in the Media). Another special trait of German private television regulations are the obligations regarding content, for example national private TV channels may be obliged to broadcast regional programmes for half an hour per day, or give a minimum of broadcasting time to a company independent of the owners of the TV channel in order to support the plurality of content. These obligations depend on the private broadcasting authorities, *Landesmedienanstalten*, of the federal state in which the channel is licensed, even if it is a national private TV channel.

Moreover, in some federal states local open channels for TV and radio were founded to promote media literacy and access for every interested citizen. States with a Social Democrat government were especially in favour of these open channels.

More TV channels were founded in the early years of the dual (PSB and private commercial) broadcasting system but they remained on a national level and were usually distributed by cable and satellite. It was not until recent digitalization that television became less expensive and the distribution became easier so that numerous new channels were founded, especially those with a special interest concept. Recently, private local television became commercially interesting and some stations were licensed.

Private radio in Germany

Radio developed in a different way. It is not economically necessary to broadcast on a national level and there are still no private national radio channels on the relevant FM band. Due to the fact that broadcasting is regulated on a federal state basis, the German radio landscape today is very heterogeneous. In Schleswig-Holstein and Lower Saxony, for example, commercial radio is only allowed on the state level, not on a local level. Neither state is densely populated so that around 1990, when private broadcasting was introduced, media policy assumed that the local advertising markets were too small to finance local broadcasting and that another competitor would harm the local newspaper market. In Lower Saxony, in addition to state-wide commercial radio stations, non-commercial local radio stations as well as several non-commercial local TV stations were licensed. They are financed partly by the private broadcasting authorities (*Landesmedienanstalten*), partly by donations, and have to offer several hours of open channel. This open channel idea also plays an important but disputed role in North Rhine-Westphalia, where commercial radio stations have to offer two hours per day to interested citizens who can broadcast whatever they want, as long as it is not against the penal law. Usually the open programmes get the low-audience slots in the evening. In densely populated North Rhine-Westphalia the then SPD-government invented a special radio model, trying to integrate local content plurality, social responsibility and the interests of the strong regional newspaper publishers who were afraid of having to share their local advertising market with a radio competitor. The authorities license only one radio station per area, which can be a town or small rural area. The *Betreibergesellschaft*, the operating company, is in charge of the economic side of the radio station and is often controlled by local or regional newspaper publishers. The *Veranstaltergemeinschaft*, the host community, is in charge of the programme and is the employer of the journalists. Only the editor-in-chief has to be accepted by the *Betreibergesellschaft*. The *Veranstaltergemeinschaft* is led by a committee of relevant social groups, like the broadcasting councils of PSB stations. The problem with this two-column model is that the *Betreibergesellschaft* works much more professionally than the voluntary *Veranstaltergemeinschaft* and over time several changes have been made in favour of the *Betreibergesellschaften*. Berlin, in contrast, favoured a market liberal model with minimum obligations for the licensees. The result is a highly competitive and continuously changing radio market. In most federal states in Germany, private radio usually has to fulfil content obligations such as a minimum of local information or a short news programme every hour. Nevertheless, almost all studies examining the content of private commercial radio broadcasters state that the content regarding information is only marginal compared to music, advertising and small talk from the presenters (see for example Vowe and Wolling 2004).

The transformation of East German broadcasters into reunified Germany

In the early 1990s, the privatization of broadcasting was, in terms of the TV market, a fact. With regard to the private radio market, it was planned in all federal states but realized in only some. Public service broadcasters reacted to the new private radio stations with further formatting (especially Adult Contemporary, Contemporary Hit Radio and news formats), and to private TV by planning new special interest channels and PSB co-operations (see ARD 2008a).[16] The West German broadcasting system had still not totally transformed into a dual system when, in 1990/91, East German radio and television had to be integrated in a reunified Germany. Up to then the GDR had operated two TV channels as well as several radio channels[17] designed according to the Soviet model. In line with the socialist state ideology, the media system was centralized and biased towards the government, for example the Socialist Party (SED, Sozialistische Einheitspartei Deutschlands). This media system was, of course, incompatible with democratic concepts. During the negotiations for the Unification Treaty, it was agreed that the West German broadcasting system should be the model for reunified Germany. The East German TV channels DDR1 and DDR2, having just been renamed as DFF1 and DFF2,[18] stopped broadcasting in December 1990 (DFF1) and December 1991 (DFF2). Two radio stations were integrated into the new PSB stations in the new eastern states: Deutschlandsender[19] was transferred into Deutschlandsender Kultur and became the twin channel of Deutschlandfunk, which broadcasts from Cologne, offering comprehensive information, while Deutschlandsender Kultur from Berlin focused on cultural topics.[20] The other East German radio channel, which was not closed down after the reunification, was DT 64, the GDR youth channel, which was renamed as *Sputnik* and integrated into the new PSB Mitteldeutscher Rundfunk (MDR) broadcasting for Saxony, Saxony-Anhalt and Thuringia. The other PSB station which was founded after difficult negotiations between the new East German states of Berlin and Brandenburg was Ostdeutscher Rundfunk Brandenburg (ORB) for Brandenburg. Berlin continued with Sender Freies Berlin (SFB) until in 2003 ORB and SFB merged to form Rundfunk Berlin Brandenburg (RBB). Mecklenburg-Western Pomerania is covered by Norddeutscher Rundfunk (NDR). The private radio scene in the Eastern states today is as heterogeneous as in the Western states.

This transformation process was also conflict-riddled because there was a surplus of staff in East German broadcasting[21] and the journalists had been socialized in a communist society. From one month to another they had to follow the role model of journalism in a democratic society; later it was discovered that a considerable number of East German journalists had co-operated with the Ministry of State Security, the *Stasi*, spying on their colleagues and interviewees. Up to today, journalists have had to resign because of new information about Stasi-activities, which often comes to light as they advance in the hierarchy.

Current challenges: Broadcasting and the Internet
The recent dispute over the German public broadcast fees between the EU-Commission and the private broadcasters on the one hand and the German states and the public broadcasters on the other hand (Ridder 2006), is a good example of differing views on how to guarantee independence of the state and, moreover, show how this discussion is used to pursue economic interests. In Germany, the broadcast fees are determined by state-independent commissions and collected by an independent agency, the *Gebühreneinzugszentrale*, GEZ, which belongs to the public broadcasting stations. EU-Commissioner Neelie Kroes made the accusation that the German broadcast fees must be considered as state subsidies which hinder competition. As a somewhat paradoxical remedy, Kroes wanted the state governments rather than the state-independent regulatory bodies to decide about the licensing of new channels and broadcasting activities, for example expansion into the Internet. In December 2006, a compromise was found between the Commission and the German states: the regulatory bodies would remain in charge, but the states gained more involvement in the decisions than they had before.

There has been, to date, no decision made about the fees themselves – the question whether they constitute a state subsidy or not has not been clarified. The question behind this conflict is also whether the fees are necessary to make an independent pluralistic TV programme possible or whether economic liberty supports (external) pluralism in the media market. The German government is currently planning to change the model of raising the fees, but a new model would have to be endorsed by the EU Commission – which may start the discussion anew.

The big current conflict in German broadcasting is the question of how far the public broadcasters should develop their Internet activities. According to the States Treaty on Broadcasting in Unified Germany (*Staatsvertrag über den Rundfunk im vereinten Deutschland*), public service broadcasters are allowed to use all new technologies concerning production and distribution of new forms of broadcasting. Nevertheless, private broadcasters as well as printed press publishers claim that the mandatory PSB-fees do not allow for the financing of Internet activities, but only traditional radio and television. The largest regional newspaper publisher, the WAZ (*Westdeutsche Allgemeine Zeitung*), however, started an online co-operation in 2008 with Westdeutscher Rundfunk (WDR), the big PSB in North Rhine-Westphalia. *Der Westen* is an internet portal for the western region which offers TV reports on regional topics produced by the WDR for its own regular TV programme (see WDR 2008). The co-operation between WAZ and WDR is limited to one year for the time being. Not just media journalists are now discussing whether both are still independent enough to criticize each other, or in other words: whether pluralism is endangered and whether WDR should finance the TV reports with broadcasting fees which are then offered on *Der Westen*-online portal, owned by the rich publisher WAZ. The WDR broadcasting council speculated that WAZ wanted to bridge the period until their own regional TV channel for the Ruhr region, which is already licensed, starts broadcasting with cheap WDR video distributions. The WDR would thus finance a new competitor (see Lilienthal 2008). The WDR/WAZ co-operation is only a start – other public service broadcasters have started negotiations with publishers (Lilienthal 2008).

However, what most publishers and private broadcasters dislike is not this kind of co-operation as such, although some assume that the PSB were only trying to improve their negotiating position in the conflict with private broadcasters on the PSB's own Internet activities (see Lilienthal 2008). The real point is the PSB's own Internet portals and the question of what they should be allowed to offer. The Association of Private Broadcasters and Telemedia, Verein Privater Rundfunk und Telemedien e.V. (VPRT), are critical of the fact that the Internet portals of ARD and ZDF have, in their view, become a comprehensive informational offer which goes beyond the PSB's public mandate according to the State Broadcasting Treaty, the 'Rundfunkstaatsvertrag'. The VPRT claims that the online activities of ARD and ZDF are not covered by the 0.75 per cent of the broadcasting fee meant for online activities, but are much more expensive. Only information directly connected to the PSB's output should be allowed online, according to the VPRT (see VPRT 2008). ZDF and ARD offer a comprehensive and free of charge video on demand via Internet since 2007 and 2008, respectively. They publish information and entertainment, fictional and non-fictional programmes but also offer additional interactive and multimedia elements adequate for the online medium. To meet half way, the ZDF decided in spring 2008 to offer programmes in their online programme archive *Mediathek* (video-on-demand) for a limited time only, to renounce advertising, games and external service partners, such as hotel bookings and route planners, and to apply a three-step test to evaluate the public value of a definite content (see epd Medien 2008a). The conflict created a situation of fierce competition on a new media market regarding the Internet and mobile communication as well, and has been carried on throughout the negotiations on the twelfth change of the State Broadcasting Treaty, '12. *Rundfunkänderungsvertrag*', which was still under discussion when this article was written. Actually, the conflict is not about public service broadcasting but about public service Internet and whether it is necessary to offer information on the basis of internal pluralism on the Internet. When media-use changes in the direction of online and mobile media, PSB, limited to the traditional TV and radio distribution, would no longer be able to reach its audience. Steffen Range and Roland Schweins (2007) found, in their study on how the Internet changes journalism, that journalistic content, sponsoring and advertising are usually mixed, even in Internet spin-offs of serious political print magazines and newspapers. In this respect, an economically independent online portal for comprehensive information seems crucial.

Print Media: Increasing concentration and regional monopolization
Print media in Germany are generally private-commercially owned and much less regulated than the broadcast media. There are a high number of magazine titles (ca. 20,000) on the German market, of which 902 general interest magazines and 1,172 trade magazines are registered with the circulation monitoring agency IVW (Verband Deutscher Zeitschriftenverleger 2008). In contrast to the newspaper market, however, the weekly and monthly illustrated magazine market is highly concentrated and divided among four big publishing houses (Bauer, Springer, Burda, Gruner + Jahr (Bertelsmann) which publish about 61 per cent of the magazine circulation in Germany (Vogel 2002).

In the daily newspaper market,[22] due to relatively strict merger control, a relative diversity still exists with 352 newspaper publishing companies (Bundesverband Deutscher Zeitungsverleger (BDZV) 2008). German merger control laws have so far prevented a high concentration as, for example, on the US-newspaper market. Economic concentration has increased nevertheless. A closer look reveals that, on a local level, regional monopolies have emerged in many German regions. This is most apparent in the former East German states where the structure of large newspapers (formerly owned by the central party SED) catering to a large area was adopted after reunification, but also in many West German counties where there is only one regional newspaper or, if several competing newspapers still exist, they often belong to the same company. As a result, there is often only one source for local information.[23] Another unique feature of the German newspaper market is the co-operation of regional newspapers regarding national and international news. Many local newspapers only produce local news themselves and syndicate the national and international coverage, and often even the complete layout, from larger newspapers. Thus, the 350 newspaper publishers only publish 136 complete papers with their own international, national and local news, and several of these are owned by the same company. In fact, there are less than 70 publishing companies left who own the majority of shares in full-service newspapers.

In 1976, the German parliament passed a special regulation applicable only to print media within the merger control law. It lowered the threshold for a mandatory approval of a merger or acquisition (25 million Euro gross income instead of the 500 million Euro volume below which a merger does not have to be approved in other business sectors) and set limits on the market share that a publishing company may have (Heinrich 2001). The law was a reaction to the acquisitions of other newspapers by the *Westdeutsche Allgemeine Zeitung* (WAZ) in the Ruhr Area in the 1970s. As a consequence, acquisitions slowed down in the 1980s and 1990s, but have picked up again considerably since the alleged economic struggles of newspapers in the late 1990s. In Cologne, M. Dumont Schauberg, publisher of the *Kölner Stadt-Anzeiger,* bought the competing *Kölnische Rundschau* and now owns both daily newspapers and a daily tabloid in the city of Cologne as well as the *Mitteldeutsche Zeitung,* a large newspaper in former East Germany. The sale was approved by the authorities at the time with Dumont reasoning that by saving the competing paper from bankruptcy they were actually safeguarding plurality, an argument which had already been used by the publishers of the WAZ when they bought competing newspapers in the Ruhr Area. Both WAZ and Dumont, as well as the Axel Springer AG, which, in addition to the large tabloid *Bild*-Zeitung (circulation ca. 4 million), owns several daily newspapers in northern Germany, Hamburg and Berlin, promised to keep the newsrooms of their newspapers strictly separate and give them editorial autonomy. In the long run, however, this principle has been eroded more and more. WAZ-newspapers have common newsrooms for certain topics such as local sports; the Springer-newspapers *Die Welt* and *Morgenpost* have merged their newsrooms in Berlin (Axel Springer Verlag 2001). In an ambience of regional monopolization and the absence of competition, newspapers have fewer incentives to report critically and disclose grievances.

In Berlin in 2004, however, when Holtzbrinck planned to buy the daily newspaper *Berliner Zeitung* from Gruner & Jahr (who had bought the former communist party newspaper in East Berlin from the trust fund) the federal merger control authority would not go along with the internal-plurality argument. Holtzbrinck already owned another large (West-)Berlin newspaper, the *Tagesspiegel.* The authorities would only allow the purchase if Holtzbrinck sold the *Tagesspiegel,* because with both newspapers they would acquire a 61.4 per cent market share among subscription newspapers (not counting the tabloid *Bild* from Springer). Holtzbrinck first sold the *Tagesspiegel* to a former Holtzbrinck manager, a deal which was not accepted by the merger control authorities. Finally, Holtzbrinck was not allowed to buy the *Berliner Zeitung* (see, for example, Die Welt 2004). This case shows that the German merger control is still guided by the objective of safeguarding external pluralism of newspaper ownership. It also shows, however, that in doing so they might find themselves between a rock and a hard place: subsequently, in 2005 the *Berliner Zeitung* was sold to a foreign investor, the British private equity fund Mecom headed by David Montgomery. Mecom did not yet own any newspapers in Berlin, thus the merger control law did not apply. Mecom has since prescribed harsh austerity measures and high profit margins to the *Berliner Zeitung*; the current manager is also the editor-in-chief (a mingling of economic and editorial responsibilities unusual in German publishing houses) and many editorial staff members and managers were laid off or have left in dissent (Roether 2005; epd Medien 2008b; Meier 2008).

As these examples show, both the regional concentration processes and the increasing investment of foreign and non-publishing investors enhance the dominance of economic values in publishing companies; cost reduction and profit maximization have become the dominant goals and have pushed aside public values, such as providing diverse and well researched information.

Resources, working conditions and outsourcing of journalism

On an institutional and individual level, limitations for diversity and independent reporting are caused by the declining resources for journalistic work. With profit maximization being the main objective of media organizations, cost reduction and efficiency are striven for. When balancing expenditures and revenues, advertisements and distribution bring in the revenues, but reporters and editors only cost money. The quality they may (or may not) produce can, contrary to other goods, only be judged on the basis of expectations of the future performance and is much more difficult to evaluate for the consumer. Thus, a decline in quality is not immediately punished by the readers but is, rather, a long term process. This makes it possible for publishers to regard costs for editorial staff as a flexible lot. In addition, the traditionally high intrinsic motivation of journalists who simply work harder in order to complete the newspaper when they have to do the work with fewer people, contributes to the opportunities for cost reductions in the newsrooms.

One trend in Germany has been the 'outsourcing' of editorial staff[24] (Verband Deutscher Zeitschriftenverleger 2004; Gehringer 2007). The *Rhein-Zeitung* in Koblenz was one of the first newspapers to implement this practice in 1995: entire newsrooms were laid off, urged to found an independent company and then given a budget to 'sell' the editorial content to the newspaper as self-employed freelancers – with a smaller staff, lower salaries (by circumventing the union tariffs) and no job-, unemployment- or retirement-security. Meanwhile, almost all of the eighteen local editing rooms were outsourced. The declared goal of publisher Walterpeter Twer was to reduce staff costs by thirty per cent. Many regional newspaper publishers have since followed this example. An especially drastic case was the *Münstersche Zeitung* which is owned by the Dortmund-based publisher Lensing-Wolff. After outsourcing the newsroom there, Lensing had a parallel newsroom erected with new (younger and cheaper) staff. When they were ready to start in January 2007, Lensing, from one day to the next, took the 'order' to produce the newspaper away from the 'old' staff and gave the contract to the new newsroom.

Under such circumstances, journalistic autonomy is under great pressure. With few and usually underpaid jobs for journalists, they have a weak stance against their publishers. Editorial autonomy, once held high in Germany (and in the 1970s achieved in the form of statutes in many large newspapers which granted the journalists autonomy towards the publishers and which have since been abolished almost everywhere)[25] has been neglected in favour of a market-liberal approach granting press freedom mainly to those who own the media outlets.

It seems that the Internet could bring about change in that it provides easy access to anyone. However, the lack of resources for journalism on the Internet has raised fears that journalistic content on the Internet cannot be financed in the long run.

Social and cultural influences

As can be seen while looking at these developments, political, economic, historical and cultural influences are very much interwoven. With regard to cultural and social aspects of the German media system and plurality, we would like to point out only one example here.

In 2005, 7.2 million of the 82 million inhabitants in Germany were foreigners and an additional 10 per cent of German citizens had a 'migration background'. Approximately 3.3 million people in Germany declared to be followers of an Islamic religion (see Statistisches Bundesamt 2006). Even the larger minorities are under-represented as journalists, presenters, or in terms of content and programming catering to them in German information media.

Part of the reason is the German immigration laws (or the lack thereof) which make it difficult for even second generation foreigners to adopt German citizenship (in 2005, only 117,241 foreigners acquired German citizenship). Not being German citizens weakens the minorities' position with regard to demanding better representation in politics as well as in the media.

Conclusion

The press and other media can act largely independently from state and government influence. German legislation safeguards this independence and the jurisdiction has usually regarded freedom of the press highly. But freedom of the press in Germany is mainly seen as a commercial freedom, largely disregarding economic pressures which potentially inhibit free, pluralistic information and opinion forming. As the examples have shown, concentration of ownership is increasing in the print media market, where growing regional monopolies have formed and in many areas, local and regional information is only available from one source. In the broadcasting sector, which is also highly concentrated, a shift towards emphasizing economic objectives can also be observed, especially in the private-commercial media, which are gaining ground in terms of viewers, especially among young people. The dominance of market mechanisms in the media may allow for institutional media freedom, but it puts individual journalistic freedoms increasingly under pressure because of a lack of resources for investigative reporting, journalistic autonomy and precarious working conditions. With regard to media legislation, there have been some favourable (freedom of information act) and some less favourable developments (legalization of online searches, data retention). In the political realm, the EU deregulation policies have been very influential – ironically, by trying to lift (perceived) state influence on the media market, such measures actually pose a threat to press freedom and plurality because they challenge the diversity approach of public service media and endanger the possibilities for representation, access and participation by societal groups without buying power or lobbying influence.

Notes

1. Deutsche Telekom is the largest telecommunications provider in Germany and one of the largest in Europe. It was privatized in 1990 but the federal state of Germany still owns 14.83 per cent of the shares (September 2007), another 16.87 per cent are held by the state-owned KfW-Bank. Telekom generated a gross income of 2.5 billion Euros in 2007 and employs 242,000 people worldwide (Deutsche Telekom AG 2008).

2. The so called telecommunications data retention act is based on an EU regulation demanding the storage of telecommunications connection data for the purpose of criminal investigations and terrorism prevention. However, trade organizations have already claimed interest in the data, for example the music industry has voiced the opinion that the data could be used to track down copyright offenders. This in turn raises fears that the usage of the data, once generated and stored, could go far beyond terrorism investigations. The German law which is currently contested in the supreme court and not yet enacted (while the data is already being stored regardless, just in case), goes beyond the EU regulation in that it would allow usage of the data for all criminal investigations, not just 'severe crime' (heise online 2007; Rath 2007; spiegel online 2007).

3. The law on online searches still has to be approved by the parliament, which is expected for November 2008. In February 2008, the Supreme Court had rejected a previous proposal which it considered not constitutional. The online searches are supposed to be conducted online by implementing a Trojan virus on the 'targets' computer.

4. The western Allies finally handed over broadcasting to German authorities by signing a treaty called 'Deutschlandvertrag' in 1955.

5. These were the stations founded in 1948/49: the Bayerischer Rundfunk (BR) in Munich for Bavaria, the Hessischer Rundfunk (HR) in Frankfurt/Main for Hesse, Radio Bremen (RB) in and for Bremen, the Süddeutscher Rundfunk (SDR) in Stuttgart for Baden-Württemberg, the Südwestfunk (SWF) in Baden-Baden for Rhineland-Palatinate and northern Baden-Württemberg and the Nordwestdeutscher Rundfunk (NWDR) in Hamburg and Cologne for Lower Saxony, Schleswig-Holstein and North Rhine-Westphalia. The NWDR was soon divided into NDR in Hamburg for Hamburg, Lower Saxony and Schleswig-Holstein and the WDR in Cologne for North Rhine-Westphalia. The Saarländischer Rundfunk (SR) in Saarbrücken for Saarland was founded in 1957 after the Saar-region had become German again after a referendum. In Berlin, which was still occupied by the United States, Great Britain, France and the Soviet Union, a conflict between Great Britain and the Soviet Union led to a four-year shut down of the Berliner Rundfunk, which had been under Soviet administration albeit being situated in the British sector. In 1957 the Soviets handed over the *Haus des Berliner Rundfunks*, the traditional building of the Berlin radio stations, to the German mayor of Berlin after a four year siege by the British army. The Sender Freies Berlin (SFB) moved into the *Haus des Berliner Rundfunks* and the Soviets started a new Berliner Rundfunk in the Soviet sector. The US Information Agency had already started the Radio im Amerikanischen Sektor (RIAS) in 1945.

6. The tasks as well as the composition of the broadcasting and administrative councils differ from state to state depending on the different broadcasting laws within the federal states.

7. Translated by the author

8. Nevertheless, the German government was still in charge of offering technical distribution facilities for broadcasting. This has since been privatized.

9. In 1988 RTLplus moved to Cologne where they are still situated.

10. SAT.1 started to broadcast from Mainz, not far away from Mannheim-Ludwigshafen, and later moved to Berlin.

11. Moreover, the RTL Group owns twenty radio stations, TV/film content producers (UFA, Grundy), an important film distributor (Universum) and TV and film studios (UFA, CBC) – apart from numerous TV stations in nine other countries (see RTL-Group 2008).

12. ProSiebenSat.1 has undergone several changes of ownership after the media empire of Leo Kirch broke down in 2002 due to financial problems. Axel-Springer-Verlag, a major German print publisher, was involved in ProSiebenSat.1 as well, owning twelve per cent. The majority of Pro7Sat.1 was bought by US investor Haim Saban. In 2005, Saban attempted to sell the majority of shares to Springer, but the deal was prevented by the German merger control authority (*Kartellamt*) on the grounds that Springer, being the publisher of the largest German tabloid newspaper *Bild* with a circulation of 4 million issues per day, would control too large a share of the mass news market. In 2007 ProSiebenSat.1 merged with SBS Broadcasting Group.

13. The ARD, for example, is financed to 80 per cent by fees, three per cent by advertising and eighteen per cent by syndication, sponsoring and other sources (see ARD 2008b). ZDF is financed 85 per cent by fees, 9 per cent by advertising and six per cent by syndication, sponsoring and so on (see ZDF 2008).

14. The term '*Grundversorgung*'/'basic supply' was first invented by the Constitutional Court in its decision on broadcasting in 1987.

15. The amount of the mandatory PSB fee is set by the KEF, *Kommission zur Ermittlung des Finanzbedarfs der Rundfunkanstalten* (Commission for the Determination of the Financial Requirements of Public

Broadcasters). It has to be approved by the federal states, which has led to conflicts in the past years, because the federal state governments did not accept the legally binding proposal of the KEF.

16. TV channels in co-operation with ARD and ZDF: arte since 1992 – cultural channel in co-operation with arte France, 3SAT since 1993 – news, society, culture in co-operation with the Austrian PSB ORF and the Swiss PSB SRG, Phoenix since 1997 – news and documentation channel, KiKa since 1997 – children's channel and several digital channels (theatre, culture, documentaries, usually secondary broadcast).

17. In the 1980s there were two TV stations, DDR 1 and DDR2, and six radio channels: Radio DDR1, Radio DDR2, Berliner Rundfunk, Stimme der DDR (formerly Deutschlandsender meant to broadcast for West Germany), the youth channel DT 64 and Radio Berlin International as the East German World Service.

18. The frequencies of DFF1 and DFF2 (Deutscher Fernsehfunk) were taken over by West German PSB channels.

19. Deutschlandsender had been called *Stimme der DDR* (Voice of the GDR) up to the breakdown of the GDR and was supposed to inform West Germans about the GDR.

20. Deutschlandsender Kultur has since been renamed as DeutschlandRadio Kultur and the co-operation between the two channels is called DeutschlandRadio.

21. About 10,000 staff members of East German radio and TV were dismissed during the reunification process.

22. Newspapers are still a main source of information in Germany, especially for local and regional information. In 2007, 301 newspaper copies were sold per 1000 inhabitants on an average day; that is about half as many as in Norway (601), but close to twice as many as in France (156) and Poland (139). Readership, however, is declining, especially among young people. In 2007, only 43.7 per cent of German residents between twenty and twenty nine years of age read a newspaper regulary, in 1997, almost 60 per cent in that age group did (Bundesverband Deutscher Zeitungsverleger, BDZV 2008).

23. Local radio stations often do not offer substantial information on local topics because many have reduced information to a minimum.

24. According to a survey conducted by the German magazine publishers' association VDZ in 2004, about 40 per cent of magazine publishers have outsourced at least some of their editorial staff.

25. As of 2006, the journalists' union dju lists only nine newspapers left with such a statute, ironically among them the Rhein-Zeitung, which has outsourced all its editors, and the Berliner Zeitung, which implemented a statute in 2006 but where, under Montgomery, the editing staff's autonomy is especially under pressure (Gerloff and Schneidewind 2006).

References

ALM (2008), 'Arbeitsgemeinschaft der Landesmedienanstalten', http://www.alm.de/. Accessed 30 May 2008.

ARD (2008a), 'Gemeinsame Programme', http://www.ard.de/intern/programme/gemeinsame-programme /-/ id=54832/uh6sx0/index.html. Accessed 30 May 2008.

ARD (2008b), 'Programm für alle, Gebühren von allen', http://www.ard.de/intern/finanzen/-/id=8214/ 1g6i2ys/index.html. Accessed 30 May 2008.

Axel Springer Verlag (2001), 'Pressemitteilung: Berliner Morgenpost und Die Welt: Redaktionen und Verlage werden zusammengeführt', Berlin, 6 December 2001.

Baum, Achim; Langenbucher, Wolfgang R.; Pöttker, Horst and Schicha, Christian (eds.) (2005), *Handbuch Medienselbstkontrolle*, VS-Verlag: Wiesbaden.

Braudel, Ferdinand (1990), *Sozialgeschichte des 15. – 18. Jahrhunderts*, München.

Branahl, Udo (2006), *Medienrecht*, VS Verlag: Wiesbaden.

Buchpreisbindungsgesetz (BuchPrG) (2002), 2. September 2002, BGB I. Teil 1/2002, http://transpatent. com/gesetze/buchprei.html, pp. 3448ff.

Bundesministerium der Finanzen (2007), '21. Subventionsbericht der Bundesregierung' (Report about subventions by the Federal Government), September 2007, http://www.bundesfinanzministerium. de/nn_4542/sid_E4AA61A10FDE20C0D4BDC376118B00E3/DE/BMF__Startseite/Aktuelles/ Monatsbericht__des__BMF/2007/09/070917agmb004.html.

Bundesministerium der Justiz (ed.) (2006), 'Gesetz zur Regelung des Zugangs zu Informationen des Bundes (Informationsfreiheitsgesetz – IFG)', 1 January 2006, http://bundesrecht.juris.de/ifg/index. html.

Bundesverband Deutscher Zeitungsverleger (BDZV) (2008), 'Die Deutschen Zeitungen in Zahlen und Daten', Berlin, http://www.bdzv.de/broschuere.html. Accessed 5 June 2008.

Decker, Markus (2008), 'BKA-Gesetz: Regierung erlaubt Online-Durchsuchung.' In: *Mitteldeutsche Zeitung*, http://www.mz-web.de/servlet/ContentServer?pagename=ksta/page&atype=ksArtikel&aid=12114 61861678&openMenu=987490165154&calledPageId=1013016724320&listid=10188 81578370. Accessed 4 April 2008.

Deutsche Telekom AG (2008), 'Die Deutsche Telekom AG auf einen Blick', http://www.telekom.com/ dtag/cms/content/dt/de/8822. Accessed 30 May 2008.

Deutscher Presserat (2006), 'Publizistische Grundsätze' (Pressekodex/press code of conduct), Bonn, revised 13 September 2006, http://www.presserat.de/uploads/media/Novellierter_Pressekodex.pdf.

Deutscher Presserat (2008), 'Statistik', http://www.presserat.de/Statistik.30.0.html. Accessed 5 June 2008.

Die Welt (2004), 'Holtzbrinck darf "Berliner Zeitung" nicht übernehmen. Gericht bestätigt Entscheidung des Bundeskartellamtes', 28 October 2004.

Dussel, Konrad (2004), *Deutsche Tagespresse im 19. und 20. Jahrhundert*, Münster: LIT.

epd Medien (2007), 'Staatsanwaltschaft Hamburg ermittelt gegen vier Journalisten', *epd Medien*, no. 9, 3 February 2007.

epd Medien (2008a), 'Logik des Netzes. Ein epd-Interview mit ZDF-Intendant Markus Schächter', *epd Medien*, no. 38/39, 17 May 2008.

epd Medien (2008b), 'Mecom-Gruppe legt im Jahr 2007 kräftig zu. Deutsche Aktivitäten um "Berliner Zeitung" noch weit vom Ziel entfernt', no. 21, 15 March 2008.

Freedom House (2008), 'Freedom of the press 2007. Table of Global Press Freedom Rankings', Washington D.C., http://www.freedomhouse.org/template.cfm?page=57&year=2007. Accessed 5 June 2008.

Gehringer, Thomas (2007), 'Radikaler Umbau. In Münster und anderswo: Outsourcing bei Verlagen', *epd medien*, 37, 12 May 2007.

Gerlof Kathrin and Schneidewind, Bernhard (2006), 'Redaktionsstatute und weiter?', *Menschen machen Medien*, 11/2006.

Hanfeldt, Michael (2008), 'BND hört mit – Geheime Leser', *Frankfurter Allgemeine Zeitung*, 20 April 2008.

Hans-Bredow-Institut für Medienforschung an der Universität Hamburg (ed.) (2003), *Internationales Handbuch Medien 2004/2005*, 27th edition, Baden-Baden: Nomos.

Heinrich, Jürgen (2001), *Medienökonomie, vol. 1, Mediensystem, Zeitung, Zeitschrift, Anzeigenblatt*, VS Verlag Wiesbaden.

heise online (2007), 'Musikindustrie für Ausweitung der Vorratsdatenspeicherung', 11 June 2007, http://www.heise.de/newsticker/Musikindustrie-fuer-Ausweitung-der-Vorratsdatenspeicherung--/meldung/90978.

Heuzeroth, Thomas (2008), 'Überwachungs-Wahn – Machtgeile Manager schaden der Telekom', *welt online*, 25 May 2008, http://www.welt.de/wirtschaft/article2032594/Machtgeile_Manager_schaden_der_Telekom.html.

Holzweissig, Gunter (1999), 'Massenmedien in der DDR', in Wilke, Jürgen (ed.), *Mediengeschichte der Bundesrepublik Deutschland*, Köln; Weimar; Wien: Böhlau Verlag.

Humphreys, Peter J. (1994), *Media and Media Policy in Germany: The Press and Broadcasting since 1945*, Oxford: Berg.

Koszyk, Kurt (1999), 'Presse unter alliierter Besatzung', in Wilke, Jürgen (ed.), *Mediengeschichte der Bundesrepublik Deutschland*, Köln; Weimar; Wien: Böhlau Verlag.

Lilienthal, Volker (2008), 'Verstricktes Netz. Medienpolitik mutiert zur Wettbewerbspolitik', *epd Medien*, no. 30, 16 April 2008.

Meier, Christian (2008), 'Alles noch viel schlimmer: Depenbrock macht Tabula Rasa im Management des Berliner Verlags', *kress report*, 27 February 2008.

Müller-Neuhof, Jost (2008), 'Das Verhalten des BND beunruhigt', *Der Tagesspiegel*, 21 April 2008.

ProSiebenSat.1 Group (2008), 'Die ProSiebenSat.1 Group', http://www.prosiebensat1.com/unternehmen/. Accessed 30 May 2008.

Range, Steffen and Schweins, Roland (2007), *Klicks, Quoten, Reizwörter: Nachrichten-Sites im Internet. Wie das Web den Journalismus verändert*, Gutachten im Auftrag der Friedrich-Ebert-Stiftung, Berlin: Stabsabteilung der Friedrich-Ebert-Stiftung.

Rath, Christian (2007), 'Größte Verfassungsbeschwerde aller Zeiten – Klage gegen Vorratsdaten speicherung', *die tageszeitung*, 9 November 2007.

Reporters Without Borders (2008), 'World Wide Press Freedom Index 2007', Paris, http://www.rsf.org/article.php3?id_article=24025. Accessed 5 June 2008.

Richter, Alexander (2008), 'Journalisten-Bespitzelung durch den BND. Uhrlau bleibt, andere Köpfe rollen', *tagesschau.de*, 24 April 2008, http://www.tagesschau.de/inland/bnd34.html.

Ridder, Michael (2006), 'Lost in translation', *epd Medien*, no. 100, 20 December 2006.

Roether, Diemut (2005), 'Heuschrecken vor der Tür. Der Berliner Verlag kämpft gegen Montgomery', *epd Medien*, 83/2005.

RTL Group (2008), 'Operations in Germany', http://www.rtlgroup.com/Operations_Germany.htm. Accessed 30 May 2008.

Rundfunkstaatsvertrag (2006), http://www.br-online.de/content/cms/Universalseite/2008/03/06/cumulus/BR-online-Publikation-95597.pdf. Accessed 24 June 2008

Schäfer, Gerhard (2006), Gutachten für den Deutschen Bundestag, 'Bericht des Sachverständigen zu den in der Presse erhobenen Vorwürfen, der Bundesnachrichtendienst habe über längere Zeiträume im Inland Journalisten rechtswidrig mit nachrichtendienstlichen Mitteln überwacht, um so deren Informanten zu enttarnen, wie auch zu den Vorwürfen, der BND habe Journalisten als Quellen geführt' (Report to the German parliament about the allegations that the secret service had illegally observed journalists in Germany in order to reveal their sources, as well as about the allegations that the secret service had used journalists as sources), Berlin, 26 May 2006, http://www2.bundestag.de/bnd_bericht.pdf.

Schmitz, Henrik (2006), 'De officiis', *epd Medien*, no. 93, 25 November 2006.

Schrag, Wolfram (2007), *Medienlandschaft Deutschland*, Konstanz: UVK.

Schuler, Katharina (2008), 'BND – Uhrlau bleibt – vorerst', *Die Zeit*, 24 April 2008.

Schütz, Walter J. (2005), *Zeitungen in Deutschland. Verlage und ihr publizistisches Angebot 1949–2004*, Vistas: Berlin.

Spiegel online (2007), 'Vorratsspeicherung – Bundestag verschärft Datenkontrolle', 9 November 2007, http://www.spiegel.de/politik/deutschland/0,1518,516482,00.html.

Spiegel online (2008), 'Spionageskandal: Telekom-Schnüffler jagten vermeintliche Verräter im Aufsichtsrat', http://www.spiegel.de/wirtschaft/0,1518,555283,00.html. Accessed 25 May 2008.

Statistisches Bundesamt (2006), *Datenreport 2006 – Zahlen und Fakten über die Bundesrepublik Deutschland*, Wiesbaden.

Stöber, Rudolf (2005), *Deutsche Pressegeschichte*, Konstanz: UVK.

tagesschau.de (2008), 'Entscheidung des Bundesverfassungsgerichts: Enge Grenzen für Bundestrojaner', http://www.tagesschau.de/inland/onlinedurchsuchung32.html. Accessed February 2008.

Verband Deutscher Zeitschriftenverleger (VDZ) (2004), 'Zeitschriftenverlage wollen mit Outsourcing Kosten senken. Mehr als die Hälfte lagert heute schon aus', 4 May 2004, http://www.vdz.de/betriebswirtschaft-nachricht.html?&tx_ttnews[backPid]=7&tx_ttnews[pointer]=5&tx_ttnews[tt_news]=1472&cHash=f1a68e7801&type=98.

Verband Deutscher Zeitschriftenverleger (VDZ) (2008), 'Der deutsche Zeitschriftenmarkt', http://www.vdz.de/branchendaten.html. Accessed 5 June 2008.

Vogel, Andreas (2002), 'Publikumszeitschriften: Dominanz der Großverlage gestiegen', *media perspektiven*, vol. 9, p. 433.

Vowe, Gerhard and Wolling, Jens (2004), 'Radioqualität. Was die Hörer wollen und was die Sender bieten', *TLM series*, vol. 17, Munich: kopaed.

VPRT (2008), 'Anmerkungen des VPRT zum Entwurf des 12. RÄndStV', http://www.vprt.de/index.html/de/positions/article/id/58/?or=0&year=%7B0%7D&page=1. Accessed 31 May 2008.

WDR (2008), 'Eckpunkte für eine Zusammenarbeit mit WAZ-Mediengruppe in Düsseldorf vorgestellt', http://www.wdr.de/unternehmen/presselounge/pressemitteilungen/2008/03/20080311_pk_wdr_waz.phtml. Accessed 31 May 2008.

ZDF (2008), 'Finanzen', http://www.unternehmen.zdf.de/index.php?id=26. Accessed 30 May 2008.

zdf heute.de (2008), 'Spitzel-Affäre: Ermittlungen gegen Ricke und Zumwinkel', http://www.heute.de/ZDFheute/inhalt/16/0,3672,7245680,00.html. Accessed 29 May 2008.

The Austrian Media System: Strong Media Conglomerates and an Ailing Public Service Broadcaster

Martina Thiele

'Two giants dominate the Austrian media scene: the government-influenced Austrian Broadcasting Company (ORF) and an enormous print family' (Fidler 2004: jacket text). These were the concise conclusions of *Standard* journalist Harald Fidler, who has documented and commented critically on media policy developments of recent years. Communications scientists speak of a highly concentrated market and one which, in comparison to the international scene, has been slow to implement a dual broadcasting system.

Nevertheless, in the area of press and broadcasting there have been a few important developments since the 1990s. Since 2001 there has been a new broadcast law, intended to regulate the relationship between private, commercial, and public service broadcasting corporations. In the same year, however, there occurred a merging of the print media which has been worrisome, as more than 60 per cent of the daily and the weekly press, and 100 per cent of the production of political magazines, are issued by this media conglomerate Media Print AG. There can therefore be only a limited sense of varied and various independent publishers and broadcasters supplying the people of Austria with information. Rubina Moehring, the Austrian President of Reporters Without Borders, sees this as one reason why Austria ranks 16 worldwide in terms of concentration of media and of political influence on ORF (see Fuith 2006: 36).

The Press in Austria

A positive sign is that 72.7 per cent of Austrians over the age of fourteen read a newspaper daily. These mostly read the tabloid *Neue Kronen-Zeitung* with its specific federal states' editions. With a circulation of 847,320 copies, representing a share of 43.8 per cent, the

Neue Kronen-Zeitung is the most successful newspaper in the country, followed in second and third places by the 269,000 copies of the *Kleine Zeitung* and the *Kurier* with 169,000 (see OeAK 2006).

Despite the market leadership of the *Neue Kronen Zeitung*, the strong position of the regional daily papers is apparent. The nationwide quality papers such as *Die Presse* and *Der Standard* reach a national readership which is as great as that of the *Oberoesterreichischen Nachrichten* or the *Tiroler Tageszeitung*, both regional newspapers. The political party press, which was so strong in the fifties, has largely disappeared; today they reach only two per cent of the daily press market. However, it is not only the party- and confessional-related press which has come under economic pressures: Many other smaller newspaper publishers have been swallowed by the larger ones. This disguises the decline of the actual numbers of the publishing companies and editorial units. Others can secure their survival only by attracting foreign or non-media investors. The *Kurier*, founded in 1954 by Ludwig Polsterer, is now 54.9 per cent owned by the Raiffeisen-Konzern, the biggest Austrian bank; small investors hold 0.1 per cent of the shares and 49.41 per cent belongs to the Essen-based German media company WAZ-Konzern, which has been engaged in the Austrian markets since 1987. They first acquired 45 per cent, then 50 per cent of Hans Dichand's *Neue Kronen Zeitung*, then the 49.41 per cent of *Kurier*. In 1988 the firm Mediaprint AG Press, Marketing and Advertising was founded for marketing and advertising on behalf of *Neue Kronen Zeitung* and *Kurier*. Several other firms also involved in broadcast, newspapers and advertising belong to Mediaprint.

Despite the tendency towards concentration, there have been attempts to establish new newspapers and magazines in the last two decades. One of the successes has been that of Oscar Bronner, who founded the political magazines *trend* and *profil* at the beginning of the 1970s, and thereby decisively changed the Austrian news magazine market. In 1988 he founded, in cooperation with the Axel Springer publishers, the liberal newspaper *Der Standard*. After Springer retired in 1995, a new partner had to be found: since 1998 this has been the *Sueddeutsche Zeitung*, a leading German national quality newspaper owned now by the Stuttgarter Südwestdeutsche Medienholding publishing house, which holds a 49 per cent interest in *Standard*. Less successful was the former co-publisher of the *Neue Kronen-Zeitung*,

Table 1: Decline of Editorial Units (EU).

Year	EUs	Circl. (Millions)
1946	34	2.54
1956	31	1.30
1966	26	1.88
1976	19	2.43
1991	15	2.55
1996	16	2.88
2004	13	2.52

Source: Melischek; Seethaler and Skodascek (2005: 247).

Kurt Falk, with his popular paper *Taeglich Alles,* which appeared between 1992 and 2000. The economic newspaper *Wirtschafts Blatt,* founded in 1995 and in which the Swedish firm Bonnier held a majority interest, was able to maintain its market place.

Helmut and Wolfgang Fellner's project to found a new daily paper for Austria was announced in 2004 and was eagerly awaited. On 1 September 2006, one month before national elections, *Oesterreich* appeared – to largely disappointed readers. Too many expectations had been awakened: innovation, exclusivity and the development of new target audiences had all been spoken of. However, the immediate general impression was simply 'more of the same'. There were, in addition, business and organizational problems. *Oesterreich* was not always available all over Austria. Many thought 50 cents for the paper was too much. Others were offended by the name of the newspaper. Principal among these latter, as reported in the competing *Kronen-Zeitung,* was Hans Boech, once the chief of the programme supplement *tele* and advertising editor of the free newspaper *Heute,* who initiated a suit before the Patents Office, and established a website, http://www.oesterreichistunserlandundkeineZeitung.at ['Austria is our country and not a newspaper'].

Further confusion was provided by the first published circulation figures for *Oesterreich* by the Austrian Circulation Control (Oesterreichische Auflagenkontrolle – OeAK) agency. Competitors asked how the many free copies were to be counted. At any event, the claim by Wolfgang Fellner that *Oesterreich* was second in the country and even first in Vienna could only be based on the total distribution, but not on the sales figures (see fid 2007: 29). In the meantime, the data available to the OeAK was incomplete, as the Mediaprint papers *Krone* and *Kurier* had not reported their circulation for the first quarter of 2007 (see Bentz 2007: 34).

Whether *Oesterreich* will stay in the market remains to be seen. The Fellners have already shown that they are successful managers of popular newspapers. They started with *News* in 1992, made possible by a 50 per cent investment by the German Springer publishing house. This was a news magazine, which soon overtook the competing *profil* in both circulation and advertising. They followed with *tv-media, Format, e-media* and the women's magazine *Woman.* In 1998 the Bertelsmann subsidiary Gruner und Jahr took a 75 per cent interest in the publishing group *News.* Three years later Kurier Magazine Verlag GmbH and News GmbH were merged; the merger was conditionally approved by the Vienna State Court (Oberlandesgericht Wien). One of the conditions was a five year guarantee of the survival of *profil.* The details of this deal are complex; who holds what shares can only be determined with difficulty by close observers of the Austrian media market. Fantasy names such as KroKuWaz or Mediamil-Komplex stand for this scarcely transparent conglomerate. The journalist and publisher of Viennese city magazine *Falter,* Armin Thurnher, is one of the few who sense in this a danger for the freedom of the press and who has spoken out. Each week he ends his column in *Falter* with the sentence: 'I remain of the opinion that the Mediamil-Komplex must be smashed.'

What appears at first glance to be a good opportunity lies with the regional weekly newspapers. At the level of the federal states, the *Niederoesterreichische Rundschau,* with 27 editorial editions and an expanded circulation of 158,000, and the *Oberoesterreichische Rundschau* with thirteen editions and a circulation of 245,000, are especially successful. These figures are actually enhanced by a multiplicity of supplements: advertising, community and regional papers, albeit of varying quality. The weekly papers are often distributed free by the publishers, who are often also active in the daily market. Thus in Salzburg there is, in parallel to the daily *Salzburger Nachrichten*, the *Salzburger Woche* as a supplement plus the advertising insert *Salzburger Fenster*.

There are attempts to approach the issue of press concentration by official means in that certain publications and their publishers are financially supported. These legally regulated press subsidies have existed since 1975. As a result of constant criticism of the criteria for receiving support, the then current guidelines for allocations were modified in 2004 and a 'Three Columns' model was introduced. The new model envisages a special 'Marketing Incentive'; a 'specific incentive for the maintenance of variety in regional daily newspapers' and there are also incentives for raising journalistic standards, such as a specific 'Incentive for Quality and Future Security'. In addition to these provisions, there are incentives for training and further education of journalists. In 2005 there were 12.8 million Euros available, nearly half of which flowed into 'specific incentives' with which it was intended to at least maintain, if not increase, the variety of regional newspapers. For the allocation of resources the 'super regulatory body' called KommAustria was established in 2001.

Press subsidies find considerable acceptance in Austria. Especially in concurrence with criticism of foreign media influence in Austrian media concerns, general acceptance of federal intervention is found. Critics, on the other hand, regard state support for the press as a fig leaf for acceptance of cartel policies, and thus tending towards a reactive media policy. Official negotiations were necessarily in the forefront of mergers and acquisitions, as in 1988 with the founding of Mediaprint and in 2001 with the merger of Kurier Magazine Verlag GmbH and News GmbH.

An observer of the Austrian media scene would be dubious about the institution for self-regulation of the press, the Austrian Press Council, inactive since 2002. This organ for voluntary self-control allowed its functions to lapse due to the too-great differences of opinion between the concerns of the publishers and the unions. This meant that the concerns and complaints of the citizens were not considered, and publishers' offences against the ethical code of the Austrian Press Council went unrebuked. If and when the Council might resume its functions is not clear. Discussion at this time concerns a Chief Editor-model or an Ombudsman-model. Equally unclear is how the independence of an Ombudsman/woman would be maintained.

Broadcasting in Austria

The situation of the Austrian press gives little cause for optimism. Can Austrian broadcasting fill the gaps to provide the people with balanced and comprehensive programming? The public service broadcaster ORF can, as a result of the Regional Radio Law (Regionalradiogesetz) of 1993 (which enabled private commercial broadcasting), no longer function as a quasi-monopoly. Private commercial providers compete with the public broadcasters and with a so-called third sector, the independent non-commercial stations, and not just in the area of radio. Something similar is occurring in the television market as well. Contributing decisively to this are a host of technical and economic developments, chief among these being digitalization, and the convergence of the previously separate areas of broadcasting, telecommunications and information services. This has occurred in part due to judicial rulings by the Constitutional Court and the coming into force of European rulings, and in part due to media policies such as the distancing of the public broadcasters from the government, and more competition.

In 2001 the Austrian Parliament approved certain laws concerning broadcasting in Austria which had far-reaching consequences for the terrain of Austrian broadcasting in general and in particular in respect to the ORF. Thus, the public structure has developed into a foundation, the objectives of which lie in the fulfilment of the public goal in which the beneficiaries are the general public. The public mission is threefold: a support service, which is to include two television stations, four radio programmes and an online service provider; a programme mission, which is to include information, education and entertainment; and a special mission, which is to include, for example, consideration of ethnic minorities and access for the sight- and hearing-impaired.

Changes in the internal organization of the ORF should limit the influence of political parties, nevertheless the Foundation's Council ('Stiftungsrat') is largely made up of political appointees, even though members of the Council may be neither employees nor representatives of political parties. Nine of 35 members are appointed by the federal government, nine are from each of the nine regional governments, six are nominated by political parties represented in parliament, six from the Viewers' and Listeners' Council ('Publikumsrat') and five from the ORF's labour organization.

Like the Foundation's Council, the Viewers' and Listeners' Council consists of 35 members and is similarly appointed for a term of four years. Six members are also members of the Foundation's Council; three of these six also recruit six members each from those paying broadcast fees. However, fewer than ten per cent of the fee payers avail themselves of this opportunity to participate. The manager of the corporation is the Director General, who is chosen by the Foundation's Council. He has the right to make personnel decisions, to determine remuneration and advertising fees and to propose guidelines for the development of the foundation.

In hindsight, in the election year of 2006 a few things did change in the Austrian media landscape. One month before the elections the new daily paper *Oesterreich* commenced circulation, and in mid-August there were elections for the Director General of the ORF. Discussion about the ORF had intensified early in the year. The putative cause of this was the speech of the ORF reporter Armin Wolf at the presentation of the Robert Hochner Prize in which he vehemently criticized certain attempts at political influence. The independence of the ORF was, and is, also at the core of an initiative of the same period entitled 'SOS ORF'. In a very short period, 70,000 persons had signed an appeal for the ORF to be removed from the clutches of politics, and for a programme of reform for more information, better quality and balance to be instituted, as well as provision for public hearings and wide-ranging discussion before the election of the Director General of ORF (see Initiative S.O.S. ORF 2007).

The favourite candidate of the conservative OeVP (Oesterreichische Volkspartei – Austrian People's Party) was the incumbent Director Monika Lindner. However, she was not re-elected. Instead the Sales Director of ORF, Alexander Wrabetz, won 20 of 35 votes in the first round. A rainbow coalition of Foundation councillors, among them those associated with the Austrian Socialist Party (Sozialdemokratische Partei Oesterreichs – SPOe), the Greens as well as the right wing populist Federation for the Austrian Future (Bündnis fur die Zukunft Oesterreichs – BZOe) and the right wing populist Austrian Freedom Party (Freiheitliche Partei Oesterreichs – FPOe), had voted for him. The new Director General immediately promised to fill important positions exclusively in accordance with journalistic criteria and a reform programme which was to provide improvements to information and entertainment. Wrabetz took office on 1 January 2007, and the new programme scheme went into effect on 10 April. It was soon apparent, however, that the new programme, which had promised an interesting early evening programme, more domestic productions, more information and a better platform for more demanding programmes, was perceived by the public as mere appearance packaging. Criticism was directed at the new early evening show, *Mitten im Achten* ['Mid Eight'] and noted that the main news programme, *Zeit im Bild* ['Time in the Picture'] was no longer the same on ORF 1 and 2 channels.

The 'SOS ORF' initiative, as well as countless letters from the public and comments on various Internet fora, demanded that the public profile of ORF be sharpened instead of just imitating the content of the private competitors. The competitors of the ORF are the foreign cable and satellite stations, plus domestic local and regional stations and, since 2003, Austria Television (ATV) – the first Austrian private television station received nation-wide. ORF reacted to the growing competition with a strengthened organization for entertainment and a display of upgraded formatting. There was a noticeable difference in a splitting of the two ORF stations: while ORF 2 retained the traditional public broadcasting format, with strong regional programming, ORF 1 featured talk, sport and films. An expansion of public content is presumed by critics to be in response to the various cooperative measures encountered by ORF. These include, for example, 3Sat, in which Swiss and German public broadcasters are involved, together with BR-alpha, the educational channel of the Bavarian Broadcasting, ZDF (Zweites Deutsches Fernsehen –

Table 2: TV Market Share December 2007.

TV Broadcaster	Market Share
ORF total	40.8%
ORF 1	16.0%
ORF 2	24.7%
ATV	3.1%
RTL A+G	5.4%
RTL II A+G	2.8%
Super RTL A+G	1.7%
VOX A+G	4.4%
Sat 1 A+G	7.7%
Sat1 Austria	5.3%
Pro Sieben A+G	4.4%
Pro Sieben Austria	3.1%
Kabel 1 A+G	2.5%
Kabel 1 Austria	1.9%

A + G = Sum Austrian + German Channel
Source: AGTT (2007).

Second German TV Programme) Theatre Channel and the German-French culture channel, arte. In response ORF, has initiated its own digital channel, TW 1, which can be received by cable, satellite and Internet and which principally covers tourism, weather and sport.

The adaptive and expansionist strategies of ORF have some opponents in the public broadcasting foundation, who advocate the abolition of one ORF channel, thus effectively combining ORF 1 and 2. At present, these recommendations are being heard, but so far have not attracted a majority. At any rate, the establishment of the second ORF programme was one of the most important results of the 1964 petition for a public referendum on broadcasting, which was signed by 832,000 persons. Although the administration of the previous Director General Lindner was referred to as the 'Era of Stagnation', the amalgamation of ORF 1 and 2 was at least prevented at that time.

The fact that ORF has had to struggle to maintain its position of market leadership in this way has a lot to do with the technical infrastructure, which has been so altered in recent years. In 2004 46.5 per cent of Austrian households received programming by satellite, 38.5 per cent by cable and the remainder by antennae. However, even the households with satellite receivers continue to receive 90 per cent of their ORF programmes by terrestrial antennae, because although ORF 1 and 2 have been encoded and digitalized for transmission via the Astra satellite, only 10 per cent of subscribers have registered with ORF for this form of reception. The majority of Austrian television households continue to receive ORF by terrestrial transmission. This should change as digitalization proceeds. Following the preparatory phase and the supply in urban centres, 'step three' of digitalization has been reached: In 2007 the analogue turn-off began – region by region the analogue frequencies will no longer be maintained. In 'step four', the period which will ensue after the analogue systems are switched off, further so-called 'multiplex platforms' will be tendered and allotted.

The competition with the private stations, along with the requirement to provide content and technical innovation, has had its effect on the financing of ORF. The budget share of advertising is, at over 40 per cent, almost as large as the subscription charges. Approximately 16 per cent of the income results from 'special proceeds', for example, licensing and rights. This financing model is explained by the small population of Austria. With just 8 million inhabitants, the user fees will never be sufficient, although the Austrian fees, averaging around 20 Euros, correspond to the European norm. These fees are comprised of several elements and vary among the federal states because, in addition to radio and television user fees, television remunerations, and artistic incentives and sales taxes, individual states' charges are also included. The recommendation to raise fees by the ORF Director General collided principally with the miscarried reform programme on account of the major sports events of 2008 plus the requirements to introduce new technology, and has met little agreement, even within ORF. The editors do not wish to be drawn into a debate on user fees without addressing the 'structural' problems of ORF. They apparently do not mean by this the fact that, despite all promises, the number of permanent employees at ORF has, in the past ten years, risen from 2,600 to 4,500.

The financing of ORF is thus a major problem. Criticism has given rise to so-called 'Ad Specials', such as 'product placement'. This does not appear to be of great concern to those responsible at ORF – and that includes in recent years, among others, the then Sales Director of ORF, Alexander Wrabetz, – although it is in direct contrast to the 2001 regulations governing ORF. This clearly prescribes that, only in specific exceptional circumstances and for very small remuneration (less than 1,000 Euros), may a product be specifically identified in a show. The cause for this clarification was the song-show *Starmania*, in which the stars of the future were shown not only singing and dancing, but also eating chips of a particular and identifiable brand. However, when ORF asked for a tenth of what would have been asked for by their private competitors for this 'product placement', there were complaints that ORF has forced down prices. Wrabetz as Director General remains of the opinion that advertising and special advertising reforms such as product placement are indispensable sources of income for ORF.

How economically the ORF is managed is subject to audit by the office of the Federal Auditor (Rechnungshof). The Federal Communications Senate, as the responsible legal advisory and enforcement body, will determine if an offence against the ORF governing regulations has occurred. Besides the possibility of a direct accusation by the Federal Communications Senate, a popular complaint may also arise, which must be placed on behalf of at least 120 people. Infractions subject to censure might include, for example, failure to maintain objectivity, or failure to maintain independence from political parties, as well as meeting the requirement to remain cognisant of diverse opinions and to maintain balanced programming.

With the promulgation of new broadcast regulations in 2001, it was intended that broadcasting management and oversight become more effective and transparent. Thus, the 'super regulatory body' KommAustria was created. This is to be the licensing, legal supervision, administration and disciplinary authority for private broadcasters, and for ORF, the frequency allocating authority, as well. The Broadcast and Telecommunications Regulatory Corporation (RTR) functions as an office of KommAustria and as the Telecom Control Commission, which is, since the ending of the monopoly period in 1977, intended to ease the entry into the market of new providers. It is also intended thereby to ensure the provision of modern, inexpensive telecommunications services. The use of mobile telephones and the regular use of the Internet have since then expanded enormously. More than two thirds (68 per cent) of Austrians aged over 14 are online each day.

Conclusion

The sources of information are not just the 'classical' media of newspapers, magazines and broadcasting. To arrive at a reasonably accurate assessment of the state of press and media freedom in Austria, it would be necessary to have a deeper evaluation of the media available in different fields. In addition to the press and television, radio, news agencies, movies and theatres, books and publishers, recording, telecommunications and Internet and advertising also have to be considered. Data on media use, official guidelines, ownership, methods of financing, media orientation and media culture must be assembled, and in a second step compared with others. In the literature of communications science, Austria is numbered among the 'central European, democratic-corporate mixed models' (see Hallin and Mancini 2004: 143), in which both liberal market and public service elements are found. Public subsidies also play a role, as in press and films. This state influence is generally accepted by the public and is justified by the challenge of the small-state environment in its encounter with the otherwise overwhelming influence of foreign publishers and broadcasters. Contrastingly, attempts at just such a state involvement in public broadcasting would be perceived as violating the freedom of broadcasting. When in 2001 new broadcast regulations were enacted with the intent to reduce political party influence, this was seen as lip service only and it was assumed that the political party wrangling over public broadcasting would continue unabated. The chances for greater media freedom in Austria are therefore not good. The media echo of the Worldwide Press Freedom Index referred to earlier remains. Sixteenth place does not seem so bad – in comparison to Italy in 40th place, or the United States, which as 'liberal-investigative model' has long been an example, and which now rests in place 56.

References

AGTT (2007), 'Arbeitsgemeinschaft Teletest (AGTT)', http://www.agtt.at/daten/agtt_ma_sender.pdf. Accessed 4 December 2007.

Bentz, Ulrich, (2007), Liste der Verweigerer, *extradienst*, 5/2007, 34–5.

Bundespressedienst Wien (2006) (ed.), *Medien in Österreich*, 2nd revised edition, Wien.

Duffek, Karl A.; Filzmaier, Peter and Plaikner, Peter (eds.) (2007), *Mediendemokratie Österreich*, Edition Politische Kommunikation volume 1, Wien; Köln and Weimar: Böhlau.

fid (= Fidler, Harald) (2007), '3079 Menschen mehr kaufen den *Standard*. ÖAK akzeptiert weniger „Österreich"-Abos', *Der Standard*, 27 February 2007, p. 29.

Fidler, Harald (2004), *Im Vorhof der Schlacht. Österreichs alte Medienmonopole und neue Zeitungskriege*, Wien: Falter Verlag.

Fuith, Ute (2006), 'Demokratie ist anstrengend', *extradienst*, 11/2006, p. 36.

Hallin, Daniel C. and Mancini, Paolo (2004), *Comparing Media Systems. Three Models of Media and Politics*, Cambridge et al.: University Press.

Hans-Bredow-Institut für Medienforschung an der Universität Hamburg (ed.) (2003), *Internationales Handbuch Medien 2004/2005*, 27th edition, Baden-Baden: Nomos.

Initiative 'Österreich ist unser Land und keine Zeitung' (2007), http://www.oesterreichistunserland undkeineZeitung.at. Accessed 1 December 2007.

Initiative 'S.O.S.-ORF' (2007), http://www.sos-orf.at/show_content.php?hid=1. Accessed 3 December 2007.

Kelly, Mary; Mazzoleni, Gianpietro and McQuail, Denis (eds.) (2004), *The Media in Europe. The Euromedia Handbook*, London; Thousand Oaks and New Delhi: Sage.

MA (2007), 'Media-Analyse' (MA), http://www.media-analyse.at. Accessed 5 December 2007.

Melischek, Gabriele; Seethaler, Josef and Skodascek, Katja (2005), 'Der österreichische Pressemarkt 2004: hoch konzentriert. Strukturen, Marktpotenziale, Anbieterkonzentration', *Media Perspektiven*, 5/2005, pp. 243–54.

OeAK (2006), 'Tagezeitungen im Jahresschnitt 2006, verkaufte Auflage', Austrian Circulation Control = Österreichische Auflagenkontrolle, http://www.oeak.at. Accessed 5 December 2007.

RTR (2007), 'Rundfunk und Telekom Regulierungs-GmbH', http://www.rtr.at. Accessed 2 April 2007.

Steinmaurer, Thomas (2003), 'Die Medienstruktur Österreichs', in Bentele, Günter; Brosius, Hans-Bernd and Jarren, Otfried (eds.), *Öffentliche Kommunikation. Handbuch Kommunikations- und Medienwissenschaft*, Wiesbaden: Westdeutscher Verlag, pp. 349–65.

Pluralism in the French Broadcasting System: Between the Legacy of History and the Challenges of New Technologies

Thierry Vedel

Introduction

Broadcasting pluralism is a notion which, at first glance, seems hardly disputable. Everybody agrees that plurality and heterogeneity of sources, channels and programmes are desirable in modern societies and are a prerequisite to a sound democracy. Most governments emphasize pluralism in media as a key objective and media diversity is a normative requirement in many countries.

However, when it comes to determining which techniques and mechanisms can best ensure pluralism, or when one has to evaluate and measure the degree of pluralism in a media system, definitions of pluralism are increasingly ubiquitous (Freedman 2008). There is no consensus on whether diversity can only be brought forth through market mechanisms, and many advocate a strong role of public authorities both as regulator and programme providers. Moreover, media pluralism is usually treated as a supply-side phenomenon (Huysmans and De Haan 2005). While governments and regulators have devised substantial legislation to promote diversity in the content as sent, they generally pay little attention to the diversity of content as received. Finally, technological developments challenge, in many ways, traditional conceptions of broadcasting pluralism.

Historical background

The history of the French broadcasting system can be broken down into four distinctive periods, closely linked to the evolution of French politics (Table 1).[1]

The first period (state television) went from the advent of television until the beginning of the 1970s. It was characterized by a tight political control of the Office of French Radio and Television (Office de la radio-télévision française – ORTF). Entirely funded by licence fees until 1968, the ORTF enjoyed a triple monopoly: on signal transmission, programming and production. Its employees had a status equivalent to that of civil servants and private management methods were deeply mistrusted. During this period, broadcasting was highly prescriptive. Television was viewed as an instrument to promote culture and education and was not supposed to cater to the tastes of the majority. As a consequence, there was little audience research and no accountability. The government frequently used television to justify its policies and openly interfered with news content. From the government's point of view, political control and cultural ambition went hand-in-hand. This conception was clearly expressed by President Georges Pompidou when he said in 1970 that television was 'the voice of France' at home and abroad, meaning that television had to represent both the views of the legitimate government and the cultural resources of the French nation.

The second period (commercialized state television) began in 1968, when French broadcasting was opened to advertising revenues. But it really fully developed after the decision was taken to break the ORTF up into seven public companies[2] in 1974, following the election of President Valéry Giscard d'Estaing. This reform was intended to bring greater variety and quality of programming, as well as political independence, by introducing competition among public broadcasters. It was also hoped that the specialization of functions would reduce costs. While the 1974 reform did open the way for competition for advertising revenues and audiences among broadcasters, it did not increase their political independence. The Government maintained its right to appoint broadcast executives and still drew the line at private broadcasting.

The third period (regulated television) started in 1982 as a consequence of the Law on Audiovisual Communication, which abolished the state monopoly on broadcasting.[3] In an attempt to set up a buffer between the government and public television stations, the law also established an independent regulatory agency for broadcasting, the High Authority for Broadcasting (Haute autorité de l'audiovisuel),[4] which was responsible for appointing the heads of public channels. In 1984, a licence for a Pay-TV channel was awarded to Canal+, the first private station in the history of French broadcasting. In 1986, a few weeks before the general elections, two more private television channels were granted licences by the government.[5] The change of government in March 1986 pushed the liberalization of French broadcasting a step further. The Law on Freedom of Communication 1986[6] set up a general regulatory framework for a dual broadcasting system, in which private and public television stations coexisted. The responsibilities of the regulatory agency for broadcasting – first renamed the National Commission for Communication and Freedoms (Commission nationale de la communication et des libertés), then in 1989 the High Council for Broadcasting (Conseil supérieur de l'audiovisuel – CSA) – were broadened. Finally, in 1987, TF1, the leading broadcaster, was privatized, which gave the private sector a growing role in French broadcasting. Yet, while commercial concerns became increasingly dominant, the French broadcasting system did not turn into a full marketplace and remained highly regulated as will be shown in the next section of this chapter.

France entered a fourth period with the launch of digital terrestrial television in April 2005 and the transition from analogue to digital technology. This fourth period is characterized by an increase of the number of available channels, a further development of pay-TV (to which twenty eight per cent French household currently subscribe), and a diversification of the delivery

Table 1: History of French broadcasting.

	1959–1974	1974–1982	1982–2005	2005 to present
Model	State television	Commercialized State television	Regulated television	Toward market television?
Organization	ORTF as a single body for broadcasting Second channel: 1964 Third channel: 1969	Breaking up of ORTF into 7 public companies: TF1, A2, FR3, Radio-France, SFP, TDF, INA	Authorization of private television: Canal+ (1984), M6 (1986), ARTE (1992) Privatization of: TF1 (1987), TDF (2002). Development of new channels on cable and satellite	Launch of DTT (April 2005) and authorization of new digital terrestrial channels. Development of television on the internet.
Governance and politics	Tight and direct political control of broadcasting by government.	Introduction of specialization and competition within the public broadcasting system.	Establishment of a regulatory agency for broadcasting: Haute autorité (1982) CNCL (1986) CSA (1989)	No change so far, but growing debate about the role, place and financing of public broadcasting.
Financing and economics	ORTF is mainly financed by licence fees, but modest introduction of advertising from 1968 on.	Development of advertising revenues and consequently of audience research.	Growing competition in production, programming, advertising. Emergence of pay-TV.	The broadcasting system is becoming a combination of 4 marketplaces: production programming advertising delivery Further increase of pay-TV.
Conception of broadcasting and viewers	Normative definition of broadcasting as a public service. Viewers are citizens who are to be informed, educated, cultivated and entertained.	Television is not just a public service but also an industry. No clear conception of viewers, but more attention is given to audience ratings.	Television is an industry providing services. Yet, this industry must be regulated and public service obligations may apply in certain circumstances.	Tendency to consider viewers as sovereign consumers who buy television services.

modes (DTT, cable, satellite, Internet, mobile communication). The latter move is especially important as it has introduced more competition in the broadcasting system, which has become a combination of four distinct marketplaces:

■ The marketplace for programmes, where broadcasters buy programmes from production companies.
■ The marketplace for commercials, in which advertisers buy airtime from broadcasters.

- ■ The delivery marketplace, in which broadcasters buy transmission capacities (cable, satellite or free-to-air) from infrastructure operators.
- ■ The marketplace for television services, where viewers buy (in the form of subscriptions or pay-per-view) programmes from broadcasters.

The French policy kit for pluralism in broadcasting

The dimensions of broadcasting diversity

Media diversity can take different forms which can be ordered along a continuum from production to consumption and include source (or support) diversity, channel diversity, diversity of content-as-sent, diversity of content-as-received, and audience diversity (McQuail 1992; Napoli 1999). However, in what Grant and Wood termed the 'cultural policy toolkit', that is, the set of techniques, measures and tools that public authorities can use to promote culture (Grant and Wood 2004), pluralism broadcasting encompasses two main dimensions.

The first one, which, depending on authors, is called structural, source, organizational or external pluralism, refers to the diversity of channel operators. It relates to concentration issues and is mostly associated with ownership and cross-ownership regulation aimed at preventing one single company from dominating the television system.

The second dimension, respectively called behavioural, content, editorial or internal pluralism, refers to the diversity of programmes provided on each channel. It deals with what is shown on screens and can be analysed through a great variety of indicators, either quantitative or qualitative (Hoffman-Riem 1987; McDonald and Dimmick 2003). These generally include the measure of programme functions (such as information, education, entertainment), genres (movies, news, music shows and so on) formats, social representations (who takes part or who is portrayed in programmes) or geographical coverage.

External diversity is certainly an important condition for pluralism in programming. With a single, monopolistic operator, it is obviously more difficult to offer a large variety of programmes than with many operators. In addition, the concentration of decision making within one authority might be dangerous when it comes to news or political coverage. Yet the degree of competition in the broadcasting system does not necessarily guarantee content diversity. The existence of many owners may not translate into pluralistic diversity if owners hold similar views and values. Market forces can push even diverse owners toward providing similar content, if a large part of the audience prefers the same type of programmes.[7] This is why it is generally considered that pluralism is best ensured through an appropriate set of regulatory measures aiming at internal pluralism and at the diversity of the content provided by each outlet. This is the dominant approach in France.

Regulations for external pluralism

External pluralism is mainly reached through ownership and cross-ownership regulations which aim at ensuring a plurality of operators. The specific missions assigned to public broadcasters are also part of external pluralism, since they contribute to a diversification of the programmes provided to French viewers.

Ownership and cross-ownership regulations

Ownership and cross-ownership in the media sector are governed by the Law on Freedom of Communication 1986, supplemented by subsequent laws and decrees.[8] On the one hand, various provisions impose limits on concentration of ownership for each type of medium (terrestrial television, terrestrial radio, satellite platform and cable systems). For instance, one company may not hold more than one licence for national analogue service, and the number of licences that a company may hold for digital television services is limited to seven. There is no limitation on the number of cable or satellite channels that one single company may own. Foreign ownership (for example non-European) is also limited to a maximum share of 20 per cent in one broadcasting company. On the other hand, cross-ownership is limited by the so-called 'two-out-of-three situations' rule (2/3 rule) applying both at national and regional levels.[9]

While these provisions seek to ensure political and programming pluralism through plurality of media corporations, they have been criticized on several grounds. Their effectiveness has been questioned, since neither the CSA nor any other specialized agency has the authority to approve ownership changes in the media sector.[10] Thus, when Suez sold most of its share in M6 to the RTL Group, the CSA could only remind RTL of the obligations placed on the channel at the moment of its licensing. Ownership limitations are also said to be excessively rigid and do not allow for quick necessary adjustments in such a fast-developing sector as broadcasting. Finally, there is a constant tension in France's ownership regulations, as they seek to reconcile the creation of major communication groups able to compete with other multinational holdings at an international level (which requires some concentration), with pluralism and diversity of the media (which requires anti-monopoly regulation). Successive governments have coped with this challenge in different ways in the past. When the (then) public broadcaster TF1 was sold off to private interests in 1987, the Hachette group's bid failed, in part because of its strong presence in print media. Ten years later, both President Jacques Chirac and Prime Minister Lionel Jospin applauded and supported the acquisition of Seagram (Universal) by Vivendi.

To date, the main effect of cross-ownership regulations has been to keep broadcast media apart from print media. These regulations have not closed the audiovisual market to foreign companies, as is demonstrated by the rampant Americanization of cable operators and in the takeover of M6 by the RTL Group.

The specific role of public broadcasters
Regarding pluralism, the broadcasting law of 1986 assigns very broad missions to public broadcasters.[11] As a general principle, they must:

> supply a wide range and diversity of programmes, covering the areas of news, culture, knowledge, entertainment and sports. They must contribute to the democratic debate within French society as well as to the social inclusion of citizens. They must ensure the promotion of the French language and reflect the diversity of cultural heritage in its regional and local dimensions. They must contribute to the development and diffusion of ideas and arts. They must also spread civic, economic, social and scientific knowledge and contribute to media literacy.[12]

In addition to the general programming obligations applying to all television broadcasters, public television and radio stations have specific obligations, which are stated in their terms of references (*cahier des charges*). These can be divided into three categories: public service missions, the expression of political, social and religious forces, and requirements for cultural programmes.

Public service missions: Public broadcasters must air general interest messages, such as health and road safety information, programmes to inform consumers about their rights (ten minutes per week in primetime on France 2 and four minutes per week in primetime on France 3), and programmes aimed at integrating foreign residents. Public broadcasters are also required to take part in public welfare campaigns by providing free airtime to organizations designated by the government to be in charge of defending an issue of national interest.[13] Public broadcasters may also be required by the government to broadcast at any time any official declarations or messages of the government to the French people.

Expression of political, social and religious forces: Public broadcasters must provide free airtime to political parties represented in Parliament and to those unions and professional associations considered to be representative at a national level. The amount of time allocated to these broadcasts and their format are determined by the CSA. For political parties, the time allocated is proportional to the number of their MPs.[14]

These provisions have raised two sorts of criticism. Political parties and unions have complained that their broadcasts are not scheduled at convenient times. More importantly, no airtime is provided for political parties not represented in Parliament or to unions that are not considered as representative under French law. This illustrates how, in France, the notion of political or social representativeness follows an institutional approach, rather than taking into account the actual influence of organizations.

France 3 is also obliged to cover the activity of Parliament through a weekly live broadcast of Parliamentary sessions devoted to MPs' questions to the government. France 2 has to broadcast religious programmes. These are mainly broadcast on Sunday mornings, but also in late-night shows, and amounted to a total of 193 hours in 2002, including Catholic (78 hours), Protestant (31 hours), Jewish (26 hours), Muslim (25 hours), Orthodox (18 hours) and Buddhist (13 hours) rites.

Requirements for cultural programmes: Finally, public broadcasters must broadcast a minimum of fifteen public musical, dance or drama performances per year. They also have to broadcast music programmes – two hours per month on France 2 and three hours per month on France 3 – with at least 16 hours per year devoted to concerts. Finally, France 2, France 3 and, above all, France 5 must regularly broadcast programmes on science and technology and the social sciences, although there is no quantitative requirement for this kind of programming.

The cultural programming of France 2 and France 3 represent between 9 and 12 per cent of their total schedule. For France 5, which has a special focus on knowledge and education programmes, it is almost 50 per cent of total programming. Public broadcasters are doing better in this area than private broadcasters. Yet, it should be noted that only a small part of this offering is scheduled at peak hours (from 18.00 until 23.00 o'clock). In this respect, the cultural programming of commercial broadcasters at peak hours is higher than that of France 2.

Overall, as a combination of their programming obligations and of their editorial strategies, the output of public broadcasters is somewhat distinctive from that of commercial broadcasters.

Public channels air regular political shows which are nonexistent on commercial broadcasters. Unlike commercial broadcasters, public broadcasters have so far refrained from going into reality television. Some of the programmes of France 3, including *Des Racines et des Ailes* ['Roots and Wings'], a magazine exploring the artistic heritage of landmark cities throughout the world, and *Thalassa*, a discovery magazine covering a wide array of stories related to oceans and seas, are widely acclaimed for their quality. However, public broadcasters' programmes do not gain high ratings[15] and their differentiation from commercial broadcasters is not necessarily perceived by viewers. According to a poll taken in September 2006, 26 per cent of French viewers considered there to be major differences between public and private broadcasters, 30 per cent some differences, 33 per cent little difference and 7 per cent no difference. In addition, 30 per cent of viewers thought that the ideal of public service broadcasting was best embodied by private broadcasters (TNS-Sofres 2006).

Regulations for internal pluralism
Internal pluralism relates to the diversity of programmes, which is also one of the CSA's remits. It is intended to promote information fairness in the coverage of politics, to protect the French culture and, more recently, to ensure the representation of minorities within the French society.

Political pluralism
Regarding political pluralism, the CSA has set up several guidelines, basically all revolving around the idea of equal time provision. Until 2000, all television stations had to comply with the so-called 'three-thirds rule' when covering political activities. This meant that stations had to devote one third of their airtime to government officials, one third to the political parties represented in Parliament which supported the government, and another third to the political parties that represented the opposition in Parliament.

In January 2000, the CSA amended its policy on political pluralism on television and established new standards, known as the 'reference principle'. On the one hand, the CSA adjusted the three-thirds rule, by requiring an 'equitable' access to television for those political parties not represented in Parliament. On the other hand, the CSA stated that, besides quantitative indicators focused on politicians' public statements, a more qualitative evaluation of the coverage of politics by the media was needed. This meant that television channels had to take other parameters into consideration, such as the duration, format and audience of programmes devoted to politics.

Practically, it seems that the new reference principle inaugurated in January 2000 has only changed the 'three-thirds rule' into an 'about 30 per cent-30 per cent-30 per cent and roughly ten per cent' rule. Judging by the official statements of the CSA, it is not clear how the qualitative assessment of political coverage has been implemented.

During electoral campaigns a special regime applies, the details of which are set up by the CSA depending on the nature of the election. For instance, for the presidential election (the major election in France), three periods are distinguished. In the first period, which covers the so-called pre-campaign or non-official campaign, broadcasters must ensure that all candidates for public offices have 'equitable' access to the screen. The term equitable has not been precisely defined by the CSA, but from the observations and comments made by the CSA, it can be inferred that it means proportional to the public support gained by candidates as registered in opinion polls. The second period starts when the list of candidates has been officially established by the Conseil Constitutionnel (the High court in charge of supervising the election), about one month before the first round. During this period broadcasters must give equal time to the public statements of candidates and cover, in an equitable fashion, the rest of the candidate's activities. The third period concerns the official electoral campaign which starts two weeks before the first round of voting. From this point on, an equal time provision applies and broadcasters have to devote equal airtime to each candidate.

Formerly a major issue in French broadcasting, the coverage of politics is now much less debated. The major parties are generally content with the current situation. However, opposition parties criticize the fact that the airtime devoted to the President is not regulated and claim that it should be counted with the time allocated to the government.[16] This makes sense if one considers that the President often behaves as the head of the majority in the Parliament. However, the CSA as well as the current government argue that there is no reason to limit the President's airtime since, under the French constitution, he represents the whole nation and not a specific political current.

Cultural diversity: The defence and promotion of French culture is a cornerstone of French broadcasting regulation. Successive governments, of the right and left alike, have constantly held the view that cultural and media products are different from other forms of merchandise because they encapsulate part of the country's identity. As a result, France – backed by some other countries such as Canada – has become the leading exponent of a 'cultural exception' to free-trade principles and championed the right to support and protect the development of a local, creative and pluralistic cultural life (Cocq and Messerlin 2005). It should be noted that in an interesting tactical move initiated in 2000, the notion of cultural exception has been rephrased more positively as 'cultural diversity'.

This concern is reflected in various programming obligations and restrictions as well as in provisions to encourage French-language productions or to support the production of French movies.

Diversity in the offering of movies and TV series: French broadcasters are subject to various programming and production obligations and to a complex system of quotas, which have been primarily designed to benefit French cinema. Some 60 per cent of the movies and series broadcast by television channels have to originate from European countries and 40 per cent from French speaking countries, which include non-European countries, notably Canada.[17] Moreover, free-to-air broadcasters must allocate a minimum share of their total revenue from the previous year (3.2 per cent since 2002) to the production of European movies.[18]

In addition, since 1986, France has established a subsidy scheme to support the production of French movies and audiovisual works. All television channels, whether terrestrial or distributed on cable and satellite, must contribute around five per cent of their net revenue from the previous year to the Fund for Support of Programmes Industry (Compte de soutien aux industries de programmes – COSIP), which also draws cash from taxes on movie theatre tickets, video rentals and text messaging by telephone. The COSIP then allocates grants and subsidies to French movies and producers of audiovisual works. The COSIP therefore operates as a cross-subsidy mechanism between advertisers and producers, and also between foreign and French producers. For instance, the more successful an American movie is at the box-office (and hence, the greater the collected tax), the more significant the subsidies to French producers will be. The COSIP can be ironically described as a system through which American cultural imperialism nourishes French cultural diversity. Some suggest that the COSIP, by making cinema the privileged branch of the French culture industry, has contributed to a comparative weakness of French TV fictional programmes (Dagnaud 2006). It has nevertheless helped to protect and nurture the French movie industry, 'making France one of the few international points of comparatively successful resistance to Hollywood' (Gibbons and Humphreys 2008).

Representation of multiculturalism in contemporary France: The representation of multiculturalism in contemporary France only became an issue – although not a prominent one – in the late 1990s as part of the general political agenda on the social inclusion of people coming from foreign countries (about ten per cent of the total population (see Haut Conseil à l'Intégration 2005)). Media observers and analysts have often underlined that the multicultural diversity of France is very poorly reflected on French television. The conference 'Colourless screens' organized by the High Council for the Integration and the CSA on 26 April 2004 noted that, despite positive changes in the depiction of French society's diversity in youth programmes and fictional programmes, people with foreign origins were under-represented among journalists and show hosts.

While there is a consensus on this issue, it is not clear how regulation in this field can be implemented, given the traditional opposition of France to any form of communitariansm. Under the French Constitution, all citizens are considered equal whatever their origin. Ethnic groups must not be identified as such and cannot be counted in any way.[19] Consequently, policies on positive discrimination cannot be implemented and are opposed by many political parties, as they are considered a first move toward a 'communitarian' society at odds with the French republican ideal. From a legal perspective, only negative discrimination – for instance, denying a person a job on the grounds of their origin – can be combated, which is often difficult since evidence can rarely be gathered.

Within this peculiar context, a new obligation was nevertheless added in 2001 to the terms of reference of France 2 and France 3, whereby the two public service broadcasters had to promote 'the different cultures constitutive of the French society without any kind of discrimination'.[20] Similarly, the licensing contracts of the private broadcasters were changed to ensure that their programming reflects 'the diversity of origins and cultures within the national community'. Besides its general and somewhat abstract obligations, as of January 2004, France Télévisions implemented an action plan (see France Télévisions 2004) that includes measures to increase the representation of foreign people who live in France in programmes and debates. Since 2001, France 3 has had a special week to promote integration and fight discrimination, during which the programming schedule of the public broadcaster is focused on foreign people living in France and French people with an immigrant background. The station has also established a training scheme for young journalists with an immigrant background, in cooperation with two schools of journalism. Similarly, private broadcasters have committed themselves to the promotion of diversity. Thus, TF1's Annual Report for 2007 states that

TF1 sustained the efforts of previous years towards the diversity of cultures and racial origins in the audiences and the candidates in television game shows. Reality TV programmes systematically include candidates who reflect the diversity of the French population. For TV drama, in-depth work has been carried out with producers and casting agencies to enhance the visibility of actors from minorities in roles of identifiable professions (doctors, judges, lawyers...) The editorial teams now include a number of incumbent journalists and presenters who are visibly from minorities. (TFI 2007: 27)

New technologies: Opportunity for, or challenge to, pluralism?

Over the last 20 years, the French broadcasting system has come to know an increasing commercialization. However, its structures have changed little and have been only marginally affected by the development of new communication technologies. The implementation of new communication technologies has been a difficult process in France. In contrast with some other European countries, and despite an ambitious plan launched in 1982 (Vedel and Dutton 1990), only 2.1 million of French households subscribed to cable television at the end of 2006 (CSA 2007). Similarly, satellite reception has slowly developed in the last decade and is doing just a little better than cable with about 3.8 million households subscribing to Canalsatellite, the French satellite operator, and an estimated 2 million accessing channels available through Eutelsat or Intelsat satellites. In other words, this means that in 2006 around 70 per cent of the 25.1 million French households would only watch the five free-to-air channels available in France.

This situation is nevertheless changing. This is, first, due to the introduction of Digital terrestrial television (DTT), which began in April 2005 and allowed the introduction of twelve additional free channels. As of March 2008, it is estimated that 37 per cent of French households are equipped to receive digital TV. According to government plans, the full deployment of DTT will take place by the end of 2011. In effect, the transition from analogue to digital has been used by the French government and the CSA as a way to smoothly introduce more competition and new players in the broadcasting system. Because it is gradual, DTT does not appear as a big bang in the system and its development over several years should allow old players to adjust to a more open environment by offering additional channels themselves.

Second, the Internet is becoming a new medium to carry TV services. After a slow beginning, the penetration of the Internet has dramatically increased since 1998 and by the end of 2007 about half of French households had an Internet connection. This growth is linked to the fierce competition among French access providers that pushed down the connection rates and also led to a steady development of broadband connections. As a result, watching TV or video excerpts on the Internet has become quite popular. Surveys by the consulting firm Médiamétrie have shown that over twenty per cent of French Internet users do so regularly.

By allowing access to an increasing number of channels, DTT and the Internet contribute to a greater diversity of choice for viewers. More generally, the development of a digital environment offering a multiplicity of sources seems to support pluralism in broadcasting. However, new technologies also undermine media pluralism in several respects. First, as already stated above, the quantity of available channels does not necessarily result in an increased variety of content. When, as in broadcasting, media are dependent on advertising, there is a tendency towards product homogeneity and to under-serve minorities (Doyle 2007). Moreover, the growth in television channels will mean more outlets chasing programmes and, in many countries, this will result in more imports from the US. Because of their limited resources, many new channels will schedule cheap programmes or they will adapt already-popular formats in order to minimize their investments and financial risks. Second, the digitalization of communications logically leads to convergence strategies, the same content being carried over different networks. This will inevitably push towards consolidation and concentration of ownership in the media industry. To remain competitive in a multimedia world and recoup huge investments in infrastructure and programmes, media companies will have to make alliances or to merge (Sanchez-Tabernero and Carvajal 2002). Third, the expansion in the supply of programming as a result of DTT and other technologies will inevitably lead to a reduction in the audience-share of public broadcasters. This will make more acute the traditional dilemma that public broadcasters face: if they try to emulate the output of their commercial rivals, they are criticized for not fulfilling their public service mission; conversely, if they schedule more demanding and highbrow programmes to highlight their educational spirit or to foster the quality of public debate, they are criticized for being elitist, boring and spending too much money on very few viewers. In any case, the place and role of public broadcasters will be questioned. Finally, the multiplication of channels and conduits for TV services weaken the capacity of governments or regulatory agencies to regulate the contents provided on new channels. DTT will bring about a more complex and heterogeneous system in which quotas or scheduling regulations will be difficult to design and implement. Nobody knows how the hundreds of video services available on the Internet, and originating from individuals or from outside France, can be regulated or even monitored. More essentially, new technologies put to question the intervention of public authorities in broadcasting. Traditionally, the role of public authorities in broadcasting has been justified by two main reasons (Pool 1983): spectrum scarcity[21] and public interest linked to the political and cultural effects of television and radio services on society. With the development of digital technologies and the Internet, there is no longer spectrum scarcity and no longer a bottleneck that would justify the action of public authorities. If television regulation is needed in a digital world, it may only be for reasons of public interest. But, then, it remains to be determined how public interest in broadcasting can be best identified.

Conclusion: Broadcasting pluralism from a viewer perspective

As noted by Denis McQuail (McQuail 1992), the notion of public interest is quite elastic and may be given different meanings. However, all approaches to public interest recognize that the notion is closely linked to values and norms which are considered as central by a society. Consequently, regulating broadcasting pluralism in the name of public interest implies a set of normative preferences in terms of media content: which kinds of programmes are considered essential for the society?

In France, these preferences have long been established by political authorities. It was the time of the ORTF when television was defined in a prescriptive fashion (see first section of this chapter). There are now growing pressures to determine the preferences through market mechanisms. As private broadcasters assert, the market is in itself a democratic medium: viewers vote with their remote control and programmes that cannot secure an audience are replaced. This concept may be appealing to a new generation of French audiences which has always known broadcasting as a competitive and commercial system. However, this approach is not fully satisfying. Audience ratings do not measure viewer preferences, but only which programmes viewers chose within a limited offering. In addition, audience ratings give more weight to heavy viewers.

Between the market and a hierarchical imposition of programming priorities by public authorities, another approach is possible. It would consist of involving citizens in broadcasting regulation. So far, in France, citizens' participation in broadcasting regulation has been very low. Citizens are rarely involved in the CSA's decision-making process. Hearings are often closed to the public and the CSA's action mainly involves experts and professionals. Viewers are not represented in the governance structures of the public broadcasters. Some simple steps could change this situation. For instance, citizens' consultation could be made mandatory when broadcasters' licenses are to be renewed; the CSA could request public comments when reviewing the programming activities of broadcasters; the development of viewer associations could be encouraged through public subsidies and free-airtime allowing them to promote their action. In any case, as Des Freeman suggested, 'we need to win back a notion of diversity that is based on citizens' engagement with and interrogation of the world rather than the idea that diversity can be measured simply through the number of organizations and channels' (Freedman 2008).

Notes

1. For additional data on the history of French broadcasting and another perspective, see Bourdon 1994.
2. Three television companies – TF1, Antenne 2 and FR3; one radio company – Radio-France; Télédiffusion de France – a company in charge of managing the technical process of broadcasting; Société française de production – a production company in charge of providing high cost programmes to broadcasters; Institut national de l'audiovisuel – entrusted with maintaining public broadcasters' archives of programmes, professional training of public broadcasters' employees and research in the field of new broadcasting technologies.
3. Law No. 82–652 of 29 July 1982 on Audiovisual Communication.
4. For a history of the High Authority, see Chauveau 1997.
5. The two stations were La5 and TV6. La5 was run by the Italian media mogul Silvio Berlusconi, and then bought by the French Lagardère media group. La5 went out of business in 1992. It should not be confused with La cinquième, the public channel set up in 1994. TV6 was replaced by M6.
6. Law no. 86–1067 of 30 September 1986 on Freedom of Communication. This law remains the basis for the regulation of French broadcasting although it has been modified and supplemented by 38 other laws. This can be confusing for outsiders since specialists may either refer to the initial law of 1986, as modified by subsequent laws, or to a specific law passed subsequently, modifying the 1986 law.
7. For example, assume that two thirds of the audience like a programming of type A, twenty per cent like type B, and fourteen per cent like type C. In such a situation, three competitors tend to offer the same type of programming A in hopes of getting a twenty two per cent share of the audience, which is more than they could get by offering either programming B or C. See: Owen and Wildman 1992, Baker 2002.
8. For a detailed presentation, see Vedel 2005; Derieux 2008.
9. A company may not meet more than two of the following criteria: holding a licence for one or several terrestrial television services reaching more than four million viewers; holding a licence for one or more radio services reaching more than 30 million viewers; publishing or controlling one or several

daily newspapers with a national market share over twenty per cent. (An equivalent rule applies at the regional level.)

10. The CSA must be just notified of significant changes (over ten per cent of capital) in ownership. Law on Freedom of Communication 1986, Art. 38.

11. The public TV broadcasting sector currently comprises five channels: two general interest channels (France 2 and France 3), and three specialized channels (France 5: education and culture; France 4, live shows, music and special events; France Ô: devoted to French regions outside metropolitan France).

12. Excerpt from the Article 43–11 of the Law on Freedom of Communication of 1986.

13. Each year, a national cause is chosen by the government: action against the Alzheimer disease in 2007, equal opportunity in 2006, action against AIDS in 2005, promotion of fraternity in 2004, integration of disabled persons in 2003.

14. For instance, in 2006, the Communist Party was awarded the right to use five broadcasts (overall, 18 minutes) while the Socialist Party was given twenty five broadcasts (90 minutes overall) and the Union for a Popular Movement (*Union pour un mouvement populaire*, UMP), which had the majority in Parliament, 45 broadcasts (162 minutes overall). For unions and professional associations, a similar regime applies. In 2006, each of the twelve selected organizations of national importance was allocated ten broadcasts (36 minutes overall).

15. On average, out of the top 100 most popular television programmes, only four to five originate from public broadcasters (see Médiamétrie 2007).

16. In January 2008, the three major TV channels devoted more than three hours to the President's public statements in their news edition. Altogether, the President, the government and the majority party in the parliament received some 7h30 as opposed to about 3h for the opposition parties at the Parliament.

17. This requirement applies to the entire schedule and also specifically to primetime hours, from 20.30 to 22.30, in order to avoid the programming of European or French-language programmes only during late night hours.

18. With the exception of Canal+ which must devote twenty per cent of its annual revenues to movie production. France 5 is exempted from this obligation because it does not broadcast movies.

19. Any mention of ethnic origin, colour or religion in official documents and reports of private or public companies is illegal according to the French Penal Code. For example, a company is not allowed to keep records of its employees' national or ethnic origin, even for private purposes. The notion of 'visible' minorities, that some people use, has been sharply criticized because it would legitimate discriminations based on the color of skin or physical traits.

20. Article 2 of the terms of reference of France 2 and of France 3 (same text for both).

21. The argument goes as follows: given the limited number of frequencies, uncontrolled use of the spectrum would result in chaos or in the domination of the most powerful actors. Regulation by public authorities is therefore necessary and takes the form of licences to operate stations. In exchange for licences, TV operators agree to comply with programming requirements.

References

Baker, C. E. (2002), *Media, Markets, and Democracy*, Cambridge: Cambridge University Press.

Bourdon, J. (1994), *Haute fidélité: pouvoir et télévision, 1935–94*, Paris: Seuil.

Chauveau, A. (1997), *L'audiovisuel en liberté. Histoire de la Haute Autorité*, Paris: Presses de Sciences-Po.

Cocq, E. and Messerlin, P. (2005), 'French Audio-Visual Policy: Impact and Compatibility with Trade Negotations', in P. Guerrieri, et al. (eds.), *Cultural Diversity and International Economic Integration:*

The Global Governance of the Audio-Visual Sector, Cheltenham, UK; Northampton, MA: Edward Elgar, pp. 27–51.

CSA (2007), 'Bilan 2006 de l'économie des chaînes payantes' (2006 Report on pay TV), http://www. csa.fr/actualite/dossiers/dossiers_detail.php?id=125206&chap=3073. .

Dagnaud, M. (2006), Les artisans de l'imaginaire. Comment la télévision fabrique la culture de masse?, Paris: Armand Colin.

Derieux, E. (2008), Droit des médias: droit français, européen et international, Paris: LGDJ.

Doyle, G. (2007), Understanding media economics, London: Sage.

France Télévisions (2004), 'Plan d'action positive pour l'intégration' (Affirmative action plan for inclusion), http://www.francetelevisions.fr/recup_data/recup_8.php?id=37&lg=fr&mode=html&year=2004&a rticle=0&month=10. Accessed 4 May 2008.

Freedman, D. (2008), The politics of media policy, Cambridge: Polity Press.

Gibbons, T and Humphreys, P. (2008), 'Globalization, Regulatory Competition and Audiovisual Regulation: the Canadian, French, German and UK Cases', Unpublished report, University of Manchester.

Grant, P. S. and Wood, C. (2004), Blockbusters and trade wars: popular culture in a globalized world, Vancouver: Douglas & McIntyre.

Haut Conseil à l'Intégration (2005), 'Diversité culturelle et culture commune dans l'audiovisuel. Avis à Monsieur le Premier Ministre' (Cultural diversity and common culture in the broadcasting sector. Note to the Prime Minister), Paris, 17 March 2005, http://www.premier-ministre.gouv.fr/IMG/doc/ Avis_HCI_audiovisuel.doc.

Hoffman-Riem, W. (1987), 'National Identity and Cultural Values: Broadcasting Safeguards', Journal of Broadcasting, 31:1, pp. 57–72.

Huysmans, F. and de Haan, J. (2005), 'Media diversity from a user's perspective in the Netherlands, 1975–2000', Communications, 30:3, pp. 320–4.

Médiamétrie (2007), 'Médiamat annuel, Année 2007', http://www.mediametrie.fr/resultats. php?rubrique=tv&resultat_id=490. Accessed 28 May 2008.

McDonald, D. G. and Dimmick, J. (2003), 'The conceptualization and measurement of diversity', Communication Research, 30:1, pp. 60–79.

McQuail, D. (1992), Media Performance. Mass Communication and the Public Interest, London: Sage.

Napoli, P. M. (1999), 'Deconstructing the diversity principle', Journal of Communication, 49:4, pp. 7–34.

Owen, B. M. and Wildman, S. (1992), Video Economic, Cambridge: Cambridge University Press.

Pool, I. d. S. (1983), Technologies of Freedom. On free speech in an electronic age, Cambridge, Mass.: Belknap Press.

Sanchez-Tabernero, A. and Carvajal, M. (2002), Media concentration in the European market. New trends and challenges, Pamplona: Servicio de Publicaciones de la Universidad de Nevarra.

TF1 (2007), 'Annual Report 2007 (English version)', http://www.tf1finance.fr/documents/publications/ 312_EN.pdf, p. 27.

TNS-Sofres (2006), Les Français et la télévision. Poll conducted among a representative sample of 1002 individuals from September 7 to September 12.

Vedel, T. (2005), 'Television regulation, policy and independence in France', in EUMAP (ed.), Television across Europe, Budapest; New York: Open Society Institute, pp. 637–728.

Vedel, T. and Dutton, W. H. (1990), 'New media politics: shaping cable television policy in France', Media, Culture, and Society, 12:4, pp. 491–524.

THE FREEDOM OF THE SPANISH PRESS

Ingrid Schulze-Schneider

The press in twentieth century Spain has been shaped by two crucial events: the Civil War and the nearly forty year dictatorship of General Franco. Following the victory of the Francoist forces in the Civil War in 1939, the government exercised strict control over all forms of the media. Newspapers and magazines had little opportunity to express dissent, and those that attempted to do so, most often found themselves harassed or closed.

After Franco's death in 1975, the Spanish newspaper market can be described as definitely artificial. It was characterized by the political background as well as by the uncertain future. The old official media maintained by the government still existed, just as the press law from 1966. The dismantling of the dictatorial structures got going rather slowly. At the same time, several new newspapers appeared that wanted to take into account the exceptional interest of the population in the political events.

The laws

After the liquidation of the so-called press 'of the movement', a new age for the Spanish media began, which would be sanctioned in the Constitution of 1978 (La Constitución Española 1978). Freedom of speech and the press were guaranteed in Article 20 that states as follows:

Article 20 [Specific Freedoms, Restrictions]
(1) The following rights are recognized and protected:
  a) To express and disseminate thoughts freely through words, writing, or any other means of reproduction.
  b) Literary, artistic, scientific, and technical production, and creation
  c) Academic freedom
  d) To communicate or receive freely truthful information through any means of dissemination. The law shall regulate the right to the protection of the clause on conscience and professional secrecy in the exercise of these freedoms.

(2) The exercise of these rights cannot be restricted through any type of prior censorship.

(3) The law shall regulate the organization and parliamentary control of the means of social communication owned by the State or any public entity and shall guarantee access to those means by significant social and political groups, respecting the pluralism of society and the various languages of Spain.

(4) These liberties find their limitation in the respect for the rights recognized in this Title, in the precepts of the laws which develop it and, especially, in the right to honour, privacy, personal identity, and protection of youth and childhood.

(5) The seizure of publications, recordings, or other means of information may only be determined by a judicial resolution.

The Article grants four fundamental rights on information: (a) the individual right for which there is no exception; (b) the professional one which refers to the possibility of seeking, getting and spreading information and which is limited by personal or social protection rights; (c) the right to equal treatment on a national scale, which means that all autonomous regions benefit from the same rights; and (d) the information right for print and audiovisual media enterprises.

Though this Article – the longest in the Constitution – seems to enclose all important aspects of the liberty of the press, an important number of Spanish journalists united in different professional associations have criticized the wording of the Article as it does not differentiate between the right of citizens to get information and the professional rights and obligations of journalists to look for information and to transmit it (Sánchez 2006). On account of the ambiguities of the text, there have been constant problems regarding the question of whether every citizen has the right to become a journalist or if only a special title obtained through university studies enables one to practice in a journalistic profession.

Furthermore, the Law respecting the civil protection of honour, privacy and personal image, proclaimed in 1982, provoked a lot of opposition for putting private individual rights far above the information right, thus granting the courts too great a margin to intervene so that celebrities could actually profit from their 'personal image right' (Ley de Protección Civil del Honor, de la Intimidad y de la Propia Imagen 1982).

The Law of Rectification was passed in 1984, assuring citizens the right to public reply in the media in the case of publication of false news or statements about his/her person or the misrepresentation of his/her words (Ley Reguladora del Derecho de Rectificación 1984).

In 1995 the Penal Code was reformed in an unfavourable way for journalists (Ley Orgánica 10/1995 de 23 de noviembre 1995): Matters like insults and slander were newly and less precisely defined, leaving the judges more room for individual convictions when applying the law.

In 1997 the regulation of the law regarding the 'Clause on Conscience' (Clausula de conciencia 1997) followed. Due to the conscience protection guaranteed in the Constitution of 1978, journalists have the right to end the contract with their employer if the latter fundamentally changes its ideological orientation.

Criticism

However, all of the aforementioned regulations do not satisfy most of the Spanish journalists, who have been demanding the approval of a special professional Statute from the Government, pointing out that Article 20 contains items that require more legal accuracy, and arguing that there should be mention of constitutional rights that refer especially and only to them and not to all citizens.

The professional journalistic associations require specific regulations of rights and duties. Furthermore, the creation of organs with the capacity to apply the law in possible conflicts relating to the mass media and their juridical relations with society and constituted media groups is necessary.

According to this demand, a draft of the 'Statute of the Professional Journalist' was sent to the Spanish Government in 2004 (Proyecto del Estatuto del Periodista Profesional 2004), but, as the Journalists' Convention has complained recently, all attempts to date to achieve the processing of the corresponding Law in Parliament have come up against a wall of managerial power and denial of the parliamentary majority groups related to these.

Therefore, it is no surprise that the *Asociación de la Prensa de Madrid* (Madrid Association of the Press) unanimously approved on 1 April 2006 a Declaration regarding the 'Liberty of Speech' (FAPE, LXV Asamblea General 2006), and denouncing the difficult situation of the Spanish journalists, in the following terms:

The information freedom is menaced in Spain, which makes the professional exercise of journalism more difficult each day. In defence of the citizen's basic right to obtain correct and true information, we denounce events that limit the freedom, degrade the journalists and damage the credibility of the media, such as:

- The opportunism of some publishers who offer something as journalism that has nothing to do with information or with the interpretation of the topical subjects.
- The abusive procedures of employment, including cases of exploitation, especially of the young employees.
- The conflicts of interests that condition the journalistic work limit the freedom and impose a kind of censorship.
- Governments' and media editor's performances, especially in the audiovisual sector, that use the media for making propaganda of people or political parties.
- The granting of licenses with criteria of ideological affinity or special interests; unjustified contracts of advertising or sponsorship and other abuses that create dependence.
- The arbitrary disqualifications and accusations against media and persons which damage the reputation of the journalists before the citizens...

For all that, the journalists claim from the company editors:

- A firm commitment to the freedom of expression and critique and firm support of the free exercise of the journalistic profession in conformity with ethic requirements and good practice.
- The accomplishment of all legal labour rules; no wage abuse and the guarantee of stable employment.

The Manifest is much longer and also contains claims directed at the government, the judicial powers and society, but all requirements end in a demand for more liberty, ethic and respect for journalists and their work.

On the other hand, the 'Annual report of the Journalistic Profession 2006' (Casanueva 2007: 61) mentions the 'yellowism' of the 'pink press' and the sectarianism as the predominant evils of the Spanish journalism.

Certainly, a look from the outside confirms many of the problems mentioned.

The activity of the press is free, subject only to the Constitution, the Penal Code and the laws protecting honour and individual privacy. Consequently, there are no limitations to the ownership of publications. However, the participation of press companies in conventional radio and television is regulated in order to guarantee the plurality of these two media and to avoid monopolization. In 1998, this limit to the ownership in terrestrial television was increased by law from 25 to 49 per cent. There is no limit for investments in digital television. In 1986, the ban on foreign capital in Spanish press was lifted (Schulze-Schneider 2005: 67–8).

Over the last decades the structures of the Spanish media landscape have changed substantially. Concentrations and fusions on a national and international scale leave the most important print and audiovisual media in very few hands. A special mention must be made of PRISA, the biggest Spanish media enterprise founded in 1972. Its principal shareholder Jesús Polanco was, until his death on 21 July 2007, the most powerful Spanish 'Media-Mogul', who maintained excellent relations with the socialist government. PRISA could then be called the 'Fourth Power' in the Spanish state, and on certain occasions it occupied an even higher political range. Some enemies do not hesitate to call PRISA 'a state in the state' (Schulze-Schneider 2005: 81).

Now things seem to be changing under the new President of the PRISA group, Polanco's son Ignacio. Lately, El País shows itself much more critical than before towards the Zapatero Government.

PRISA is the editor of Spain's most important daily El País, as well as of the sports daily AS and the economic Cinco Días, apart from its participation in the audiovisual market, especially in digital Pay-TV Channels.

Other predominant media groups are Vocento, Recoleto and Unedisa. Actually, twenty owners control about 70 per cent of the total newspaper circulation and about 60 per cent of all these newspapers are owned by regional daily press groups.

Over the past few years, the market has seen a decline in sales and circulation figures of weekly TV and political interest magazines, while the celebrity magazine market remains stable. At the same time there has been a visible increase in monthly magazines, particularly in the more recent segments such as decoration, travel and lifestyle.

Distribution of the Spanish press market (2006):

Vocento Group	25.7 %
PRISA	15.1 %
Unidad Editorial	10.0 %
Prensa Ibérica	9.3 %
Grupo Zeta	7.4 %
Others	32.5 %

(BBC NEWS 2006).

Foreign investment has entered the Spanish market with great difficulty and is much lower in the Spanish daily press than in the weekly magazines. Today, the foreign groups (for instance, Bertelsman, G & J, VNU, Hachette) have the largest magazine sales, together with some Spanish-owned companies.

The daily press

In Spain, some 155 dailies exist, the majority of which are local or regional. There is no yellow press like in Great Britain or similar to the German *Bildzeitung,* but the so called 'serious press' is less serious than in other countries. Sports dailies and 'pink' woman magazines are much better adapted to the Spanish taste than sex and crime newspapers.

The major leaders in sales, *El País, El Mundo* and *ABC* are dailies of national circulation published in Madrid, although they have regional editions in some of the Autonomous Communities. They are followed by *La Vanguardia* and *El Periódico,* published in Barcelona and read essentially in Catalunya and, to a much lesser extent, in other parts of Spain.

Within the daily press, the sports newspapers stand out for their very high readership. Among the ten most widely sold dailies, two papers are exclusively dedicated to sports, *AS* and *MARCA.* Another type of newspaper which has experienced extraordinary success in the last few years is the economic journal. Not only have a large number of publications devoted to this theme appeared, including dailies, but the most important newspapers are also publishing special supplements centred on economic topics.

The greatest problem confronting Spain's daily press over the past years has been its technological restructuring, which was successfully surmounted by the majority of newspapers, thanks to, in great part, the financial support of the Administration that has helped to subsidize them.

Over the last few years, Spain has also seen the appearance of free newspapers, which began with the arrival of the Scandinavian groups Metro and 20 Minutes. In the meantime, publishers of paid-for newspapers have started publishing free newspapers such as Qué (Recoletos) and *ADN* (Płaneta). As the circulation figures of these free papers have rapidly increased, the paid-for dailies try to increase sales by introducing all kinds of promotional products – especially books, CDs and DVDs, which are sold together with the papers. By now, this has become normal practice.

Profiles of the principal daily newspapers (OJD 2007)

El País
Based: Madrid
Founded: 1976
Net Average Circulation June 2006 – July 2007: 425,927 copies
Owner: Group PRISA

It is no coincidence that this daily emerged only after Franco's death and fast became the top circulation paper in the country, backing the popular socialist government of Felipe Gonzalez. Nearly 30 years later, *El País* (*The Country*) continues to support the socialists and was one of the most vociferous critics of the country's involvement in the 2003 Iraq war. Like its main

Madrid rivals, *El País* is tabloid size and comfortably straddles the line between authoritative and entertaining. It has a number of regional and international editions.

El Mundo
Based: Madrid
Founded: 1989
Net Average Circulation June 2006 – July 2007: 337,172 copies
Owner: Unidad Editorial

Another of Madrid's three major general news tabloids, *El Mundo* has managed to establish itself as a popular alternative to *El Pais* and *ABC*. With a right-wing political perspective, the daily was originally a virulent critic of the socialist government and a keen supporter of the Popular Party. It is now arguably the most independent-minded of the big Madrid dailies.

ABC
Based: Madrid
Founded: 1903
Net Average Circulation June 2006 – July 2007: 230,422 copies
Owner: Group Vocento

Founded in 1903, *ABC* became a daily in 1905, and sees itself as the doyen of Madrid journalism. It considers itself a staunch supporter of the monarchy as 'the most harmonious system for Spain'. During the Civil War of 1936–9, circumstances forced the publication of two editions, one in Madrid backing the republicans and another in Seville supporting Franco's forces. Now, it claims to be independent, though it has been a consistent supporter of the Popular Party, advocating the politics of a 'modern, reformist and European centre-right' Party. But it subsequently distanced itself from the Popular Party after failing to obtain the government support it had hoped for in a battle for control of the digital TV sector. Lately, the incorporation in the Vocento group and the following slight ideological turn to the left has brought about considerable reader losses to the daily.

La Vanguardia
Based: Barcelona
Founded: 1881
Net Average Circulation June 2006 – July 2007: 209,735 copies
Owner: Group Godó

Of the widely read Spanish dailies *Vanguardia* is the granddad of them all, having been founded in 1881. Its conservative line allowed it to continue publishing independently under the Franco regime, and it proved adaptable enough to become Spain's top circulation daily for a brief period after his death. It was subsequently eclipsed, especially outside Catalonia, by the success of *El Pais*, but still remains one of the top-selling dailies. It gives critical support to regional parties and causes. It is particularly popular among the Catalan middle classes, and is seen as providing well-balanced coverage of regional, national and international events.

El Periódico de Catalunya
Based: Barcelona
Founded: 1978
Net Average Circulation June 2006 – July 2007: 177,830 copies
Owner: Grupo Zeta

Barcelona's second major daily is published in Barcelona in Spanish and Catalan, unlike its venerable rival *La Vanguardia*, which only publishes in Spanish. However, unlike the latter's backing for regional parties, *El Periodico* has tended to support the socialists, although not uncritically. It has managed to capture a sizeable share of the regional market since its comparatively recent arrival on the scene, appealing to a blend of students, office workers and young professionals. Readership is largely confined to Catalonia.

El Correo
Based: Bilbao
Founded: 1910
Net Average Circulation June 2006 – July 2007: 119,140 copies
Owner: Group Vocento.

El Correo is a long-established, independent Spanish-language daily which has traditionally supported an accommodation between the Basque Country and Madrid. Its conciliatory stance has angered the Basque separatist group ETA, which has targeted it on a number of occasions. In one attack in March 2001, about twenty Molotov cocktails were thrown at its offices in Bilbao. Most of its estimated 500,000 readers are from the middle and upper classes.

La Razón
Based: Madrid
Founded: 1998
Net Average Circulation June 2006 – July 2007: 149,559 copies
Owner: Group Płaneta

La Razón is the newest Madrid daily offering general information. It was created in 1998 by Luis María Anson and belongs to the group Płaneta. The editorial line is liberal in economics and conservative in politics, reflecting the opinions of the classical Spanish right wing population. *La Razón* has substituted *ABC* as a reference paper of the right after the purchase of *ABC* by the Vocento group and its subsequent ideological change as mentioned above. After a very difficult start, *La Razón* is today one of the principal Spanish dailies with a consolidated place in the market, and enjoys a small but faithful readership.

Negative aspects
There are two especially negative aspects of the Spanish system of communications: the ideological and political fixation and the low circulation of the daily press. Less then 100 daily newspapers are sold per thousand inhabitants. In 2006 the number was 98. In order to gain an advantage, the Spanish press regularly offers other 'values' besides the daily news, such

as books, movie and music-CD's, and other collections at very low prices which raise the sales figures for a short time.

These circumstances decisively influence the relationship between journalists and their employers. Another handicap to more liberty for journalists is the fact that there are over thirty institutions – public and private universities and professional schools – offering communication studies in Spain, which means a total of more than 32,000 students in this area. The result is that the demand for jobs related to information and communication activities is much higher than the offer. 'Stubborn' journalists, who do not follow the guidelines of their bosses, have, therefore, very a low chance of keeping their jobs. The concentration of the media in a handful of large-holding groups frequently produces self-imposed censorship or slanting of coverage in the major media, favouring certain business interests or political parties.

The audiovisual media (Schulze-Schneider 2005: 95–100)
Post-Franco Spain inherited a broadcasting structure unique in Europe: a mixed commercial and public radio system and state-run national television, financed by both public funds and advertising. News content in all sectors was tightly regimented by the government. Newly democratic Spain broadened the scope of public television and created regional television corporations in the 'Autonomous Communities'. Despite agreement in principle that broadcasting should be democratized, in practice public television remained dominated by the political parties in power. Subsequent legislation approving commercial television led to a battle for advertising and audiences, and has sparked a financial crisis in state television as well as undermining its identity as a truly public service. The financial crisis, the growing national importance of the now federally-organized 'Autonomous Community' network, and the phenomena of local and cable television, demand a fresh approach to Spanish broadcasting policy.

The ownership of the companies operating television channels and radio stations is public and private. There is Radiotelevisión Española (RTVE), controlled by a central administration, which operates the two public national television channels (TVE-1 and La 2), TVE Internacional (broadcasting by satellite to Western Europe and Latin America), several thematic digital television channels by satellite, a teletext system, and Radio Nacional de España (RNE) which has about 459 radio stations. About 105 of these stations are AM stations working in a network and about 354 of them on FM, working in four networks. RNE also owns Radio Exterior de España, the first short wave station in the Spanish language and the third largest in the world, after BBC and Radio Vaticano.

The regional third channels are also managed by public (regional) companies and dependent on the regional (CCAA) parliaments. Basque (ETB) and Catalan (TV3) channels started broadcasting in 1983. Two years later, the Galician channel (TVG) followed. Since then, third channels have been created in Andalusia (Canal Sur), in Valencia (Canal 9) and in Madrid (Telemadrid). Second channels were established in the Basque Country, Catalonia, Valencia. The regional television channels also broadcast via digital satellite platforms. Every regional (CCAA) radio and television corporation owns a regional FM radio network.

There are about 500 local public radio stations depending on municipal councils.

In 1989 three private national television channels started to broadcast through a terrestrial network (Antena 3, Tele5 and Canal+, a subscription TV channel). All of them have frequently changed ownership and management personnel; Tele5 did so in 1996 and 1997.

In 1997, the two digital satellite platforms began operation: Canal Satélite Digital (CSD) belonging to Sogecable (Prisa) and Vía Digital. Via Digital did not succeed and finally fused with Canal Satélite in 2002.

In the near future there will be new licences for private and public regional and local terrestrial digital television. The present terrestrial televisions also have to change to the digital system.

The cable services, which include Internet and television, began working in 1998 but its presence is very low to date. There are about 700 public and private local television stations, most of them broadcasting terrestrial but also via cable networks. In most cases their legal situation is not quite clear.

Today's proliferation of public and private channels, at national, regional and local levels, generates fierce competition for available advertising revenue. The massive deficits run up by government and community-controlled broadcasting, together with the deterioration of their cultural content, have brought about an ongoing debate on how publicly-owned broadcasting should be funded. In order to solve the problem, the Spanish Parliament passed a new Law and Statute of the Public Radio and Television in June 2006 which introduces a complete reorganization of the anterior model and aims at offering the Spaniards a truly independent public broadcasting system for the first time in history. The *State Radio and Television Act* transforms RTVE as a public institution into a state corporation with special autonomy (Council of Europe/ERICarts 2007: 36):

> The new law aims, on the one hand, to provide a legal framework for public radio and television that guarantees their independence, neutrality and objectivity, and establishes organisational structures and a model of funding that enables them to carry out their mission as a public service. On the other hand, it aims to reinforce the role of Parliament and foresees the supervision of the Corporation's activity by an independent audiovisual authority.

Press freedom controversies

Terrorism

As the International Press Institute states (Freelance Spain 2006), Spain, a European Union member and signatory to the European Convention on Human Rights, is a modern democratic country with a 'lively media environment. However, there are difficulties for the media when reporting on certain taboo subjects; one of these subjects is terrorism.' Certainly, all information concerning the Spanish terrorist group ETA and also the Islamic fundamentalists like Al Qaeda, who committed the worst terror attack in Spain on 11 March 2004 causing the death of 173 innocent victims, is considered partly secret because of its implications for National Security.

Without any doubt, the most serious recent incidents concerning press freedom have been the attacks by the Basque terrorist group ETA on journalists critical of their ideas. Journalists both in the Basque Country and elsewhere in Spain have been the recipients of threats and letter bombs. In May 2000, an ETA gunman shot José Luis López de la Calle, a columnist for the Madrid daily *El Mundo* in his hometown of Andoain. In November 2000 a couple in the Basque city of Bilbao, both journalists, and their eighteen month-old son narrowly escaped death when a bomb planted in a flower pot outside their home failed to explode. More than

100 journalists in the Basque country are forced to use bodyguards or request police protection due to threats from ETA, according to the organization Reporteros Sin Fronteras (Reporters Without Borders).

On the other side of the dispute, in a controversial decision Spanish investigating judge Baltasar Garzón ordered the closure of the Basque daily newspaper *Egin* and its associated radio station *Egin Irratia* in 1998, on the grounds that it was a mouthpiece of the ETA terrorists. Egin's role has since been taken up by a new title *Gara*.

With respect to Islamic terrorism, in September 2005, Al Jazeera journalist Tayssir Alluni was sentenced to seven year's imprisonment for aiding Al-Qaeda. First arrested in September 2003, Alluni was accused of collaborating with the terrorist group by acting as the group's financial courier during his time in Afghanistan. The prosecution of Alluni has caused considerable problems for press freedom organizations, which have found it difficult to discover the truth behind the assertions and contra-assertions. Indeed, Alluni's case is symptomatic of many other cases in which specific allegations are made, but in which, because of their nature, it is extremely difficult to test the evidence.

The Royal Family
Until last year, there was another taboo in the Spanish media: the taboo on the Royal Family. Very little is known about what really goes on behind the curtains in the Royal Palace and nobody talks about details regarding the financial situation of the Royals, the money they receive from the Spanish state, the obligations of the members of the Family and so on. Nearly all journalists practised self-imposed censorship on the matter. But things changed dramatically in 2007.

In January, an embarrassing incident concerning King Juan Carlos and the liberty of the press occurred, when the Basque newspapers *Gara* and *Deia* used inappropriate words referring to the King and the affair with the drunken Russian bear Mitrofán. Authorities in the Russian region of Vologda began an investigation into reports that he had shot a tame bear that had been plied with vodka to make him an easy target.

A spokesman of the Royal Family dismissed the report as absurd and refused to discuss any details. In consequence, the public prosecutor Zaragoza took legal action against both dailies, arguing that the journalists used annoying and humiliating expressions when calling the King a 'whippersnapper', 'irresponsible', and a 'relapsed bloodthirsty tourist' (Marraco 2007: 17). Though the incident was minimized, a few months later a large scandal concerning the Royal family went through the international press.

The facts
On 20 July 2007 the Spanish judge Juan del Olmo ordered the withdrawal of the satirical magazine *El jueves* (http://www.eljueves.es/) published two days before. The cause was a sexually explicit cartoon on the front page depicting Prince Felipe and the Princess Leticia having sex in an 'irreverent' pose, and the judge argued that it contravened the law. A speech bubble issuing from the Prince's mouth made a joke about the recent decision by the Government to award mothers Euro 2,500 for each child they bear, leading Prince Felipe to say to his wife: 'Do you realize what it means if you get pregnant. This is going to be the closest thing to work that I've ever done.'

The public prosecutor's office said in its writ that the cartoon was 'clearly denigrating and objectively libellous'. Spanish police were ordered to raid newsagents across the country to remove all the copies of the magazine and also the 'printing plates'. The court also planned to issue an injunction to stop websites or other media from reproducing the cartoon, but finally refrained from doing so (Cat 2007).

Articles 491 and 504 of the Spanish Penal Code say that insults and calumnies to the King or any of his ascendancies or descendants, or the use of the image of any member of the Royal Family carry a prison sentence from six to twenty four months.

The cartoonist Guillermo expressed his amazement at the ban, saying that printing plates ceased to exist years ago and the best thing would be for the prosecutor to cut off his right hand.

Following del Olmo's ruling, news of the cartoon – containing the offending image – was immediately published in newspapers' and radio stations' websites, clearly breaking the unspoken pact among the media not to damage the image of the monarchs in a country accustomed to feasting on harmless gossip about a largely respected royal family,.

The magazine's director, Albert Monteys I Homar, condemned the ban as a direct attack against freedom of expression. He added that he was surprised by the official reaction because, during its 30 years of publications, *El Jueves* had often been critical of Spain's royals without being punished. This is not quite true, however, because the magazine had been asked before by the royal household to 'reflect' on its contents, as the newspaper *El País* reported on its website (Haines 2007: 1).

Indeed, today, media censorship is rare in Spain. The last publication to be censured was another satirical magazine, *El Cocodrilo*, in February 1986, also for a reference deemed disrespectful to the head of state.

The reaction of the media
The judicial ruling set off a political storm in Spain. All the papers agreed that pulling the royal cartoon only served to draw attention to it and spread it around to many more people than *El Jueves'* usual 80,000 readers. Most newspapers criticized the cartoon as crude and in bad taste but, as *El País* wrote in an editorial, 'it is hard to say it intended the sort of damage that would make it a crime'. Right-leaning *El Mundo* said the cartoon could offend people but insisted it was 'within what is permissible in a society where freedom of expression is a fundamental value'. Some days later *El Mundo* added:

> The picture, which had been seen by thousands of people, was posted on numerous websites in Spain and abroad and will now have been seen by tens of millions of people. Not even the Crown's worst enemy could have had that effect.

Barcelona-based *El Periódico* went further and slammed the decision as anachronistic and a flashback to the years when Francisco Franco pulled papers for criticizing his dictatorship.

Only right wing *ABC* supported the ban – the first in about twenty years – saying the cartoon was symptomatic of 'a climate in which civic and moral values are ever more relaxed and seen as relative' (Agencies 2007a: 1).

Finally, on 13 November 2007, the two cartoonists were convicted of insulting the heir to the throne and fined 2,730 Euros each. The Judge, José María Vazquez Honrubia of the National Court, said that the two men 'vilified the Crown in the most gratuitous and unnecessary way', adding that they should learn that they may have any ideas they like, but cannot attack the basic institutions of the State (Agencies 2007b).

A week later, on 21 November, the International Press Institute (IPI) stated in a Press release that the 'global network of editors, media executives and leading journalists in over 120 countries, strongly condemns a Spanish Judge's decision to fine two journalists under a criminal code prohibiting insults to the King or members of his direct family' (IPI Public Statements 2007). 'Although I make no comment on the cartoon itself, the decision to publish such material is one for the editor, not the courts' said IPI Director Johann P. Fritz. 'As a result of expressing themselves, Torres and Fontdevilla have now been unfairly stigmatized as criminals. No law should turn irreverence into a crime, especially in a modern democracy such as Spain'.

Important side effects
Why did the cartoon cause such media-frenzy? Until July 2007 the media tended to report only the royal family's official engagements and almost nothing negative about King Juan Carlos has made it into print since he was crowned in 1975 after the death of Franco. But now it seems that not only the journalists but many other people as well believe that Spain's three decade taboo against criticizing the Royal Family is on the point of collapse, with a huge public appetite for gossip being met increasingly by internet sites that are harder to control.

The unequal marriage in 2004 of Prince Felipe to Letizia Ortiz, a divorced commoner and former television journalist, has greatly contributed to the loss of glamour of the royal family. When Letizia's sister died earlier this year, many newspapers disregarded pleas by the Royal Family to be discreet and mentioned police theories that she committed suicide.

Far more important than the gossip is the fact that the scandal has roused in the serious press the question of the monarchy as a form of state in Spain.

In all public demonstrations republican flags appear and republican voices are also increasing in Spanish websites.

Luis Maria Anson, famous journalist and member of the Royal Spanish Academy, goes as far as accusing the Prime Minister Zapatero of ordering the ban on the magazine, knowing that the media would claim against it and thus creating a hostile climate against the royal heir Felipe, with the intention to prepare the people for a future Republic after the death of Juan Carlos (Anson 2007: 2).

Another journalist, David Gistau, said in his column in *El Mundo* on 25 July that the Spanish government intervened in the affair in order to be sure that the cartoon would not pass without receiving public attention. After the explosion of the scandal, the debate turned to general comments against monarchy as a state system (Gistau 2007: 5).

Only the summer holidays interrupted a debate in which the defendants of the liberty of speech were much more numerous than those who applauded the ban.

Victoria Burnett from the International Herald Tribune said in an article published on 11 October 2007 and reproduced in the Boston Globe (Burnett 2007):

For more than three decades, King Juan Carlos of Spain has enjoyed the unquestioning loyalty of his subjects and the discrete respect of the media. But the era of deference during which the royal family's jet-set lifestyle and personal affairs were free of public scrutiny could be drawing to a close.

Other incidents
Apart from the royal scandal, the liberty of speech in the media has also been questioned in other cases.

In Catalonia, in 1998, the regional government refused to renew broadcasting licenses for radio stations sponsored by the Catholic Church, thus effectively closing them, because they allegedly did not comply with regional regulations regarding the use of the Catalan language.

More recently, the director of Spain's national library, Rosa Regas, named by the government as guardian of the country's reading heritage – including the country's newspaper archive – scandalized journalists by admitting she doesn't read newspapers and is glad their sales are flagging. 'I haven't read the press for two months. I don't watch television or listen to the radio because the tension they express upsets me so much I can't work', said Rosa Regas in an interview published in the *Tribuna de la Administración Pública*, a magazine published by the civil service union affiliated to the pro-communist Workers' Commissions. Spanish newspapers are too critical of the Government, Ms. Regas said, and added she was glad their sales were falling (R.G.G. 2007). Her comments prompted a wave of outrage from Spain's media representatives who rushed to defend the high ground of press freedom. A few weeks later, when a new Minister of Culture was named, Regas resigned her post.

These examples show that the freedom of the Spanish media, although guaranteed in the Spanish Constitution, is sometimes not accepted by public authorities. Its limits probably have to be defined more precisely by new laws. Until this happens, it is quite possible that the growing competition in the media sector and on the Internet will bring about other conflicts and will sharpen the debate regarding freedom of the Spanish press and its possible limitations.

References

Agencies (2007a), 'Spanish Cartoon prompts legal ban. Media criticism', *MWC News* , 21 July, p. 1, http://mwcnews.net/content/view/15594/52/. Accessed 17 August 2007.

Agencies (2007b), 'El juez declara culpables de injurias al Príncipe de Asturias a los autores de la viñeta de El Jueves', *Estrella Digital*, 13 November, http://www.estrelladigital.es/diario/artículo.asp?sec=med&fech=13/11/2007&name=j. Accessed 14 November 2007.

Anson, Luis María (2007), 'Canela fina', *El Mundo*, 27 de Julio, p. 2.

BBC NEWS (2006), 'The press in Spain', http://bbc.co.uk/hi/world/europe/3909491.stm. Accessed 24 November 2007.

Burnett, Victoria (2007), 'Free pass fades for Spanish royal family. Protests spark debate on role of the monarchy', *Boston Globe*, 11 October, http://www.boston.com/news/world/europe/articles/2007/10/11/free_pass_fades_for_spanish_royal_family/. Accessed 12 October 2007.

Casanueva, Mariví (2007), 'Informe Anual de la Profesión Periodística 2006', *El Mundo*, 4 December, p. 61.

Cat, Thomas (2007), 'Cartoonist draws wrath of royalty with satire on sex', *Times online*, http://www.timesonline.co.uk/tol/news/world/europe/article2112719.ece. Accessed 17 August 2007.

Clausula de conciencia (1997), Ley Orgánica 2/1997 de 19 junio, http://www.noticias.juridicas.com/base_datos/Admin/lo2-1997.html. Accessed 14 January 2007.

Council of Europe/ERICarts (2007), 'Compendium of Cultural Policies and Trends in Europe', 8th edition, E-1, www.culturalpolicies.net/down/spain.pdf. Accessed 28 January 2007.

El jueves (2007), 'Se nota que vienen elecciones, ZP. 2.500 Euros por niño', Title page 18 July 2007, http://www.eljueves.es/. Accessed 20 July 2007.

FAPE, LXV Asamblea General (2006), 'Declaración sobre la Libertad de Expresión', http://www.apmadrid.es/node/727/print. Accessed 15 January 2007.

Freelance Spain (2006),'Press Freedom in Spain', http://www.spainview.com/media3.html. Accessed 28 December 2006.

Gistau, David (2007), 'La viñeta', *El Mundo*, 25 July, p. 5.

Haines, Lester 2007, 'Spanish satire mag savages over royal sex cartoon', *The Register*, 17 August, p. 1, http://www.theregister.co.uk/2007/07/22/el_jueves_rumpus/print.html. Accessed 17 August 2007.

International Press Institute (IPI) Public Statements (2007), 'IPI condemns use of archaic Spanish criminal law to justify cartoon censorship', Press Release 21 November, http://www.freemedia.at/cms/ipi/statements_detail.html?ctxid=CH0055&docid=CMS. Accessed 24 November 2007.

La Constitución Española (1978), http://www.mtas/es/insht/en/legislation/constitution_en.html. Accessed 23 July 2007.

Ley de Protección Civil del Honor, de la Intimidad y de la Propia Imagen (1982), http://www.noticias.juridicas.com/base_datos/Admin/lo1-1982.html. Accessed 14 January 2007.

Ley Orgánica 10/1995 de 23 de noviembre (1995), http://www.noticias.juridicas.com/base_datos/Penal/lo10-1995.html. Accessed 16 January 2007.

Ley Reguladora del Derecho de Rectificación (1984), http://www.noticias.juridicas.com/base_datos/Admin/lo2-1984.html. Accessed 14 January 2007.

Marraco, Manuel (2007), 'El fiscal se querella contra "Gara" y "Deia" por injuriar al Rey sobre el oso borracho Mitrofán', *El Mundo*, 5 January, p. 17.

OJD, La Oficina de Justificación de la Difusión (OJD) (2007), http://www.ojd.es/ojdx4/diarios2.asp. Accessed 24 November 2007.

Proyecto del Estatuto del Periodista Profesional (2004), http://www.congreso.es/public_oficiales/L8/CONG/BOCG/B/B_044-01.PDF. Accessed 15 January 2007.

R.G.G. (2007), 'El modelo "Granma de Rosa Regâs"', *El País*, 7 August 2007, http://www.elpais.com/artículo/sociedad/modelo/Granma/Rosa/Regas/elpepusoc/20070807elpepisoc_7/Tes. Accessed 7 August 2007.

Sánchez, Victor (2006), Agrupación General de Periodistas de UGT, *El Estatuto del Periodista Profesional*, 23 de octubre de 2006, http://www.agp-ugt.org/actualidad/050503_libertadprensa.htm. Accessed 14 January 2007.

Schulze-Schneider, Ingrid (2005), *Spanische Medienkultur gestern und heute*, Berlin: Vistas Verlag GmbH.

Pluralism of Information in the Television Sector in Italy: History and Contemporary Conditions

Cinzia Padovani

Introduction

The history of pluralism of information in Italy illuminates the complex set of relationships among media, political, and legislative powers that have defined the evolution of electronic media, in particular, television. This history illustrates the ideological nature of pluralism by showing that this principle, fundamental for democracy, is never a natural outcome of progress in communication technologies; in fact, the concept and practice of pluralism change and adapt depending on political and industrial interests. Moreover, the history of pluralism in Italy underlines the consequences of insufficient public policies in the sector of broadcasting. Instead of protecting the citizens' rights to be informed in a media environment where 'media pluralism [is] respected' (Art. 11, Comma 2, the Charter of Fundamental Rights of the European Union), legislation has often protected the interests of broadcasting companies to consolidate and maintain their dominant positions in the market place.[1]

According to Antonio Gramsci, there are '[t]wo aspects to every question: how it has been treated theoretically and how it has been dealt with practically' (Gramsci 1992: 125). In this chapter, I will address those two aspects (the theoretical and the practical) as they relate to the question of pluralism of information: I will look at how the Italian Constitutional Court has historically dealt with pluralism – namely, the theoretical treatment of pluralism; and how the legislature has responded to the court's sentences – that is, the practical treatment of pluralism. More specifically, I will focus on the history of pluralism of information as it relates to the terrestrial broadcasting television market.

The Italian context

The European Federation of Journalists notes that '[t]he narrowness of control of the Italian media is striking' (2005: 82). Indeed, Italy is a country whose media system is defined as 'one of the most complex in the European context for the set of interrelationships among political, sociocultural, and economic variables' (Richeri 2005: ix). Its broadcasting television market – defined as a duopoly – is dominated by two major players: RAI Radiotelevisione Italiana, the public broadcaster, and Mediaset, the commercial competitor. By 2006, the two broadcasters still controlled 84 per cent of national audiences (Marzulli 2007: 9), with Mediaset's three terrestrial channels commanding 40 per cent of the audience in 2007 (Vivarelli: 2008a).

Since the end of 1993, when Silvio Berlusconi (owner of media giant Fininvest/Mediaset[2]) entered the political arena, the lack of pluralism in the broadcasting sector has become a cause for great concern. The fact that the media mogul-turned politician (Berlusconi has been Prime Minister of Italy in 1994, 2001–6, and 2008–) controls, directly and indirectly, six out of eight national TV channels is a constant threat to pluralism of information. The results of some investigations, brought to public attention by the national daily *La Repubblica* in November 2007, are examples of the profound malaise of the information sector in Italy. Indeed, according to those investigations, between 2004 and 2005, RAI and Medaset's top managers and TV executives regularly consulted among themselves to decide on the items to be put on the respective news bulletins, how to conceal negative results (for Berlusconi's coalition) of the regional elections of spring 2005, and how to improve Berlusconi's image when his popularity was declining.[3]

Homogenization of television programs

Instead of promoting diversity, competition between the two broadcast operators has in fact brought about homogenization of programming output. Indeed, as the history of Italian television illustrates, 'an increase in the number of broadcasters [does] not necessarily imply a wide variety of suppliers, genres and formats' (Richeri 2003).

Since the 1990s, the rising costs of TV productions, of imported films, and rights to broadcast live sporting events, have made the competition for audiences a fundamental goal for the public broadcaster. Counter scheduling has often been the public broadcaster's main strategy in the struggle against its commercial counterpart, and the public service broadcaster has frequently been accused of failing to play an innovative role. In fact, instead of raising the bar of quality programming and thereby initiating a 'virtuous cycle', RAI (especially its second channel, and, to a lesser extent in more recent times, its flagship channel) has often filled its prime time slots with imported TV series (or old films during the summer months), imported children's cartoons, flashy news bulletins, reality and game shows. Indeed, according to a research prepared by the Group of Specialists on Media Diversity and presented to the Council of Europe on 27 February 2006, the genre composition of RAI and Mediaset's output remains strikingly similar. At the time when the research was completed, 60 per cent of the schedule on RAI's flagship channel, RAI1, was made up of news, talk shows, light entertainment, drama and game shows; 65 per cent of the output of Canale5 (Mediaset's flagship channel) was also characterized by the same genres (Group of Specialists 2006: 41–2). As media analyst Francesco Siliato predicted, heterogeneity of programming output on Italian terrestrial broadcasting TV 'continues to be the exception, rather than the norm' (Siliato 2001).

The homogenization of TV programmes is especially disturbing in a country where 'more than half [the population]...gets its information exclusively from television' (D'Avanzo 2007), and where television is still the most used medium, with 92.1 per cent of users in 2006 (CENSIS 2007: 1–2). The concentration of political and media power is particularly worrisome if we consider that, during political campaigns, television becomes even more important. During those times television is 'absolutely the only source of information, [with] 77.3 percent [of Italians] trusting [TV] completely and only 6.6 percent accessing other sources' (D'Avanzo 2007).

Political pluralism
In a country like Italy, historically characterized by highly polarized political and media systems (Hallin and Mancini 2004: 89–98), by a wide range of political parties playing the intermediary role between citizens and state institutions (Scoppola 1991), and by a wealth of local, regional, and immigrants cultures, a plurality of voices, opinions, and political perspectives, is very important. In fact, 'proper access to the different media by all political and social actors' (Polo 2004: 2) is the *conditio sine qua non* for both 'Internal Political Pluralism' and 'External Political Pluralism', indicating respectively the 'diversified supply of political views within each single medium...and [with]in the market' (Polo 2004: 1). As Polo explains, not even a differentiation in the 'content of the media companies...[would] necessarily [mean a broader]...representation of political opinions and views' (Polo 2004: 30). In fact, given the concentrated structures of media markets and the political interests at stake, the 'market will hardly satisfy the need [for] external [as well as internal] pluralism' (Polo 2004: 30).

Media pluralism in Italy: A history
Proper public policies aimed at reducing market concentration are an absolute necessity, indeed, the history of media regulation in Italy serves as an important lesson to learn about the consequences of poor legislation in this sector. As this history points out, laws regulating the TV market have usually been too slow in coming, and those pieces of legislation that have been passed often supported the interests of political and industrial elites, protecting corporations' freedom of expression and competition (in particular, Fininvest/Mediaset's freedoms), rather than supporting and promoting citizens' rights to be informed and entertained in a pluralistic media environment.

The monopoly over broadcasting
In Italy, television has represented a formidable tool for the linguistic and cultural unification of the country after World War II (De Mauro 1962), and for political part(ies) to establish and solidify consensus (Padovani 2005; Mancini 2006; Pinto 1980; Cesareo 1970). This last aspect, namely the relationship between television and the political establishment, is critical to understanding how pluralism first developed in the country. A practice known as *lottizzazione* (i.e., the sharing of position of powers among political parties within the public service broadcaster) at times functioned as a practical application of pluralism and could be seen as a 'recognition of the existence of many groups (exclusively political groups in Italy's case) in competition and their need to express and circulate their points of view' (Mancini 2006: 6). Political pluralism within the public broadcaster often improved because of *lottizzazione*, a quota system that allowed representatives of the most important parties (including the

opposition) to intervene in the administration of the broadcaster as well as in the making of programming.

In order to understand how *lottizzazione* developed, it is necessary to understand the history of public service broadcasting in Italy. Far from considering RAI's role as that of a public sphere where information could be provided in order to promote rational and informed debates among citizens (Habermas 1989; Garnham 1983, 1986, 1992, 2003), the governing parties often saw television as a tool to establish and maintain their cultural and political hegemony. Indeed, from its early days in the 1950s, the public broadcaster was conceived not as a place for enlightenment according to the tenets of liberal democracies, but 'as a terrain of ideological struggle' (Padovani 2005: 6). From the time it obtained rights over television broadcasting in 1952[4] until the mid-1970s, the control of the broadcaster was firmly secured in the hands of the government, which, directly and indirectly, appointed most of the members of the board of directors. Not only local and national broadcasting was under state monopoly, 'complete government control was guaranteed as all appointments were...negotiated among the various currents of the Christian Democratic Party (DC)' (Padovani 2005: 68). The DC was later joined by a variety of small parties (including the Italian Socialist Democratic Party and the Italian Republican Party), negotiating power inside the broadcaster.

Pluralism and the end of state monopoly

By the early 1970s, an unprecedented grass roots movement, comprised of national unions, citizens and consumers' organizations, print journalists, as well as RAI journalists and programmers, was advocating for the liberalization of the airways and the end of the state's monopoly over radio and television broadcasting.

Ruling in 1974 on a series of cases regarding private citizens, who, between 1971 and 1973, had been accused of illegally installing television receivers to access international broadcasts, the Constitutional Court (Sent. N. 225) urged the legislature to provide new rules for the broadcasting sector. The high court took the opportunity to underline that the only reason for justifying the legitimacy of the state's monopoly over broadcasting (a monopoly established in 1952) was for the public broadcaster to ensure cultural and political pluralism. On that occasion, the court emphasized that 'access to radio and television [broadcasting] should be impartially open...to all political, religious, cultural groups, through which the various ideologies present in society express themselves' (Art. 8, Comma F). The court envisioned a new law that would free RAI from its dependence on the government of the day and promote pluralism.

Opening the broadcaster to diverse instances in society, decentralizing RAI's production centres, and making its programming more relevant and representative of regional cultures, were the goals of the reform movement. Law No. 103 of 14 April 1975 acknowledged the growing demands coming from the high court as well as from the body social, and, in its opening statement, declared that the fundamental principles of public broadcasting were to provide 'independence, objectivity, and openness to the diverse political, social, and cultural instances' (Art. 1). An *ad hoc* sub commission was established to secure access to the broadcaster (to air time and production facilities) for underrepresented groups and ensure a 'plurality of opinions and of political and cultural orientations' (Art. 6). After years of monopoly of the Christian Democratic Party over RAI, pluralism – political and party pluralism in particular – was finally required by law.

Lottizzazione and pluralism

In an effort to respond to the court's directions emphasizing the need for more pluralism, the law of the 1975 assigned new important functions to the Commissione Parlamentare di Vigilanza RAI (founded in 1947 but rather inactive since then). In order to remove RAI from the direct control of the government, it was established that the Committee's 40 members would be nominated by all parliamentary parties, thereby broadening the governance of the public broadcaster. Among other tasks, the Committee was given the responsibility of electing more than half of the sixteen members of RAI's board of directors, while the remaining members would be nominated directly by the Parliament. Moreover, in order to ensure more diverse programming and promote a more open, de-centralized broadcaster, the law makers established that at least five per cent of TV air time (and at least three per cent of radio broadcasting time) should be reserved for 'political parties and parliamentary groups, local administrative institutions, national unions, religious organizations, political movements...[and] ethnic groups' (Law N. 103, Art. 6).

Although complete decentralization was never achieved (RAI continues to be primarily a Rome-based broadcaster, although in 2003 its second channel was moved to Milan in an effort to please the federalist requests of Berlusconi's political ally, Lega Nord), political and party pluralism was religiously implemented as a result of the 1975 reform law. RAI1 remained the channel of the ruling party with its populist and more conservative programming, while the second channel, RAI2 (founded in 1961) was assigned to the Italian Socialist Party (PSI). Finally, in 1989, RAI3, at the time a struggling regional channel, was given to the Italian Communist Party (PCI), the second most important party in the country.

Historically, *lottizzazione* played a very important role and had a positive function: in an environment that, until the mid-1970s was still defined by RAI's monopoly in the broadcasting sector, the practice of sharing positions of power among the various political parties secured both internal and external pluralism. *Lottizzazione* ensured external pluralism because each channel was assigned to one of the two (and then three) most important political parties; it provided internal pluralism, because, as an effect of rather sophisticated *lottizzazione* formulas, positions were shared among the representatives of all major parties within each channel and newsroom.

Even though most of the old mass parties of the post war era, including the DC, the PSI, and the PCI, disappeared in the wake of the so-called Clean Hands scandal of the early 1990s,[5] the practice of allocating political party quotas inside the public broadcaster continued. RAI1, the flagship channel, including Tg1, its national news bulletin, remained in the hands of the main government party (the most important party of the governing coalition); RAI2 went to the second most important party (or the other parties in the coalition); and RAI3 to the opposition.

Consolidating the duopoly

Whereas the Constitutional Court had agreed that state monopoly over local broadcasting was unconstitutional (Sent. 202/1976), it continued to uphold state monopoly over national broadcasting based on the argument that 'public broadcasting service...is a service of general utility...[and that] the general interest [is realized] by the need to avoid the concentration of broadcasting in a monopoly or oligopoly' (Sent. 148/1981, Comma 2). Addressing those who claimed that technological advancements had in fact made the state monopoly obsolete and that there was no risk of consolidation in what appeared to be a lively and competitive growing market (in 1978 there were more than 2000 private, or 'independent' radio stations, and, by 1981, 800 television stations), the high court clarified its position in a subsequent sentence:

> The necessity [of the state monopoly] does not emerge only in relationship with the more or less available broadcasting frequencies, rather it derives from the nature of the broadcasting phenomenon, seen in the socioeconomic context in which it is destined to develop. (Sent. 148/1981, Comma 2)

On that occasion, the court underlined the need for proper regulations. In fact, unless appropriate legislation were put in place to prevent the formation of monopolies in the TV sector, the state's reserve over national broadcasting had to be maintained in order to protect a service of 'general utility'. However, when the legislature intervened, it did so primarily to protect the interests of Fininvest, the private TV operator. In the fall of 1984, after a few judges had ordered Berlusconi's channels to be shut down because of being in breach of two Constitutional Court sentences (202/1976 and 148/1981) banning private operators from broadcasting nationally, the government, then headed by Prime Minister Bettino Craxi, passed a decree law to quickly overturn the magistrates' decisions. In that decree (known as the 'Berlusconi decree' and converted into Law N. 10 on 4 February 1985), the legislator established that: (1) the channels that were in operation by 1 October 1984 could continue their broadcasts; (2) each existing broadcaster would be allowed to air pre-registered programmes at any time; and (3) each local broadcaster would be allowed to transmit its signals to other local TV stations across the country. These norms were custom-made to cater to Fininvest's needs. In fact, in an attempt to circumvent the state monopoly over national broadcasting, the private broadcaster's stratagem was to send pre-recorded tapes to all Fininvest-owned stations across the nation and broadcast those tapes almost simultaneously. Although this was not, technically, 'national' broadcasting, it obviously contributed to creating a national audience for a de facto national broadcaster.

The juridical principles used by the Craxi government to legitimatize its support of private initiative in national broadcasting were those of freedom of expression and pluralism (Art. 1, Comma 2 of Law N. 10, 4 February 1985). Without addressing the Constitutional Court's position, according to which concentration in the TV sector had to be prevented because it was not conducive to promoting broadcasting as a 'service of general utility' (Sent. 148/1981), the legislator used the principle of freedom of expression to justify its support for the private broadcaster's own freedom of expression. While internal pluralism within RAI continued to be practised thanks to an increasingly rigid lottizzazione, external pluralism now meant that instead of one national monopolist (RAI), there would be two, although only two, national broadcasters.

In a subsequent sentence of the Constitutional Court, a fundamental one for the history of Italy's jurisprudence on pluralism of information (Sent. 826/1988), the court called on the Parliament to take action and insisted that 'an appropriate legislation [was needed] to avoid the dangers of monopoly or oligopol[ies]' (Zaccaria 1996: 5). The court warned that once national broadcasting was left in the hands of private investors in monopolistic or oligopolistic markets, those investors would be able to 'exercise, from a position of prominence, influence over the collectivity and that would be incompatible with the rules of a democratic system' (Constitutional Court, 826/1988, Comma 9).

In the same sentence, the court clarified its view on pluralism:

[P]luralism of radio and television broadcasting means...the possibility, on the part of as many voices as technically possible...to access the public as well as the private broadcaster. In order to make sure that external pluralism is real and not simply [theoretical], such access to the private broadcaster must be a concrete possibility. [Indeed] those who bear different opinions [shall] be able to express themselves without the risk of being marginalized because of the processes of concentration of technical and economic resources in the hands of one or a few. (Constitutional Court Sent. 826/1988, Comma 11)

According to the court, in order to ensure real pluralism it was necessary to foster an environment supportive of citizens' rights to be informed and entertained from a variety of media outlets. The high court explained this principle:

Pluralism manifests itself as the concrete possibility for all citizens to choose among a multiplicity of informational sources, a choice that would not be realistic if the public targeted by audiovisual communication were not in the condition to access, in the public as well as in the private sector, programmes that guarantee the expression of heterogeneous tendencies. (Constitutional Court 826/1988, Comma 11)

The court underlined that 'national [or external] pluralism [could] never be reached if the competition continue[d] to be only between one public and one private broadcaster' (Comma 19). Once again, the court urged the legislator to take action. Lawmakers were warned: 'an [impending] formal declaration of unconstitutionality [was going to be issued] unless an organic law disciplining the whole sector were to intervene in a reasonable time' (Zaccaria 1996: 7).

In fact, the prolonged inactivity of the legislator had already caused 'serious difficulties to the few publishing firms that had entered the market in the early 1980s' (Zaccaria 1996: 6). In an environment often referred to by the popular press as the far west of the airwaves, the TV market was consolidating in the hands of Silvio Berlusconi, then a young entrepreneur from Milan and owner of Canale5, who had acquired Italia1 in 1983 and Rete4 in 1984. By 1986, RAI and Fininvest were already in control of 85 per cent of the national audiences and 90 per cent of available resources. Moreover, Fininvest owned shares – up to 82 per cent of them in the 1990s – of the national daily *Il Giornale* (a newspaper founded in Milan in 1974 by journalist guru Indro Montanelli); by 1989, Berlusconi's holdings had obtained a majority share of the prestigious Mondadori publishing house.

A law to legitimize the duopoly

Law No. 223 of 6 August 1990 confirmed the inability, or unwillingness, of the political establishment to stand up in favour of a more open and diversified TV sector. Instead of regulating the market in support of citizens' right to be informed from a variety of sources, as the high court had often recommended, the law limited itself to simply describing the existing situation. As customary, the legislator paid lip service to the principle of pluralism, stating that:

Pluralism, objectivity, complete and impartial information, openness to diverse opinion, political tendencies, social, cultural and religious [tendencies]...represent the fundamental principles of the radio and television broadcasting service, [a principle] that is realized thanks to the competition of public and private operators...(Art. 1, Comma 2)

In reality, 'competition of public and private operators' only meant the competition between one public broadcaster and one private broadcaster. In this sense, the law 'put [serious] obstacles to pluralism in a fundamental way: by limiting the plurality of voices, which is the best guarantee of pluralism' (Gambaro and Silva: 162).

Article 15 of the Mammì law (named after Oscar Mammì, the communications minister at the time), forbade cross-ownership (Comma 1), but left the broadcasting sector untouched. Indeed, it set the anti-trust limits to 'no more' than three national channels (Comma 4) – three was exactly the number of channels operated by RAI and Fininvest respectively – and established that no single operator could access more than twenty per cent of the available resources for the entire mass media sector, including those for the print media, advertising, and the licence fee for the public broadcaster (Comma 2 and 3).

Technological advancements and pluralism

In an attempt to address the issue of political interference within the public broadcaster – increasingly unpopular at the time of the Clean Hands scandals of the early 1990s – Law N. 206, of 25 June 1993 (also known as the anti-*lottizzazione* law), was passed to free RAI from its dependency on the political party system. As Mancini notes (2006), the law reduced the number of members of RAI's board (from sixteen to five) in order to prevent the proportional division of those positions among parties, and established that board members be appointed by the speakers of the Senate and the House of Deputies instead of the Commissione Parlamentare di Vigilanza RAI in an effort to ensure political independence.

However, the problems afflicting the Italian TV and media sector went well beyond the relationship between RAI and the party system. Indeed, the concentration of the TV broadcasting market and Berlusconi's conflict of interests were pressing concerns. Unfortunately, not even the centre-left government of Romano Prodi (1996–8) did much to address either of these issues. Law No. 249 of 31 July 1997 (the so-called 'Maccanico Law', named after Communications Minister Antonio Maccanico) established the Communications Authority and assigned to it the task of 'adopting the necessary measurements to eliminate or impede [dominant] positions... [colliding with] pluralism' (Art. 2, Comma 7). The law also set new anti-trust limitations forbidding national broadcasters from controlling more than thirty per cent of the available resources in the television sector or utilizing more than twenty per cent of the analogue national television channels.

In an attempt to break down the duopoly (both RAI and Mediaset collected more than thirty per cent of the available resources and occupied more than twenty per cent of the television channels), the legislator imposed (Art. 3, Comma 6) the transition of the exceeding channels to other platforms (satellite or cable). However, it failed to set a deadline for the migration, a task that was instead assigned to the Communications Authority (Art. 3, Comma 7). Widespread expectations about the advent of digital terrestrial TV (a delivery technology that would have overcome the limitations dictated by the spectrum scarcity and cured the ills of a concentrated market), were some of the reasons for not pushing the migration of RAI and Mediaset's third channels to satellite. After all, with a future of abundant digital channels just around the corner, why worry?

Expectations for a fast transition to digital-only television failed to materialize and, four years later, the Communications Authority finally set 31 December 2003 as the deadline for compliance with the anti-trust limitations established by the Maccanico law of 1997 (Resolution 346/2001). In 2002, the Constitutional Court declared Art. 3, Comma 7, of the Law 31 July 1997, unconstitutional for failing to 'provide a deadline, certain and unchangeable' (Sent. 466/2002), and confirmed the deadline set by the Authority. The court underlined that:

> external pluralism...cannot be...achieved based [just] on the fact that there is competition between a public and a private pole, [and when] the private [competitor] is [in] a dominant position. This is because [in such a situation] access to the broadcasting sector on the part of the 'highest possible number of diverse voices' cannot not be [fully] realized. (155/2002)

Meanwhile, motivated by a similar intent to maintain the status quo, both the public and the commercial broadcasters found themselves agreeing on what they saw as a useless imposition. RAI's perspective was exemplary: indeed, representatives from the public broadcaster argued that the 'reduction of an exceeding operator would not in itself be sufficient to ensure pluralism' (RAI's defence quoted in Constitutional Court, Sent. 466/2002, Art. 8). The technological transformation of the broadcasting sector was perceived as the solution to the lack of external pluralism and many hoped that the upcoming 'technical innovation in digital terrestrial [transmission] would allow an unlimited increase of available frequencies, with the consequence of increased pluralism of information' (RAI's defence quoted in Sent. 466/2002, Art. 8).

Pluralism as the right of the minorities

In reality, the full transition to digital TV, first scheduled for the end of 2003, then postponed to 2006, is now expected to be completed in 2012. Meanwhile, RAI and Mediaset have continued to dominate the broadcasting market. In a sign of urgency and concern, even Carlo Azeglio Ciampi (President of the Republic from 1999 to 2006) addressed the Parliament on two occasions in July 2002 and December 2003.

In his July 2002 address, the president emphasized that 'there [can be] no democracy without pluralism and impartiality of information' (Ciampi 2002). He also underlined that the existence of dominant positions in the field of communication and media, is, in itself, an 'objective obstacle to the effective actualization of pluralism', and reminded the lawmakers of their duty to 'secure pluralism of voices, expressions of freedom of thought, and to guarantee, in this way, the fundamental right of citizens to information' (Ciampi 2002).

The Italian President applauded technological advancements in the field of broadcasting transmission, but warned that 'pluralism and impartiality of information will not be the automatic consequence of technological progress'. Lawmakers – he told the Parliament – should work on public policies in order to guide technological processes. Ciampi also called attention to cultural pluralism (a fundamental component of Italian culture) and recommended to his audience that 'pluralism and impartiality of information are fundamental factors to balance the rights of the majority with those of the minorities'.

In his second parliamentary address in 2003, Ciampi explained the reasons why he had refused to sign a bill, proposed by the Berlusconi government and approved by the Parliament, to reform the media and television sectors. The president called the lawmakers' attention to the fact that the bill had failed to impose the migration of analogue broadcasting channels in excess of anti-trust limitation as demanded by the Constitutional Court's sentence No. 466 of 2002. Moreover, Ciampi underlined that the proposed law did not provide, as requested by another sentence (420/1994), 'appropriate legislation that would prevent dominant positions' (Ciampi 2003). Finally, the head of State criticized the legislator for proposing a new system to calculate the 'relevant market' (out of which anti-trust percentages would be calculated). This system, called 'integrated system of communication' or 'SIC', would include not only TV ads and the licence fee, but also resources generated from books, movies and the Internet. In fact, Ciampi believed that the SIC, 'taken...as the baseline for calculating the profits of each operator...could cause...even for those in control of [only] twenty per cent of the resources...to be in a dominant position' (Ciampi 2003).

The Gasparri Law

In its opening remarks, the Gasparri Law (named after Communications Minister Maurizio Gasparri and approved on 3 May 2004 with only minor adjustments), the legislator celebrated 'freedom and pluralism of the means of communication, and the tutelage of freedom of expression for every citizen' (Law N. 112, Art. 3, Comma 1), and guaranteed 'the user's access...to an ample variety of information and content offered by a plurality of national and local operators...in conditions of pluralism and freedom of competition' (Art. 4, Comma 1a). The law also stated that in order to guarantee pluralism of the means of communication, the broadcasting sector would have to strictly adhere to the principle of market competition, thereby forbidding 'the constitution or the maintenance of positions that [could be] damaging to pluralism' (Art. 5, Comma 1a). It is important to notice that freedom of competition rather than citizens' freedom of expression and their right to be informed and entertained in a pluralistic media environment, were, once again, the legislator's main concerns. In fact, 'there is no doubt that [this law] was conceived to protect Berlusconi's broadcasting empire' (Tonello 2007: 246), and the existing duopoly.

The Gasparri law established that no single operator could access more than twenty per cent of total available resources, but significantly enlarged the 'relevant market' out of which this percentage ought to be calculated (Art. 15, Comma 2 and 3). Indeed, the Integrated System of Communication would include resources generated by the 'printing press...electronic publishing, INTERNET, radio and television, cinema,...and advertising' (Art. 15, Comma 2 and 3). As one commentator wrote, Mediaset could even buy the national newspaper *Corriere della Sera* (the Milanese daily with the highest circulation in the country) and still be in compliance with the 20 per cent anti-trust limitations (Rampini 2003)!

Moreover, in an effort to secure a fast transition to digital terrestrial television (DTT), Article 25 of the Gasparri law established that, by January 2004, the public broadcaster would cover 50 per cent of the population with its digital terrestrial channels; 70 per cent by 2005. According to the law, such new delivery technology would solve the problem of spectrum scarcity, implicitely eliminating the need for sending existing analogue channels to other platforms.

As Ezio Mauro (editor in chief of the daily *La Repubblica*) wrote, the law 'deformed information, pluralism, and the market of consensus,...sanctifie[d]...the absolute supremacy [of Silvio Berlusconi]...[and] alter[ed] the rules of the political game by transforming television in the last Italian ideology, the perpetual source of Berlusconi's power' (Mauro 2003). For Giuseppe Tesauro, president of the Italian Antitrust, 'the anti-concentration norms [set by the Gasparri law]...risk to transfer the...duopoly [from the broadcasting market] in the digital era' (Tesauro, quoted in *La Repubblica*, 2003). Indeed, given the prolonged transitional period from analogue to digital TV, the uncertainties of the new digital terrestrial television market, and the existing operators' advantage over delivery networks, programmes acquisition, and content development, both RAI and Mediaset find themselves positioned to enjoy their privileged positions on into the future.

The Gentiloni Bill

Understandably, the Gasparri Law became a target of the European Commissioner for Competition that declared the law as illegal in one of its notes addressed to the Italian government (then led by Romano Prodi) on 19 July 2006. Indeed, according to European Commissioner Neelie Kroes, the law contained:

> unjustified restrictions for new operators and unjustified advantage for the existing ones – which could, according to Kroes – preclude those who are not active in the analog broadcasting market from experimenting with the creation of digital transmissions and... digital networks. (Maggiore 2006).

The second centre-left Prodi government (May 2006 – January 2008) was prompt to respond and, in fact, Communications Minister Paolo Gentiloni assured that a new law would soon be designed to reduce RAI and Mediaset's dominant position, set new anti-trust limitations, and govern the transition to digital television. The minister also ensured that a long overdue national database for broadcasting frequencies would be prepared to rationalize the allocation of frequencies.[6]

A bill approved by the government in October 2006 required TV broadcasters with more than two analogue national channels to send the surplus channels to a digital platform by 2009; it established that in the future, all-digital environment, content providers would not be allowed to utilize more than twenty per cent of available transmitting capabilities, and that content providers should be separated from network providers. The bill also set a new anti-trust ceiling of 45 per cent of advertising revenues for television. This was a noteworthy step forward, considering – as Polo (2006) explains – that Mediaset, in 2006, controlled as much as 60–5 per cent of the TV advertising market, and RAI controlled between 30 and 35 per cent. Unfortunately the Gentiloni bill, presented to the senate on 29 May 2007, was never approved.

Conclusions

Political interference in the television sector in Italy has a long history. At times, such interference has served as a positive force for pluralism of information, by promoting, thanks to the practice of *lottizzazione*, a variety of voices and perspectives to be heard on television. However, through the years, the consolidation of media and political power has encouraged the formation and continuation of the duopoly in the TV market. The absence of appropriate legislation in support of citizens' rights to be informed and entertained in a pluralistic media environment has *de facto* encouraged the process of consolidation of the broadcasting market since the early 1980s. While the public broadcaster has been able to maintain a considerable portion of the audience share and a strong presence in the analogue broadcasting market, Silvio Berlusconi has embodied the worst aspects of the historically close relations between the political system and the television system in Italy.

The negative impact on Italian democracy is evident: as Jürgen Habermas underlines, Berlusconi has been able to use his considerable 'economic clout as a switch to immediately convert media power into public influence' (Habermas 2006: 19). The unresolved conflict of interests between Berlusconi's public duties as prime minister and his private interests has warped Italy's public debate on media-related issues for more than a decade, and will continue to do so in the future. This has given birth to a situation in which the media mogul has 'used his media empire to back dubious legislation in support of the consolidation of his private fortunes and political assets' (Habermas 2006: 19). As Alexander Stille bluntly puts it, Italy might continue to be 'a nation of 58 million people held hostage to the interests of one man and his company' (Stille 2006: 351). For this to change, laws that protect and favour citizens' right to be informed in a pluralistic media environment are vital.

Unfortunately, given the history of the legislation in the field of broadcasting and media, and Berlusconi's extraordinary political and media power (he became Italy's prime minister again after his coalition won national elections in April 2008), it is more than reasonable to not expect, in a foreseeable future, any law that might seriously reform the TV and media sector, break the duopoly, or prevent the same duopoly from casting its shadow over the digital TV market. Reciting the same old mantra celebrating technological advancements as the solution to market concentration, those who support the status quo dismiss concerns over the duopoly as something that belongs to the past. In their opinion, Mediaset and RAI will be players, just like any other, in the new all-digital media environment. The future is in the pay-TV sector (including pay DTT channels, a sector where Mediaset is aggressively expanding), where there will be plenty of competition.

In reality, terrestrial free-to-air TV is still a very strategic asset for Mediaset. Berlusconi's TV channels control high percentages of advertising resources for television, and although audience share for terrestrial TV channels is diminishing (Marzulli 2007: 9), terrestrial free-to-air TV is crucial for the resources that it brings in (of the $6.25 billion revenues posted by Mediaset for fiscal year 2007, 85 per cent was from TV advertising (Vivarelli 2008b)), and for the political and ideological clout that it has.

Perhaps Mediaset might even be able to finally purchase Telecom Italia, the telecommunication giant which operates La7, the small seventh TV channel in the Italian broadcasting market. In fact, talks about this possibility have been making the headlines on trade publications since early 2007 (see, for instance, *The Times* 2007: 48; *Variety* 2008: 16; Lyman 2008). Certainly, if this were to happen, the new 'merged entity would be one of the world's largest communications and media companies' (Lyman 2008), and this, as Lyman naïvely notices, might never happen because of anti-trust restrictions. But when, throughout the history of Italian media legislation, have regulations failed to favour Berlusconi's private interest?

Notes

1. The Italian Constitution supports freedom of expression in its Art. 21, where it reads: 'everybody has the right to manifest their own thinking...via any means of communication'.
2. According the European Federation of Journalists, the Berlusconi family owns 96 per cent of Fininvest, a private financial holding company founded by Silvio in 1978 ('Media Power in Europe: The Big Picture of Ownership'). Fininvest controls 36 per cent of Mediaset (established in 1996), which owns the three national broadcasting channels Canale5, Italia1, and Rete4, in Italy; Telecinco in Spain; and the advertising giant Publitalia '80.
3. This story was broken by the daily *La Repubblica* on 21 November 2007 (see *La Repubblica* 2007a; see also *La Repubblica* 2007b; D'Avanzo 2007; Merlo 2007).
4. See Concession of 1952 *Approvazione ed esecutoreità della Convenzione per la concessione alla Radio Audizioni Italia Società per azioni del servizio di telediffusione su filo* [Concession of 1952 between the state and RAI for radio and television broadcasting services], approved by Presidential Decree N. 180 on 26 January 1952.
5. The Clean Hands scandal of the early 1990s refers to a series of investigations carried out by a pool of Milanese magistrates over the illegal financing of political parties. The magistrates unveiled many cases of corruption of political elites and party leaders; as a result, many of the old politicians were forced to step down and most of the post war mass parties (including the Christian Democratic Party and the Italian Socialist Party) disappeared.
6. The Communications Ministry and the Communications Authority announced the national database of broadcasting frequencies on 4 June 2007 (see Italian Government 2007).

References

CENSIS (Centro Studi Investimenti Sociali) (2007), 'Rapporto sulla situazione sociale del paese, 2007. Comunicazione e Media', [Annual Report 2007 on the country's social conditions. Communications and Media], http://www.censis.it. Accessed 2 May 2008.

Cesareo, G. (1970), *Anatomia del potere televisivo*, Milan: Franco Angeli.

Ciampi, C. A. (2002), 'Messaggio alle camere in materia di pluralismo e imparzialità dell'informazione' [Message to the parliament on the issue of pluralism and impartiality of information], Rome, 23 July 2002, http://www.quirinale.it/ex_presidenti/Ciampi/Discorsi/Discorso.asp?id=20101. Accessed 1 February 2008.

Ciampi, C. A. (2003), 'Messaggio alle camere' [Message to the parliament], Rome, 15 December 2003, http://www.aeranti.it/altrepag/normativa/legisl_base/20031215_Mess_Ciampi_legge_Gasparri.htm. Accessed 10 May 2008.

Constitutional Court (1974), 'Sentence N. 225/1974', http://www.giurcost.org/decisioni/1974/0225s-74.html. Accessed 2 January 2008.

Constitutional Court (1976), 'Sentence N. 202/1976', http://www.giurcost.org/decisioni/1976/0202s-76.html. Accessed March 2007.

Constitutional Court (1981), 'Sentence N. 148/1981', http://www.giurcost.org/decisioni/1981/0148s-81.html. Accessed 10 May 2008.

Constitutional Court (1988), 'Sentence N. 826/1988', http://www.giurcost.org/decisioni/1988/0826s-88.html. Accessed 10 May 2008.

Constitutional Court (1994), 'Sentence N. 420/1994', http://www.giurcost.org/decisioni/1994/0420s-94.html. Accessed 1 June 2008.

Constitutional Court (2002a), 'Sentence N. 466/2002', http://www.uonna.it/466-2002-sentenza-corte-costituzionale.htm. Accessed 21 December 2007.

Constitutional Court (2002b), 'Sentence N. 155/2002', http://www.giurcost.org/decisioni/2002/0155s-02.html. Accessed 10 May 2008.

D'Avanzo, G. (2007), 'Operazione Verità', La Repubblica, 23 November 2007, Rome.

De Mauro, T. (1962), Storia Linguistica dell'Italia unita, Bari: Laterza.

European Federation of Journalists (2005), 'Media Power in Europe: the Big Picture of Ownership', http://www.ifj.org/assets/docs/245/202/08737f5-ec283ca.pdf. Accessed 10 May 2008.

European Union (2000), 'Charter of Fundamental Rights of the European Union', Official Journal of the European Community, (2000/C 364/01) http://www.europarl.europa.eu/charter/pdf/text_en.pdf. Accessed 10 May 2008.

Gambaro, M. and Silva, F. (1992), Economia della televisione, Bologna: Il Mulino.

Garnham, N. (1983), 'Public Service Versus the Market', Screen 5, No. 1 (1983), pp. 6–28.

Garnham, N. (1986), 'The Media and the Public Sphere', in P. Golding, et al. (eds.), Communicating Politics: Mass Communication and the Political Process, Leicester: Leicester University Press, pp. 37–54.

Garnham, N. (1992), 'The Media and the Public Sphere', in C. Calhoun (ed.), Habermas and the Public Sphere, Cambridge, Mass.: MIT Press, pp. 359–76.

Garnham, N. (2003), 'A Reply to Elisabeth Jacka's Democracy as Defeat', in G. Sussman (ed.), Rethinking Public Media in a Transitional Era. Special issue of Television and New Media, 4:2 (May 2003), pp. 193–200.

Gramsci, A. (1992), Prison Notebooks, Vol. 1 (J. A. Buttigieg ed.), New York: Columbia University Press.

Group of Specialists on Media Diversity (2006), 'Final report on the study commissioned to Mr. D. Ward by the MC-S-MD', Media Division Directorate General of Human Rights, Strasbourg, 27 February 2006, http://www.coe.int/t/e/human_rights/media/1_Intergovernmental_Co-operation/MC-S-MD/MC-S-MD(2006)001_en.pdf. Accessed 21 April 2008.

Habermas, J. (1989), The Structural Transformation of the Public Sphere, Cambridge, Mass.: MIT Press.

Habermas, J. (2006), 'Political Communication in Media Society – Does Democracy still enjoy an epistemic dimension? The impact of normative theory on empirical research', Communication Theory, 16 (2006), pp. 411–26.

Hallin, D. and Mancini, P. (2004), Comparative Media Systems: Three Models of Media and Politics, Cambridge: Cambridge University Press.

Italian Communications Authority (2001), Resolution n. 346/2001, 'Termini e criteri di attuazione delle disposizioni di cui all'art. 3, commi 6, 7, 9, 11, Legge 31 Luglio 1997 n. 249', http://www.agcom.it/provv/d_346_01_CONS.htm. Accessed 10 November 2007.

Italian Constitution (1947), http://www.quirinale.it/costituzione/costituzione.htm. Accessed 2 May 2008.

Italian Government (2006), 'Disegno Legge Disposizioni per la disciplina del settore televisivo nella fase di transizione alla tecnologia digitale presentato dal ministro delle comunicazioni Gentiloni' [Proposed law to discipline the television sector during the transition to digital technology, presented by Communications Minister Gentiloni], Rome, 16 October 2006, http://www.comunicazioni.it/binary/min_comunicazioni/normativa/ddl1825.pdf. Accessed 15 April 2007.

Italian Government, Ministry of Communications (1975), Law 14 April 1975, n. 103, 'Nuove norme in materia di diffusione radiofonica e televisiva' [New norms about radio and television broadcasting], http://www.camera.it/_bicamerali/rai/norme/listitut.htm. Accessed 21 April 2008.

Italian Government, Ministry of Communications (1985), Law 4 February 1985, n. 10, 'Conversione in legge del Decreto-legge 6 Dicembre 1984, n. 807, recante disposizioni urgenti in materia di trasmissioni radiotelevisive' [Conversion into law of the decree law 6 December 1984, n. 87, regarding urgent dispositions about radio and television broadcasting], http://www.aeranti.it/altrepag/normativa/legge40285.htm. Accessed 4 June 2008.

Italian Government, Ministry of Communications (1990), Law 6 August 1990, n. 223, 'Disciplina del sistema radiotelevisivo pubblico e privato' [Discipline for the public and private broadcasting system], http://www.agcom.it/L_naz/L223_90.htm. Accessed 19 April 2008.

Italian Government, Ministry of Communications (1993), Law 25 June 1993, n. 206, 'Disposizioni sulla società concessionaria del servizio pubblico radiotelevisivo' [Norms for the public service broadcaster], http://www.camera.it/_bicamerali/rai/norme/l206-93.htm. Accessed 21 April 2008.

Italian Government, Ministry of Communications (1997), Law 31 July 1997, n. 249, 'Istituzione dell'Autorità per le garanzie nelle comunicazioni e norme sui sistemi delle telecomunicazioni e radiotelevisivo' [Institution of the Communications Authority and norms on the telecommunications and broadcasting systems], http://www.agcom.it/L_naz/L_249.htm. Accessed 21 April 2008.

Italian Government, Ministry of Communications (2004), Law 3 May 2004, n.112, 'Norme di principio in materia di assetto del sistema radiotelevisivo e della RAI- Radiotelevisione italiana S.p.A., nonché delega al Governo per l'emanazione del testo unico della radiotelevisione' [Norms for the restructuring of the broadcasting system and of RAI], http://www.agcom.it/L_naz/L_112_04.htm. Accessed 10 May 2008.

Italian Government, Ministry of Economic Development, Communications (2007), 'Arriva il Database unico delle frequenze televisive nazionali', 4 June 2007, http://www.comunicazioni.it/aree_interesse/televisione/televisione_news/pagina257.html. Accessed 20 December 2008.

La Repubblica (2007a), 'La rete segreta del cavaliere che pilotava Rai e Mediaset', 21 November 2007, Rome.

La Repubblica (2007b), 'Rai-Mediaset, indaga l'Authority', 21 November 2007, Rome.

Lyman, E. (2008), 'Mediaset, "Telecom Italia merger speculation grows"', The Hollywood Reporter, 11 March 2008.

Maggiore, M. (2006), 'La TV di Gasparri tre volte fuorilegge', La Repubblica, 20 July 2006, Rome.

Mancini, P. (2006), 'La lottizzazione. Between pluralism, consociational democracy and clientelism', Paper presented at the conference of the International Association for Mass Communication Research, Cairo, Egypt, 23–8 July 2006 [author's manuscript, no page numbers].

Marzulli, A. (2007), 'Televisione', in F. Barca and A. Marzulli (eds.), L'Industria della comunicazione in Italia Decimo Rapporto IEM. La domanda dei contenuti dei broadcasters generalisti, Turin: Guerini & Associates, pp. 7–22.

Mauro, E. (2003), 'Il contratto con se stesso', La Repubblica, 3 December 2003, Rome.

Merlo, F. (2007), 'I Tartufi del giornalismo', La Repubblica, 23 November 2007, Rome.

Padovani, C. (2005), A Fatal Attraction, Public Television and Politics in Italy, Boulder, CO: Rowman & Littlefield.

Pinto, Francesco (1980), Il modello televisivo. Professionalità e politica da Bernabei alla Terza Rete, Milan: Feltrinelli.

Polo, M. (2004), 'Regulation for Pluralism in the Media Markets', Paper prepared for the conference 'Regulations of Media Markets', Toulouse, Spain, 1–2 October 2004, pp. 1–33 [author's manuscript].

Polo, M. (2006), 'Si può fare di più', *Lavoce.info*, 16 October 2006, http://www.lavoce.info/articoli/pagina2397.html. Accessed 23 April 2008.

Rampini, F. (2003), 'Rossi: Antitrust e magistratura possono fermare la Gasparri', *La Repubblica*, 4 December 2003, Rome, http://www.repubblica.it/2003/k/sezioni/politica/gasparri2/guidorossi/guidorossi.html. Accessed 10 May 2008.

Richeri, G. (2003), 'Digital Television in Europe: What Prospect for the Public?', Rome, 3 November 2003, http://www.coe.int/t/e/human_rights/media/links/events/CONF(2003)004_en.asp. Accessed 16 March 2007.

Richeri, G. (2005), 'Foreword', in Padovani, C., *A Fatal Attraction, Public Television and Politics in Italy*, Boulder, CO: Rowman & Littlefield, pp. ix–x.

Scoppola, P. (1991), *La Repubblica dei partiti Profilo storico della democrazia in Italia (1945–90)*, Bologna: Il Mulino.

Siliato, F. (2001), telephone interview with author, 3 October.

Stille, A (2006), *The Sack of Rome*, New York: Penguin Press.

Tesauro, G. (2003), quoted in 'Legge Gasparri ecco le frasi dello scontro sulle TV', *La Repubblica*, 1 December 2003, Rome, http://www.repubblica.it/2003/k/sezioni/politica/gasparri2/parole/parole.html. Accessed 3 May 2008.

The Times (2007), 'Berlusconi "preparing Telecom Italia bid"', 18 April 2007, London, p. 48.

Tonello, F. (2007), 'The Italian Media Landscape', in G. Terzis (ed.), *European Media Governance. National and Regional Dimensions*, Bristol, UK: Intellect, pp. 239–50.

Variety (2008), 'Italo Telecom shareholder favors merger', 14 April 2008.

Vivarelli, N. (2008a), 'Cable TV, Italian Style. Berlusconi breaks Murdoch monopoly on pay TV', *Variety*, 25 January 2008.

Vivarelli, N. (2008b), 'The Empire of the Son', *Variety*, 23 March 2008.

Zaccaria R. (1996), Radiotelevisione, in G. Santaniello (ed.), Trattato di diritto amministrativo, XV, Padova, Cedam, XIX+714pp.

THE AUTHORS

Auksė Balčytienė *(Vytautas Magnus University, Kaunas, Lithuania)*
Auksė Balčytienė, Ph.D. is professor of Journalism at Vytautas Magnus University in Kaunas, Lithuania. She had been Head of the Department of Journalism for 8 years and in 2006 she assumed the position of the Secretary of the University with responsibilities in information management and communication. Her research and teaching activities focus on comparison of media structures and journalism cultures, media policy and journalism online. She is interested in the role of the media in development of European Public Sphere. She has been teaching as a visiting professor at universities of Dortmund, Madrid, Ulster, Tampere, Copenhagen, Valencia and Tartu. In 2001/2002, she held the Erich-Brost Professorship in international journalism at the University of Dortmund. She has international experience in project coordination and management (in COST and Nordplus Neighbour programs as well as 6th FP projects 'Adequate Information Management in Europe – AIM)' and 'CINEFOGO'); she provides consultancy to the media on the impact of the Internet on journalism. She is editorial board member of journals European Journal of Communication, Informacijos mokslai, Informatics in Education and Journal of Maltese Education Research. Her publications include 3 books (most recent is *Mass Media in Lithuania: Changes, Development and Journalism Culture*, Vistas 2006) and over 70 articles.

Markus Behmer *(Ludwig-Maximilians-University, Munich, Germany)*
Markus Behmer conducts the Journalism Programme at the Institute of Communication Science and Media Research at the Ludwig-Maximilians-University of Munich. His main research interests are communications and media history, cultural communication and international communication policies. His recent publications include a book about broadcasting history after 1945 (2006, with Bettina Hasselbrink). Markus Behmer has been a postdoctoral research and teaching associate in Munich since 1992 (dissertation in 1996). In 2002 and 2004/05 he was a visiting professor at the University in Leipzig. From 2003–6, he chaired the Communication History section of the German association of communication sciences (DGPuK).

Mihai Coman *(University of Bucharest, Romania)*
Born in Fagaras, Romania, in 1953, Mihai Coman graduated from the College of Letters within the University of Bucharest (1976), and holds a PhD in Letters (1985). He was the first Dean of the School of Journalism and Mass Communication Studies within the University

of Bucharest, being considered the founder of journalism and communication education in Romania. Until 1989 he specialized in cultural anthropology studies on Romanian folklore. He has published four volumes of mythology studies and a vast synthesis on animal mythology (*Bestiarul mitologic roman*, 1986, 1988, second edition published in 1996). Other mythology studies have appeared in scientific journals 'L'Ethnologie francaise', 'Etudes indo-europeennes', 'Kurier'. From 1989 he published the reference volume *Introducere in sistemul mass media* and he has started to elaborate the theoretical and analytical framework of the mass media anthropology. In 2003, as a synthesis of these investigations, he published with Presses Universitaires de Grenoble the book *Pour une anthropologie des medias,* and in 2005 he co-edited (with Eric Rothenbuhler) the pathbreaking reader *Media Anthropology* at Sage Publ. He has also published numerous scientific studies in journals and collective volumes dedicated to the transformations in the mass media in post-communist countries and the books *Media in Romania* (A Sourcebook), Berlin, Vistas Verlag, 2004, and *Mass Media and Journalism in Romania* (with Peter Gross), Vistas, Berlin, 2006 etc.

Andrea Czepek (*University of Applied Sciences, Wilhelmshaven, Germany*)
Andrea Czepek has been a Professor of Journalism at the University of Applied Sciences in Wilhelmshaven, Germany since 2003. She studied Journalism at the University of Dortmund, Germany (Diploma in 1992, Dissertation in 2001) and International Studies at the University of Wyoming, USA (M.A. in 1999). She was trained as a journalist at the daily newspaper *Kölner Stadt-Anzeiger,* worked as a freelance journalist in the U.S. (1992–4) and as an editor for the publishing business journal *Buchreport* in Dortmund (2001–3). In Zambia and Zimbabwe, she worked for a journalism training centre in 1991, and at the University of Wyoming, U.S.A., she was a Graduate Assistant in International Studies (1994–6). She has gathered European research experience as an Assistant at the Institute of Journalism at the University of Dortmund, Germany, from 1996 until 2001. Her research background includes a study about press freedom and pluralism in Zambia, for which she developed an index of press freedom that considers the four factors legal provisions, structural framework, pluralism and participation as indicators for the degree of press freedom. (*Andrea Czepek: Pressefreiheit und Pluralismus in Sambia, Demokratie und Entwicklung Bd. 47, Lit Verlag: Münster 2005; Andrea Czepek: "Journalismus als Motor der Demokratie," in: Patrick Rössler/Friedrich Krotz (eds.): Mythos Medien, UVK: Konstanz 2005*)

Ryszard Filas (*Jagiellonian University, Cracow, Poland*)
Ryszard Filas, Press Research Centre of the Jagiellonian University, b. in 1949, PhD in Social Sciences, MA in Sociology, member of the Polish Sociology Society, co-author of the research on *Poles and mass media*. Selected articles in collective publications: *The Readership of Newspapers and Magazines in Poland at the beginning of the 1990s* (1990), *The Changes of Press Readership in Poland in 1989–95* (1996), *The Media and Culture Activity of Poles in 1978–95* (1996), *Who Reads Press in Poland? What Kind of Press? What Do They Look for in It?* (1997), *Magazines and Their Audience* (1996), *Ten Years of Changes of Mass Media in Poland* (1989–99). The Periodization.(1999), *The Domination of Electronic Media Grows – the New Phase of Media Market Changes in Poland* (2003), *The Market of Daily Press in Poland before and After 'Fakt'* (2005), *From Press Reading to Its Viewing and from Press*

Viewing to Press Surfing, i.e. How the Usage of Press Changes in Poland Under the Influence of the New and Newer Media (2006), *The Situation of Polish Press Market and the Influence of Newspapers and Magazines on Public Debate* (2007), *Polish Magazines in the 21st Century: Development or Crisis?* (2007). Research interests: sociology of education, sociology of mass communication, public opinion, mass media reception, mass media market, traditional mass media towards new technology of communication.

Melanie Hellwig *(University of Applied Sciences, Wilhelmshaven, Germany)*
Melanie Hellwig has a Master's degree in History and Political Sciences with an emphasis on European politics. She has been an Assistant at the University of Applied Sciences in Wilhelmshaven since 2003.

Peter Humphreys *(University of Manchester, United Kingdom)*
Peter Humphreys studied Modern Languages with Politics at Bristol Polytechnic, during which time he also obtained a Diplôme d'Études Françaises from the University of Caen, France. Subsequently, Humphreys completed a Master's degree in West European Politics at the LSE and obtained his PhD – on the subject of Pluralism and the Mass Media – from Bradford University, where he spent a period as a research assistant between 1984–6. Since then, he has been at The University of Manchester as Lecturer (1986–92), Senior Lecturer (1992–7), Reader (1997–2001) and Professor (since 2001). He has published extensively in the area of comparative media and telecommunications policy: five authored or co-authored books, three edited collections, and numerous scholarly articles, book chapters, and contributions in handbooks, textbooks and scholarly encyclopaedias. Notable among his publications are: Peter Humphreys and Seamus Simpson, *Globalization, Convergence and European Telecommunications Regulation*, Edward Elgar, 2005. 228 pp; Peter Humphreys, *Mass Media and Media Policy in Western Europe*, Manchester: MUP. 358 pp; and Peter Humphreys, *Media and Media Policy in Germany: the Press and Broadcasting since 1945*, Oxford/Providence, USA: Berg, 1994, pp. 381.He has held three major ESRC funded research awards. Between 1996–9, he was Principal Investigator on an ESRC research award for a three-year project entitled Regulating for Media Pluralism: Issues in Competition and Ownership. Between 2000–3, he was Co-Investigator on the project "The European Union as a Medium of Policy Transfer: Case Studies in Utility Regulation." Humphreys is currently Principal Investigator on a third three year research project entitled "Globalization, Regulatory Competition and Audiovisual Regulation in Five Countries."

Guido Keel *(Zurich University of Applied Sciences, Winterthur, Switzerland)*
Guido Keel is the Research Coordinator at the Research Department of the Institute of Applied Media Studies (Zurich University of Applied Sciences). He studied social and cultural anthropology as well as Communications at the University of Zurich. After earning his masters degree, he worked in various positions as journalist and PR-consultant, before joining the Zurich University of Applied Sciences. His research is focused on media in developing countries (field work in Armenia and Liberia), online communications, as well as various quality management projects in Switzerland. He is currently involved in research project analysing the media coverage of topics relating to religion in Switzerland.

Elisabeth Klaus *(University of Salzburg, Austria)*
Prof. Dr. Elisabeth Klaus is professor and chair of the Department of Communication at the University of Salzburg; she studied mathematics and social sciences at the University of Münster and holds a PhD in sociology in 1986 from the University of Notre Dame/USA. In 1996 she finished her "Habilitation" at the University of Dortmund. She was a visiting professor at the Universities of Hamburg, Vienna and Klagenfurt and a research fellow at the Department of Communication of Dublin City University. From 1996–2003 she was professor for Empirical Communication Research at the University of Göttingen. Her focus in research and teachings are communication and journalism research, feminist media studies, popular culture, and theories of the public sphere. Her most recent book publication is *Kommunikationswissenschaftliche Geschlechterforschung. Zur Bedeutung der Frauen in den Massenmedien und im Journalismus* (2005).

Beata Klimkiewicz *(Jagiellonian University, Cracow, Poland)*
Beata Klimkiewicz is Assistant Professor at the Institute of Journalism and Social Communication, the Jagiellonian University, Cracow, Poland. She received her Ph.D. from the Institute of Political Sciences, Jagiellonian University, and studied at the Oxford University and the Columbia University. Since 2000, she has been a member of the Advisory Panel of Experts on Freedom of Religion and Belief for OSCE. She has co-operated with Open Society Institute in Budapest, Media Diversity Institute in London, Peace Institute in Ljubljana and provided an expertise for the European Parliament. Since 2006, she has been a member of the Steering Committee of COST Action A30 East of West: Setting a New Central and Eastern European Media Research Agenda. Recent research interests include media pluralism and diversity, media policy in Europe, media reform in Central Europe, media representations of minorities and minority media.

Eva Nowak *(University of Applied Sciences, Wilhelmshaven, Germany)*
Eva Nowak is a Professor for Journalism at the University of Applied Sciences in Wilhelmshaven. She specialised on radio and TV journalism while studying journalism at Dortmund University and working as a journalist. Eva Nowak holds a Ph.D. in Journalism from the University of Dortmund. Her research interests are focused on journalistic professionalisation, quality management and international communication policies. From 1995 to 2000 Eva Nowak researched and taught at the Institute of Journalism at the University of Dortmund, where she implemented a students' radio station for training purposes and organised a number of pan-European production and research workshops with students and journalism trainers. From 2000 to 2006 she was a teacher and manager at the Cologne based journalism school "Kölner Journalistenschule für Politik und Wirtschaft e.V.". In her recent book, Eva Nowak develops a quality model for journalism training: 'Quality model for journalism training: Competences, institutions, didactics' (Dortmund: Eldorado, 2007).

Cinzia Padovani *(Southern Illinois University at Carbondale, U.S.A.)*
Cinzia Padovani is an Assistant Professor in the School of Journalism, Southern Illinois University at Carbondale. Her publications include *A Fatal Attraction: Public television and politics in Italy* (Lanham, MD, Rowman & Littlefield, 2005), also published as *Attrazione Fatale: Televisione pubblica e politica in Italia* (Trieste, Italy, Asterios Editore, 2007). She has also published various articles in peer reviewed international journals such as *Javnost/The Public*, *Television*

and New Media, *The International Journal of Media and Cultural Politics*, and *The Asian Journal of Communication*. Her current research focuses on the transition to digital TV and the impact of this transition on public service broadcasting institutions in various countries.

Paweł Płaneta *(Jagiellonian University, Cracow, Poland)*
Paweł Płaneta, Press Research Centre of the Jagiellonian University, b. in 1969, PhD in Social Sciences, MA in Politics and Journalism, co-author of research on the image of election campaign in the Polish press, one of the authors of the *Polish Alternative Press Catalogue in the 1990s*, member of the editorial board of *Polish Media Catalogue*, member of the editorial board of *Zeszyty Prasoznawcze*. Selected publications: *bruLion (1987–92)*. *The Generational Manifest in Art* (1994); *The Image of the World in Polish Press in 1994* (1995); *Computer game as a means of cultural transmission* (1996); *The Image of the presidential election in Poland in Polish Press* (1996), *Kosovo on the Web* (1999), *The Language of the Youth Magazines: the image of the world, values and persuasion* (2000), *Chaos in the Global Network of Persuasion* (2002), *Media and Communication Landscape in Poland*, series Working Papers in International Journalism, Bochum, Projekt-Verlag 2002, *Das Mediensystem Polens* [in:] Internationales Handbuch Medien, Nomos Verlagsgesellschaft, Baden-Baden 2002 (co-author: Ryszard Filas), *The Image of Macedonia in Polish Press in 2000–7* (2008). Research interests: media technologies, the media images of the world, political communication, visual communication and photojournalism, international relations.

Lilia Raycheva *(St. Kliment Ohridski University of Sofia, Bulgaria)*
Dr. Lilia Raycheva is a member of the Council for Electronic Media (the regulatory authority for radio and television broadcasting in Bulgaria). She has been a Vice-Dean for Scientific Research and International Affairs and Head of Radio and Television Department at the Faculty of Journalism and Mass Communication of the St. Kliment Ohridski University of Sofia. She has been lecturing home and abroad. She has been extensively published. She has successfully participated in a number of international projects on mass media issues.

Inka Salovaara-Moring *(University of Helsinki, Finland)*
Dr Inka Salovaara-Moring is a Post-Doctoral Researcher with the Academy of Finland (University of Helsinki). She studied social and political sciences at the University of Helsinki and was awarded a PhD in Communication in 2004. Her research is focused on media geography (localization, Europeanization and identity politics), political economy of media and Nordic/Eastern European Media systems. In addition to her own research project "Beyond East and West: Comparing Media Geographies of New Europe" (2007–9 funded by the Academy of Finland), she is currently collaborating in the research project "European Public Sphere," which is also funded by the Academy of Finland. At the moment she is engaged in editing two books: "Media and Nation in the Global Era with Anna Roosvall (forthcoming 2008); and "European East and West: Public Sphere(s) and Media" (forthcoming Nordicom 2008). She has been the President of the Finnish Association for Mass Communication Research and is a member of Euromedia Research Group, and TIEKE decision-makers' index (Finnish Information Society Development Centre). She is on leave from her position of Associate Professor in Communication at the University of Tallinn.

Ingrid Schulze-Schneider *(University Complutense, Madrid, Spain)*
Ingrid Schulze-Schneider has been director of the department Historia de la comunicación Social for eight years. Furthermore she is teaching amongst others the courses "history of propaganda" and "history of international journalism" at the faculty Ciencias de la Información of the University Complutense in Madrid. In the summer semester 2002 she held the Erich-Brost-Foundation Professorship of International Journalism at the University of Dortmund.

Martina Thiele *(University of Salzburg, Austria)*
Dr. Martina Thiele graduated in 1994 in Slavonic Studies, Communication Science and Politics. She worked as a tutor and assistant at the Universities of Göttingen and Dortmund from 1993–2003. In 2005 she was appointed Professor of Journalism and Communication Science at the University of Göttingen. She is currently Assistant Professor at the Department of Communication, Paris-Lodron University of Salzburg, and also teaches at the Universities of Bern and Krems. Her teaching and research interests include media and politics, communication theories, and the role of media in identity construction. She has published in each of these areas, her most recent book is *Journalistic Controversies caused by Holocaust Films* (2001).

Thierry Vedel *(National Centre for Scientific Research (CNRS), Paris, France)*
Thierry Vedel is a Senior Research Fellow with the National Centre for Scientific Research (CNRS), based at the Centre for Political Research (CEVIPOF) in Paris. His research interests cover media policies and regulation, the transformation of political communication in modern democracies, and internet and politics. He is currently conducting research projects on the use of the internet during electoral campaigns and on the impact of ICT on traditional media. Thierry Vedel has been a visiting fellow at the Oxford Internet Institute in 2005. Other involvements: COST action "Government and Democracy in the Information Age" (1999–2003), the Open Society Institute's project "Television across Europe: regulation, policy and independence" (2004–5), partner of the EU Network of excellence "E-participation in Europe" (2006–9). Thierry Vedel is a member of the editorial boards of *Communication & Strategies, Information Communication and Society,* and *Réseaux.* He teaches political communication at Sciences-po Paris and at the University of Paris 2. His recent publications related to media regulation include: "Les effets de l'information télévisée sur les évaluations politiques et les préoccupations des électeurs" (en coll. avec V. Tiberj), *Cahiers du CEVIPOF,* n°46, avril 2007, pp. 27–46. "The Idea of Electronic Democracy: Origins, Visions and Questions". *Parliamentary Affairs.* Vol. 59, n° 2, April 2006, pp. 226–35. "Television regulation, policy and independence in France". In EUMAP, *Television across Europe.* Budapest, New-York: Open Society Institute, 2005, pp. 637–728.

Vinzenz Wyss *(Zurich University of Applied Sciences, Switzerland)*
Dr. Vinzenz Wyss is a professor of journalism and media research at the Zurich University of Applied Sciences where he heads the Research Department of the Institute of Applied Media Studies. He studied German literature, Sociology and Communication Science at the University of Zurich and was awarded a PhD in Communications in 2002. His research is focused on journalism theory, newsroom quality management and media performance assessment. He is currently involved in applied research projects and furthermore acts as consultant for media quality management issues for Swiss National Television and private broadcasters.